Library Manual : A Practical Approach to Management

Library Manual : A Practical Approach to Management

AASHISH WAREKAR

CYBER TECH PUBLICATIONS
4264/3, Ansari Road, Daryaganj, New Delhi-110002 (India)
Ph.: 011-23244078, 011-43559448 Fax: 011-23280028
E-Mail: cyberpublicationsdelhi@yahoo.com
Website: www.cybertechpublications.com

LIBRARY MANUAL : A PRACTICAL APPROACH TO MANAGEMENT

AASHISH WAREKAR

First Edition 2011

Published by :

G.S. Rawat for **Cyber Tech Publications**
4264/3, Ansari Road, Daryaganj, New Delhi-110002 (India)
Ph.: 011-23244078, 011-43559448 Fax: 011-23280028
E-Mail: cyberpublicationsdelhi@yahoo.com
Website: www.cybertechpublications.com

CONTENTS

Preface

The purpose of management is to enable the organization to produce the best possible results under the best possible conditions. The world situation today is so difficult and changing that no organization can attain this objective by relying on habit or intuition. There must be a systematic effort: (a) to analyse situations; (b) to define objectives; (c) to select the most economic means of attaining them; (d) to organize resources in consequence; (e) to monitor results; and (f) whenever the need arises to adapt the objectives, resources and organization in the light of the results obtained, new circumstances and new tasks. The management and policies of any information unit must deal with the following areas: organization of services, personnel, equipment, collections, services for users, production, relations with users, relations with the parent organization and relations with other organizations (especially other information units).

The responsibility for management lies with the head of the information unit. In most cases it is, at a certain level, shared with higher authorities outside the unit itself (the directors of the parent organization) or not involved in its daily routine (the board of governors or advisory committee of a large unit). When the unit is large enough, managerial responsibility is also shared with the heads of each section and the staff. Policies are guidelines or general principles which help to express objectives in terms of actions by establishing codes for the taking and implementation of decisions.

The structures of an organization are an essential concern of management, whatever its size. Indeed, the smaller it is, and therefore the more limited its resources, the more efficiently it must be run.

—Author

1

Introduction

Management is the process of directing individual skills and energies and allocating material resources to attain an objective.

It can also be regarded as a set of techniques for reaching rational decisions ensuring that all available resources are fully utilized in their implementation, and checking their effectiveness.

These techniques are based on: quantitative methods, or the use of measurements that are as objective as possible, the need for efficiency, the careful preparation of decisions in accordance with firm criteria, and teamwork and leadership.

Modern management is also a state of mind and an attitude to work centred on effectiveness and rationality. It cannot be effective unless all members of the group or organization feel involved: each individual has a vital role to play and must therefore understand its principles while accepting that the final decision at each level must be the clear responsibility of a particular person or group of persons.

Owing to their wide range of activities, their human and material resources, rapid technical progress and, above all, the many different functions they have to perform in backing up the productive activities of their users, information services must lay great stress on management.

MANAGEMENT

Management deals in varying degrees with: (a) all the personnel and all the material components of an organization; (b) all its activities: routine tasks (the sale of products and services), or organization of the whole (staff promotion regulations). This does not mean to say that management is concerned with all the minor details that crop up.

The purpose of management is to enable the organization to produce the best possible results under the best possible conditions. The world situation today is so difficult and changing that no organization can attain this objective by relying on habit or intuition. There must be a systematic effort: (a) to analyse situations; (b) to define objectives; (c) to select the most economic means of attaining them; (d) to organize resources in consequence; (e) to monitor results; and (f) whenever the need arises to adapt the objectives, resources and organization in the light of the results obtained, new circumstances and new tasks.

Policies are guidelines or general principles which help to express objectives in terms of actions by establishing codes for the taking and implementation of decisions.

The structures of an organization are an essential concern of management, whatever its size. Indeed, the smaller it is, and therefore the more limited its resources, the more efficiently it must be run. These structures form a complex whole and can be regarded:

- As internal (organization of the various subdivisions and assignments of tasks) and external (links with the parent or other organizations).
- As functional (arrangements for the proper execution of tasks) and relational (links between the subdivisions of the organization).

Communications are very important in the life of any information unit, yet they give rise to a great many problems. There are various types of communication:

- Vertical communication, that is, from top management down through each level of responsibility, or from the bottom up.
- Horizontal communication, between people with the same level of responsibility, or of different levels when hierarchical considerations are ignored.

- Controlled (or official) communication, from a person in authority and in the proper form, as against spontaneous communication.
- Formal communication, which uses specific predetermined channels, forms and carriers, as against informal communication.
- Communications that differ in content (administrative or technical), in target (internal or external, individual or general communications), in purpose (an instruction; the minutes of a meeting), and in form (oral, written, posters, etc.).
- Management must pay special attention to communication in order:
- To ensure as far as possible that the organization disposes of all the types of communication needed for it to function smoothly.
- To establish communication circuits that cover all needs, are as direct and short as possible, familiar to all staff and fully utilized.
- To see that the communication work smoothly, *i.e.* that there are no breakdowns, that people are not by-passed and that the messages fulfil their functions, come from a competent authority and are put into effect.

The management and policies of any information unit must deal with the following areas: organization of services, personnel, equipment, collections, services for users, production, relations with users, relations with the parent organization and relations with other organizations (especially other information units).

The responsibility for management lies with the head of the information unit. In most cases it is, at a certain level, shared with higher authorities outside the unit itself (the directors of the parent organization) or not involved in its daily routine (the board of governors or advisory committee of a large unit). When the unit is large enough, managerial responsibility is also shared with the heads of each section and the staff. All staff members in fact have some say in the various aspects of management, even though general supervision, evaluation of activities, and choice of policies and plans are the responsibility of senior staff.

The legal status of a unit affects its choice of policy. Some units come under public administration and must therefore respect official regulations which are not always geared to their managerial problems; moreover, they must provide the same quality of service for all users, in many cases free of charge, or respect certain general obligations (preservation of the national heritage, for instance) which can limit their freedom of action.

Other units are private concerns and operate in a context of competition. For example, certain information searches from external sources might reveal the commercial strategy of the firm.

Many information units have been set up to serve the information needs of a larger organization. Their problem is to know how far they can serve users from outside the parent organization and what links can be established with other units.

Lastly, certain units from the start, or soon afterwards, depend entirely on the proceeds obtained from selling their services and are therefore restricted to profitable activities.

Policies have to be formulated, and regularly updated, for the main aspects of the unit's work. Their purpose is to provide the clearest possible guidelines on: the target clientele; priority needs; the limits and scope of the unit's field; the types of services; the creation and management of collections, the nature and organization of technical operations; relations with users; the use of material resources; personnel management; the system of administration; relations with other units and with the parent organization, etc.

The analysis on which policies are based must not be restricted to the unit alone but take into consideration all aspects of its current environment and how this is likely to develop, including the branch of activity with which the unit is concerned, the national and international information infrastructure, information technology and so forth. This will make it possible to clarify the user services to be provided and the most effective methods not only for immediate purposes but in the longer term. It should also be stressed that policies cannot be formulated unless user needs have been adequately defined.

Planning is the means whereby the unit's resources are marshalled over a given period of time in order to attain predetermined objectives.

Plans and programmes can be regarded from. two points of view:

- First, their time-span: for example, a unit might have a long-term plan to develop into a specialized national documentation centre and the hub of a full-fledged network, medium-term plans for the successive stages involved, and short-term plans for expanding each service in the context of these stages.
- Secondly, their scope: for example, a strategic plan covering the full development of a system designed to satisfy 80 per cent of potential users, operational plans for establishing a range of services (such as the selective dissemination of information), and functional plans covering particular tasks in a given stage of the unit's development (such as the intellectual processing of documents with a view to building up a minimal data base).

As all these levels are naturally interdependent, more complex and comprehensive plans must be drawn up, or at least outlined, before the others. The plans of an information unit must be consistent both with those of the parent organization (which are in turn geared to plans for the branch of activity concerned and the national plans) and with national plans for scientific and technical information.

For large units, the planning process will probably require the assistance of specialists and special machinery such as working groups, advisory committees, a planning committee, and so on. In smaller units, it is one of the normal managerial tasks of those in charge.

The planning process itself goes through several stages: definition of objectives, analysis of the present situation and available resources, assessment of the required changes, elaboration of alternative proposals and determination of the resources needed in each case, evaluation of the various proposals and recommendation of a particular plan, its adoption, implementation and subsequent regular revision and updating.

It is advisable for the objectives of the plan to be quantified. Though it is not always possible to do this with a high degree of precision, the plan should at least contain estimates that can subsequently be compared with the actual results obtained.

Organization of an Information Unit

The organization of the unit is not an abstract construction reflecting a purely administrative logic; neither is it settled once and for all. It is another means of helping the unit to perform its function as well as possible. It must not, of course, be constantly altered but it should be possible to make adjustments whenever necessary.

The structure of an information unit can be envisaged in accordance with the following criteria:

- The functions of the documentary chain (acquisition, bibliographic description, retrospective searches, etc.).
- Fields covered (for example, an agricultural documentation centre would deal with crop production, animal production, rural engineering, etc.).
- Types of document (books, reports, periodicals, audiovisual documents, special collections, legal documents, regulations, patents, etc.).
- In the case of a large unit, the location of each service (central service, the services attached to the various branches of the parent organization, the computer-processing department, the central repository of documents, etc.).
- The clientele (for example, a development bank would have a general director's office, a studies division, a legal service, an industrial loans division, an agricultural loans division, etc.).

- Services (library, documentation centre, translation service, publications service, industrial information service, liaison service, etc.).

Naturally, these criteria can be and in practice usually are combined so as to meet user needs more effectively. At all events, it is always important to study, clarify and monitor the distribution of functions because this governs the smooth execution of operations.

Basing organization solely on the functions of the documentary chain facilitates standardization and control, and makes for greater homogeneity in the division of work, but tasks tend to be more fragmented, and it becomes more difficult to staff each section with people who are familiar with different types of document, subject and clientele. Other methods of organization result in more interesting tasks with staff members covering at least one of these different areas, but there is a greater risk of overlapping, and standardization and control are rendered more difficult.

The selected structure should minimize efforts; in other words, each operation should serve directly for as many subsequent operations as possible and everything needed for each service provided should be quick and easy to obtain. Each section should be given a clearly defined role that is logical and interesting. The communication circuits should be as direct as possible and avoid pointless duplication for both staff and users.

If the unit is large (the information service of a ministry working for institutions in different places, for example), it will have to choose between centralization and decentralization. With a centralized organization, the services can be fully integrated and are simpler and cheaper to run, but the unit is often located far from its users and even runs the danger of becoming completely cut off. Decentralization presents the opposite advantages and drawbacks. In many cases a compromise is worked out in which technical operations such as cataloguing and the production of bulletins are centralized and input and output functions located close to the user.

It is useful, not to say essential, to have a sufficiently clear and detailed description of the unit's structure and mode of operation for each staff member to know where he fits in, what he has to do, and how and why. This is the point of organization charts.

Task Analysis

Task analysis and the organization of work are major concerns with a vital role in maintaining the productivity of units faced with the steadily growing mass of information.

By careful observation of all the work performed in an information unit and a detailed analysis of the processes Involved, it is possible to distinguish elementary tasks, the series of tasks that make up an operation and the set of operations that comprise a function or service.

Tasks are discrete acts which cannot be broken down any further and which have a specific location in the documentary chain or administrative procedures; they effect a single transformation (for example, marking the accession number on a document or identifying the main keyword). The degree of skill required depends on the nature of the task. Tasks are differentiated according to this degree of skill, the amount of freedom left to the performer and the responsibilities implied in regard to other members of the staff.

A work unit or job is composed of a varying number of tasks. The distribution depends on the amount of work, the size of staff and the unit's organization. They should normally involve a set of closely related tasks or consecutive operations at the same level. In principle, no task should be performed by a more qualified, or less qualified, person than the work involved calls for.

Work units can be organized in accordance with the same criteria as those mentioned above for the unit as a whole. A division on purely functional lines might well prove monotonous for the staff, but this danger can be avoided by alternating duties from time to time. On the other hand, a division based on the type of public, product or specialist field-often preferably in combination with a functional division sometimes tends, especially in smaller information units, to result in too many tasks performed by under-qualified staff. As all the functions of an information unit are interdependent, it is better for all the staff to be perfectly familiar with all the unit's work. This can be arranged in providing a thorough introduction for new staff and by job rotation. Since most information units have a small staff, it is advisable to be able to cope with any eventuality, to define jobs with some flexibility and ensure that all staff members are as polyvalent as possible.

Information units offer many employment opportunities: (a) administrative jobs (typing, bookkeeping, legal services, personnel department, etc.); (b) technical jobs (reprography, binding, computer processing, etc.); (c) specialized jobs in scientific and technical information (archives, librarianship, documentation, etc.).

These jobs can be filled at different levels of execution, supervision or management. They should be accurately described so that candidates or staff members know exactly what is involved. This 'job description' covers the hierarchical level, the responsibilities, the amount and kind of work, the qualifications required, salary and administrative status.

When information specialists have an officially recognized administrative status, the job description must mention the fact.

Personnel management is of particular importance in information; in many countries, career prospects are still all too often limited. Staff must be recruited with great care and efforts made to keep up their enthusiasm by arranging meetings, discussion groups, etc., and continuing in-service training.

The salary scale and increments should reflect the general conditions of the profession, growing responsibilities, further qualifications and improved performance. Salaries are sometimes supplemented by other payments (,allowances, bonuses, etc.). It is most important that members of the staff have clear salary and career prospects.

Costing and performance evaluation is fundamental to most managerial activities. There are direct costs, which are those related to a particular documentary function (for example, the salaries paid to indexers) and indirect costs which are chargeable either to documentary functions in general (the indirect costs of the system: thesaurus maintenance, for instance) or to general overheads (the indirect costs of the organization: lighting, for instance). There are three categories of direct cost: staff costs, materials (documents, supplies) and equipment (amortization, operation and servicing). Costing calls for the analysis of transactions and the time taken.

The transactions cover the quantity and cost of purchased items (for example, the number and total cost of microfiches bought in one year), intermediate products (number of documents indexed), and the products and services delivered to users (number of photocopies). The other element is the time spent on executing each task, for the measurement of which a unit of time and a nomenclature of the tasks involved are required (time spent on indexing a document of twenty pages, for example'). The time spent implies certain labour costs and the cost of using equipment

The costs are measured on the basis of bookkeeping vouchers and records which are analysed systematically or over a given period of time. In some cases a general estimate ",ill suffice, bu good management requires them to be broken down into cos units, that is, according to the functions stated in an accountin scheme. The accounting scheme is a double-entry matrix whic shows the various types of cost for each function. The definitio of functions depends on the organizational structure of the uni

Another important aspect of performance is the time taken This can be checked by recording the dates when documents c queries (individually or in sets) pass through each work place c function. These data can then be noted on a planning chart facilitate analysis. Even though information work is of a intellectual nature, it is preferable to treat it like normal productic activities and to make sure that capacity' is being full) utilize This is done by establishing the normal work load for each job ar each piece of equipment in the form of a chart which states, f a given period, the theoretical production capacity, the expect amount of activity and the actual production. This will sho where performance has been good or poor, help identify the reaso and make it possible to take advantage of success or put the mat right.

The qualitative aspect of performance evaluation is mc delicate to handle. If the unit has no arrangements for monitori each task or operation, it will have to resort to sample surveys or artificial tests. With monitoring procedures-which cannot be recommended too highly-the proportion of products rejected and the reasons why (for example, 5 per cent of Indexing operations for lack of specificity) are recorded. A useful form of control, which can provide a partial and subjective indication of performance, is based on user reactions, which can and should be systematically requested. It is also possible to establish special criteria for each function, service or product and to measure performance on a regular or occasional basis. For example, the effectiveness of a question-answer service could be assessed in terms of speed, exhaustivity, precision and case of use. These data, together with the cost structure, will provide enough information to improve this service and the unit as a whole.

Budget control integrated planning data (that is, the estimated volume of activity: the number of SDI profiles planned for the Year, for example) and accounting data (the actual number profiles served, the rate of production and the cost). This will point to ways of Improving the unit's mode of operation and make it easier to foresee the consequences of decisions or other factors likely to have an influence. Unfortunately, available data on costs and performance are at present in short supply and difficult to compare. They obviously depend on the situation and organization of each unit and on the methods of calculation, which vary, consider ably. Disparities in the available figures are too great for the conclusions to be significant.

Budget and Financing

The budget and financing of information units depend on their legal status and their type: clearly, there will be a considerable difference between a computerized national centre and the library of a small university research laboratory, but their budgets have much in common.

The main items of expenditure are as follows:

1. Staff salaries and related charges; this is the largest budget item in all units and often accounts for over half the total expenditure.

2. Purchase of documents; this is the second largest item though it occasionally-all too rarely-exceeds staff costs.
3. Expenditure on processing (use of the computer, production of bulletins, etc.).
4. Supplies.
5. Equipment (amortization, servicing and replacement).
6. Premises (only significant for large units).
7. Communications (mail, telephone, telex, transport, etc.).
8. General overheads (electricity, cleaning, etc.).
9. Expenditure on sub-contracting. This item can be quite important if certain functions (computer processing) are performed by other organizations or if certain jobs (elaboration of a thesaurus) are contracted out.

In normal circumstances, Items 1 to 9 account for only a small proportion of the total budget, two-thirds of which is devoted to 1, 2 and 3. In most cases, the unit's resources are in the form of budgetary allocations from the parent organization. The amount generally depends on needs and possibilities but there also exist certain standards and ratios for determining the desirable level of a unit's resources in relation to its clientele and the overall budget of the parent organization. Unfortunately, the actual allocation is sometimes simply what is left over after the requirements of other departments have been met. This explains the need for accurate accounting and efficient financial administration to help the unit defend its requests more effectively, and for high-quality management in general to provide a clear justification for the sums involved.

For some units, especially those which benefit from legal deposit, the various types of free acquisitions can make a significant contribution. Lastly, many units are deriving more and more resources from the sale of products and services.

It should be observed that the separate items of the budget are relatively inflexible: it is not easy to make much change in the distribution of expenditure or to increase overall resources. At the same time production costs, in particular for staff and acquisitions, are rising steadily. This obliges units to pay special attention to management, and in particular to policy formulation and increased productivity.

The budget is prepared in conjunction with the plan and takes the financial data and results into account. It can either start with available resources, distribute them among the items of expenditure and it' necessary try to make cuts or find additional resources, or it can work in the other direction. In many cases the two approaches are combined.

Payment of services: here a frequent problem is that many information units are in one way or another public services expected to function free of charge or come under the general services of their parent organization. Another difficulty with charging is the widespread view that information should be freely available to everyone, or that it is a right. This is perfectly true, but health is also a right and this does not exclude medical fees. Even where no actual charge is made, however, payment can be used as an administrative technique for the unit and its partners, since it is a simple and effective way of measuring the usefulness and utilization of services. In this case, the payments would be fictitious or returned at the end of the financial year.

When information services which have been free begin to make charges, even a very small fee will at first lead to a drop in the number of users. Even services that were free only for a trial period and whose users are perfectly aware that the time will come when they will have to pay experience this. Nevertheless, if the service proves its worth, it should quickly make up the lost ground and then find the number of users rising. The fact is that users are read),, at least those in productive activities, to pay a fair and even a high price-and often do so-for really useful information that reaches them in time and in acceptable form. Often the refusal to pay is simply a sign that the service is being rejected because of low quality or unsuitability.

Information units can charge for admission to the unit, for their various products and services (publications, SDI profiles, answers to questions, translation, etc.), for photocopies or microcopies, for postage, or to help defray the cost of meetings, visits or other activities that they organize. Payments can take the form of dues, subscriptions or a charge for each service rendered. Regular users would have an account and pay the bill at fixed intervals.

The charges made can cover all the direct and indirect costs of each product or service, but this system is still only practised by a few commercial units, whose prices also include a profit margin. Another approach is for the charge to cover all production costs but not the initial cost of setting up and running in the system and its products. Sometimes only direct production costs or a varying proportion of them will be demanded, while other units require payment only for certain products or services, particularly those which involve extra work in addition to what they regard as normal services: for example, they might make no charge for a retrospective search but demand payment for a selective bibliography.

In each case, once the production cost is known, the price should be set bearing in mind that if it is too high it will be out of the reach of the user however much he is interested in the product or service. The prices of similar products and services available elsewhere should also be taken into account, the aim being to make the unit's activities as profitable as possible or at least to obtain the maximum amount of income.

Promotion and Market Research

All information units, even those whose usefulness seems self-evident, must pay careful attention to these if they do not want to go into a gradual decline.

Market research involves an integrated set of activities whose purpose is to determine:

- The potential clientele of the various products and services, together with their characteristics, needs and motivations.
- The characteristics of the products: nature, content, presentation, quality, availability and possibly price.
- The standing of a product in relation to other similar products (for example, the advantages of a national abstracts bulletin in relation to equivalent foreign publications).

- The possibilities of a broader clientele (,attracting new groups of potential users) or of consolidating the clientele (taking action to convert as many potential users as possible into actual users).

Strategies for the promotion and dissemination of the products.

In business concerns, for example, the library is often regarded as a possibly useful luxury. By studying the various categories of potential users it is possible to find out the reasons for this image., what the people would like the library to contain and how they would like to utilize it. This will suggest how the library should be laid out, how it should be run and what documents it should acquire. The next step could be to see what other libraries offer the same services and whether they have any particular advantages. An attempt would then be made to discover how many potential users could be attracted to the library and the best way of going about it, and whether the library should be opened up to outside users and, if so, how to attract them. The reorganized library would then be promoted along lines that the preceding research had indicated.

The promotion of an information unit is represented by an interrelated set of activities whose aim is:

- To publicize the unit, its products and its services among potential users.
- To encourage them to utilize the unit; to make its products and services attractive.
- To show potential users how to make use of' the various products and services and what advantages they offer.
- To maintain contact with the users with a view to keeping them informed about the unit and obtaining their reactions.

A wide range of methods is used: advertisements in newspapers, leaflets given or sent to potential users, the organization of visits to the unit, demonstrations and open days, posters, offers of products and services on a trial basis, and personal contacts with individual users and their superiors.

Though personal contact is the most effective approach, a unit will in practice often find it worth while combining several of these methods to form a promotion programme. Efforts to promote the unit should not be restricted in time, for instance, to when the unit is created or a new product introduced, but should be kept up at a high level. The aim should be to put the dialogue with users on a permanent footing, one possibility being to organize a club or association so that users can be directly or indirectly associated in the management of the unit as actively as possible.

A natural part of promotion activities is user training, with the unit providing appropriate instruction by means of documents or theoretical and practical training sessions to show how the unit's products and services can be employed to the best advantage.

The unit's links with the parent organization often have a decisive influence on the way it is run. They can be seen from two points of view: the unit's official place in the hierarchy and organization chart of the parent organization as a whole, and its informal working relations with other departments and individuals.

For its official standing, a number of requirements have to be taken into consideration. There is the need for it to be close to the users and especially the most important ones, which explains, for instance, why information units are frequently' attached to research departments; to have fairly direct and effective links with all the other departments; to be of central importance or at least highly respected, especially if the unit's task is to collect the documents produced by the organization; to offer satisfactory conditions of employment for the staff, particularly in regard to status, and to be able to count on stable resources over a long period. Clearly, there exists no ready-made solution to these problems.

In practice every possible kind of approach is encountered: units attached to research and development services, to technical services, to administrative services or to general management; units regarded as less important than or as the equal of the other departments. Each organization makes its own arrangements and its decision in this respect has to take into consideration the objectives, policies and resources of the unit and the structure, policies, operation and general life of the organization. These last two aspects can make the situation appear highly satisfactory on paper but much less so in practice, for example, when the unit comes under general management and other departments are kept strictly separate from each other and jealously watch over their privileges. In many cases the unit itself has little say in the arrangements made on its behalf.

These decisions are taken either when the unit is set up, which clearly has important consequences, or in the course of a subsequent general reorganization if the unit wants its position to be changed.

The relative position of the unit in the organization's hierarchy has a pervasive but not decisive influence on its informal relations with the other departments. Owing to the nature of its work, it functions in parallel with production and administrative activities. It has to make sure that it has links with all parts of the organization at all levels and find ways to getting round any reluctance to cooperate on the part of certain sectors or at a particular level. Through paying systematic attention to these links the unit could become the unofficial hub of the organization, a standing that could well make up for its possibly unsatisfactory position in the hierarchy.

Links with the outside: the unit can establish relations with, as the case may be, users not belonging to the parent organization, the authorities responsible for national information policy and the development of information infrastructure, other units, and the profession.

There is no problem with external users unless it is desired to give internal users special advantages. This would make it necessary to restrict the former's access (special opening times, limited borrowing privileges, certain services excluded) or to charge more (a small charge or entirely free to internal users with a varying charge for the others). Such discrimination is only worth considering if the unit is unable to extend its clientele. However, every effort should be made to associate external users with the running of the unit in the same way as internal users.

The purpose of establishing relations with the national authorities responsible for national information policy is to ensure that the unit has a recognized role in the information infrastructure, is invited to take part in policy formulation and the preparation of programmes, particularly through the working groups and commissions of the national plan, and is thus enabled to base its own policies and development on these national actions.

Links with other units can serve a number of purposes: first, to establish friendly relations that will allow the units to exchange information and back each other up; secondly, in case of need, to exchange services, perhaps under preferential conditions; and thirdly, to promote cooperation, which can range from task sharing or a simple division of labour in the field concerned to the setting up of joint services or even a network. Whatever the arrangement, it is essential for the senior staff of units working in the same field or located in the same area to keep in close touch with one another. More often than not cooperation proves indispensable, if only to avoid pointless overlapping (for example, the purchase of rarely requested costly books which can be borrowed from another unit). Even in the absence of a national programme, information units are increasingly tending to share out tasks (in regard to acquisitions, their clientele, and the provision of joint services such as bibliographic bulletins or data bases) and to form networks involving adoption of the same techniques and methods of operation.

When it is only a matter of helping each other, the relations can be kept informal, but joint initiatives should preferably be based on a formal agreement stating the rights and duties of each party. Sometimes, however, the unit's official status rules this out, and it is also possible for the conditions on which the cooperation was based to change quite quickly,. When the situation is favourable, two units can develop very close relations without a formal agreement and thus avoid temporary legal or political obstacles. For example, two information units belonging to organizations which themselves are reluctant to cooperate could quite easily adopt the same documentation system and the same equipment and thus in actual practice work together.

It is just as essential to establish and maintain relations with the profession. Contacts through professional organizations will enable the unit to exchange technical information, join in cooperative research on methodology, and so forth. Conversely, the unit's active participation will strengthen these organizations and contribute to the general progress of the profession itself.

Evaluation of Activities

This is not a theoretical and purposeless exercise but one of management's essential instruments, which should be applied to all aspects of a unit's work.

One method is to check a unit's operations and functions by regularly monitoring some of their essential aspects. The number would depend on the type of operation or function: for example, 5 per cent of the queries processed each month could be taken to ascertain whether the time needed for the answers, their precision and exhaustivity and the procedure followed were in accordance with the standards fixed. From time to time however, particularly, when a medium-or long-teem plan is being prepared, it is a good idea to undertake a systematic evaluation.

There are three levels of evaluation: the evaluation of effectiveness, of the cost-effectiveness ratio and of the cost-benefit ratio. The first level attempts to assess how far the unit is meeting its objectives or, in short, how far it satisfies its users. The second attempts to determine the cheapest and most efficient way of running the unit while the third is focused on the benefits derived by, users of the service or services and whether they justify, the cost.

Evaluation is a form of research states its hypotheses and objectives, defines the objects to be examined, collects the necessary data (by means of documents, observation, measurement and interviews), analyses them and draws conclusions. Each operation or function has its own special methods of evaluation, which can be adapted as necessary. It is also possible to employ advanced techniques such as models, simulation or operational research. The evaluation can be centred on some or all of the functions of an information unit, and each function calls for special evaluation techniques and criteria. The sectors with which evaluation is most often concerned are the holdings, the provision of primary documents, question-answer services, information retrieval, data bases and documentary products, catalogues, technical services computerization, and management.

The most usual criteria include standards costs effort (,amount and complexity of the work involved for staff and users), response time, qualitative criteria such as exhaustivity precision, recall, novelty and relevance and the various signs of user satisfaction.

When these studies are carried out by or for information units, they have a very specific and practical purpose: either to detect and put right any weaknesses or to help select and organize new activities, and in many cases both.

Clearly, the cost of an evaluation and the effort involved must be commensurate with the advantages to be derived from its conclusions; it would hardly be reasonable to allocate resources at the expense of production itself. But this argument is no reason for the systematic refusal to undertake evaluations, which is often in reality a refusal to change. Without evaluation, arty information unit is likely to take the wrong direction, lose its adaptability or become obsolete.

ORGANIZING AND OPERATING AN INFORMATION AND DOCUMENTATION CENTRE

General Organizational Aspects

As in all tasks involving organization, the purpose of an IaD centre must be the decisive factor in determining the most rational form of organization. The IaD centre is a business concern which provides services. In organizational terms, it regulates and directs relations between the highly varied 'market' of information sources and the equally varied 'market' of Information needs. This applies equally to public and private IaD centres, but we shall concentrate here on the requirements of IaD centres In the private economy. The 'market' concept Is used in this context to make it easier to draw parallels with other economic activities, for example trade. In commercial concerns, familiarity with the producer market and with consumer needs determine turnover and hence economic success. Optimum organization helps to keep a business's costs as low as possible.

Similarly, in the case of an IaD centre familiarity with information needs and information sources is the most important factor in ensuring an efficient information supply service. Proper organization will also ensure that the costs of this service are kept at an economically rational level.

In practice, many different approaches are now adopted to the organization of IaD centres, depending on the function they perform. Specialized libraries are frequently linked with IaD centres whose services include the provision of information and literature.

However, only IaD centres engaged essentially in providing information are dealt with below.

Activities and Functions

Users expect an IaD centre to provide the following services:

A. Information through the supply of original documents, *e.g.*:

Newspaper Circulation

- supply of research papers, reports on meetings, etc.;
- book lending;

B. Information on specific subjects, *e.g.*:

- bibliographical research;
- data inventories;
- product and producer listings;

C. Current information on the state of the art through Information services, *e.g.*:

- in-house bibliographical information services;
- profile services;
- abstract sources;
- information on application techniques;
- market data.

The activities of central specialized information establishments as independent service enterprises are on a far larger scale than those of subsidiary establishments.

The range of services required by users has a decisive influence on the various procedures that need to be efficiently combined in the work routine of an IaD centre.

Each IaD centre may be said to perform three broad functions related to the flow of information from the producer (information profile) to the user (profile of interests):

a. acquisition;
b. documentation;
c. information.

An additional field 'word processing and reprography' is usually superimposed on these basic functions.

The Information System as a Simple Feedback Control System

Information systems can be represented as a simple feedback control systems (diagram 65) operating between the producer of information and the user. The feedback control system is made up of the following functions: acquisition, documentation, information and management.

The purpose of the system Is to select from a wide-ranging supply of Information the elements that match the user's profile of interests. The information system is controlled by the regulator (management) by means of constant adjustment. Changes In user requirements, for example, lead to corresponding changes in individual functions.

Each and every change in and addition to the IaD task necessarily calls for an Investigation of the consequences for the entire system. A really smooth flow of information can only be achieved on the basis of an overall review of the system.

Organization Chart

On the basis of the sequence of steps involved in providing an information service, an IaD centre may be divided up into the following fields:

1. *Functions*
    1. source collection (specialized library)
    2. documentation
    3. Information
2. *Management and related fields*
    1. management
    2. central services
    3. coordination and systems development

A detailed organization chart is shown in diagram 66. It is applicable to almost every kind of enterprise, with possible variations in the prominence assigned to individual fields.

Provision of Services (Dissemination of Information): The Problems

The services provided by IaD centres have hitherto been based essentially on primary publications. They have played a decidedly secondary role In the normal process of disseminating information through the mass media, the specialized press, specialized literature, etc. They concentrate instead on processing and organizing information in the light of users' interests. However, an IaD centre's supply of services Is in competition to some extent with the acquisition of information by users themselves. It is therefore essential, if the supply is to be accepted by the user, to ensure that an IaD centre's information potential is greater than the user's information stock. An efficient system is expected to be able to supply information from virtually all relevant sources, shedding light on the particular problem concerned. Users also expect the supply of information to adapt itself to changes in interests without entailing major expense.

The resulting qualitative expectations of a more or less anonymous 'user market' exert an important influence on the planning and efficiency of an information system.

Planning and Organization

Planning is a prerequisite for organization. Analysis of interests, identification of service expectations and selection of the sources to be consulted for that purpose (information profile) provide the basic data needed for the efficient organization of an IaD centre. The establishment and organization of this kind of operational field may be divided into the following three stages:

a. planning;
b. systems development;
c. testing of the system and attainment of 'maturity'.

Planning

In the planning stage, guidelines are drawn up for the actual design of the system. An attempt is made to illustrate the interdependence of system components and user-dependent factors in the form of a matrix.

User-dependent factors		System components
scope		user
level of information	influence	storage
type of service desired	on	documentation
user frequency		sources

Exercise consists in identifying the specialized field for which documentation is required. It is important to know (field-user relationship) whether the subject to be dealt with is narrow (plastics in motor vehicles) or wide ranging (car manufacturing). This will have an influence (field-source relationship) an the selection of sources to be consulted (important: existing stock and growth rate).

The next set of questions concerns the level of information for which services are to be provided. If it is exclusively for research and development purposes, this will affect the structure of the publications to be covered by the documentation (patents, research reports, scientific journals, legislation, etc.), the factual content and the detail of cataloguing. If the service is to cover a more general field of information, this will have a qualitative effect (structure of sources) and an effect on data selection (factual content, cataloguing).

In this connection, it is also useful to know the number of persons to be informed:

- A further aspect to be taken into account in designing a system is, broadly speaking, the type of services desired. This influences the type of storage facilities to be provided and has implications for the factual content and detail of cataloguing.
- A final question concerns expected frequency of user recourse to the services. This may have implications for storage design and search strategies.
- The planning stage concludes with a rough preliminary estimate of staff needs for setting up an IaD centre in the

following two stages: development and testing. A rough estimate of financial needs is also made at this stage.

Systems Development

The system must in any case be designed in such a way as to be expandable in any desired direction.

It must be possible, therefore, to make the transition from manual documentation to mechanical procedures with the minimum disruption. The sequence is more or less as follows: selection of the optimum organizational procedure (classification, thesaurus, etc.):

- preliminary design of the storgage system;
- design of a data-gathering sheet for recording data and reports;
- drawing-up of guidelines for formal data collection and cataloguing;
- decisions regarding the installation of technical equipment;
- revision of staff needs.

Testing of System

During the test period, the system must be tested to ensure that it is providing users with a largely satisfactory service and developed until it reaches 'maturity'.

The steps in the process may be as follows:

- documentation-formal compiling and cataloguing;
- building up a storage system;
- use of forms to direct and control the work process;
- training of documentation staff;
- training of users;
- research work;
- supply of periodically produced information services;
- analysis of relevance;
- improvements to the system;
- establishment of cost indicators for evaluation of the system.

A Mature Information System?

The steps in setting up an information system set out chronologically above are very difficult to carry out in practice in the same sequence. There is heavy overlapping of the individual phases during the development process. User needs should be the overriding consideration in all cases during the development and testing stages.

As user needs always evolve in the light of progress, information systems are also subject to structural fluctuations. A system's 'maturity' is therefore limited in time.

Internal Documentation Work or Reliance on Outside Services

As information and documentation are highly labour-intensive activities, it is advisable in designing the system to consider what kind of outside services might be used by the new information system. This calls for market analysis to determine whether IaD work is already being wholly or partially executed elsewhere.

It should prove less costly to purchase required services from outside suppliers and concentrate on internal aspects of the documentation project (*e.g.* Independent research, etc.). Indeed the expected increase in specialized information centres, providing services ranging from print services to magnetic tape services and linking up terminals to the ADP store, will make it possible to reduce the scale of independent documentation work.

General Observations on the Low-cost Organization of IaD Centres

The following 'maxims' are key considerations to be borne In mind in organizing an IaD centre. They are Intended as a 'summary' of the preceding sections.

1. Necessary personal services arc to be organized in terms of the expertise required.
2. Considerable division of labour, with the possible use of temporary staff or outside services where they prove cheaper.
3. Control of steps in the work process through form-filling.

4. Development of storage and information supply, making substantial use of external services.
5. Full use of all opportunities for cooperative agreements with other IaD centres operating in the same field.
6. Constant reappraisal of the work process with a view to simplification.
7. Development of indicators through cost-benefit analysis with a view to controlling costs and evaluating performance.

Staff costs are the main component In the overall cost of running an IaD centre, accounting for about 75 to 80 per cent of the total in the case of small-and medium-scale enterprises. In the interests of low-cost organization, therefore, all measures required to fulfil users' requests must be critically investigated from the standpoint of their impact on staff costs.

RECORDS MANAGEMENT

Not all archives services carry out a records management programme, though in principle most would have the possibility of introducing one to cover the records created by their governing authority. Where an archive service has the primary duty of serving an employing authority or institution, the records management aspect is of major importance, and affects all the processes which come after it. Records management can also be considered as a function exercised independently of archival management, but the two logically go together and either may suffer from the absence of the other.

Records management is a field which has attracted increasing attention in recent times. The growing sophistication of administrative practices, and the increasing complexity of organisations, together with the enormous expansion of the quantity of records produced, has made it necessary to introduce conscious management into this area, and to develop it as a set of techniques or as a discipline.

Historically, interest in records management has arisen from different points of origin. In some cases the initiative has come from archivists, whose main concern is the control of material passing out of current record systems into archival care. Records management in this tradition is concerned mainly with retirement of records from currency and their appraisal. In other cases the initiative has come from organisation and methods or management advisory units, whose main concern has been the reduction of administrative costs. In other cases again the records management system may have originated in central secretariat departments, whose main concern has been to regulate the flow of information and documentary media within the central offices. There may also be cases where records management has begun with legal advisers, whose concern has been to preserve and retrieve official documents. Finance departments have also had to develop systems to serve the needs of audit.

The historical point of origin impresses its character on the resulting programme, and it may determine where the main thrust of management effort is placed. The present study takes as its starting point the view that records management is a branch of information management. The quality of the information it supplies is the main criterion for an RM programme, and this information supply is radically affected by its relationship with in archives service.

RM is a field of management whose material is the data, media and systems used in the record-making and record-storing processes in any organisation. Its aim is to achieve the best retrieval and exploitation of the data held in these media and systems, and incidentally to reduce the cost and improve the efficiency of record-making and keeping processes.

The relationship between archives and records management can be illustrated by two models: Figures 1 and 2.

Two recent developments reinforce the validity of an information-centred approach to RM. One is the advent (more gradual thin at one time foreseen) of office automation; the other is the increasing tendency of legislators to introduce specific legal requirements for record retention and access.

Office Automation: A useful recent summary of developments in the automation of administrative processes has been published by a working party of the Records Management Group, headed by S.C. Newton. This investigation divides the automation of office processes into four groups: electronic data processing; word processing; micrographics; and telecommunications. Each has a distinct influence on record processing.

Electronic data processing usually involves using a machine-readable data base. From the archivist's point of view, there are two kinds of these, the accumulated and the regenerative. Accumulated data banks consist of collections of data used as a whole at one time.

Regenerative data bases are constantly, or at least periodically, updated with new information, so that there is never a moment when the information is in a definitive state. Data base management systems are in frequent use today.

The Newton study gives examples of integrated ledger systems, personnel records systems, automated pensions programmes, and documentation systems containing textual records. When an organisation introduces any form of data base management, it is necessarily involved in some form of administrative restructuring, aimed at assimilating the newly necessary data processors, but also taking into account the consequences of the central data base being shared by various sections or departments.

Word processors are rapidly replacing typewriters as the main means of storing words on paper. They are inherently more efficient and flexible. When an organisation introduces word processing, it inevitably finds that it has begun a process which leads, once again, to change in its administrative structures. This is because word processors are only a small step away, technologically, from integrated electronic office communication systems. In the first stage, manually generated pieces of writing are translated into formal shapes by typing them on a word processor.

In the second stage, the administrators write directly on to the word processor, which is capable of transmitting their words to colleagues or addressees, and also, if required, storing them electronically. Thus a system originally thought of as meant for formalising text ends as one for transmitting it. It will be noticed that writing and transmitting messages has always constituted a large proportion of all administrative work.

Micrographics have now developed far from their origin as storage media, into technological components of information systems. Automated retrieval of data from microforms is now advanced, either by electro-mechanical means or by using computers. Computer output is also often in microform. Recent applications include pensions records, insurance claims, purchase invoice control, and incoming correspondence.

Telecommunications is likely to be important in combination with the data transmission processes mentioned with word processors. It is already technically possible to extend these automated communication systems by means of telephone lines, and this extends into the transmission of visually read data (view-data). Together with document facsimile transmission and teleconferencing, these are developments which are likely to change the whole work environment of administrators.

All four sectors of automated recording interrelate, and all are rapidly advancing. It is interesting to notice that all concern the management of information, and the media which retains it. Whether or not we are to see the advent of a 'paperless office' (and this has been questioned), it is clear that the advance of information technology has reinforced the importance of RM as central to management planning. An extreme view might be that in high-level administration only two kinds of managers are needed at the centre: the decision-makers, who rely on the data provided for them by the service; and the records managers, who devise and maintain it.

The design and retention of automated data bases is subject to statutory control much more closely than similar records kept in hard-copy form. Many governments, including the British, have appointed officials to supervise them, and have instituted legal codes to protect the individual.

Data protection legislation is based to a great extent on international accords, and supplements the increasingly detailed requirements of law over other forms of record. Records managers must of course be equipped to observe the law in these respects, and to design their systems in accordance with relevant codes of practice.

All this shows that RM has an increasingly important role in an automated administration, and that the design of the records series to be generated, stored and accessed is a central concern of management.

Newton's study concludes with a model for the positioning of an RM service within an automated organisation.

Legal Control: The second recent development is that in all countries, but especially in North America and in the European Community, the law is taking an increasing interest in specifying the retention of records and in allowing litigation to be based upon record evidence over longer periods of time.

There is no comprehensive summary of these legislative requirements, which would indeed be difficult to assemble from a wide variety of statutes and legal decisions. A recent brief survey, also by S.C. Newton, covering recent changes to the law of criminal and civil evidence, and of contract, is a useful guide. J. Smith's study of the law covering records of drug manufacture illustrates the importance and the complexity of the subject as it extends into technical areas. Health and safety legislation has tended to specify the retention of personnel records, and to dictate the creation of records of accidents and hazards, all with long periods of currency. As mentioned above, machine-readable data bases are specially regulated.

The Structure of an RM Service: Records are information media which are generated by an administrative system. They include data which originated outside the organisation (for example in incoming letters), but are essentially an internal information source. Most organisations need also to provide and manage information services which seek for and use information of external origin: books and documents. No single source of information will by itself satisfy the total information requirement of any organisation, so that the RM service depends for its success on building up a workable relationship with four other facets of the organisation:

- the administration (financial, legal, general and specialist) in which the records originate;
- the special library service;

- the technical documentation centre; and
- the archives.

The *administration* generates records which carry the information it acquires and uses in the course of business. It arranges these records in systems which are the stock-in-trade of administrative departments. The RM unit must be able to build up a relationship with these administrative units which will allow the records manager a degree of responsibility for the design and maintenance of record systems, and for the disposition of particular series. The relationship should also allow the administrative departments to become accustomed to using the RM system and to call on it for information.

It is often difficult to define the concept of administration. Most organisations have a central office, the headquarters of overall management. It is common to find that there are also important administrative centres outside this. Some will be specialist or technical departments or units; others will be branches or sub-organisations, often situated away from the main administrative centre. Processing or manufacturing units also generate records, and may be administratively distinct. If it is to deal with all these, the RM programme has to be able to enter into relationships with all the different kinds of administrative entity.

The internationally accepted model for RM within government and business administrations proposes that it should be responsible for the design and maintenance of what have traditionally been the three main types of record created. Under this model RM should include mail, reports and forms 'management. Mail management covers not only systems for receiving, distributing and storing incoming mail, matching it with mail sent out in reply, but also extends into the design of form letters and even into campaigns for improving the language used in official letters.

It is clear that mad management also involves the design of systems for filing. A filing system is essentially a practical application of a classification scheme covering the organisation's area of interest; but it also has another dimension. This is the control of movement of documents round the office, plotting a lifecycle for each letter. Incoming documents are filed, the file placed before the official who is to take action, and the resulting outgoing document takes its place next on the file. In this way a full and retrievable record is available on the whole transaction: but to set it out in this way involves a good deal of structural organisation in the office.

Reports should of course be succinct and accurately expressed, should conform to established standards, and be available to any proper user for reference. Forms must be well designed, must make the data they carry easily usable, and (as is often remarked today) should be understood by those who have to fill them up.

The *special library service* assembles books, journals and published materials, including non-book materials, on subjects relevant to the information needs of the organisation and its staff, and runs a service based upon these. The *documentation centre* assembles published and unpublished technical papers of relevance to the organisation and its staff, obtaining these from sources outside the organisation itself, and running a service based upon these materials. An automated documentation service, common today, provides the organisation's access to international, local or specialised data bases. Clearly, reports generated from within the organisation should also be dealt with in a documentation system.

All these services may have a similar structure, consisting of input, store, and user services. The arrangements for input differ between the different services, but it is easy to suggest that store and output could be combined. In particular finding aids, systems for disseminating information, and the arrangements for communicating data have no theoretical need to be separate. The *archives service* receives all or some of its material from the RM programme, as a result of the process of appraisal. which is the interface between them. It shares with the RM programme a concern over the completeness of the documentation assembled by the system, because in the end this is what determines the value of the archive. Looked at from the other direction, the RM service uses the archives for the storage and use of its most valuable materials, over long periods.

In view of the closeness of the relationships suggested above, one could hardly suggest an RM system which does not incorporate them as an essential feature. RM systems ought to function hand in hand with the other information services.

Surveys and Registers of Classes: The first important job of a records manager is to find out what records are being produced by his employing organisation, and what systems are being used for their deployment.

Previous writing on RM has sometimes neglected the second half of this statement. Walk-through surveys are often recommended, as an alternative to, or backed by, surveys by questionnaire. These surveys identify classes of records, and note details of thew on field work sheets. This is a good way of doing a survey which notes the existence of particular records series, but it is not sufficient if the objective is to evaluate systems.

It is possible, therefore, that an RM survey should be carried out in two parts, one to establish what classes of record are being produced, and the other to determine the production processes used. The normal method in the first case would be for the survey team to use worksheets which can later be turned into a register of classes. In the second case the survey might use flowcharts, indicating the contributory flows of manpower which lead to the production of record classes.

PLANNING THE SERVICE

Specialized Problems of Practical Librarianship: Planning

Management in socialist society is inconceivable without planning. The principle of the planned development of the new society and of its economy, science, technology and culture was emphasized even in the works of the classical authors of Marxism-Leninism, and in their resolutions the party and government pay much attention to improving the planning system. Librarianship in Czechoslovakia forms an integral part of-and is an active factor in-the political, economic and cultural development of the advanced socialist society on the basis of planning, *i.e.* pursuing a given course and a long-term objective.

The work of libraries must be so organized that it is geared as closely as possible to the implementation of the party programmes and influences effectively, by means of its specific forms and methods, further development of our society. With a view to improving the quality Of Planning in the library sector, both the Ministry of Culture and lower administrative echelons issue directives, methodological guidelines and principles as to what should be planned, when and how.

Let us take a look at how we are coping with these essentially simple questions in practice.

First, a little theory. Planning is a systematic balancing of the aims and resources of the object of planning in accordance with the directives and decisions of the agent of management. The result of planning, or rather of the planning process, is a plan in the shape of a system of binding organizational measures, procedures and stipulations which lead to the achievement of the set aim. Thus the plan is a binding directive, a specifically approved norm which applies at all levels of management entrusted with the plan's implementation, which organizes the object of planning and its activity and which prompts it to achieve a socially desirable aim.

The object of planning is in our case the entire library sector, a library network or an individual library, while the agent of management might be the Ministry of Culture as the central management authority, or a national committee, etc. By activity we mean the services offered by libraries and by socially desirable aim the fullest possible satisfaction of library users' information requirements. This is a rather simplified way of looking at things, but it is quite adequate for our purpose here.

Librarianship in Czechoslovakia draws on long-term and short-term plans. Long-term plans (outline plans) are mostly compiled for a term of five years and are based on studies and forecasts that look 10-20 years ahead. The source of information about the object of planning is the forecast, which takes a broad view of the object's possible future and establishes basic development trends and the emergence, growth or decline of environmental influences affecting the object of the forecast, such as education, publishing and so forth. On the basis of the forecast development concepts are elaborated which then find their concrete expression in the plan.

The forecast sets out a number of alternatives for the future and different ways of reaching them, while the concept, which stems from the forecast, sets out the optimal alternative for the future; and the plan, which stems from the concept, specifies the most effective way of implementing the optimal alternative.

The characteristic feature of the plan, as distinct from the forecast, it is feasibility, which, however, depends on the realism with which it was drafted, on an objective assessment of the material, manpower and other potential of the object of planning. Long-range studies and forecasts ensure the continuity of the planning process, while the five-year plan provides more precise data for the given five-year period and in turn provides the point of departure for executive plans. While long-term studies are concerned with general formulations, the five-year plan specifies concrete tasks and quantified indicators to be achieved by the object of planning during the set period, and it indicates the resources by which this is to be done.

The prerequisite for systematic and planned management is the short-term plan (executive plan), which specifies the aims and resources of the object's activity for the set period and helps to tap unused potential to provide opportunities for further development. The most important plan in library management is the annual plan, which, through its highly concrete specification of aims, resources and forms of work, provides every opportunity for subsequent strict verification of its implementation.

The annual plan as a rule specifies a library's main tasks for the set period as well as other concrete tasks, depending on its size and organizational structure. The plan's basic structure is as follows: the plan of main tasks; the executive plan, including special tasks; and the organizational and material backup plan. (For further information see bibliography.)

After our excursion into the realm of theory, let us return to our initial questions, which, having learned our lesson, we shall be able to answer with no difficulty. When do we plan? We plan at the end of the year for the next year and at the end of the five-year plan for the next five-year plan. How do we plan? Responsibly, of course, compiling long-or short-term plans depending on our position and seniority. What do we plan? We plan the work of a library, a network, or the entire sector. Essentially very simple answers to very simple questions, but... that is exactly where the problem lies. Plans are indeed drawn up by libraries within the set deadlines and, what is more, dispatched to superior organs or institutions on time; and they comply with the directives of the higher authority in respect of set indicators and percentages.

However, let us ask again: when is it done? At the last minute so as not to miss the deadline! How? At fast as possible so as to have done with it! What is planned? What is asked and required of us and no more! Does this not call to mind a paraphrase of Hamlet: To plan or not to plan, that is the question! Of course, we must plan. If our thoughts and actions are to be meaningful, we must have a certain long-term objective against which we can measure our results and assess the success or failure of our work. Why, then, do librarians view the plan as a necessary evil, why do they not exploit its indisputable managerial advantages and why do they frequently attent to the plan only when verification is due? Verification that the plan has been compiled, I hasten to add, not verification of its execution. Probably because we do not plan the right indicators, or do not plan them correctly.

In addition to general formulations on the lines of 'we will fully satisfy users' information needs during the target period', or 'we will actively contribute to the development and enhancement of the population's cultural and educational standards', indicators whose implementation is very difficult for a higher authority to verify (polling users, perhaps), the plans contain indicators that refer to library statistics-library stock in quantitative terms and its content structure, the number of readers, loans, visits, exhibitions, discussions, staffing and financial provision and so forth.

These indicators are quantifiable: hence they are easy to plan and, naturally, their implementation is subsequently not difficult to verify either. At the end of the year we can compare the results achieved with the plan, tick off the relevant sections and consider the job done and finished. Finished? Yes, of course, done and finished, what else? Sometimes we manage to forget that verification is part and parcel of management and that due attention must therefore be paid to it. However, let us digress a little and pay an imaginary visit to XY-a small town with a small library. There is not much industry, it is more of a recreational area where people have their weekend houses and cottages. A nice library with a devoted librarian, good premises and a good structure and range of library stock, very good working conditions-yet the number of readers has again declined. Loans have been 'bumped up', it is true, by lending magazines, but where are we to find people? There are none. The library organizes talks and exhibitions, it invites citizens to visit the library, yet the growth indicator is completely out of reach.

People come here to relax and do not give much thought to the library, either in summer or in winter. You may say that the librarian should have considered external circumstances when compiling the plan. Yes, she should have done, but this is not only a purely fictitious example but also a greatly simplified one. The library's efforts to attract readers may be frustrated not only by a natural decrease in population or a change in the locality's functions, but also by a change in potential readers' interests.

The decline in cinema audiences can be cited as an example. No, I am not trying to claim that our people are giving up reading, but they are less prepared to make an effort, they are spoilt by their own libraries or even by other forms of entertainment. To attract a reader today, a library must expend considerably more energy than, say, 10 or 20 years ago, and these efforts, this energy are not revealed by a mere figure, which gives the numerical information and nothing else. It is not my intention to militate against planning and statistics as to the number of readers, loans, library visits, or exhibitions, but it is my humble opinion that they give virtually no indication of the value and quality of librarians' work.

The Package of Measures to Improve the System of Planned Management of the National Economy after 1980, approved by the Czechoslovak Government in its Resolution No. 42 of 31 January 1980, considerably changed the situation in our economy, science and technology. Its purpose is, on the basis of an improved planning system, to make maximum use of all intensive factors for economic growth and to enhance the effectiveness and quality of all work.

Throughout our society utmost emphasis is placed on the intensive development both of the economy and of science and technology, yet in the library sector the trend towards extensive development has still not been halted. The constant pursuit of the biggest possible number of loans and readers is, alas, characteristic of us. True, according to Unesco statistics our country holds the world record for per capita number of loans. However, the question is: are our readers really satisfied with the service we offer.

The statistically-proven quantitative indicators specified in the plan currently tell us virtually nothing about the quality of library services, thus depriving our plans of their incentive function. Our library sector must react promptly to the new situation. We face the difficult task of establishing new indicators or of retaining the old ones but enhancing their ability to reflect quality. This would result, of course, in greater demands being made not just on the librarians themselves but also, and above all, on library management. Without the appropriate management we cannot expect high-quality results.

Let us imagine that the indicator specifying the number of readers for a given year was further broken down into fully satisfied readers, partially satisfied readers and those dissatisfied with the library's services: and the indicator for exhibitions and discussions organized by the library not only indicated the number of events held and the number of people they attracted but also reflected the extent to which they were satisfied with these events. It would, of course, be a very demanding task to ascertain the level of reader and library user satisfaction, but it would undoubtedly furnish valuable information about libraries' performance which could subsequently be used during the verification and assessment of the institution's fulfilment of its tasks, besides producing an overall improvement in the quality of the services offered, which is our main aim. The relevant scientific and methodological institutions should engage in a quest for qualitative indicators and methods of ascertaining and interpreting them.

By improving our planning system, giving it a new content, enhancing its ability to reflect more information and thus ensuring more effective management, we shall promote a more intensive development of our library sector and a greater contribution on its part to the development of the advanced socialist society. We must not forget that the plan is the basic instrument of management, but also no more than that. There still are 'executives' among us who invoke Pythia's counsel when drawing up plans, 'executives' who during the verification of plan fulfilment pull out of their sleeve a trump card in the shape of objective difficulties. If we fail to objectively assess our potential and decide our priorities, then, naturally, we must bear the consequences.

When do we plan? At the end of the year for the next year and at the end of the five-year plan for the next five year-plan.

How do we plan? Responsibility, of course.

When do we plan? The work of a library, a network of libraries, or the entire library sector.

And so we are back where we started. Or are we?

Archive Planning

The peaceful idyll once enjoyed by the archivist and Court Counsellor Grillparzer has been thoroughly destroyed. The archivists of today and tomorrow have to work in an environment in which science and technology impose their law and their rhythm. It is no accident that in recent years the question of the archivist's job, his status and career prospects and the problem of delimitation from others, such as the documentalist, has been posed with ever greater insistence. But a satisfactory answer can be worked out only with difficulty. The aim and function of this profession and the associated problem of a training pattern to meet the needs of the time have become permanent features of conferences and international congresses on archives. The job definition has become hazy and in need of clarification and amendment in two dimensions, depth and breadth.

The archivist's present list of worries does not end here, however. Going through the annual reports of national and foreign archives quickly reveals three problem areas common to all archive administrations:

1. The discrepancy between staffing levels and constantly growing tasks.

2. The discrepancy between the available storage space and the overwhelming inflow of archive material.
3. The difficulty of convincing budget experts, and in the final analysis elected representatives, of the need to provide an adequate archive budget, which would make it possible not simply to cover operating costs and the staff and infrastructure expenditure required to deal with the virtually chronic backlog in archives, but also provide for the tasks of tomorrow.

We do not deny that there are many factors contributing to this state of affairs that the archivist can do nothing about and is not responsible for, but we are not convinced that archivists have really done everything within their powers to create a sound basis for mastering the problems and tasks facing them.

2

Advances in Archival Management Science

INTRODUCTION

Once specialized State Archive Services have been established there is a need for archives administration, and the number of countries lacking such services is gradually being reduced to a minimum.

A rational system of archives administration may be introduced most easily in countries with a single State collection: this is the case in Bulgaria, Hungary, the German Democratic Republic, Poland, Romania, the Union of Soviet Socialist Republics and many other countries.

In the USSR, the decree of 1 June 1918 submitted by the Soviet of People's Commissars 'On the reorganization and centralization of archives' was signed by V. I. Lenin, founder of the Soviet State, and was an act of revolutionary importance which marked the beginning of the socialist system of archives organization. The decree stipulated that all the archive material in the country was to be considered public property. This measure led to the establishment of a new scientific category, the 'State Archive Collection'. The General Archive Directorate, which was responsible for managing the collection, was set up at the same time. A series of laws subsequently confirmed the application of the 1918 decree, particularly the 'Status of the USSR State Archive Collection' of 1958, which reinforced the principles of centralized management and storage and consolidated the links between the

State Archives and the institutions responsible for the production of documents.

By virtue of their statutes and functions the State Archives are not only repositories of documents but also scientific research establishments and institutions forming an integral part of the State's administrative services. They are responsible for managing the archives of ministries, institutions, firms and other bodies (generally known as 'current records'). Intercommunication in the functioning of these two types of archives which pursue different aims is the result of the natural continuity between the three stages of document processing: office work, current records and the State Archives.

The ultimate aim of archive services is to carry out retrospective searches as required by the public services, the national economy, culture, science, private individuals and society in general. To be able to do this archives institutions and current records must perform five major functions: collection, organization based on scientific principles, conservation, classification and the organized use of the documentary information provided by retrospective searches. The performance of these functions taken as a whole and in their various forms makes up the task of managing the State Archive Collection,

Archives consequently conduct three fundamental types of activity, corresponding to the general classification of aspects and types used in scientific work: organization, research and information.

These three aspects of archives administration are closely linked to one another, each of them being based on the other two. They none the less differ and have varying aims, and will consequently bear individual examination as aspects of archives administration.

THE SCIENTIFIC ORGANIZATION OF ARCHIVES ADMINISTRATION

The scientific organization of archival management involves a wide range of issues which include personnel management, planning the development of archives and the archival sciences, regulations, coordination and accounting. The study of these problems is closely linked to archival economics, an expanding archival discipline which deals with the organization of work, efficiency, determining the grades at which archive staff are to be recruited, etc. Economic analysis is applied to all the different aspects of archival work designed to make rational use of material and human resources and ensure constant improvements in organizational methods, in order to chance the quality of such work and make it more effective.

The need to tackle the organization and division of archival work in the USSR in a scientific manner led to the compilation of a table in which all the categories of work carried out in State archives are clearly set out. This table facilitates operational studies of the work and serves as a basis for establishing model procedures.

The scientific organization of personnel calls for uniform working conditions and a series of documents setting out the functional distribution tasks, the structures of archival institutions, and the area of activity covered by each post.

The scientific bases of archives administration entail the introduction of new recruitment norms in the State Archives. Soviet archivists are researching this problem, using mathematical statistics (the multiple correlation method). These standards make it possible to determine not only recruitment levels but also the number of archivists required to carry out a given task, and to improve the monitoring methods to be applied to archival work.

Planning and accounting constitute a second group of problems connected with the administration of archives. Archives in the USSR have developed an integrated planning system based on the principles used in national economic planning.

At the basis of this planning system are the five-year development plans for the State archives, reflecting the decisions of the executive bodies, the objectives of economic planning and the need to develop and improve archives.

During the five-year period that has just begun (1976-1980), following lines laid down by the XXVth Congress of the CPSU, special attention is being paid to enhancing the scientific dimension of archives work, as well as its quality and effectiveness, to storage conditions and to the rational use of material, financial and human resources. The five-year plan for archives development is made up of several sections defining the practical tasks allocated to different projects.

The scientific research work carried out by VNIIDAD is based on annual and five-year plans. There are other plans covering coordination of the approach to major problems (in which the other institutions participate), the work of the Academic Council and its sections and the application of research findings. All these plans are linked and constitute a single organizatory and planning system governing the development of scientific research.

Forecasts of scientific growth are an important factor in planning and management. An outline of the forecasts concerning the basic problems in documents management archival science and archeography up until 1990 is made available to Societ archivists.

The coordination of scientific research has become extremely important in recent years. This is due to the complexity of the most advanced scientific work, which requires the attention of several institutions covering different areas. The Commission for the Coordination of Scientific and Systematic Research of the USSR General Archive Directorate has a large part to play in this process. The Commission revises the plans coordinating VNIIDAD's research work and that of other archival institutions, establishing the requisite contacts with the different institutions and the Academy of Sciences of the USSR. It monitors the progress of research into complex problems and assesses its findings. Coordination is the responsibility of VNIIDAD, which is the leading institution and prepares the methodological and organizational documents for the coordinating bodies (specifications, research schedules, work schedules), organizes conferences with their representatives, examines their work, etc. These are complex tasks with a high labour coefficient, and they are taking up more and more of the time of those concerned.

The plans for the implementation of completed research work provide for the establishment of methodological norms to be applied for experimental purposes, as well as the dissemination of the findings; talks given by specialists, conferences, seminars, the preparation of exhibitions and of articles, etc.

The accounting system is complemented by the planning structure. The book-keeping for each piece of scientific research work is done separately, according to a system whose structure, order and lay-out are the subject of a special State norm.

In recent times, a trend towards the constitution of scientific research groups and committees to encourage the effective use of labour in archival institutions has been observed in State archives (Poland, Croatia, Romania, Czechoslovakia).

Scientific organizations of this kind mainly study the problems connected with the internal organization of archives, the development and correct grouping of the collections, and the standardization of documents dealing with archives administration.

THE SCIENTIFIC BASES OF ARCHIVES ADMINISTRATION

Each of the branches of archival science and records management is linked in one way or another to archives administration. This link is determined above all by the nature of the scientific research, whose considerable diversity may be reduced to three essential categories: theoretical or basic research, applied research, methodological research. In the USSR, this classification is strengthened by the 'Basic guidelines for the organization of scientific research in archival institutions' (Moscow 1975).

The aim of theoretical research is to develop scientific theories and promote the acquisition of systematic knowledge concerning specific scientific problems. They contribute to the detailed development of research work. The purpose of applied research is to use theoretical knowledge in order to solve specific practical problems. Methodological research is the result of archivists' scientific activities, which are reflected in general and consultative methodological handbooks and in mandatory standard-setting texts.

The Importance of Scientific Archival Research into Archives Administration: Among the effects of scientific archival research on archives administration mention should be made in the first place of the effect of such research on the most important function of archives: collection and selection. This function is supported by special theoretical research and methods of assessing the usefulness of documents.

These problems attract the attention of archivists the world over. Many countries are organizing research and devising a methodology for a low-cost system of selecting and preserving genuinely useful documents, which can be applied to a constantly expanding flow of documents. It was precisely this aspect of studies that directly influenced archives administration in several countries.

The methods used to evaluate documents are based on theoretical concepts of the informative role of documents. Generally, the role and importance of an institution in a hierarchical government system is a crucial factor when determining the content and historical value of the documents it has produced. In the USSR, documents are assessed on the basis of this principle, after drawing up a list of institutions to be taken into account. The process of selecting the institutions is carried out by means of 'sample lists', prepared for this purpose. These lists classify the institutions in groups. They are standard-setting documents which directly influence the workings of the process whereby historic documents are incorporated in archives.

The need to select the documents that are stored in archives with care because of the increasing quantities of public records has obliged archivists in several countries to formulate basic evaluation criteria. There is a noticeably tendency to make these more detailed and to have recourse to other disciplines linked to archives science. Research of this kind is connected to applied research in archives science and thanks to specific methodological texts, it has an influence on archives administration.

The need to reduce the number of documents to the minimum while maximizing their information content has led archivists in several countries to study the phenomena of the absorption and reproduction of information in contemporary documentary systems. Research is being carried out in this field in Great Britain, the USSR, the U.S.A., France, Sweden and other countries. In the USSR documents are evaluated by the Committee of Experts of the State Archives and by institutions, organizations and business concerns. The archive services of the federated and autonomous republics and their archives departments also have committees of experts which evaluate documents. These committees are the various links in the administrative chain that controls the selection of documents. The supreme authority, the Central Committee for Expert Inspection (TsEPK) of the General Dictorate of State Archives of the USSR, is an organizational and methodological centre which directs the methodological side of document assessment at the level of the State Archive Services: it draws up model lists of documents and approves the draft lists of documents intended for the different departments.

Research and management functions are both represented on this committee, as is demonstrated by the participation of VNIIDAD representatives in the relevant studies. Not only do the findings of scientific research work influence organization and practical content, but they are themselves influenced by the administrative bodies which, by handing over their records to the State Archives, at the same time determine the direction and the intensity of this research. The TsEPK is thus an administrative mechanism governing the interaction between theory and practice in the expansion of archives. Mention should also be made of the effect of contemporary research into the reference system on archives administration. These studies are intended to facilitate the retrieval of data in retrospective searches.

The usefulness of the differential method of describing documents on the basis of their information category should be stressed. From the standpoint of archives administration, this type of classification facilitates the planning of descriptive work, reduces the time and labour required to carry it out and provides a more detailed description of the collections which contain the most information. The application of the differential method means that the acquisition of documents by archives is directly determined by their quality as sources of information (diversity of documentary data, historical importance, state of preservation, frequency of use).

In the majority of countries the need for serious scientific research into the use of archives has also been recognized. Efforts have been made to define the problem of the use of documents (Canada), to undertake a systematic examination of users' information requirements by analysing their requests (Archives of the Federal Republic of Germany), to establish links between the ways in which the documents are used and the selection of the corresponding personnel (Great Britain), to include archival information in the network of scientific/historical information and documentation (German Democratic Republic), to create a stock of data which will subsequently be translated into machine language (Poland), to develop objective criteria for assessing the effectiveness of research from the standpoint of the tasks of 'social management', the development of the national economy, science, etc. (USSR).

The Importance of Research into Records Management for Archives Administration: From the standpoint of archives administration, the main significance of research into the creation of records is that its findings contribute to one of its most important functions of archives, *i.e.* the acquisition of highly informative documents.

Scientific and technical progress, together with the increase in documents on the subject and the emergence of new types of media (audiovisual, computerized and others) call for a new, universally valid approach to the problems raised by the creation of records. In most countries, archivists have joined forces with management specialists (the German Democratic Republic, Denmark, Canada, France, Great Britain, Poland, USSR, U.S.A., Sweden and others).

In the USSR studies of the procedures and principles of the handling of records in administrative systems have made it possible to create the nucleus of a new scientific discipline, the science of records management, which is an application of the science of 'social management', and is connected with archival science and contemporary studies on information.

It should be noted that a broader definition of records management has been adopted. It now covers all handling of documents in administrative systems. This is the theoretical basis on which Soviet archivists, together with legal and other specialists have built up a unified records conservation system (EGSD).

This system is a code of rules, recommendations and norms for the conservation of records at every administrative level. It has been designed as a uniform method that will have an influence on management procedures as it guides, regulates and standardizes the handling of records from their creation until the time comes to store them in archives.

The establishment of this system led Soviet archivists to give closer attention to the standardization of administrative documents. As a result, two norms concerning administrative documents have been issued: 'System of documents on organization and administration. Basic principles' and 'System of documents on organization and administrations. Model'. These certain specifications regarding the drafting and typing of documents and the optimum layout for each component of the document. A number of documents are thus based on a single model matrix and their quality as sources of management information is improved.

The idea underlying the unified system and the norms for administrative documents is the idea that at the very conception of a document, even before its creation, its value as a source of information for the future must be taken into account. The application of these norms constitutes a link between records management and the State Archive Collection. The latter thus benefits from improvements in records management. The establishment of the unified system and of norms for administrative documents gave an impetus to the development of the administrative sciences and made it possible to consider a unified system for documents on organization and administration which could be used both in automated administrative systems and in traditional ones.

A unified system of this kind (USORD) is currently being developed by VNIIDAD in conjunction with several other archival institutions in the USSR; it will give rise to a complex network of documents designed to carry out one of the basic administrative functions, *i.e.* the organization of administrative systems and processes. Similar research is under way in other countries. For instance, the Central Archive Directorate and the State Archives in Bulgaria are also setting up a unified system for the conservation of the State Archives (EGSD).

The Importance of Research in the Natural Sciences for Archives Administration: An important feature of contemporary archives administration is the wide-ranging application of discoveries in the natural sciences and of advanced techniques. The role of research in this field is constantly expanding, so that theoretical and applied research serves as a base for the preparation of norms and manuals designed to improve conservation processes and rationalize reprographic and reduction techniques.

Several countries are planning to develop their existing scientific research centres and establish new ones. Czechoslovakia is building a centre for applied research in document conservation and restoration, which will use the most up-to-date techniques. In the USSR, this type of research is carried out by VNIIDAD, which is responsible for the methodological supervision of the network of microfilm and restoration laboratories working for the State Archives. The Croatian State Archives in Zagreb are planning an archival research centre, in which research in the natural sciences will play a clearly defined part. Two further laboratories dealing with documents hygiene, conservation and restoration have been built in Bulgaria, in addition to the one already in existence. In Poland, the specialized laboratories of the conservation service of the General Directorate of State Archives play an important role. Other countries are also well advanced in this field.

Large-scale research projects generally require close cooperation with other experts who are engaged, to a greater or lesser extent, in research on paper, ink, film, their environment, biological agents which can damage documents and even the dangers inherent in documents themselves. Archivists in the United States work together with scientists specializing in restoration and reprography. They apply the findings of their work on the development of artificial aging methods, the use of laser beams, refrigeration techniques atomization with non-acid aerosols, etc.

In the USSR, the VNIIDAD laboratories work together with

institutions of the Academy of Sciences and the major State libraries. A number of countries have research programmes whose aim is to create durable media (paper, film, ink) and use them to solve the problem of document conservation (Great Britain, GDR, USSR and others).

The laboratory of W.D. Barrow (U.S.A) has studied the agents which hinder book and documents conservation, and ways of producing long-lasting paper.

In recent years, there has been a good deal of interest in synthetic paper (U.S.A and Japan). According to the information published on the subject, this type of paper is extremely stable and long-lasting but there is a problem of electrostatics to be dealt with. Great Britain has produced a type of paper called 'archival quality paper' which is guaranteed to last 500 years. The USSR has produced an experimental batch of long-lasting paper with a life of approximately 850 years. Research is being carried out into paper made from cotton fibres which would have a life of 1,000 years and could be used for particularly important documents.

However, the physical conservation of the paper does not as yet guarantee the conservation of the text. It has in fact been shown that ink often actively contributes to the destruction of a text. The interrelationship between the medium and the text thus had to be investigated with reference to conservation conditions, as did the parameters of the 'medium/text' system.

Scientific research and practical measures designed to combat infectious biogenic substances, particularly fungi, have also been given a fresh impetus. The objective is to protect not only paper documents but also films and photographic plates. The danger of placing infected documents in storage is particularly great in a tropical climate. Recent discoveries in the field of antisepsis open up major possibilities for the treatment of archival documents.

As a result of research into existing methods of mass disinfection the use of formation has gradually given way to more effective treatment with gas, using ethyl oxide, methyl bromide and other chemical products. Archivists in many countries also consider the physical method, which consists of disinfecting documents with high frequency currents, to be promising. Several countries (Bulgaria, France, Czechoslovakia) use ionizing radiation for this purpose.

Studies concerning the properties of computerized, audiovisual and other documents are a particular focus of interest at the moment. So far little is known about their durability or optimum storage conditions. The problem of the durability of the microfilms used in automatic data reduction systems (COM) is one of great urgency. The archives of several countries possess large collections of films and microfilms, and methodological guidelines for their storage and conservation are needed.

It is often necessary to reproduce the colours of documents by photographing them. It is thus essential to create new types of photographic media for the purposes of microfilming or photography, as well as optimum conditions for the chemical treatment and conservation of these materials.

The financing of means of observing certain ecological parameters should be considered in the light of the cost of protective treatment on the one hand and of the equipment of restoration laboratories on the other. Economic criteria must outweigh purely technical considerations, particularly as regards the choice of methods. Archivists require detailed information on new techniques in order to choose the most suitable materials. Several countries, particularly the USSR, have begun to draw up selection and assessment criteria for new materials intended for the State Archives and to prepare summary catalogues of these materials adapted to the specific aims of archives.

The question of what would constitute the 'ideal archives' has been discussed for some time now. Archivists in most countries associate this concept with the archives administration of the future. In countries where archives are considered to be part of the State's information potential the '"ideal archives' are seen in the context of a task to be carried out by archives either following their integration in a single national information system (Japan), or as a result of greater interdependence between the networks of archives, libraries and documentation centres (Great Britain) or finally, following the constitution of a computer 'network covering the whole country' (U.S.A.).

Archivists in the German Democratic Republic associate the definition of the 'ideal archives' with a definition of the role and functions of State Archives in a developed socialist society. In Czechoslovakia, the idea of 'ideal archives' is bound up with the project for the construction of an archives complex in Prague, of State Archives in Bratislava and of new archive buildings in other towns which would use the most up-to-date administrative techniques and information systems.

Archivists in the Federal Republic of Germany have outlined a model which the Federal Archives should, in their view, comply with by 1980. The Archives are considered as a cultural centre that stores a minimum of documents with the maximum content in a more compact form, and uses the latest techniques to satisfy the information requirements of the whole of society.

Soviet archivists believe that the traditional methods of archival storage call for improvements that go beyond changes in technological procedures and in the technical equipment used in archives. The research undertaken in this field aims to develop technological criteria for each technical operation. The specifications of projects relating to 'ideal archives' are being prepared, and studies are being carried out on recommendations concerning the equipment in archival repositories.

Great importance is now attached to the updating of technical and standard-setting documentation applicable to the construction and equipment of archives, together with the standardization of architectural design. Most countries consider it reasonable when building archives to take into account the physical constitution of the documents that are to be stored in them (paper, film, magnetic tapes) and to follow standardized plans.

In Great Britain, the U.S.A., France and the Federal Republic of Germany, it is felt that documents that have not been sorted, and most of which will be destroyed after a short space of time, need only be preserved in intermediate repositories, which are built and equipped at a low cost and are clearly distinguished from archives proper. Structures of this kind already exist in a number of countries. Their main advantage is the relatively low cost of storing the documents, combined with the possibility of making maximum use of the space. As for models of the ideal archives building and their construction, Soviet archivists take as their basis the fact that new trends in the field of archives point above all to the mechanization and complete automation of technological procedures such as data processing and collection, the conservation and use of documents, and to the introduction of new types of data carriers that make it possible to reduce archives to a very small scale and aŭtomate them.

THE USE OF THE COMPUTERS AND OF MICROFILM IN ARCHIVES ADMINISTRATION

One of the main tasks of archives administration is the establishment of automated systems which use computers to store, process and retrieve information.

In a number of countries, this has become a matter of urgency due to the rapid increase in the amount of documents that are preserved and recent advances in computer technology. The national archives in the United States are one of the main archival centres for the use of computers. There the automatic SPINDEX indexing system is used to process staff files and includes name, post, date and the document reference number.

The Public Record Office in London uses computers to store and produce data describing its collections and is thus able to publish directories using a photo-typesetter. A topographical index arranged by codes of groups of documents, by classes and by location is issued twice yearly for internal use.

The East Sussex County Record Office uses computers for cataloguing and records management (ARCAIC) and PARC systems. The Archives of the Federal

Republic of Germany are using a STAIRS system to retrieve data from stored documents and to compile indexes of names of persons, places and subjects. The Italian State Archives use an automatic indexing system to retrieve and produce summaries of notarial documents. The Canadian Federal Archives use the document indexing and monitoring system RECODEX, which was created with the assistance of the State bureau of computer services. The ALPHATEXT system has made it possible to draw up a standardized description of private archive collections (manuscripts) preserved in the Canadian Archives (30,000 items). The Belgian State Archives have introduced automatic cataloguing for the science library and printed records. Similar projects are under way in Austria, France, Japan, and in several other countries.

The Member States of COMECON are investigating the possibility of developing AIRS for archival purposes. These countries can draw on the experience of very large automated information centres. For instance, the Romanian State Archives have adopted the SARIAS descriptive system using a third generation computer. The system which uses an open thesaurus, operates on a two-pass principle, and is linked to a summary and a search facility recorded on magnetic tape. Czechoslovakia and the German Democratic Republic are using automated information systems and have computerized the whole sequence of document storage, retrieval and production (PENTAKA system in the GDR).

The USSR is working on the implementation of an automated scientific and technical information system which covers the documents of all the State Archives in the country. An automated scientific and technical documentation subsystem for the State Archives network will be established within this system. Document storage and processing will be carried out by means of a three-pass circuit designed to carry out the following functions:

- retrospective subject searches requested by an individual user or group of users;
- the selective circulation of information to a limited number of regular users;
- the statistical treatment of data.

The Central Catalogue AIRS (AIRS/CFC) will constitute a further part of the general automated documentary information system of the USSR State Archives. Its purpose is to store information on all the archive documents in the USSR, including their title, location, the amount of room they occupy in the storage units and several other factors.

The use of magnetic tape cassettes that are identical to the compact cassettes used in portable recordings opens up a wide range of possibilities. These cassettes are easy to store, transport or send by post. A mini-computer cassette can store from one to two million alphanumeric characters. Most minicomputers also have visual display units for both text and graphics.

In the major modern archive repositories effective document retrieval is based on the use of microfilms as information carriers. Microfilming reduces storage space and computer time in a rational way, and less paper is thus required.

For some time now there has been a clear tendency to use computerized data production systems employing a microphotographic medium (roll microfilm and microfiches), instead of separate microfilm units.

The AIRS/CFC is classed as a two-pass factographic documentary system. A variant of this system will use an information retrieval language of the descriptor-classification type with a position-based grammar. The two systems will be used together to assess collections of scientific and technical documents.

The development of programming systems for third generation computers has made it possible to set up effective integrated information systems bringing together the documentary collections of several archives. The exchange of data between archival centres can then be organized by location or communication networks.

AIRS specialists are showing great interest in the use of low-power computers ('mini-computers'), designed to handle relatively small numbers of documents. The mini-computers used in a number of local AIRS have already demonstrated their cost effectiveness chiefly on account of their lower price-and given satisfactory performances. Should the number of documents increase or more intensive use be made of the machines, the system's reserve of power may be supplemented by replacing certain components without incurring major expense. This adds to the system's flexibility.

The advantages of microfilm as an information carrier and of minicomputers as a means of processing this information have led to the establishment of relatively cheap specialized mini-systems for the storage, retrieval and production of copies of microfilms or of graphic documents. The application of these systems is, however, limited with regard to the number of documents that may be stored, the length of the index, the research algorithm, etc. The Miracod (Kodak, U.S.A.) Odelcod Filmdata Bank (De Oude Delft, the Netherlands) and Cezam (Cifal and Sait Data System, France) mini-systems have established their reputation. The Miracod system is used by the Canadian State Archives.

The retrieval of information on magnetic tape or in electronic memory banks direct to the user's console will become increasingly common. The automatic indexing of documents, real-time dialogue, and the establishment of a link between the computer and the communication system would make possible further significant improvements in the effectivenss of AIRS.

THE NEED TO DEVELOP A SCIENTIFIC ARCHIVAL TERMINOLOGY

Efficient archives administration is conditional upon the development of a special instrument of communication: scientific archival terminology. This will involve improvements in the definition of traditional concepts and the interpretation and assimilation of new terms adapted to the special nature of archival work.

The influence of terminology on administrative objectives is by its very nature informative; only its forms differ. In any case, a unified and unambiguous terminology encourages sound decision-making and makes it easier to carry decisions out. In addition, it makes scientific literature and informative publications less arduous reading.

The publication in the USSR of the 'Concise dictionary of archival terms' (1968) and the 'Concise dictionary of types and varieties of documents' (1974), which contain a considerable number of terms, marked a great stride forward in the unification of the theoretical aspects of archival science and records management in this country.

Several countries have established norms for archival terminology. In Sweden, this is done by the National Standardization Committee, on which sit representatives of the

State Archives. In the USSR, a 1971 terminological bulletin contains 49 basic terms relating to the conservation of documents and archives whose use is compulsory in standard-setting documents and in specialized, technical and reference works.

Terminological research has repercussions beyond national frontiers, contributing to understanding among specialists on an international level and helping to surmount terminological barriers. Archivists in Poland, the GDR, Czechoslovakia, Hungary and Bulgaria are revising their terminological dictionaries and the latest editions already contain new terms.

The COMECON countries are at present engaged in terminological research which highlights the need for a common terminology that can only be achieved on the basis of a comparative analysis of the definitions used in the different national archival terminologies.

The compilation of an international dictionary under the aegis of the International Council on Archives, which would include archival terms in the Council's different working languages, would appear to be highly desirable, if not essential, for the future of archival science throughout the world.

Library Administration and New Management Systems

MONSIEUR JOURDAIN, Molière's *Bourgeois Gentilhomme,* was surprised and pleased to learn that he had been speaking prose all his life without knowing it. I felt the same way when I finally learned that I had been a manager for 20 years without knowing it. Well, I always knew that I was a library *administrator*, but somehow I never thought of myself as a *manager* because that term connoted a kind of modern professionalism that the more familiar term *administrator* lacked.

Ten years ago I attended the University of Maryland's excellent two-week development programme for library administrators and was deeply impressed by the introductory courses and readings which covered the full range of subjects like McGregor's Theories X and Y, Management by Objectives (MBO), Programme Budgeting (PPBS), Decision Theory, Cost-Benefit Analysis, Mathematical Modelling, Management Information Systems, etc. I came away thinking, somewhat naively, that business and other managers had mastered and were routinely using that arsenal of sophisticated management systems and techniques in their daily work, and that it was only library and perhaps academic administrators that were struggling along with the traditional methods. It was clear that we librarians had a lot of catching-up to do.

It was with some hesitation that I accepted the directorship of a large library in 1970 because I believed that research libraries were becoming increasingly costly and complex organizations and that I lacked the formal management training and skills that the job required. Determined to remedy my lack of formal training, I enrolled in the Harvard Business School's Advanced Management Programme, a prestigious and expensive three-month programme especially designed for high-level business, government, and military executives. I thought the ''B-School" would work its magic and convert me from a self-taught library administrator into a certified modern manager, but I was disappointed.

Early in its history, the Harvard Business School developed the case method of instruction and it has used it almost exclusively in its teaching ever since. The case method can be very effective, but it was overused in the executive development programme. In three months, we never read anything but cases, and since the cases were all efficiently reproduced and distributed in convenient packets, we never had the need or the occasion to use the rich resources of the Baker Library. In fact, we seldom had to read from a real book or journal.

The classics of management science were rarely mentioned, and with the exception of a few sessions on decision theory and computer simulation, almost no mention was made of any of the new management systems that had been developed and were presumably being used routinely everywhere but in libraries. The Harvard programme was useful, but it did not give me the management knowledge and skills that I needed and wanted; so I continued to read about management and to attend management institutes and workshops. (Among the best and most useful are the short programmes offered by ARL's Office of Management Studies.) This reading and supplementary training helped me to develop and sharpen my management skills over the years. At the same time, I was gaining confidence and maturity and getting a lot of practical on-the-job experience.

I was also called upon to serve on a number of boards, commissions, and committees; this gave me the opportunity to work closely with and observe a peer group of top managers and executives, not only in libraries, but in universities, business firms, and government offices. I found that most of them, like me, had no special management training or education and were struggling, each in his or her own unscientific way, to do the management jobs to which they had been appointed. Some were more competent and effective than others, but previous formal management training seemed not to make any significant difference. Indeed, it was hard to tell who had training and who didn't. I noticed that there were few trained management experts in top level management positions. Instead, they were working as specialists in staff positions or as teachers, researchers, or consultants.

I could not see any real difference in what I was doing as a library director and what my peers in other fields were doing. After a while, I began to suspect that the reality of what we managers were experiencing in our day-to-day activities had more validity than the theoretical world of management that was being described in books and articles written by management professors and social scientists.

How do Managers Manage?

The studies by Mintzberg and other researchers showed that from street gang leaders to the President of the United States, managers do not spend their time planning, organizing, coordinating, and controlling as the French industrialist, Henri Fayol said they did in 1916 and as most writers on management have continued to repeat ever since. They are not like the orchestra leader who directs the component parts of his organization with ease and precision. Instead, they spend their time reacting to crises, seizing special opportunities, attending meetings, negotiating, talking on the telephone, cultivating interpersonal and political relationships, gathering and disseminating information, and fulfiling a variety of ceremonial functions. Mintzberg says:

> *I was struck during my study by the fact that the executives I was observing-all very competent by any standard-are fundamentally indistinguishable from their counterparts of a hundred years ago (or a thousand years ago, for that matter). The information they need differs, but they seek it in the same way-by word of mouth. Their decisions concern modern technology, but the procedures they use to make them are the same as the procedures of the 19th Century manager. Even the computer, so important for the specialized work of the organization, has apparently had no influence on the work procedures of general managers. In fact, the manager is in a kind of loop, with increasingly heavy work pressures but no aid forthcoming from management science.*

The Mintzberg view is by no means unique. There is a growing number of management scholars who are questioning the conventional view of management and what managers do. In a critical review of *On Management* (Harper, 1976), a book of articles selected from 25 years of the *Harvard Business Review,* Albert Shapero, a management professor at the University of Texas, strikes a similar note:

> *The term management conjures up images of control, rationality, systematic: but studies of what managers actually do depict behaviours and situations that are chaotic, unplanned, and charged with improvisation. The Managerial life at every level is reflexive-responding to calls, memos, personnel problems, fire drills budget meetings, and personnel reviews. Occasionally, however, we find at managerial levels individuals who go 24 hours without being interrupted by meetings or phone calls. They are the long-range planners the people in O.R.. E.D.P., financial or market planning, or market research. Management is really for them. The bulk of the articles in On Management are concerned with ideas from the world of the staff functionary.*

Are Management Systems Really Used?

What about the claims of widespread use of new scientific management systems and techniques? Is it really true that managers in business, government, and other institutions are using them extensively while we library administrators are lagging far behind?

Let's first look at what a few of the management experts say about the use of these systems in general, and then we will look at their use in libraries.

William R. Dill. dean of the Graduate School of Business Administration at New York University, makes this sober assessment:

> *For all the progress we have made in developing good approaches to planning, forecasting, budgeting, and control, and for all the enthusiasm we in schools of management have helped to build for these approaches their use has been fitful and sporadic even in the most analytically sophisticated and goal-oriented institutions. In corporations that are pointed out as models for what can be accomplished, the outputs of planning, budgeting and modelling staffs are often quietly ignored by operating people when times are good; these outputs often seem irrelevant in times of sudden challenge or change. Analysis and planning are still far from foolproof ways to anticipate change and potential crises.*

Aaron Wildavsky, dean of the Graduate School of Public Policy at the university of California, Berkeley, has written a number of articles in which he argues convincingly, citing evidence and authorities, that the major modern information systems like PERT, MBO, PPBS. Social Indicators, and Zero Based Budgeting have not worked and cannot work. About PERT (Programme Evaluation Review Technique), he says that "the few studies that exist suggest that outside of construction, where one activity tends to follow another, PERT is rarely successful."

On MBO (Management by Objectives), he says: "The trouble with MBO is that the attempt to formalize procedures for choosing objectives without considering organizational dynamics leads to the opposite of what was intended-bad management, irrational choice, and ineffective decision-making." "The main product of MBO, as experience in the United States federal government suggests, is, literally, a series of objectives. Aside from the unnecessary paper work, such exercises are self defeating because they become mechanisms for avoiding rather than making choices. Long lists of objectives are useless because rarely do resources remain beyond the first few." On PPBS, Wildavsky is equally harsh. He says that "Programme budgeting does not work anywhere in the world it has been tried," and that "no one knows how to do programme budgeting." His assessments of Social Indicators and Zero Based Budgeting are in a similar vein.

These realistic assessments that we are getting from authorities like Mintzberg, Shapero, Dill, Wildavsky, and others should serve to remind us to maintain a healthy skepticism whenever we read about the effectiveness and widespread use of new management systems and techniques. We librarians should guard against the tendency we have to look for panaceas and to accept uncritically the claims and promises made on behalf of each new management theory or system that appears.

Consider the minimal impact on libraries as compared with the initial promise, for example, of PPBS, Operations Research, MBO, and even Participative Management.

To the best of my knowledge, PPBS has not been successfully implemented in a single library and I doubt that it ever will be. Interest in it is rapidly waning.

The practical application of Operations Research in libraries has been extremely limited to date. One of the earliest and best known economic analyses of library decision making was done in the MIT Libraries in 1969. The report of that study came to this sobering conclusion: "Although helpful, an economic analysis of a university (or public) library is insufficient because libraries operate as political systems and thus improving libraries requires political analysis." In an excellent article on library decision making, Jeffrey Raffel, an economist and co-author of the MIT study begins by saying that "in general, the more important the decision, the less beneficial a cost-benefit analysis is to library decision makers," and concludes by saying that "it is time that we all recognized the politics of libraries and acted accordingly."

In a classic paper on Management by Objectives in academic libraries, lames Michalko, after a thorough, critical review of the literature, recommends against the use of MBO in libraries on the grounds that it is a limited approach which is costly and difficult to implement and which yields uncertain results.

Participative management is another "new" management technique that has been particularly oversold in the last decade. In fact, it is considered by many librarians to be the perfect management system. Good management has always included consultation and participation, it is just the name the faddishness, and some of the formal structures that are new. When used properly and honestly, participative management is a useful process at all levels, and not just by top managers on major decisions as is sometimes assumed. It is essential that there be appropriate consultation and participation of interested and competent staff members on important decisions affecting them. But participative management will not bring on the management millenium in libraries.

Participative management is not decision making by committee or by staff plebiscite. Good management requires that when all the facts have been gathered and analyzed and all the advice is in, the appropriate administrator has to make the decision and take responsibility for it.

Knowing when and how to seek and take advantage of consultative advice and prior approval of decisions where appropriate is one of the most important managerial skills. Decisions should be made at the lowest competent level. The library's critical strategy decisions involve a world outside the library and must usually be made by the director and his chief associates. Staff committees can give good advice on such matters, but they simply do not have the information, the knowledge, or the perspective required to make those decisions-and they cannot take responsibility for the results.

One extreme form of participative management, the collegial or faculty system of governance, was developed for academic departments; it works badly there and worse or not at all in libraries. Where it appears to work, it is because those involved have tacitly made concessions to traditional hierarchical systems and the demands of the environment while preserving the collegial form. A library is not an academic department, it is a service organization and should be so administered. A librarian by any other name is still a librarian and it is time for mature acceptance of that fact.

Perhaps the reason that participative management has been embraced so enthusiastically and uncritically by librarians in recent years is not because of its management benefits, but because it appears to be the model that best justifies faculty status. It is assumed that because faculty members participate in a collegial academic decision-making process, that model is the appropriate one to use in libraries-if librarians are to achieve faculty status.

Much of the library-based management literature since 1970 is self-serving and reflects a direct or indirect preoccupation with matters of staff status and benefits frequently hidden behind arguments for participative management. It is time that we recognized this natural bias and took steps to overcome it by giving more attention and weight to the more objective management literature from outside the library field.

Two recent articles on participative management in libraries, one by James Govan and the other by Dennis Dickenson, give encouraging evidence that the library profession is beginning to take a more realistic and balanced view of the advantages and limitations of participative management and collegial governance. Govan reminds us that:

> *Librarians cannot afford to degrade services nor alienate their users in an effort, however enlightened or well intentioned, to make their jobs more challenging and satisfying. Participation and consultation cost time and money and often, like faculty deliberations, produce rather conservative results. In this connection, it is useful to remember Masiow's belief that Theory Y is possible only in periods of affluence. It is also healthy to recall Drucker's statement that service institutions do not operate for the people who work in them.*

In his perceptive article, Dickenson tries to provide "an antidote for some of the more extreme and sometimes naive interpretations of participative management that appear from time to time in library literature".

Peter Drucker summed up an important truth about management when he said in response to an interviewer's question about the efficacy of new management techniques: "The young people today expect to see business run by theory, knowledge, concepts, and planning. But then they find it is run like the rest of the world-by experience and expediency, by who you know, and by the hydrostatic pressure in your bladder".

This is not just the way business is run it is the way libraries are run as well. And it is the way they will continue to be run despite the current rhetoric about the managerial revolution that is being ushered in by the use of new quantitative and psychological management systems and theories.

Why? Because a library operates in a political environment and nearly all the really important decisions that are made at the highest levels have an overriding political component. They are rarely the product of cost benefit analysis or Operations Research where the various factors are weighed and compared and the "best" or most cost-effective course is chosen. These management techniques can be useful sometimes to implement a programme or a project in the most effective manner *after* the political decision to proceed has been made.

They can also be useful in providing a rationale to support some essentially political decision that is being proposed or advocated, or to impress higher authorities or constituents with the competence of the managers and the rationality of their decision making process. Management systems, particularly PPBS, ZBB, and PERT are used in government and military bureaucracies largely because they are mandated by law or regulation.

In the library world, as in education, business, and government few major programme decisions are made solely or even largely on the basis of careful studies of needs and costs. Consider, for example, decisions to build a new library building, to open a new departmental or branch library, to achieve excellence in some special subject discipline, or to embark on a major automation programme. These programme decisions are usually the result of an initiative or vision by an imaginative and powerful person, perhaps a library director a dean a president, a mayor, or other official. They are political, emotional or even personal decisions-justified, rationalized, and perhaps implemented with the assistance of various kinds of analyses and studies, but seldom derived from them.

It is important that librarians understand how and why these really critical decisions are made so that they will not be disillusioned or discouraged when they discover that the "best", the most efficient, or the least expensive solution frequently loses out to the one that is the most politically expedient or attractive.

The Quantitative Approach

I think it is important to make a distinction between the claims made on behalf of complex quantitative management systems such as Operations Research and Cost-Benefit Analysis and the collection and analysis of quantitative data in libraries to assist in rational decision making.

I am questioning the validity and usefulness of these complex systems, but I am not questioning the need for and use of quantitative studies for measuring and evaluating library services. Quite the contrary, we need to know more about libraries, their resources, and how they are actually used. We have relied historically upon input data, *e.g.*, the number of books acquired the number of serials subscribed to, the number of books circulated, the dollars spent, etc. The qualitative characteristics of these data are dubious; we desperately need reliable measures of library effectiveness.

Following the pioneering work by Fremont Rider in 1940 on the growth of research libraries, there has been an increasing number of extremely valuable quantitative studies like those by Fussler, Lancaster, Buckland, and other works of solid quality. The findings of such studies provide the theoretical foundations and practical knowledge that working library managers need to draw on to help them think clearly and creatively about library management and to make sound decisions based on valid data. This is especially true in this time of transition when the conventional wisdom of our profession will not suffice to see us through.

As one of the library managers for whose benefit and use such studies are presumably made, I thank the authors and urge them on to greater productivity and precision. I also urge them to try to keep their studies as simple as possible and to summarize their findings in readable English.

Unfortunately, a good deal of the quantitative research that is done in the library field is unintelligible, irrelevant, or too complicated and theoretical for any practical use in libraries. Much of it is written in the language of higher mathematics which is incomprehensible to most managers. This is particularly true of studies that are made by academics outside the library field such as statisticians, economists, psychologists, Operations Research people, etc. Their goal is not necessarily to do studies that are useful, but to demonstrate their mathematical prowess, to test theories and methodologies, to get published, and to award doctoral degrees to deserving graduate students. They select the library as their laboratory because it is convenient and because they think it is virgin territory ready for easy exploitation. They are more interested in the process than in the results.

The most useful library research is done by librarians or others with a serious long-term interest and involvement in libraries who work with librarians in a spirit of genuine collaboration. They are trying to make an impact. It is the difference between a class assignment and the real thing, between war games and war.

A notable exception to this criticism of academics is the landmark work by William J. Baumol and Matityahu Marcus, *Economies of Academic Libraries* (American Council on Education, Washington, D.C., 1973). These two economists went to unusual lengths to explain their statistical methods and to summarize their conclusions with refreshing brevity and clarity. As a consequence, their work is widely read and frequently cited.

Management scientists and other quantitatively oriented researchers frequently wonder why the results of quantitative research studies are not used more by practicing library managers in the decision making process. One reason is that the mathematics and the methodologies required are far too complex and difficult for operating managers to learn and apply in their busy work environments. Few senior library administrators have the kind of staff support needed to successfully carry out complex analyses. Another and equally important reason is that the quantitative approach does not and cannot take into sufficient account the complex of political, organizational, and psychological factors that characterize the real work where people are more potent than numbers or logic. The quality of many decisions could be significantly improved if we had more and better data, but many of the more important decisions have a relatively small quantitative component. As a library director, I seldom have a critical need for more quantitative data than are available from regularly kept statistics or by having someone make a special and usually simple survey and analysis of the problem. When the data are simply not available or too difficult to assemble, I can usually find a satisfactory way to manage without them. My real problem has nearly always been to correctly assess the political rather than the economic or quantitative factors.

It is fairly easy to determine the most cost-effective course of action with or without detailed data. It is much harder to map out and implement a successful strategy for achieving it, to assess how the various persons and groups affected will perceive the manager's intentions, and how they will react to the decision. Someone said that quantification is not synonymous with management. Finding the best or most cost-effective course of action is not the same as getting it accepted. Sometimes the quality of a decision is critical, other times, it is acceptance.

Effective decision making processes in large academic and public libraries involve complex sets of policies, procedures, and problems which require a variety of different kinds of information and approaches. Some decisions will be authoritarian some will he collegial, some will be made by committees, and some will be made by combinations of the above. Library directors are not all knowing, nor are the collective judgments of library faculties and committees infallible. Different situations call for different approaches. There are no simple formulas and no easy answers.

The new management systems that I have been discussing in this article divide into two general categories. There are *quantitative systems* such as Operations Research, PPBS, and ZBB, end *psychological* or *behavioural* systems such as Theory Y (and its variants) and MBO. In each system there are a number of concepts, ideas, tools, and techniques that have validity and can be used to advantage by library managers, but as comprehensive systems they are all far too theoretical, complex, and simplistic to be applied successfully by ordinary managers in the day-to-day work environment. Few managers have the time or the specialized knowledge and skills required to make these systems work, and those that do are probably astute enough to manage as well or better without them.

In the hands of amateurs-and this is most of us-the quantitative systems frequently produce misleading and wrong solutions, while the psychological or behavioural systems can lead to the manipulation and misuse of people. The real danger with both kinds of management systems is that they offer mechanistic formulas for dealing with complex realities and keep us from thinking about and solving our management problems in practical, realistic, and common sense ways.

Despite the many claims to the contrary, management is not yet a science. It is still an art, but is very much an art that can and should be mastered and practiced by librarians.

CASE STUDY: MANAGEMENT OF INFORMATION IN CHINA

Management Development and its Practice in Chinese Library and Information Services

Management, as a human organized activity, has been in existent e in organized society throughout all civilized history, although its systematic study as a branch of science is fairly recent. It emerges and develops along with the development of social productivity and obviously the management approaches have become more advanced and progressive to correspond with the progress of human society. That is to say the management approaches have a very close relation with social productivity and the economic formation of society. The library as a part of the social fabric, has existed in all ages of organized society. Management approaches in business, industry and social administration have inevitably influenced library management, and 50 would the past approaches influence the recent grits. The influence between one part of the world and other parts is extremely evident in modern society because of the advanced means of transportation and communication.

According to some hooks on management, the development of management in western countries can be roughly divided into four periodis: the prescientific period (before 1800), the scientific period (1800 1927), the human-relations period (1927 50) and the synthesis period (1950 present). Library management practice has generally followed the same pattern of development, several years later than business and industry. A study of the development of management in China and in Chinese libraries has revealed that it by and large follows the same basic lines. Therefore, it would be beneficial to take a short look at the development of business and library management in western countries first before dealing with the management approaches in China in general and in Chinese library and information services in particular.

The prescientific management approach existed during the period of slavery and feudal society. The word for these periods would be autocratic. To become a manager throughout these periods one only needed authority, power and coercion. There were no human rights as we speak of today, no willing participation and cooperation between manager and the managed. The industrial revolution beginning with the invention of Watt's steam engine and the spinning Jenny promoted the development of modern industry in the eighteenth century and brought with it the first glimmer of understanding in terms of management skill. Many principles and methodology of modern sciences were applied to problems of administration. In this context, the scientific management approach came into being. But most of the managerial concepts of the time emphasized organizational aspects, especially those relating to the production of goods. Attention was focused on production, efficiency, and the prevention of waste. Human factors were neglected. In contrast to this, the main emphasis of the human relations approach was on the individual and the informal group in the formal organization. This approach was concerned with integrating people into a work environment. The phrase "personnel administration" came into prominence at this time, and increased efforts towards democratization and staff participation were evident.

This period was a reaction against the overemphasis on productivity during the scientific management period. In order to overcome the one-sidedness of both the scientific management approach and the human relations approach, most of the effort expended in developing management thinking and concepts has, since the early 1950s, been toward refining the work started by F. W. Taylor (the scientific approach advocate) and 1,. Mayo (the human relations approach advocate) and combining elements of both with ideas from other fields such behavioural sciences. Thus management theory and practice has entered into a new stage the synthesis period. This approach pays more attention to individual ego needs besides economic and social needs for work motivation and also attaches importance to the work situation which consists of three elements: people, organization and environment. Only if all these six factors are in balance can a harmonious and pleasant work situation be achieved and increased productivity as well.

The development of library management can also be roughly divided into three basis periods, *i.e.* pre-1937, the scientific (1937-1955) and the human relations (1955 present). However, these time divisions art somewhat arbitrary, as the overlap between one period and another is very great, although there is some evidence that the periods identified do represent an effort on the part of library administrators to pick up some of the ideas coming out of the disciplines of business management and public administration.

Most libraries in the period before 1937 tended to be small. As the concern was simply to keep the libraries open, there was very little need to be concerned about costs and management. The chief librarian was expected to run the library and to make the decisions in almost all stages of its operation. Libraries had been run with a rather traditional and conservative approach. In the late 1930s, a number of changes in library services took place and in some respects there were great strides forward. Studies on cost analysis, technical services, cataloguing and use of edge cards appeared about this time.

Then people began to look seriously at some of the work done by Taylor and others to see whether or not there were sonic techniques applicable to the library, situation. After the Second World War, with the rapid development of science and technology, and the urgent needs for scientific information and education, the budgets of libraries increased as well as new library building and collections. To cope with this new situation, libraries began applying a combination of the scientific management approach of the Taylor school with some of the new mathematical operations research techniques developed during the War and began to emphasize, efficient operation. However, being administrators of non-profit making institutions they had little or no idea about how much it cost to carry Out various library activities during this period, until in the mid-1960s computer application and systems analysis became more feasible for the library situation.

The human relations school in library management came into being about 1955 and has had a continuing influence on library administration up to present time. In most libraries, human relations management means democratic administration, participative administration and involvement in the decision-making process, although there are several difficulties and problems in its practice.

More and more evidence demonstrates that the synthesis management approach is not only a theoretical concept, but a practical method employed in many libraries in recent years. As a matter of fact, no library administrator confines himself to one definite management style or school, but usually combines several styles or schools with scientific approach as the core. The Introduction of computers and modern facilities of communication and other electronic technology into libraries has had a profound effect on library management. No doubt, library management will continue to improve. Managers or administrators of libraries will have the background to make better selections from the developments in management and related fields. As this takes place the libraries should become a more basic part of the community arid a pleasant environment in which to work.

MANAGEMENT DEVELOPMENT

As stated above, management development has a close relationship with social development. T. F. Mention's great contribution to social sciences is his discovery, that human society in all parts of the world has by arid large gone through the same stages of social formation. Management development in China can also be roughly divided into three basic periods as in western countries, but with some differences.

The main differences are: firstly, the prescientific period is rather long in China and the approaches of that period have strong influence on the approaches which followed, because of the long history of feudal society in China and the long dominant influence of Confucianism on Chinese ideology and ethics. Secondly, China went through semi-feudal and semi-colonial society, *i.e.* a mixed social formation of feudalism and colonialism, in the last century, which makes the scientific approach in China during this period somewhat different from the western one. Thirdly, the new democratic and socialist revolution in China inevitably marked a new stage of management development in China.

As for the temporal divisions, the whole period of Chinese slavery and feudal societies is prescientific; the scientific period began with the first attempt at introducing techniques of capitalist production (called the-Westernization-Movement-initiated by comprador bureaucrats in the latter half of the nineteenth century) till the founding of the People's Republic in 1949. Then began a new approach of socialist scientific management which is a different concept, but somewhat similar to human relations or synthesis approaches, and is the one that still needs to be developed and perfected.

Being one of the most ancient civilized countries in the world, China was outstanding in administering state affairs, organizing military operations and managing great projects such as the Great Wall and the Grand Canal in ancient times. Administrative affairs were systematized arid regularized as early as Xia Dynasty, (21-16th century, BC.) according to historical recordings.

During the periods called the Spring and Autumn, and Waring States (770-221 BC), there was a period of time called the "Contention of a Hundred Schools of Tought Of, these schools, Legalists and Confucianists were in a dominant position and had a strong influence alternatively on the approaches of state administration. Legalists advocated reform and-"ruling by law". Qin Xiao Gong, the Duke of the State of Qin appointed legalists as his senior officials and carried out reform. Very soon, his state became stronger than the other states and finally defeated all of them. In the end, the whole of China was reunited by his grandson Qin Shi Huang, the noted first emperor of the Qin Dynasty in 221. Confucianists advocated "Following the previous kings' practice" which was rather conservative. Because of the needs to consolidate the centralized feudal monarchy, Emperor Wu of the Han Dynasty (206BC-AD220) implemented a policy of "Banning the other schools of thought and solely esteeming Confucianism".

Since then, Confucianism dominated Chinese ideology for about two thousand years. The doctrine of obedience and loyalty to superiors benefited the ruling classes, but hampered people's initiative and creativity and fettered the productive forces. That is the reason why China could not move from a feudal society to a capitalist society in modern history, though the seeds of capitalism emerged long before they did in western countries, *i.e.* the thirteenth century, at the end of the Yuan Dynasty and the beginning of the Ming Dynasty. Autocracy in tile feudal society of China was so strong that even successive peasant uprisings could not shake its foundation until the invasion of foreign imperialism in the last century.

The repeated defeats in the wars between feudal China and foreign aggressors completely exposed the corrupt nature of the Qing Dynasty. These events on the one hand promoted the Reform Movement within the ruling classes and bourgeois democratic revolution of the people, and on the other hand introduced the ways and techniques of capitalist production and management. The rising of comprador-bureaucratic capitalism and the presence of foreign capitalism turned feudal China into a semi-feudal and semi-colonial country politically and economically. Management approaches in industry and business in this period were, in the main, scientific ones, but more autocratic. Workers had to work long hours, for low wages and in poor working conditions. Management in some enterprises during this period still relied heavily on coercion.

In discussing management in new China, two facts that make the nature of management differ from the western one must be noted. One is that China had abolished feudalism through land reform and later, capitalism through socialist transformation. All land, natural resources and means of production now belong to the people. Another fact is that the working people are politically masters of their own country.

The principle of "cadre participation in collective productive labour and worker participation in management" ensures their position in production being equal to that of managers. Most of them work conscientiously and enthusiastically. This was especially true during the 1950s when planning, efficiency and economic results, in a sense, were emphasized, while labour emulation and voluntary labour were also encouraged. People were motivated mainly by spiritual reward in the early years. The participation in decision making. and the supervision over the management by workers are the striking characteristics of socialist management.

In the early 1950s, China stood politically on the side of the Soviet Union and learnt economically from the Russian. To some extent, China just copied the Soviet model in management as in other fields, which did not quite accord with China's real situation in many respects. It is wise for any country to learn from others' experiences and apply them in a creative way so as to develop her own. The "Charter of the Anshan Iron and Steel Company" was a systematic and comprehensive set of management regulations in industry stipulated by China in the early 1960s, which was then summarized into "70 Regulations" called Management Regulations for Industries, Mines and Enterprises-. Unfortunately, these regulations, influenced by left political idea had several defects. For example, while exaggerating the situation of class struggle in socialist society and overemphasizing the importance of mass movement in industry, scientific rules and methods were not respected adequately.

The authorities concerned were simply after a high production quota, high output and quantity, while quality, efficiency, cost unit, economic results and the law of value were overlooked. That is what people usually called "too much enthusiasm and too little scientific consideration".

However, for many years since the early 1950s, Sun Yefang, the former director of the Institute of Economics of the Academy of Social Sciences and a noted economist, has established a series of socialist economic principles in management in the context of China, such as those on achieving maximum economic results with minimum labour consumption; on paying attention to the law of value and profits in a planned economy; on enlarging enterprises' rights of management; and on the correct application of economic levers and raising the position of profit in management.

His theories divined correctly that the mechanical copying of the Soviet model and the "left" deviation policies would do no good to Chinese economy. Unfortunately, Sun's theories were not accepted by the former authorities, and instead, he was criticized and accused of being revisionist just at that time, scientific laws and economic rules were not fully observed and people's socialist enthusiasm was abused, thus causing two great setbacks during 1959-61 and 1966-76 in economic construction.

The penalty for that is heavy: the huge waste of time, natural resources and human energy, especially the people's enthusiasm. The most successful enterprise in the early 1960s was Daquing Oil Field which was regarded as an example of scientific management in industry by the whole of China for many years. One of its management principles, the system of personal responsibility, is still adopted by all factories. In recent years, things have been changing a lot.

Scientific management is reemphasized in addition to economic system reform and technical transformation. Efficiency and economic results are again the vital norms for evaluating the success of a unit's management. People's material interests are linked with production. They are encouraged to do more work, get more pay and be well off before others. Since individual interests have a lot to do with the interests of the units, every one is very much concerned with what is going on in his units and has a great say in decision making. Equalitarianism is rejected in the salary system nowadays.

Instead, differentials are established according to kind of work and the quantity and quality of work done, and thus the socialist principle of product distribution, *i.e.* "from each according to his ability, to each according to his work", is really carried out. People are thereby motivated and inspired, and the relations between the managed and managers, and among colleagues and follow workers, are thus improved.

On the other hand, each production unit has more rights of self'-management. That is to say it is more independent than it was, and assumes sole responsibility for its own profits and losses, which directly concern the income of both managers and staff. Under this situation, the initiative and enthusiasm of the people are brought into full play and thereby productivity is raised and output increased.

China is now experiencing a period of transformation through which some defects in the existing system will be overcome and some new approaches suitable to China's specific condition will be found on the basis of other management approaches for her modernization. Library and information services, as part of society, are sure to apply some of the principles of industry and business management to their own management, with some modifications in order to suit their own needs.

LIBRARY MANAGEMENT IN OLD CHINA

The existence of libraries in China can be traced back as far as the Shang Dynasty (1600-1100 BC). Although China has been noted for her prosperous imperial and private libraries for thousands of years, the main function of these early libraries was to collect and keep books, as in other countries. The use of these libraries was restricted to imperial families, senior officials and noted scholars, not for the general public. However, the prosperity of Shu Yuan (academy) libraries and private libraries in the Ming (AD 1368-1644) and especially the Qing Dynasty (AD 1644-1911) played an important role in spreading literacy and knowledge and in preserving rare editions of ancient books.

The former libraries were designated only for the reference use of teachers and students. Books could not be taken out of the library premises. The latter were merely for book collection, but sometimes could be consulted by friends and noted scholars. These collectors were usually bibliographers or experts on textual criticism, examination and correction and were sometimes also book publishers. Book lending was generally impossible. Because of the relatively small size of most private libraries, almost all operations could be done by one person.

A few private libraries such as the Tian Yi Ge and the Xi Gu Ge which had existed for several hundred years, had very, large collections by the standards of those years. For example, the Tian Yi Ge had 70000 volumes and the Xi Gu Ge 84000 volumes. Unfortunately, war, damage and financial problems made the existence of these libraries very difficult in old China. Finally, all of them were taken over by the state.

There are few records about the management of imperial libraries, and yet the development of Chinese classification such as the *Si Bu Fa* (the Four Division Classification Scheme), the compilation of large encyclopaedia such as the *Yong Le Da Dian,* and national bibliographies such as the *Si Ku Quan Shu* in feudal China indicate certain success in managing these libraries.

Modern libraries in China began with the establishment of the first public library in Wuhan, Hubei Province and especially the founding of the Metropolitan Library, now the Beijing National Library, in 1910. The transition from traditional library functions to modern ones took place thereafter. The main trends during this period are as follows:

1. The functions of the library were no longer merely for collecting and keeping but also for using books.
2. Libraries were gradually used by everyone and not only by the privileged few.
3. The collection of books on modern sciences and technology rather than the Chinese classics was stressed.
4. Better service and satisfaction for users were required.
5. Books were no longer classified by languages but by subjects.
6. More attention was paid to the division of work and specialization as well as professional training in management.

The open shelf system was popular in many libraries. Book from catalogues were replaced by catalogue cards. Modern decimal classification, *i.e.* Dewey's scheme was introduced to replace the traditional Chinese *Si Bu Fa,* which was no longer suitable for modern scientific and technical literatures. Library science was also introduced into China and studied during this period. Many noted scholars and librarians made great contributions to the development of librarianship and library services in old China.

For example, Professor LI Dazhao, one of the earliest propagators of Marxism-Leninism in China, was the former director of Beijing University Library from 1918 to 1922. He strongly advocated that the library should not be a book storage, but a place for research, and education; a librarian should not be a book keeper, but a researcher and instructor; the library should open to the labouring class free of charge. He took a lead in introducing open shelves in his library for the convenience of students. For this purpose, he changed shelving from traditional dictionary form, or alphabetical order into subject classification and organized catalogue cards of books in western languages by following Dewey's classification. He also paid great attention to statistics in order to improve the quality of service and satisfy the users needs.

Tile great contributions of the Beijing National Library to tile culture of modern China lies in its effort and success in collecting, preserving and sorting out Chinese classics, rare editions of ancient books and important documents, and in building a large collection of scientific and technical literatures in foreign languages, despite foreign aggression, civil wars, disasters and the corruption of previous governments. As for management during this period, it was mainly traditional.

LIBRARY MANAGEMENT IN NEW CHINA

Library services in new China have expanded rapidly in the last thirty years and a national network has been formed. Now, there are already about 20000 libraries of various types with more than 100000 staff. Take the public library and the university library as examples. By 1981, there were 1731 public libraries above county level with a staff of 19641 and 670 university libraries with a staff of 17000. Both types of libraries have total collections of about 190 million volumes. By comparison in 1956 there were only 96 public libraries above county level, with 3714 staff and 28-9 million volumes and 212 university libraries with 3568 staff and 37-28 million volumes.

The Administrative Bureau for Library Services at the Ministry of Culture, a central agency for the planning and coordinating library development of all types, was set up in 1981 to suit the new situation brought about by the modernization drive in China. Furthermore, each type of library has a central unit for coordinating its activities, *e.g.* the Beijing National Library for public libraries. The Academy of Sciences Library for science libraries, and the Ministry of Education for university libraries. The expansion of library services in China demonstrates that libraries have played an important role in economic construction and education and are already an indispensable part of society. At the same time, Chinese librarians have gained some experience in library management and made some progress in the study of librarianship. For instance, the central authorities concerned have in the last two years sponsored a number of conferences, at which several working regulations have been formulated or revised respectively for public libraries, science libraries and university libraries in order to improve working efficiency and the quality of service.

Another important event is the promulgation by the state Council in 1981 of "The Temporary Provisions of Professional Titles for Library, Archive and Information Personnel", which is of tremendous significance for improving personnel management and inspiring stair enthusiasm.

Standardization of documentation is the key link for library management. Since its founding in 1979, the National Documentation Standardization Technical Committee of China has done a lot in this field. It has sponsored several workshops in cooperation with the China Society of Library Science and the China Society of Scientific and Technical Information to examine "The National Standard Entries for Cataloguing" prepared by the Standardization Group of Beijing National Library, "The Abstract and Title-list Entry Formats for Retrieval journals" prepared by ISTIC, and suggest the use of "The Classification Scheme for Chinese Libraries" (including both the detailed version of the-Classification Scheme for Documents" and the simplified version) and of-The Chinese Thesaurus". This Committee also worked out-Tape Formats for Catalogue Information Exchange",-Name Codes for Nations and Regions", "Sex Codes for People", "The Codes for Administrative Regions of PRC" and-The Standardized Codes of Chinese Characters for Information Exchange". The latter two, already Chinese National Standards, are being prepared for submission to ISO/TC97/SC2 for approval as international Standards.

Research in information methodology, and in the theory and practice of library science were started years ago. There is a Section for Information Methodology in ISTIC and 12 research groups under the China Society of Library Science including those for research in fundamental theory, bibliography, classification, cataloguing, reader service, staff training, rare and ancient books, standardization, information: services, children's library and foreign library work. Some progress has been made in recent years. Scientific management, efficiency and economic results and the application of computers in libraries and information institutes are also receiving great attention and sonic initial successes have been achieved in these respects.

In summing up past experiences and lessons, library services in China have suffered setbacks twice during the last thirty years. One was in the years of so-called "Great Leap Forward", another in the "Cultural Revolution". Both were caused by the trend of neglecting scientific management as in industry and by the influence of a depressed economy as well. There is not a slightest doubt that scientific management in China is as important as in any other country. As everybody knows, the fact that the rapid advance of science and technology produces large amounts of documents, makes it more difficult for librarians to select, collect, process, store and report, and for users to access them quickly and precisely. Only scientific management and scientific methods in addition to modern facilities can solve this problem to some extent. The library itself is an integrated system consisting of different functional departments doing different jobs.

The coordination and cooperation between departments and jobs, and the contact between the library and users are essential for a library to fulfil its social functions or to attain its objectives; and the library services or library undertaking in this country as a whole, including different types of libraries, also from an integrated system. Centralized planning with overall consideration for healthy development, rational geographic distribution, and effective cooperation among different or same types of libraries demands the introduction of scientific ways to analyse the needs and possibilities of the economic situation as important basis for allocating funds and facilities.

From a long term point of view, it is imperative for a nation like China with so large a territory and the biggest population in the world, to establish a retrieval network which includes data bases, communication systems and terminal facilities in order that a quick and precise service can be offered to users, as in the United Kingdom and the United States. This is the aim of the modernization of the Chinese library and information services. But first of all, they must be well managed. Without good management, any resource cannot be given full play, no matter how intelligent the staff, how advanced the facilities and how large the collections.

Owing to the fact that some Chinese librarians are fully aware of their weakness and the importance of scientific management in libraries, they have been vigorously committing themselves to the study of its theory and practice in recent years. A number of seminars have been held to discuss its definition and principles, especially in the Chinese situation. Here is a-definition of scientific management based on recent discussion. It is defined as "giving full play to manpower, material and financial resources in order to raise operational efficiency and the quality of services by applying the principles and methods of modern science and technology and observing the objective laws of librarianship, for the purpose of achieving optimum social results of services".

This definition includes two concepts: efficiency and the social results of service. As a matter of fact the first one is the means and methods, the second is the objective of scientific management or the objective of library services. There is a controversy about the measurement of efficiency and social results.

In fact, the measurement of efficiency is possible for most of library work, *e.g.* the repetitive and mechanical routines such as ordering, cataloguing, cards filing, binding, circulation and shelving. But social results are more difficult to measure. The satisfaction of users and the application of new technology or the improvement of education and culture in localities may be generally regarded as social results of library services. Cost and profit cannot generally be taken as criteria to measure the performance of libraries as they are for business, but these factors must be taken into consideration for good management.

As far as scientific management itself is concerned, this means good planning, rationalization and standardization of library work and documentation It also involves highly organized activities relating to administrative, professional, personnel and equipment management, such as planning, organizing, stalling, budgeting and directing.

Scientific management in Chinese libraries and information services is ideally characterized by the following principles.

The Principle of Centralization and Unification: China is a country with a planned economy. The development of her industry, agriculture and all other public services is carried out in a planned way. Therefore, the expansion of library and information services in this country cannot go beyond the ability or remain behind the needs of her economy. It is necessary to give overall consideration to the priority and geographic distribution of different libraries in order to make the best use of limited resources such as funds, manpower and facilities, to organize a rational national network and technically to realize standardization and unification of library work and documentation such as classification, cataloguing and automation for sharing resources nationwide.

The Principle of Democracy: Staff and some users expect to be asked to speak their views or make suggestions in the process of policy making, decision making and planning. There are two ways to do so in practice. The authorities make the draft or outline of a plan first, and then consult staff and sometimes users. This way is called "From top to bottom". Otherwise, staff and sometimes users, are asked to discuss first. Then, the authorities concerned summarize their suggestions and ideas as a basis for drawing up their plan or making decision. This is called the "from bottom to top" method in policy making. Sometimes, these processes go through several times from top to bottom or from bottom to top before a decision is made if it is not urgent. Moreover, staff and users are encouraged to make complaints or suggestions at any time in the process of carrying out of a plan or a policy in order to correct unexpected errors and mistakes because of the changing situation or carelessness when making this plan and policy. Democratic management helps the authorities overcome subjectivism and bureaucracy and inspires staff enthusiasm, initiative and creativity because their personality and opinions are respected. In addition, problems can be found and solved in a timely way. Relations between management and stair are improved and the ties between library, users and society at large are thereby strengthened.

The Principle of Economic Results: Unlike business, libraries are non-profit-making institutions. It is difficult to measure their economic results in the from of unit cost and profit. However, it is possible for libraries to use their funds as economically its possible, assign staff tasks as rationally as possible and utilize facilities as effectively as possible.

It is also possible to establish a series of optimum systems fur literature collection, storage and service, and to formulate some rules and regulations that serve the needs of these systems with the aim of costing less money to get more documents that users need most, taking less people and time to process more documents and providing users with better service. The waste of human energy, money, time and material resources is incompatible with the principles of scientific management and must be lessened or totally avoided if possible.

The System of Personal Responsibility: The social functions and relations of library with society were never so important as they are today. Society supports libraries, libraries serve society. The quality of library services directly affects both users and the whole of society. Conversely, social needs or users' needs also promote library services. Therefore, elaborate division of labour, and frequent contact and mutual dependence between departments are very important in order to offer a better service to society.

Jobs in each department and in each link of an operation must be done well. That means that everyone must be sensible of his responsibility and get his or her job done on time, in the required quantity and quality. This responsibility system, like the one used in business provides standard to assess the performance of staff and the departments and enhances their sense of responsibility in work. A better management and service can thus be achieved in the end.

The above principles are general guides or aims to be sought for better management in library and information services. As for tire present situation so far, it is not quite the case yet. There are still a lot of things to do before reaching these aims.

SOME SUGGESTIONS FOR IMPROVEMENT OF CHINESE LIBRARY SERVICES

In comparison with other countries, planning and management in Chinese library services do have some strong points, but on the whole, the managerial level is relatively low as it is in industry and for the same reasons. Some factors which affect the efficiency of library services should be improved in order to serve the information and education needs of this country and at the same time modernized library services themselves.

Geographic Distribution: For historical reasons, there are more libraries providing better services in big cities and economically developed areas than that in rural and remote areas. It is incredible that some counties even have no library services at all. Irrational distribution of libraries is of course a common problem in many other countries, and it was riot so urgent to solve this problem some years back in China because the needs for information and education in rural and remote areas were very small. Things are quite different nowadays.

The new economic policies for industry and especially for agriculture, stimulate economic development in these areas. People are becoming well off and want to learn. Small rural factories need information for technical transformation and innovation in order to increase the quantity and improve the quality of products or change the line of their products to some which may be more profitable. Peasants need information and knowledge for scientific farming. Scientific and technical books and other materials are in great demand and hard to get in many rural areas. People call this situation "science fever" which could riot be seen before. It is reported that many peasants invited experts from their neighbouring areas or professors from colleges to transfer technology, or attended technical seminars and "technical fairs" themselves sponsored by local authorities.

From a long term viewpoint, perhaps, the more effective and economical way to satisfy the information and education needs in rural areas is to improve library services. The general accepted LA standards for the provision of branch libraries are that: a population of under 1500 in a catchment area is usually better served by a mobile library; an isolated population of over 1500 normally needs a trailer library, sub-branch or branch library; in urban areas a branch should be provided in each major shopping centre. China is unable to reach these standards at present, but can do her best to improve the county central library service and at the same time to provide branch libraries in most districts and sub-branches, or mobile libraries or reading rooms of some sort at some town level grass roots.

Agriculture is of vital importance in China's economy, arid about 80% of her population are peasants living in rural areas. No one in China can afford to neglect their demand if he wishes to see agriculture well developed and enough food to feed the 1000 million people or to tap the resources in remote areas. The provision of library services must be taken into consideration by the local leadership in those areas where there are still no such services, when planning overall development in their localities. The central library authorities, on the other hand should urge the local authorities to give enough financial arid manpower support to the establishment of library services.

Regional Cooperation: Organizationally, China has already had a national library network consisting of different types of libraries. The problem is that these libraries lack close cooperation with information services, between different or even similar types of libraries, especially on a regional scale. The tasks of information services in China's situation differ from that of library services in some respects, and each type of library has its own tasks and objectives. However, their cooperation on a regional scale is very important to improve the efficiency arid quality of services and to utilize resources in a more economical way. The United Kingdom arid some other countries have set some examples in library cooperation. Their experience is helpful for China in projecting regional networks and cooperation with Beijing National Library and ISTIC as backups like the British Library's position and functions in Britain.

Regional cooperation including acquisition, cataloguing, staff training and resources sharing between libraries and information services would be organized, with provincial arid county public libraries arid local information institutes as centres. Some libraries, for instance university libraries, may have their own cooperation, like those in Changsha, Hunan Province in recent years. It should be emphasized that for a country with the biggest population in the world, regional and local networks arid cooperation in China are more important than in any other countries. Users should first rely, on their local libraries, then central libraries in this region.

National centres are the last resort. Therefore, the collection of regional central libraries should be relatively large and comprehensive according to local conditions and needs, and regional union catalogues containing holdings of the participating libraries should be prepared for this purpose and for avoiding duplication of labour. Regional cooperation is the infrastructure of national cooperation and the basis of library modernization. China should exert much effort in the establishment of regional cooperation in order to make the best use of her resources and to modernize her library services.

National Referral Services: On the basis of regional library cooperation and regional information networks which already exist, two national referral centres should be established according to the actual existing situation: one mainly for monographs on social sciences and natural sciences as well in the Beijing National Library and one mainly for scientific and technical serials in ISTIC in order to improve the exploitation of existing resources nationwide. In doing that, the preparation of the national bibliography, catalogues of different types of literature and regional union catalogues should be hastened. Abstracts and indexes, other retrieval and reference books and directories published at home and abroad should be collected as comprehensively, as possible.

At present, referral services are offered only, by mail or by personal visits. It is quite possible technically and economically, now for China to carry out these services by, direct telephone and ISTI links with big libraries and local information institutes.

When conditions are ripe, these two centres will be national data bases for automatic retrieval equipped with computers linked through telecommunication systems with terminals all over the country.

It is recommended that the centre in ISTIC also provide a business information service for the needs of foreign trade and economic cooperation with foreign companies. Local information centres should provide local product arid market information. For tins purpose, market research reports, company cards, trade and professional directories, trade and business journals from major developed countries and business publications published at home should be collected, and specialists for guiding the use of these publications should be trained.

Open Access and Opening Hours: Because of management problem and the fear of the loss of books, open access is still not popular in most libraries and information institutes except for periodicals, newspapers and children's books. Experiences have repeatedly proved that open access is the best way to facilitate users' needs and exploit literature resources. Rare books, valuable editions and manuscripts and some other materials are not suitable for open shelves.

Open access to standard materials, patent literature and trade literature has been carried out in ISTIC libraries in recent years. Monographs and technical proceedings, research reports in big libraries such as Beijing National Library and ISTIC are difficult for open access, because the shelving is arranged by accession numbers or serial numbers, riot by subjects for saving the trouble of reshelving resulting from the huge daily intake of publications. Nevertheless, this call be done in medium and small size libraries, especially ill university libraries, school libraries and local public libraries.

As for opening hours, the internationally accepted standards for urban main libraries are 60 hours per week; for branch libraries 18-60 hours per week. Urban libraries and information institute libraries in China open only eight hours a day, 48 hours per week. No services are available on Sundays and national holidays. Children's libraries arid rural libraries usually open on Sundays.

It is recommended that science libraries and urban public libraries with science open 10 hours a day, 60 hours per week. Opening hours for information documentation centres and university libraries may be longer depending on the users' real needs, and if' possible, board and accommodation should be provided for those who cannot get home on the day of a visit. ISTIC Chongqing Branch Library has offered this service for several years. Other libraries should do the same if necessary and conditions permit.

Publicily and Users' Survey: Besides reporting Journals, exhibitions arid lectures, guides and pamphlets about each kind of service and how to gain access to them and other information should be published in libraries and information centres. This is not only for the convenience of the users, but would also save much trouble for the staff and as a result, would save time for both users and stall'.

Publicity relating to user service is a weak point ill Chinese library arid information services. Most libraries do not even have a sheet of printed material for presentation to users and foreign visitors. Compare this with some other countries where libraries, even smaller ones, provide various types of pamphlets free of charge explaining their services and holdings. The results are good. Users feel quite at home, especially fresh visitors and timid users who are not confident about what to do. Publicity is very important in user services arid each library should have someone in charge of this work.

Surveys and investigations on users' needs and the level of satisfaction by existing services should be carried out regularly by specialists ill order to improve the quality of services. Little has been done about this to date in most Chinese libraries and information centres.

This kind of survey is very necessary and should he done by various means such as telephone, questionnaires, individual correspondence or even personal interview. When this is done, library policies and plans will be built on a more realistic foundation. Better services can then be achieved.

Library Education: The fact that China lacks qualified librarians is serious, especially in local libraries. This situation can perhaps be illustrated by the following statistics. Among 100000 library staff in 20000 libraries, only 3000 graduates were from the Departments of Library Science of Beijing University and Wuhan University and another 1500 persons had received correspondence courses by the end of 1980 since 1949.

This figure accounts for a very small proportion of the total staff, not more than 5% on the average even in university and science libraries and public libraries above provincial level. Eighty-one percent of the stair began working in libraries just during or after the "Cultural Revolution" (1966-76). Eighty percent among them only had middle school education.

On the other hand, quite a few technicians and research workers do not quite know how to use the library to search for documents. Of course, many staff can become professionals by training and working practice, and users get familiar with the use of the library by frequent visits or by the guidance of the staff.

However, the lack of systematic library education and training for the stair would inevitably affect the efficiency of operation and the quality of services and for the users, the effective search for useful documents and literatures or other materials for the purpose of reference and education or entertainment.

Happily, the central authorities have done something to change this situation in recent years. For example, there are already 19 universities and colleges having departments or specialities of library and archive studies. Wuhan University even has a speciality of information science in the Department of Library Science. Correspondence courses continue to be given to some stair. On-the-job and off-the-job training in Beijing National Library, ISTIC and other big libraries has been continuous except during the years of "Cultural Revolution".

The guide for users was improved recently. This is really encouraging, but not enough for a country like China with so many libraries and staff. A radical solution to this problem would be to enhance library education.

It is recommended firstly that one or two colleges of library and information science be set up for undergraduates as well as postgraduates to do research in order to supply libraries and information institutes with qualified librarians and staff and to raise the academic level of librarianship and information science. Secondly, all college and university undergraduates, science undergraduates in particular, should be given library and courses in order to make them ready to use library and information services when they become users, especially after graduation.

Personnel Management: For librarians and library stair, as part of the Chinese intellectual stratum, their social position was low, and their labour was not fully understood by society sometimes in the past. Things are getting much better now, their contributions to society are generally acknowledged and appreciated by both people and government. However, present personnel management is not conducive to bringing stair initiative and creativity into full play. Most stair are not quite satisfied with the existing cadre system, promotion and salary systems.

For example, officially there are four conditions for stair promotion and salary increment: education, length of service and experience, professional ability and contribution or performance. Generally speaking, it sounds good. In fact it is very complicated to implement. Most leaders used to emphasize the second one, *i.e.* the length of service and experience, because it is easy to measure and saves labour and argument. This "iron rice bowl" (job security) and "big pot rice" (equalitarianism) system are accepted by many people because the assessment system for stair performance is far from perfect. For quite a long time, "be red and expert" was supposed to be the lofty realm of accomplishment and the only standard for a perfect librarian, as for other intellectuals. Actually, "be red" was always overemphasized and distorted while "be expert" neglected or even criticized. Today, this slogan is given some new meanings and some more concrete standards are adopted for evaluating the performance of stair.

Following the reform in economic areas, a reform is about to be carried in libraries and information institutes. In the context of library and information services, this reform should, firstly, change step by step the life-tenure system of leadership into an election system, at least partly, so that more younger professionals may have the opportunity to play their parts and make their contributions in management positions. Non-professionals and aged leaders should conscientiously give up their posts to younger ones for the interest of the country. Secondly, the state assignment system should, at least partly, be replaced by a recruitment system so that the quality of staff can be controlled.

Their specialities can thus be matched to the job and more willingness they will give to their assignments thereby. Thirdly, working regulations and the personnel assessment system should be improved and perfected. For instance, the following factors should be considered in personnel assessment: professional knowledge, professional skill, managerial ability, working attitude, service quality and achievement.

Quality of service and achievement or working results would be always put into first place so as to encourage people to work hard and learn well. This assessment should be done in some cases by examinations, or by colleague appraisal with reference to work records. The appraisal of the leading person which in most cases is crucial and decisive should be as fair and impartial as possible without personal prejudice and discrimination. Proper material and spiritual reward is necessary for those who have good performances. When this is done, staff enthusiasm will be inspired and no or less complaints will be found then.

A Library Act: Many countries in the world have formulated library acts and practised them for many years. China does not yet have one. The history of library development has proved that it library act is very necessary and important for the healthy development and the perfection of library services.

China should by all means have a library act to stipulate legislatively the principles, social functions, financial sources, scope of activities and the forms of services of libraries; the natures and functions of the library committee and the system of leadership and administration and their tasks so that library position and development can be guaranteed by law. For instance, library services in China were always the first ones to have their funds cut and the last ones to have their funds increased in the past. Some local governments never allocate enough funds for local libraries. This situation would not have happened if there had been a library act, or at least things would not have been so bad.

The implementation of a library act, on the other hand, reflects government concern about people's welfare and their rights to enjoy education and entertainment. It also reflects the level of the development of library services of a country.

CONCLUSION

China is very aware of her current weaknesses in management both in industry and in library and information services. The existing management systems do not quite fit the new Situation created by the modernization drive. The current reform of economic systems and technical transformation, the new economic policies at home and the open-door policies towards the outside world require it reform in management systems and a lot of managers with both theoretical background and practical experience of management.

Just for this end, 1-6 out of 7 million leading cadres, managers and technicians in industrial and communication departments have received management training during the past three years, which includes economic policies, basic economic theories and fundamental techniques of business management. In addition, the China Society of Management was set up, the *Journal of Management* has appeared and a number of academic conferences on management were held during the same period. Considerable attention is also being devoted to foreign management techniques. While sending some people to study abroad, an industrial, scientific and technical training centre was jointly inaugurated in 1980 by China and the United States in Dalian, Northeast China.

Many leading cadres of libraries and information institutes have been trained at this centre. These training programmes will help library and information services improve management techniques, raise the quality of service to society, and provide a major impetus to the modernization of library and information services as well as to the nation.

3

Knowledge Management in Libraries

INTRODUCTION

Knowledge economy is a knowledge-based economy. In the knowledge economy era, the management refers to effectively identify, acquire, develop, resolve, use, store and share knowledge, to create an approach to transforming and sharing of tacit and explicit knowledge, and to raise the emergency and innovation capability by utilizing the wisdom of the team.

Since knowledge has become the driving force for social development, the attention of the society to information and knowledge is rising and people's demands for information and knowledge are increasing step by step.

This has provided a good environment for library development. Moreover, as information and knowledge has become an important productive factor for the modern economic system, the society will inevitably require intensified management of information and knowledge.

How to manage knowledge will become an important subject facing libraries in the near future. Knowledge management in libraries should be focused on effective research and development of knowledge, creation of knowledge bases, exchange and sharing of knowledge between library staffs (including its users), training of library staff, speeding up explicit processing of the implicit knowledge and realizing of its sharing.

Characteristics of Knowledge Management in Libraries

The role of knowledge management in libraries will become more and more important along with the development of knowledge economy. It is a new management mode, boasts the following superiority and characteristics incomparable with conventional management:

Human Resource Management Is the Core of Knowledge Management in Libraries

The most important resource in the knowledge economy system is the talents who grasp knowledge. The talent competition has become the focus of market competition in the knowledge economy era. In the knowledge economy era, the libraries will attach importance to vocational training and lifelong education of library staffs to raise their scientific knowledge level and ability of acquiring and innovating knowledge.

They also will and fully respect the human value, guide and bring into play wisdom potentialities of library staffs, take developing knowledge resources in the brains of library staffs as an important way for rising work efficiency. An all-round improvement of library staff's quality and positioning of the human value will become important objectives of knowledge management in libraries.

The Objective of Knowledge Management in Libraries is to Promote Knowledge Innovation

Knowledge innovation is the core of the knowledge economy society. As bases for collection, processing, storage and distribution of knowledge and information, libraries represent an indispensable link in the scientific system chain, an important link in the knowledge innovation. Secondly, libraries take part in scientific research process directly. The library work is a component of knowledge innovation. Thirdly, libraries must pay attention to diffusion and conversion of knowledge. They act as bridges for turning the results of knowledge innovation into realistic productive forces. Knowledge management in libraries is to promote relationship in and between libraries, between library and user, to strengthen knowledge internetworking and to quicken knowledge flow. In the knowledge economy era, libraries will carry out researches on development and application of information resources, construction of virtual libraries, protection of intellectual property rights in the electronic era etc., thus founding the base for knowledge innovation.

Information Technology is a Tool for Knowledge Management in Libraries

Knowledge acquisition is the starting point of knowledge management in libraries. The application of information technologies enlarges the scope of knowledge acquisition, rises knowledge acquisition speed and reduces knowledge acquisition cost. It is impossible to accomplish such important tasks by using man's brains only in the modern society in which the knowledge changes with each passing day. It will be possible to link closely knowledge sources and knowledge workers by computer networks, thus constructing knowledge networks in libraries based on realization of single-point informatization.

The knowledge acquired must be accumulated and converged into knowledge warehouses of libraries. The priority of information technologies in the field of knowledge storage not only finds expression in quantity, but also in retrieval, sorting and security of the knowledge. Information technology is also indispensable in the application and exchange of knowledge and other fields. It functions as a source and tool for knowledge innovation.

Contents of Knowledge Management in Libraries

As a completely new method of management, knowledge management in libraries leaves much to be desired in its theoretical system. In my opinion, knowledge management in libraries should include such respects as follows:

Knowledge Innovation Management

Knowledge innovation management in libraries refers to the management of the production, diffusion and transfer of knowledge as well as of the network systems constructed by related institutions and organizations. It includes three aspects, namely, theoretical innovation management of knowledge, technical innovation management and organizational innovation management. Theoretical innovation management is to enrich and enlarge the theoretical and practical research fields of library science and information science through pursuing the latest development trends in library science the world over.

Technical innovation management is to manage the network systems constructed by institutions and organizations that relate to the full course of technical innovation. In their evolution from conventional libraries to electronic libraries, or digital libraries, Libraries should make technical breakthroughs and progress and build up technical facilities to support knowledge management. Organizational innovation management is to create a set of effective organizational management systems adaptable to the requirements in the electronic library era to support and strengthen knowledge management activities, by optimizing the functional departments and operation procedures of libraries.

In these systems, it firstly requires that leaders who take charge of knowledge management activities should undertake to formulate the management plans and coordinate all knowledge management related activities. Secondly, it requires establishment of special leading groups of knowledge flow for accomplishing all tasks relating to knowledge management activities. Electronic resources committees are established composed of various types of specialists to take charge of evaluating, procuring and creating the electronic resources on the one hand, and coordinating activities of business departments and spurring them on to close cooperation in such fields as procurement and organization of the electronic information resources as well as providing services on the other hand.

Knowledge Dissemination Management

Knowledge dissemination is of equal importance as compared to knowledge innovation. Knowledge creators do not have much time and energy to look for knowledge users. Though there are a multitude of knowledge users, it is very difficult to acquire knowledge that already exists in the minds of knowledge creators as restricted by various objective and subjective conditions. Therefore, libraries may play the part of knowledge tosser, use diverse media and channels to disseminate various new knowledge.

In the 21st century, the Internet, with its mass information and extensive contents, will provide people with the main approach to searching knowledge and acquiring information.

But now there emerge absurd, salacious, false and uncivil information resulting from seeking for commercial profits and political objectives on the Net. Therefore, it is necessary to strengthen knowledge dissemination management in libraries as follows:

1. uninterruptedly strengthening the creation of libraries' own document resources and deepening the development of document information resources;
2. continuously raising the quality of libraries' staffs and strengthening continuous engineering education of working staffs;
3. giving full play to the special role of the expert system in knowledge dissemination;
4. making a comprehensive utilization of all media to ensure security of operation of networks, and prevent online criminal activities and online dissemination of inapropriate information.

Knowledge Application Management

In the 21st century libraries should also attach importance to provision of services for people to acquire knowledge and achieve maximum functions and efficiency of knowledge information. Therefore, knowledge services based on high-speed information networks should be carried out by:

1. Setting up virtual libraries or information centres for enterprises, governments, public organizations and scientific research institutions. It is difficult for an enterprise or a social organization to put sufficient manpower, material and financial resources on information gathering, organizing and developing. It is also impossible and unnecessary to spend a large amount of funds on information resources for their own use. Libraries can create virtual libraries or information centres for these organs separately according to their respective information

requirements by using abundant information resources on the high-speed information networks.

2. Setting up digitized knowledge services which is actually a development trend of libraries in the 21st century. This presupposes: creating step by step the users-oriented information service systems such as information dissemination, information search and special supply of information; quickening the creation of digitized libraries; studying the methods, means and techniques of information distribution and search with the Internet as the base and WEB technique as the core.
3. Digitizing libraries' resources. The electronic libraries or digitized libraries are the technical modes and development trends of libraries in the knowledge economy era. The knowledge services of libraries in the future will start with creation of databases comprising electronic journals and books in different languages that have discipline features and can operate on high-speed information networks. Great efforts should be made to transform all existing large non-electronic information resources into electronic information and integrate them into electronic libraries.

Human Resources Management

Human resources management takes it as its basic starting point to train high quality specialized talents and to revitalize the library undertaking. In practice, we should pay full attention to diversity and variation of library staffs' requirements, strengthened management of different library staffs by applying contingency management approach.

That is, to some people, rigid management method is applied, rigorous supervision and control imposed, and quantity and quality requirements of work according to regulations and procedures are made clear. And, to the rest of people, more flexible management method is applied to let them participate in decision-making and consultation and undertake more jobs so as to bring their management abilities into full play and realize organizational and personal objectives. Doing well in continuous engineering education of specialized staffs, which should not only focus on the theory of library science and related disciplines, but also cover the latest technical knowledge. And strengthening professional ethics education.

Technologies for Realizing Knowledge Management of Libraries

One of the aims of knowledge management in libraries is to promote the knowledge exchange among library staffs, strengthen innovation consciousness and abilities, arise the library staffs' enthusiasm and abilities for learning, making the knowledge most efficiently applied to business activities of the library, and rebuilding the library into a learning organization. Therefore, the main train of thought in realizing knowledge management of libraries is a rational design of the organizational structure and business procedures of libraries, and cultural fostering, as well as modernized information support, thus creating an environment and incentive mechanism forinnovation, exchange, study and application of the knowledge.

IN THE FIELD OF ORGANIZATIONAL STRUCTURE, BUSINESS PROCESSES AND CULTURE OF LIBRARIES

Introducing the CKO System: The Chief Information Officer (CIO) is a conspicuously high management position that has emerged successively in the government departments and large organizations in Western countries since the 1980s.

The Chief Knowledge Officer (CKO) is the highest-ranking person in charge of knowledge management, which has evolved from CIO along with the transition of information research management into knowledge management. The CKO system represents the latest development trends of the information management system of the organizations, and marks the transition of information management from the stage of information resources management to that of knowledge management..

Realizing seamless combination of library business management with knowledge management during the business process reorganization of libraries

Knowledge management integrates itself with the whole process of knowledge exchange, sharing, innovation and application of the organization, and becomes the key driving force for the knowledge innovation, exchange and application of the organization. The implementation of knowledge management will inevitably give rise to organization of library business process. This reorganization will also be the process of further combination of library business management with knowledge management.

***Rebuilding the Library Culture by using the Theory of Knowledge Management* :** Knowledge management will inject new blood into the library culture. The main contents include: mutual trust, open exchange, studying, sharing and developing knowledge operation mechanism of libraries, enjoying the knowledge management process. In a word, to make full use of knowledge, it is necessary to foster a new type of library culture suitable to its requirement. This is high level requirement of realizing technology of knowledge management.

In the Field of Information Technology

The main information technologies relevant to knowledge management includes: Internet, Intranet and Extranet; storage architectures; database management systems; metadata; data acquisition and gathering; dissemination, messaging; push and pull; information retrieval; information resources sharing; groupware; middleware; online analytical processing; multidimensional analysis and data mining. How to convert data to the object of knowledge management-knowledge is also relevant to some basic information technologies, mainly including data processing, reporting, networked communication, document management, information search and retrieval, relational and object-oriented databases, electronic publishing, work flow and help desks.

In addition, because of the differences in architecture, usage and characteristics between information and knowledge, the storage and management of knowledge are more complicated than those of information. The storage architecture technology, database management system technology and metadata are also the key technologies in knowledge management.

Conclusions

Economic environment and information environment is changing quickly today. Knowledge management has become a powerful tool for promoting innovation and realizing reengineering the various walks of life. It occupiès very outstanding position in the creation of the knowledge innovation systems of a country. How for the library circles to meet the challenge of knowledge economy and to build the knowledge management systems of libraries.is a subject that demands our urgent study and solution.

BENEFITS OF WEB SERVICES

Many businesses today are a conglomeration of disparate system architectures and technologies. Company mergers and differing departmental philosophies add to this mixture of systems and applications. Companies may even deploy multiple systems that provide overlapping or redundant business services to the organization. Web services can help you integrate your enterprise. By creating an enterprise-wide repository that registers all services, any service is available to any client, which speeds development, enables enterprise-wide access, and opens new revenue streams.

What Are Web Services?

A Web service is a component packaged and published in a service registry as a single entity that can be used by other programmes. Using the Internet, a Web service can be published at the global level, allowing other companies to access it. Alternatively, by using an existing network or intranet a Web service can be accessible to an entire enterprise. Web services can be grouped together to provide greater levels of functionality, exposing a set of business processes, or even a set of applications.

An example of a Web service is a stock quote service that returns a stock price when given a specific ticker symbol. Any business process, such as a document retrieval process or an ordering system, can be engineered with Web services.

In its simplest form, the Web services model is a message-passing system. The breakthrough in Web services is that messages can be passed across different programming languages, different architectures, and different platforms.

Web services use a combination of new and existing technologies that allows any Web service to talk to another Web service. Since existing Web technologies provide the base for Web services, an existing Web server can easily become a Web services server. This, in combination with wide industry support, makes Web services a viable commodity.

Web services allowing Company A to place an order and receive an order confirmation from Company B. The bottom part of the diagram shows internal Web services at Company B being used to fulfil the order-verifying the customer, performing credit card validation through an external provider, and integrating all the legacy systems that control inventory management.

Companies have been solving integration challenges with proprietary solutions for decades. The power of Web services lies in bringing three things to the forefront:

- Best-practice architecture
- Open standards for true interoperability
- Tools to rapidly apply the standards

Understanding the Web Services Architecture

In order to understand how Web services work, let's examine the components of Web services. Web services are deployed in a service-oriented architecture (SOA) that consists of the following:

Service Provider: Publishes the availability of its services in a registry and responds to requests to use its services

Service Registry: Categorizes published service providers and allows searching of its registry

Service Requester: Uses service registries to find a needed service and binds to that service

Even at the enterprise level, this architecture is in place (although in enterprise configurations all of these roles could be performed by the same company) in order to complete the three Web services operations: publish, find, and bind.

The company acts as service provider, publishing its Web services in a service registry. This registry can be behind the firewall for internal access or at a company portal for business partner access. Once the service is published, application developers, acting as service requesters, can access the registry in order to find the needed service and retrieve the service's interface description. The bind operation occurs as the service requester interacts with the service at runtime, using the binding details in the service description to invoke the service. In this way, valuable business processes can be shared across an organization.

Applying Web Services Technologies to the SOA

When you combine the SOA of the service provider, service registry, and service requester with service-oriented technologies, you get the Web services stack, with the upper layers of the stack building on the lower layers:

Network: At the bottom of the stack are the network layer and the basic communication protocols. A Web service must be available on a network. Communication protocols such as HTTP (Hypertext Transfer Protocol) allow transfer of data and access to applications over the network.

XML Messaging: XML (eXtensible Markup Language) allows data to be structured in a platform-and language-independent manner. Unlike HTML, which uses a fixed set of tags to specify both the content and display of information, XML allows you to define your own set of tags that accurately describe the information and enable the presentation of the information to change depending on its use. SOAP (Simple Object Access Protocol) specifies an XML-based messaging protocol and provides an envelope for transferring XML data.

Service Description: WSDL (Web Services Description Language) describes a Web service in an XML-based format.

Service Publication and Discovery: UDDI (Universal Description, Discovery, and Integration) specifies how to publish and find Web services.

Service Flow: As the technology matures, Web services will be combined to provide greater degrees of functionality. WSFL

(Web Services Flow Language) uses XML to describe how Web services interact to solve a business problem by modelling the basic workflow.

The vertical bars in represent requirements that need to be addressed by all layers of the stack: security, management, quality of service, and transactions.

DEVELOPING WEB SERVICES IN THE ENTERPRISE ENVIRONMENT

Defining Web Services : To develop Web services in the enterprise environment, you must first define in your enterprise UDDI which services you want to make available. Any existing EJBs (Enterprise JavaBeans) or COM components, which are inherently modular in nature, are prime candidates for publication in a UDDI registry. In addition, you need to examine your legacy systems. Functionality in those systems can be wrapped as message-based Web services.

Publishing Web Services : Once the Web services are available, you need to publish them. There are tools available to automate this process, writing the necessary WSDL at the specified location. For IBM WebSphere, the Web Services Toolkit and WebSphere Studio Application Developer (WSAD) contain tools that will write the WSDL. By completing the steps in WSAD's Web service wizard you can:

Define a Web service based on an existing Java class, EJB, or Document Access Definition Extension (DADX)

Generate WSDL and deployment descriptors for the Web service

Create a service proxy and client mappings

Creating the UDDI: By publishing the Web services, you create the UDDI. At the enterprise level, you can implement one or more of the following UDDI scenarios:

A private UDDI placed inside the firewall for applications within the company

An enterprise-wide UDDI placed inside the firewall for interactions within the company and with trusted business partners

A company portal UDDI placed on the firewall, allowing interested business partners to find Web services across the Internet but restricting access to published operations

Developing Service-Based Applications : Once the services are published they can be called from any enterprise application. Even though Web services can be bound dynamically, a widely accepted practice is to look up the Web service during development and use its interfaces and methods in the application.

Current Development Issues

As of this writing there are two major divisions of Web services tool sets:

J2EE technologies used by vendors such as IBM, Sun, and Oracle

Microsoft's.NET Technologies : The J2EE technologies have been around the longest, making their solutions more robust in many areas, but since Web services specifications have been agreed to by all major vendors, different technologies can work together.

There are several issues at the current stage of Web services, especially when implementing Web services at the global level:

Reliable Messaging: How to determine if a particular message was actually received and was sent only once.

Dependability: How to determine the dependability of an unknown company in a 24/7 marketplace.

Security: How to make Web services secure if they use the HTTP protocol. HTTPR is a new protocol that has been proposed to address security concerns.

Transactions: How to complete transactions in the Web's stateless environment. In the past, transactional applications used a two-phase commit structure to determine when a complex transaction was complete and ready to commit to the database. Since this model is not available on the Web, new models for transactions are being discussed.

One of these models uses a concept called dependency spheres, which allows both synchronous and asynchronous distributed messages to occur within a single transaction.

Payment for Web Services Access: How to be paid for Web services used by other companies.

As Web services evolve, expect to see answers and specification changes that deal with these issues.

Using Web Services to Integrate Technologies

To illustrate how Web services can be used to integrate disparate system architectures, the sample application described in figure uses both EJB and COM technologies. The sample application was built with:

IBM Web Services Toolkit (a version was also built using WebSphere Studio Application Developer.)

IBM WebSphere 4.0

Microsoft SOAP Library (for the Microsoft clients)

Contact information (name, address, and so on) in the sample application is stored in Microsoft Outlook and a DB2 database. Using Web services, you can update the contact information using either HTML or Visual Basic clients and those changes will be reflected in both data sources.

The sample application consists of:

Proxies: These provide directly callable methods that map to SOAP services. They contain the service names and URLs of the Web service servers.

Helper Beans: Helper beans call the proxies and hold and parse the data returned by the Web services. They contain read and write methods that make the service calls. They also contain get and set methods for data access.

JSPs: JSPs contain the user interface and call the helper beans in order to access and change all data. They also perform some data validation.

SOAP Servlets/Apache Pluggable Service Providers: These handle all incoming SOAP requests. The requests are parsed and the appropriate implementation is called. The service is defined in a deployment descriptor used when registering the service.

Accessing Web Services

When the sample application was implemented, it contained two SOAP services, one for each data source:

DemoOutlook: Provides an interface for reading and writing an entry in the Contacts section of Microsoft Outlook

DemoDB2: Provides an interface for reading and writing an Employee record from the Employees table in the DB2 sample database, which is part of IBM WebSphere

***Using a Microsoft Client*:** Access to a SOAP server through VB or VBS was done using the Microsoft SOAP library. Unlike the Java client, the Microsoft client is dynamic. By simply initializing a SOAP object with the WSDL URL, all the service methods are available to be called.

Future Directions

One of the benefits of building an enterprise-based UDDI is that it can be upgraded for other uses. Even though its initial benefit is for internal enterprise integration, with trusted business partners it can later be used to move to global Web services. Major vendors such as IBM and Microsoft provide online access to the global UDDI registry in order to publish services or to search the registry for needed services or potential business partners.

Web services are the future of e-business. Future visions of the Internet see applications primarily being hosted on Web servers, thereby encouraging access by all types of devices, not just personal computers. Web services can be used to provide access to those Internet applications, even allowing syndication of them to many Web sites.

Web services also allow for greater automation of business processes since computer-to-computer communication across systems and architectures is easily implemented. This combination of communication, open standards, and multiple vendor support paves the way for Web services not only to expand, but also to transform e-business.

4

Networked Resources

INTRODUCTION

The proliferation and the infinite variety of networked resources and their continuing rapid growth present enormous opportunities as well as unprecedented challenges to library and information professionals. The need to integrate Web resources with traditional types of library materials has necessitated a re-examination of the established, well-proven tools that have been used in bibliographic control. Librarians confront new challenges in extending their practice in selecting and organizing library materials to a variety of resources in a dynamic networked environment. In this environment, the tension between quality and quantity has never been keener. Providing quality access to a large quantity of resources poses special challenges.

This paper examines how the nature of the Web and characteristics of networked resources affect subject access and analyses the requirements of effective indexing and retrieval tools. The current and potential uses of existing tools and possible courses for future development will be explored in the context of recent research.

A New Environment and Landscape

For centuries librarians have addressed issues of information storage and retrieval and have developed tools that are effective in handling traditional materials. However, any deliberation on the future of traditional tools should take into consideration the characteristics of networked resources and the nature of information retrieval on the Web. The sheer size demands efficient tools; it is a matter of economy. I will begin by reviewing briefly the nature of the OPAC and the characteristics of traditional library resources.

OPACs are by and large homogeneous, at least in terms of content organization and format of presentation, if not in interface design. They are standardized due to the common tools (AACR2R/MARC, LCSH, LCC, DDC, etc.) used in their construction, and there is a level of consistency among them. The majority of resources represented in the OPACs, *i.e.*, traditional library materials, typically manifest the following characteristics:

- tangible (they represent physical items)
- well-defined (they can be defined and categorized in terms of specific types, such as books, journals, maps, sound recordings, etc.)
- self-contained (they are packaged in recognizable units)
- relatively stable (though subject to physical deterioration, they are not volatile)

The World Wide Web, on the other hand, can be described as vast, distributed, multifarious, machine-driven, dynamic/fluid, and rapidly evolving. Electronic resources, in contrast to traditional library materials, are often:

- amorphous
- ill-defined
- not self-contained
- unstable
- volatile

Over the years, standards and procedures for organizing library materials have been developed and tested. Among these is the convention that trained cataloguers and indexers typically carry the full responsibility for providing metadata through cataloguing and indexing.

In contrast, the networked environment is still developing, meaning that appropriate and efficient methods for resources description and organization are still evolving.

Because of the sheer volume of electronic resources, many people without formal training in bibliographic control, including subject specialists, public service personnel, and non-professionals, are now engaged in the preparation and provision of metadata for Web resources. Additionally, the computer has been called on to carry a large share of the labour involved in information processing and organization. The results are often amazing and sometimes dismaying. This raises the question of how to maintain consistency and quality while struggling to achieve efficiency. The answer perhaps lies somewhere between a total reliance on human power and a complete delegation to technology.

Retrieval Models

The new landscape presented by the Web challenges established information retrieval models to provide the power to navigate networked resources with the same levels of efficiency in precision and recall achieved with traditional resources. In her deliberation of subject cataloguing in the online environment, Marcia J. Bates pointed out the importance of bringing into consideration search capabilities "*Online search capabilities themselves constitute a form of indexing.*

Subject access to online catalogs is thus a combination of original indexing and what we might call 'search capabilities indexing'" (Bates 1989). In contemplating the most effective subject approaches to networked resources, we need to take into account the different models currently used in information retrieval. In addition to the Boolean model, various ranking algorithms and other retrieval models are also implemented. The Boolean model, based on exact matches, is used in most OPACs and many commercial databases.

On the other hand, the vector and the probabilistic models are common on the Web, particularly in full-text analysis, indexing, and retrieval (Korfhage 1997; Salton 1994). In these models, the loss of specificity normally expected from traditional subject access tools is compensated to a certain degree by methods of statistical ranking and computational linguistics, based on term occurrences, term frequency, word proximity, and term weighting. These models do not always yield the best results but, combined with automatic methods in text processing and indexing, they have the ability to handle a large amount of data efficiently. They also give some indication of future trends and developments.

Subject Access on the Web

What kinds of subject access tools are needed in this environment? We may begin by defining their functional requirements. Subject access tools are used:

- to assist searchers in identifying the most efficient paths for resource discovery and retrieval
- to help users focus their searches
- to enable optimal recall
- to enable optimal precision
- to assist searchers in developing alternative search strategies
- to provide all of the above in the most efficient, effective, and economical manner

To fulfil these functions in the networked environment, there are certain operational requirements, the most important of these being interoperability and the ability to handle a large amount of resources efficiently. The blurred boundaries of information spaces demand that disparate systems can work together for the benefit of the users. Interoperability enables users to search among resources from a multitude of sources generated and organized according to different standards and approaches.

The sheer size of the Web demands attention and presents a particularly critical challenge. For years, a pressing issue facing the libraries has been the large backlogs. If the definition of arrearage is a large number of books waiting in the backroom to be catalogued, then think of Web resources as a huge arrearage sitting in the front yard. How to impose bibliographic control on those resources of value in the most efficient and economical manner possible—in essence achieving scalability—is an important mission of the library and information profession. To provide users with a means to seamlessly utilize these vast resources, the operational requirements may be summarized as:

- interoperability among different systems, metadata standards, and languages
- flexibility and adaptability to different information communities, not only different types of libraries, but also other communities such as museums, archives, corporate information systems, etc.
- extensibility and scalability to accommodate the need for different degrees of depth and different subject domains
- simplicity in application, *i.e.*, easy to use and to comprehend
- versatility, *i.e.*, the ability to perform different functions
- amenability to computer application

In 1997, in order to investigate the issues surrounding subject access in the networked environment, ALCTS (Association of Library Collections and Technical Services) established two subcommittees: Subcommittee on Metadata and Subject Analysis and Subcommittee on Metadata and Classification. Their reports are now available (ALCTS 1999, 1999a). Some of their recommendations will be discussed later in this paper.

Verbal Subject Access: While subject access to networked resources is available, there is much room for improvement. Greater usage of controlled vocabulary may be one of the answers. During the past three decades, the introduction and increasing popularity and, in some cases, total reliance on free-text or natural language searching have brought a key question to the forefront: Is there still a need for controlled vocabulary? To information professionals who have appreciated the power of controlled vocabulary, the answer has always been a confident "yes." To others, the affirmative answer became clear only when searching began to be bogged down in the sheer size of retrieved results. Controlled vocabulary offers the benefits of consistency, accuracy, and control (Bates 1989), which are often lacking in the free-text approach.

Even in the age of automatic indexing and with the ease in keyword searching, controlled vocabulary has much to offer in improving retrieval results and in alleviating the burden of synonym and homograph control placed on the user. For many years, Elaine Svenonius has argued that using controlled vocabulary retrieves more relevant records by placing the burden on the indexer rather than the user (Svenonius 1986; Svenonius 2000). Recently, David Batty makes a similar observation on the role of controlled vocabulary in the Web environment: "There is a burden of effort in information storage and retrieval that may be shifted from shoulder to shoulder, from author, to indexer, to index language designer, to searcher, to user. It may even be shared in different proportions. But it will not go away" (Batty 1998).

Controlled vocabulary most likely will not replace keyword searching, but it can be used to supplement and complement keyword searching to enhance retrieval results. The basic functions of controlled vocabulary, *i.e.*, better recall through synonym control and term relationships and greater precision through homograph control, have not been completely supplanted by keyword searching, even with all the power a totally machine-driven system can bring to bear. To this effect, the ALCTS Subcommittee on Metadata and Subject Analysis recommends the use of a combination of keywords and controlled vocabulary in metadata records for Web resources (ALCTS 1999a).

Subject heading lists and thesauri began as cataloguers' and indexers' tools, as a source of, and an aid in choosing, appropriate index terms. Later, they were also made available to users as searching aids, particularly in online systems. Traditionally, controlled vocabulary terms embedded in metadata records have been used as a means of matching the user's information needs against the document collection. Subject headings and descriptors, with their attendant equivalent and related terms, facilitate the searcher's ability to make an exact match of search terms against assigned index terms. Manual mapping of users' input terms to controlled vocabulary terms—for example, consulting a thesaurus to identify appropriate search terms—is a tedious process and has never been widely embraced by end-users. With the availability of online thesaurus-display, the mapping is greatly facilitated by allowing the user to browse and select controlled vocabulary terms in searching. Controlled vocabulary thus serves as the bridge between the searcher's language and the author's language.

Even in free-text and full-text searching, keywords can be supplemented with terms "borrowed" from a controlled vocabulary to improve retrieval performance. Participating researchers of TREC (the Text Retrieval Conference), the large-scale cross-system search engine evaluation project, have found that "the amount of improvement in recall and precision which we could attribute to NLP [natural language processing] appeared to be related to the type and length of the initial search request. Longer, more detailed topic statements responded well to LMI [linguistically motivated indexing], while terse one-sentence search directives showed little improvement" (Strzalkowski et al. 2000).

Because of the term relationships built in a controlled vocabulary, the retrieval system can be programmed to automatically expand an original search query to include equivalent terms, post-up or down to hierarchically related terms, or suggest associative terms. Users typically enter simple natural language terms (Drabenstott 2000), which may or may not match the language used by authors. When the searcher's keywords are mapped to a controlled vocabulary, the power of synonym and homograph control could be invoked and the variants of the searcher's terms could be called up (Bates 1998).

Furthermore, the built-in related controlled terms could also be brought up to suggest alternative search terms and to help users focus their searches more effectively. In this sense, controlled vocabulary is used as a query-expansion device. It can be used to complement uncontrolled terms and terms from lexicons, dictionaries, gazetteers, and similar tools, which are rich in synonyms, but often lacking in relational terms. In the vector and probabilistic retrieval models, using a conflation of variant and related terms often yield better results than relying on the few "key" words entered by the searcher. Equivalent and related terms in a query provide context for each other. Including additional search terms from a controlled vocabulary can improve the ranking of retrieved items.

Classification and Subject Categorization: With regard to knowledge organization, traditionally, classification has been used in American libraries primarily as an organizational device for shelf-location and for browsing in the stacks. It has often been used also as a tool for collection management, for example, assisting in the creation of branch libraries and in the generation of discipline-specific acquisitions or holdings lists. In the OPAC, classification has regained its bibliographic function through the use of class numbers as access points to MARC records. To continue the use of class numbers as access points, the ALCTS Subcommittee on Metadata and Subject Analysis recommends that this function be extended to other types of metadata records by including in them class numbers, but not necessarily the item numbers, from existing classification schemes (ALCTS 1999a).

In addition to the access function, the role of classification has been expanded to those of subject browsing and navigational tools for retrieval on the Web. In its study of the use of classification devices for organizing metadata, the ALCTS Subcommittee on Metadata and Classification has identified seven functions of classification: location, browsing, hierarchical movement, retrieval, identification, limiting/partitioning, and profiling (ALCTS 1999).

With the rapid growth of networked resources, the enormous amount of information available on the Web cries out for organization. When subject categorization devices first became popular among Web information providers, they resembled broad classification schemes, but many were lacking the rigorous hierarchical structure and careful conceptual organization found in established schemes. Many library portals, which began with a collection of a limited number of selected electronic resources offering only keyword searching and/or an alphabetical listing, have adopted broad subject categorization schemes when the collection of electronic resources became voluminous and unwieldy (Waldhart et al. 2000). Some of these subject categorization devices are based on existing classification schemes, *e.g.*, Internet Public Library Online Texts Collection based on the Dewey Decimal Classification (DDC) and CyberStacks(sm) based on the Library of Congress Classification (LCC) (McKiernan 2000); others represent home-made varieties.

Subject categorization defines narrower domains within which term searching can be carried out more efficiently and enables the retrieval of more relevant results. Combination of subject categorization with term searching has proven to be an effective and efficient approach in resource discovery and data mining. In this regard, classification or subject categorizing schemes function as information filters, used to efficiently exclude large segments of a database from consideration of a search query (Korfhage 1997).

Recent Research on Subject Access Systems

Before we explore the potential directions for future development of traditional subject access tools, let us also examine some of the recent research efforts and their implications for current and future methods of subject indexing and access. A huge body of research has been reported in the literature. Three areas of experimentation that I consider to have important bearings on subject access tools are automatic indexing, mapping terms and data from different sources, and integrating different subject access tools.

***Automatic indexing*:** In the past few decades, some of the most important research in the field of information storage and retrieval has been focused on automatic indexing. Beginning with the pioneer efforts in the 1970s, various techniques, including term weighting, statistical analysis of text, and computational linguistics, have been developed and applied.

More recent examples include OCLC's Scorpion project, which uses automatic methods to perform subject recognition and to generate machine-assigned DDC numbers for electronic resources (Shafer 1997). Another OCLC project, WordSmith, (Godby and Reighart 1998), applying computational linguistics to implement a series of largely statistical filters, investigates the feasibility of extracting subject terminology directly from raw text.

An extension of this project, called Extended WordSmith, applies a similar technique to the automatic generation of thesaural terms. On the more practical side, the recent implementation of the LEXIS/NEXIS SmartIndexing Technology combines controlled vocabulary features with an indexing algorithm to arrive at a relevance score or percentage based on criteria such as term frequency, weight, and location in document in indexing LEXIS/ NEXIS news collections (Quint 1999; Tenopir 1999).

Mapping Terms and Data from Different Sources: Mapping natural-language expressions typical of end-user search queries and of automatically extracted index terms to more structured subject-language is an area that has been explored and holds great promise (Svenonius 2000). A recent example is the "Entry Vocabulary Modules" project at the University of California-Berkeley, which explores the possibility of mapping "ordinary language queries" to indexing terms based on metadata subject vocabularies unfamiliar to the user, including classification numbers, subject headings, and descriptors from various subject- or domain-specific vocabularies (Buckland et al. 1999).

On another front, numerous efforts have focused on mapping subject data from different vocabulary sources, including free-text terms extracted from full texts, controlled vocabularies, classification data, and name authority data. Because the networked environment is open and multifarious, multiple tools for resource description and subject access are often used side-by-side.

In this open environment, use of multiple controlled vocabularies within the same system is not uncommon. Harmonization of different vocabularies, similar or analogous to crosswalks among metadata schemes, is an important issue. Even before the advent of the World Wide Web, mapping subject terms from multiple thesauri was a topic of great interest and concern. An example was Carol Mandel's investigation to resolve the problems caused by using multiple vocabularies within the same online system (Mandel 1987). Much progress has been made in biomedical vocabularies.

The Unified Medical Language System (UMLS) Metathesaurus currently maps biomedical terms from over fifty different biomedical vocabularies, some in multiple languages (Nelson 1999; National Library of Medicine 2000). A general metathesaurus covering all subjects is still lacking. Outside of the library context, there are also efforts to map index terms from different sources. An example is WILSONLINE's OmniFile, which results from merging index terms from six H.W. Wilson indexes into one index file. On a broader scale, indexes from different language sources also need to be interoperable. Mapping between controlled vocabularies in different languages is an issue of great interest particularly in the international community. MACS (Multilingual ACcess to Subject), an ongoing international project involving Swiss, German, French, and British national libraries, attempts to link subject authority files in three different languages, Schlagwortnormdatei (SWD, German), RAMEAU (French), and the Library of Congress Subject Headings (English) (Landry 2000).

Mapping between subject headings and class numbers is not new. Past efforts have focused mainly on facilitating subject cataloguing and indexing. Examples include the linking of many LCC numbers to headings in the *Library of Congress Subject Headings (LCSH)* list and the inclusion of abridged DDC numbers in the *Sears List of Subject Headings* (Sears). More recently, there have been efforts to map between DDC numbers and LCSH (Vizine-Goetz 1998). OCLC's WordSmith project mentioned earlier demonstrates that subject terms can be identified and extracted automatically from raw texts and mapped to existing classification schemes such as DDC (Godby and Reighart 1998).

Diane Vizine-Goetz demonstrates how results from the research projects WordSmith and ExTended Concept Trees can be used together to enhance DDC (Vizine-Goetz 1997). The same techniques should be applicable to LCC also. With the implementation of the CORC (Cooperative Online Resource Catalogue) project, results of many of OCLC's research projects have converged in practice. Actual application includes the automatic generation of subject data and DDC numbers in metadata records. A most impressive feature of CORC that can yield great benefit is the capability of mapping names and subject words and phrases input by cataloguers or indexers or those automatically generated from websites to entries in subject and name authority files.

***Integrating Different Subject Access Tools*:** In the manual environment, subject headings and classification systems have more or less operated in isolation from each other. Technology offers the possibility of integrating tools of different sorts to enhance retrieval results as well as facilitate subject cataloguing and indexing. The merging or integration of classification with controlled vocabulary holds great potential. Numerous research projects have been undertaken and some of the designs have been tested. For example, Karen Markey's project incorporated the Dewey Decimal Classification as a retrieval tool alongside subject searching in an online system (Markey 1986). Her research was built on AUDACIOUS, an earlier project using UDC as the index language with nuclear science literature (Freeman and Atherton 1968).

In a system called Cheshire, Ray Larson, used a method called "classification clustering," combined with probabilistic retrieval techniques, to improve subject searching in the OPAC. Starting with LC call numbers and using probabilistic ranking and weighting mechanisms, Larson demonstrates that class numbers combined with subject terms generated from titles of documents and subject headings in MARC records can enhance access points and improve greatly the retrieval results. The integration of different types of access is significant, as Larson observes: "The topical access points of the MARC records used in online catalogs, such as the classification numbers, subject headings, and title keywords, have usually been treated in strict isolation from each other in search. The classification clustering method is one way of effectively combining these difference 'clues' to the database contents" (Larson 1991).

Traditional Tools in the Networked Environment

The concepts surrounding subject access have been explored in relation to the configuration of the Web landscape and retrieval models. In this context, a question that can be raised is: How well can existing subject access tools fulfil the requirements of networked resources? More specifically, how adequate are traditional tools such as LCSH, LCC, and DDC in meeting the challenges of effective and efficient subject retrieval in the networked environment?

Library of Congress Subject Headings: With regard to LCSH specifically, a basic question is whether a new controlled vocabulary more suited to the requirements of electronic resources should be constructed. The ALCTS Subcommittee on Metadata and Subject Analysis deliberated on this question and examined the options relating to the choice of subject vocabulary in metadata records.

After considering the options of developing a new vocabulary or adopting or adapting one or more existing vocabularies, the Subcommittee recommends the latter option (ALCTS 1999a). For a general controlled vocabulary covering all subjects, the Subcommittee recommends the use of LCSH or Sears with or without modifications.

Among the reasons for retaining LCSH are: (1) LCSH is a rich vocabulary covering all subject areas, easily the largest general indexing vocabulary in the English language; (2) there is synonym and homograph control; (3) it contains rich links (cross references indicating relationships) among terms; (4) it is a pre-coordinate system that ensures precision in retrieval; (5) it facilitates browsing of multiple-concept or multi-faceted subjects; and, (6) having been translated or adapted as a model for developing subject headings systems by many countries around the world, LCSH is a de facto universal controlled vocabulary. In addition, there is another major advantage. Retaining LCSH as subject data in metadata records would ensure semantic interoperability between the enormous store of MARC records and metadata records prepared according to various other standards.

While the vocabulary, or semantics, of LCSH has much to contribute to the management and retrieval of networked resources, the way it is currently applied has certain limitations: (1) because of its complex syntax and application rules, assigning LC subject headings according to current Library of Congress policies requires trained personnel; (2) subject heading strings in bibliographic or metadata records are costly to maintain; (3) LCSH, in its present form and application, is not compatible in syntax with most other controlled vocabularies; and, (4) it is not amenable to search engines outside of the OPAC environment, particularly current Web search engines. These limitations mean that applying LCSH properly in compliance with current policy and procedures entails the following requirements:

- trained cataloguers and indexers
- systems with index browsing capability
- systems with online thesaurus display
- sophisticated users (Drabenstott 1999)

In the networked environment, such conditions often do not prevail. What direction and steps need to be taken for LCSH to overcome these limitations and remain useful in its traditional roles as well as to accommodate other uses? Pondering the viability of LCSH in the networked environment, the ALCTS Subcommittee on Metadata and Subject Analysis recommends separating the consideration regarding semantics from that relating to application syntax, in other words, distinguishing between the vocabulary (LCSH per se) and the indexing system (*i.e.*, how LCSH is applied in a particular implementation).

This recommendation involves several important concepts that need to be reviewed. Semantics and syntax are two distinct aspects of a controlled vocabulary. Semantics concerns the source vocabulary, *i.e.*, what appears in the term list (*e.g.*, a thesaurus or a subject headings list) that contains the building blocks for constructing indexing terms or search statements. It covers the scope and depth, the selection of terms to be included, the forms of valid terms, synonym and homograph control, and the syndetic (cross-referencing) devices. Semantics should be governed by well-defined principles of vocabulary structure.

At the heart of the syntax concept is the representation of complex subjects through combination, or coordination, of terms representing different subjects or different facets (defined as families of concepts that share a common characteristic (Batty 1998)) of a subject. There are two aspects of syntax: term construction and application syntax. Term construction, *i.e.*, how words are put together to represent concepts in the thesaurus, is an aspect of semantics and is a matter of principle; while application syntax, *i.e.*, how thesaurual terms are put together to reflect the contents of documents in the metadata record, is a matter of policy, determined by practical factors such as user needs, available resources, and search engines and their capabilities.

Enumeration (*i.e.*, the listing of pre-established multiple-concept index terms in the thesaurus) and faceting (*i.e.*, the separate listing of single-concept or single-facet terms defined in distinctive categories based on common, shared characteristics) are aspects of term construction, while precoordination and postcoordination relate to application syntax. Term combination can occur at any of three stages in the process of information storage and retrieval: (1) during vocabulary construction; (2) at the stage of cataloguing or indexing; or, (3) at the point of retrieval.

When words or phrases representing different subjects or different facets of a subject are pre-combined at the point of thesaurus construction, we refer to the process as enumeration. When term combination occurs at the stage of indexing or cataloguing, we refer to the practice as precoordination. In contrast, postcoördination refers to the combination of terms at the point of retrieval. A totally enumerative vocabulary is by definition precoordinated.

On the other hand, a faceted controlled vocabulary—*i.e.*, a system that provides individual terms in clearly defined categories, or facets—may be applied either precoordinately or postcoordinately. A faceted scheme hence is more flexible. An example of a rigorously faceted, precoordinate system is PRECIS (previously used in the British National Bibliography). Another example is the Universal Subject Environment (USE) system, proposed in a recent article by William E. Studwell, which contains faceted terms and uses special punctuation marks as facet indicators (Studwell 2000). On the other hand, current indexing systems used in abstracting and indexing services employing controlled vocabularies are typically postcoordinated. Whether a precoordinate approach or a postcoordinate approach is used in a particular implementation is a matter of policy and is agency-specific. In the remainder of this paper, we will focus on the semantics and term construction issues.

Because of the varied approaches to retrieval in different search environments and the different needs of diverse user communities, a vocabulary that is flexible enough to be used either precoordinately or postcoordinately would be the most viable. A faceted scheme can accommodate different application syntaxes, from the most complex (*e.g.*, full-string approach typically found in OPACs) to the simplest (descriptor-like terms used in most indexes) and would also allow different degrees of sophistication. The advantages of a faceted controlled vocabulary can be summarized as follows:

- simple in structure
- flexible in application (*i.e.*, able to accommodate a tiered approach to allow different levels of subject representation)
- amenable to software applications (Batty 1998)
- amenable to computer-assisted indexing and validation
- interoperable with the majority of modern indexing vocabularies
- easier and more economical to maintain than an enumerated vocabulary

On the last point regarding efficient thesaurus maintenance, Batty remarks: "Facet procedure has many advantages. By organizing the terms into smaller, related groups, each group of terms can be examined more easily and efficiently for consistency, order, hierarchical relationships, relationships to other groups, and the acceptability of the language used in the terms. The faceted approach is also useful for its flexibility in dealing with the addition of new terms and new relationships. Because each facet can stand alone, changes can usually be made easily in a facet at any time without disturbing the rest of the thesaurus" (Batty 1998). Thus, a faceted LCSH will be easier to maintain. With the current LCSH, updating terminology sometimes can be a tedious operation. For example, when the heading "Moving-pictures" was replaced in 1987 by "Motion pictures," approximately 400 authority records were affected! (El-Hoshy 1998).

A faceted LCSH is by no means a new idea. Earlier advocates of such an approach include Pauline A. Cochrane (1986) and Mary Dykstra (1988). To remain viable in the networked environment, a controlled vocabulary, such as LCSH, must be able to accommodate different retrieval models mentioned earlier as well as different application policies.

Outside of the OPAC, most search engines, including many used in library portals for Web resources, lack the ability to accommodate full-string browsing and searching. Even among systems that can handle full strings, their capabilities and degrees of sophistication also vary. With a faceted vocabulary, it will not be an either/or proposition between the precoordinate full-string application and the postcoordinate approach, but rather a question of how LCSH can be made to accommodate both and any variations in between, thus ensuring maximum flexibility and scalability in terms of application. Mechanisms for full-string implementation of LCSH are already in place; for example, in the OPAC environment, with highly trained personnel and the searching and browsing capabilities of integrated systems, the full-string syntax has long been employed in creating subject headings in MARC records.

In the heterogeneous environment outside of the OPAC, we need a more flexible system in order to accommodate different applications. LCSH can become such a tool, and its use can be extended to various metadata standards and with different encoding schemes. Investigations and experiments on the viability of LCSH have already begun. Using LCSH as the source vocabulary, FAST (Faceted Application of Subject Terminology), a current OCLC research project, explores the possibility and feasibility of a postcoordinate approach by separating time, space, and form data from the subject heading string (Chan et al. in press).

Now we come to the question of where LCSH stands currently in becoming a viable system for the networked environment. LCSH began in the late nineteenth century as an enumerative scheme. It gradually took on some of the features of a faceted system, particularly in the adoption of commonly used form subdivisions and the increasing use of geographic subdivisions. In the latter part of the twentieth century LCSH has taken further steps, ever so cautiously, in the direction of more rigorous faceting. In 1974, the Library of Congress took a giant leap forward in expanding the application of commonly used subdivisions by designating a large number of frequently used topical and form subdivisions "free-floating," thus allowing great flexibility in application.

The adoption of BT, NT, RT in the 11th (1988) edition rendered LCSH more in line with thesaural practice. After the Subject Subdivisions Conference held in 1991 (The Future of Subdivisions, 1992), the Library of Congress has embarked on a programme to convert many of the topical subdivisions into topical main headings. Finally, in 1999, the implementation of subfield $v for form subdivisions in the 6xx (subject-related) fields in the MARC format, marking the distinction between form and topical subdivisions, moved LCSH yet another step closer to becoming a faceted system. Considering the gradual steps the Library of Congress has taken over the years, even a person not familiar with the history of LCSH must conclude logically that LCSH is heading in the direction of becoming a fully faceted vocabulary. It is not there yet; but, with further effort, LCSH can become a versatile system that is capable of functioning in heterogeneous environments and can serve as the unified basis for supporting diversified uses while maintaining semantic interoperability among them.

A faceted LCSH has a number of potential uses in the areas of thesaurus development and management, indexing, and retrieval. As mentioned earlier, to enhance the interoperability of a multitude of controlled vocabularies, a general metathesaurus covering all subjects would be most desirable (ALCTS 1999a). It will not be a trivial task, but the first question the library and information profession must agree upon is whether it is something worth pursuing. LCSH, with its rich vocabulary—the largest in the English language—can serve as a basis or core of such a metathesaurus.

From a different perspective, LCSH could also be used as the basis for generating subject-or discipline-specific controlled vocabularies or special-purpose thesauri. The *AC Subject Headings* (formerly *Subject Headings for Children's Literature*) sets a precedent. Other examples include a large "superthesaurus" proposed by Bates (1989), with a rich entry vocabulary as a part of a friendly front-end user interface for the OPAC. While many subject domains and disciplines such as engineering, art, and biomedical sciences have their own controlled vocabularies, many specialized areas and non-library institutions still lack them.

These include for-profit as well as non-profit organizations, government agencies, historical societies, special-purpose museums, consulting firms, fashion design companies, to name a few. Many of these rely on their curators or researchers, most of whom have not been trained in bibliographic control, to take responsibility for organizing Internet resources. Having a comprehensive subject access vocabulary to draw and build upon would be of tremendous help in developing their specialized thesauri.

To move LCSH further along the way towards becoming a faceted vocabulary, if indeed such is the direction to be followed, more can be done to its semantics. Aspects of particular concern that need close scrutiny and re-thinking include principles of term selection, enhanced entry vocabulary, rigorous term relationships, and particularly term construction.

Library of Congress Classification (LCC) and Dewey Decimal Classification (DDC): In recent years, with the support of the OCLC Research Office, DDC has made great strides in adapting to the networked environment and becoming a useful tool for organizing electronic resources. For example, the newly developed WebDewey contains, in addition to the DDC/LCSH mapping feature first developed in Dewey for Windows, an automated classification tool for generating candidate DDC numbers during metadata record creation.

It has taken LCC somewhat longer because its voluminous schedules have only recently been converted to the MARC format. Let us hope that the Library Congress can now turn its attention to making LCC a useful tool not only in the library stacks but also as an organizing tool of networked resources. Results and insights gained from experimental and actual implementations of Web application of DDC and other classification schemes should be applicable to LCC as well.

Existing classification schemes have already been adopted or adapted to a limited extent for use as subject categorization devices for Web resources. Examples include the adaptation of DDC in NetFirst and CyberDewey and the use of LCC outlines in Cyberstacks. In this particular role, existing classification schemes need greater flexibility and more attention to their structure. Adaptability of classification schemes can take the form of flexibility in the depth of hierarchy and variability in the collocation of items in the array.

The requirement of depth varies from application to application. As a tool for shelf-location and bibliographic arrangement, considerable depth in classification is required, as evidenced in the growth of both DDC and LCC in the past. As a navigating tool typified by the subject categorization schemes used in the popular Web directories, broad schemes are often sufficient. What is needed is a flexibility of depth and the amenability to the creation of classificatory structures focused on specific subject domains. Flexibility in depth has always been a feature of DDC and UDC, with the availability of abridged, medium, and full versions, in recognition of the different needs of school, public, and research libraries. LCC has not yet demonstrated this flexibility. This is an area worth exploring.

The principle of literary warrant, *i.e.*, basing the development of a scheme or system on the nature and extent of resources being described and organized, operates in the Web environment as well as in the print environment. In the development of subject categorization schemes used in popular Web information services, such as Yahoo! and Northern Light (Ward 1999) as well as many library portals, we have often witnessed the gradual extension from simple, skeletal outlines to increasingly elaborate structures—almost a mirror of the development of classification schemes in the early days.

Flexibility in the collocation of topics in an array would also be helpful, if the same topics in an array could be arranged or re-arranged in different orders depending on the target audiences. For example, the categorization scheme in NetFirst uses the DDC structure, but modifies the arrangement of the categories to suit its target users (Vizine-Goetz 1997).

Observing recent uses of classification-like structures on the Web and the tortuous re-inventing and re-discovering of classification principles in both research and practice (Soergel 1999a), one sees a need for both broad/general (covering all subjects) and close/detailed (subject-or domain-specific) classification schemes. Portals found on websites of general libraries, ranging from school and public libraries to large academic libraries that cover a broad range of subject domains, need schemes of varying depths with a top-down approach, beginning with the broadest level and moving down to narrower subjects as needed.

On the other hand, portals that serve special clientele often need specialized schemes with more details. These often require a bottom-up approach starting with topics identified from a collection of documents focusing on a specific theme or mission. How to organize these topics into a coherent structure has often stymied those not trained in the principles and techniques of knowledge organization.

The library and information profession can make a contribution here. Subject taxonomy schemes built around specific disciplines (art, education, human environmental sciences, mathematics, engineering), industries (petroleum, manufacturing, entertainment), consumer-oriented topics (automobiles, travel, sports), and problems (environment, aging, juvenile delinquency) can serve diverse user communities, from special libraries to corporate or industry information centres to personal resource collections.

For domain-and subject-specific organizing schemes I suggest a modular approach. In building special-purpose thesauri mentioned earlier, LCSH could serve as the source vocabulary, and DDC or LCC could be used to facilitate the identification and extraction of terms related to specific subjects or domains and could provide the underlying hierarchical structure. Where more details are needed in a particular scheme, terms can be added to the basic structure as needed, thus making the specialized scheme an extension of the main structure and vocabulary. Developing these modules with a view of fitting them as nodes, even on a very broad level, into the overall classification structures of meta-schemes such as DDC and LCC can go a long way to ensure their future interoperability.

As mentioned earlier, the merging or integration of controlled subject vocabulary with classification in order to facilitate both information storage and retrieval has great potential, because they complement each other. A subject heading or descriptor represents a particular topic treated from all perspectives, while classification gathers related topics viewed from the same perspective. Traditionally, each performs its specific function and contributes to information organization and retrieval more or less in isolation.

Together, they have the potential of improving efficiency as well as effectiveness. Schemes simple and logical in design lend themselves to interoperate efficiently with each other. How to combine the salient features of a rich vocabulary like LCSH and the structured hierarchy found in classification schemes such as LCC and DDC to improve retrieval of networked resources remains a fertile field for research and exploration.

Conclusion

The sheer volume of available networked resources demands efficiency in knowledge management. Of course, we intend to provide quality and to maintain consistency also. Content representation schemes and systems design must meet halfway—a combination of the intellect and technology, capitalizing on the power of the human mind and the capabilities of the machine. Technology has provided an impetus in the creation of an enormous amount of information; it can also help in its effective and efficient management and retrieval (Soergel 1999).

A proper balance in the distribution of efforts between human intellect and technology can ensure both quality and efficiency in helping users gain the maximum benefits from the rich resources that are available in the networked environment. Already, technology has helped create many useful devices for efficient management and application of traditional tools, for example, Dewey for Windows, the WebDewey, and ClassificationPlus. These developments are encouraging. In the near future, we may expect also new applications which can help us not only do the same things better and more efficiently, but also maximize the power of existing subject access tools hitherto not yet exploited.

ARCHIVING THE WEB: THE NATIONAL COLLECTION OF AUSTRALIAN ONLINE

Recognising online publications as an intrinsic part of the national documentary heritage, the National Library of Australia, together with a number of partners, is building the National Collection of Australian Online Publications. The purpose of the National Collection is to ensure that Australians of the future will be able to access today's significant Australian online information resources. This paper describes what we are doing, why we are doing it, and how. It also discusses the lessons we have learned, and aspects of web archiving that we have still to address adequately.

I do not need to tell this audience about the challenges to libraries in collecting, storing and conserving the digital materials for which they are responsible. You know these challenges, are facing them, and that's why we are all here today, to learn from each other. So I shall go straight on to the situation in Australia and how we have addressed them.

Background-The Australian Situation

In Australia there are three layers of government – National, State and Local-and the libraries of two of these – National and State-are responsible for collecting and preserving the documentary heritage of their respective jurisdictions. At the national level, the National Library is responsible for the published output of the nation as a whole. The State libraries are responsible for building collections of works published in their respective States. Each jurisdiction has legal deposit legislation, some of which includes electronic publications and some of which does not. I shall speak about the national legislation further on.

The print collections of these National and State libraries have necessarily remained quite separate, though resource discovery has been integrated through the National Bibliographic Database, which is a national union catalogue that records the collections and holdings of 1,100 Australian libraries.

In the online environment, the National Library quickly saw not only the possibility of, but also the necessity for, collaborating with the State libraries to build one national collection of Australian online publications. Especially in the case of freely available Internet publications, it is possible to collect just one copy of a title in order to provide access to all Australians, indeed, to everyone in the world. Since the management of electronic information resources is such an expensive business, sharing the work and the cost would enable a collection of greater scope and depth to be developed.

Legal Deposit and Building a Collection of the National Imprint

In Australia at the national level, legal deposit provisions are contained within the *Copyright Act 1968*, which is under review. In a joint submission to the Copyright Law Review Committee by the National Library of Australia and the National Film and Sound Archive, it was recommended...

> *...[t]hat the scope of publications to be covered by the legal deposit provisions of the revised Copyright Act be extended to include microforms, audiovisual materials of all kinds and electronic publications, both networked and artefactual (eg. CD-ROM), and all formats yet to be developed, in addition to the print-based publications currently included.*

This approach is supported by the International Conference on National Bibliographic Services held in Copenhagen in November 1998 which reaffirmed the value of legal deposit and recommended that 'states should, as a matter or urgency, examine existing deposit legislation and consider its provisions in relation to present and future requirements: and, where necessary, existing legislation should be revised...'

A key issue for legal deposit legislation and the libraries that administer it is the definition of 'publication', a concept that has become blurred in the online environment. Are all Web sites necessarily publications? Which documents on a government or other organisational web site are publications (to be collected and preserved by libraries) and which are organisational records (to be collected and preserved by archives)?

While it will be advantageous to have legal deposit provisions for online publications, it will not be a panacea for all our collecting problems. The Library wants the right to archive any publication it deems to be of national significance, but it does not want to be obliged to archive all Australian online publications and web sites and wants the right to remain selective.

It is likely that the Library will find itself called to account for its selection decisions more than has been the case in the print environment and we will have to be able to justify our decisions. A clear collection development policy will be more important than ever.

Legal deposit legislation will not remove the necessity for liaising with many publishers to ensure that publications are complete and accessible. We will continue to need their assistance with archiving certain types of files that are difficult for us to download. In the case of commercial publishers, we will need to negotiate access to publications that are secured in some way, for instance, by password, and we will still need to negotiate periods of restriction so as not to jeopardise their commercial interests.

Origins of the National Collection of Australian Online Publications

At the National Library of Australia, we accepted in the early years of the web that online publications are important social, intellectual and cultural resources and that, with or without legal deposit legislation, our statutory responsibilities in relation to this material were no less than for the material which we traditionally collected. Ensuring long-term access can be seen as a two-step process. First the materials have to be identified, collected and made accessible in their current format (the archiving process). Second the materials have to be managed in such a way that they remain accessible as technology changes (the preservation process.)

The National Library has always recognised the importance of both these steps and their interdependence. For practical reasons the first step received most attention when we set up the PANDORA Archive in 1996. The preservation process has, however, been the growing focus of the Library's efforts as the archive has moved beyond the 'proof of concept' stage to the operational National Collection. The name PANDORA derived from its goal of "Preserving and Accessing Networked DOcumentary Resources of Australia". For a number of years now the work has been a mainstream, operational activity and we refer to it as the National Collection of Australian Online Publications, although the name, PANDORA Archive, is still used interchangeably for it.

Description of the National Collection of Australian Online Publications

The National Collection of Australian Online Publications is a highly selective one containing to date only 2000 web sites.

Nevertheless, it already constitutes a strongly representative sample of Australian web publishing by academic, government and commercial publishers, and community organisations. A number of the web sites captured in the archive, including the official web site for the Sydney Olympic Games, have already disappeared from the live Internet. Moreover, about one-third of the sites have been captured on multiple occasions, allowing the gathering of successive issues of serials, and enabling the collection of a sequence of snapshots, which demonstrate how some sites have changed over time.

The Collection now comprises 10,600,000 files using 320 gigabytes of storage; and is growing at about 500 new titles and about 400 re-gathers each year.

The gathering of titles is undertaken by the National Library as well as its partners: the State Libraries of Victoria, South Australia, and New South Wales, the Library and Information Services of Western Australia, the Northern Territory Library and Information Service, and Screen Sound Australia, (the national film and sound archive). In addition, the National Library cooperates closely with the State Library of Tasmania and its independent web archiving venture, Our Digital Island.

A primary goal is to provide immediate as well as long term access to readers both onsite within the partner agencies and anywhere in Australia, and to this end permission of the publisher is sought and received prior to any site being included in the Collection.

All partners gather web sites and publications for the National Collection using the Digital Archiving System, which was developed by the National Library, and which I will describe in more detail later in this paper. All material, including that gathered by other partners, is currently stored on the National Library's server and its associated storage systems.

The gathered version of every publication is subjected to quality checking to ensure that all files have been correctly captured.

Every web site/publication is fully catalogued, and the catalogue entries are included in the Library's own catalogue, as well as the National Bibliographic Database. This policy is based on the Library's firm view that access to all information resources (digital and traditional) should be integrated. (This approach has been endorsed by the International Federation of Library Associations (IFLA), which supports the treatment of online publications as part of the national imprint, incorporated into the National Bibliography.)

As an alternative access pathway, titles in the National Collection are accessible via alphabetical and subject lists on the PANDORA home page.

Within the National Library, the work of building the Collection is now a routine part of the selection, acquisition and collection management processes of the Library. Organisationally, it is managed by the Electronic Unit, which forms part of the Collections Management Division of the Library.

Selection Issues for Online Publications

The Library and its partners do not attempt to capture everything published online that relates to Australia. A policy of selective acquisition has been adopted, partly dictated by resource issues but also by the determination that everything in the Collection should be accessible.

To govern the selection of online publications and web sites for which it takes responsibility, the Library has developed a set of guidelines. These guidelines take account of characteristics such as Australian content and Australian authorship, whether the publication is indexed by a recognised indexing service, and stress the authority of the author, the research value and the quality of the publication.

Up until now the selection guidelines have excluded publications with print equivalents since, in the early years of our work, we needed to limit its scope to manageable proportions. However, we are constantly reviewing the selection guidelines and aim to be as inclusive as limited resources permit.

The policy of excluding those publications with print equivalents has already been relaxed to a certain degree when two years ago we invited indexing and abstracting agencies to enter into partnership with us. These services were already finding that some URLs cited in their references to electronic publications were defunct. The Library now has arrangements with six services, whereby they notify us of publications that they are referring to and we archive them, even if they have print equivalents.

The National Library of Australia has deliberately pursued the selective approach to archiving for its advantages of quality control and permission from publishers to archive and provide access. However, we have remained interested in the work of other agencies such as the Internet Archive and the Royal Library of Sweden, which are aiming to collect and preserve entire domains. We recognise that there is value in a comprehensive approach and have had initial discussions with the Internet Archive to ascertain whether cooperation with it would enable us to extend collecting of the Australian domain.

The Digital Archiving System

To facilitate the building of the National Collection a Digital Archiving System has been developed by the Library with the latest version implemented in June 2001.

Specifications for the system were devised by the Library's Electronic Unit, and the system was built by contract staff using WebObjects as an Application Development Environment. The system is designed to support the following functions:

- manage the metadata about titles that have been selected for inclusion in the Archive or rejected, for instance, title, URL, publisher details, gathering schedule, whether access conditions apply;
- initiate gathers of titles to be archived;
- manage the quality checking and problem fixing process;
- prepare the item for public display and generate a title entry page;
- manage access restrictions; and
- provide management reports.

This digital archiving system is a web-based tool that uses Internet Explorer 5.5 to enable the partners to achieve a more efficient workflow without the need for special desktop software. While currently all titles, including those archived by partners, are stored and delivered from the National Library's server, the system will support distributed content as an option for the future.

Persistent Identifiers

The publications stored in National Collection are to be preserved for posterity and they may be cited in many places including other web documents, in scholarly articles, in library catalogues and databases, in indexes and abstracts, and in bookmark files within browsers. They therefore need to be accessible indefinitely and require persistent identification.

In 2000, the Library engaged a consultant to provide advice on the direction it should take in relation to persistent identification of digital objects. The report produced by the consultant has been valuable in assisting the Library to determine its policy on naming standards and its procedures for managing digital information resources for persistent access.

In the absence of a global, operational system of persistent identifiers meeting the National Library's needs, the Library has implemented the guidelines for persistent identification developed by the consultant and reproduced in the appendix to this paper. The resulting persistent identifiers are automatically assigned to titles and component files in the Collection. They are not dependent on a domain name to provide unique identification of the resource but could be used as the namespace specific string in the context of any naming system implemented at a later date.

This standard aims to ensure that each file will have a persistent unique identifier, that there will be sufficient granularity of identification to support preservation activities, and that there will be sufficient "intelligence" to enable a measure of grouping and relating of versions.

Since June 2001, the Digital Archiving Software has enabled the persistent identifier to be cited on the title entry page for every title in the PANDORA Archive. While this has been an important step forward in the promulgation of the use of persistent identifiers, it does not assist those researchers or indexing and abstracting agencies that need to refer to part of a publication, for instance, an article in an e journal. The new version of the Digital Archiving Software coming out in March will provide the persistent identifier for every file in the Archive.

Access Control

Access restrictions are applied to a number of titles in the Collection and are managed by the Digital Archiving System. Restrictions may be applied for commercial reasons, for privacy or cultural reasons, or as part of a policy decision for certain categories of material. Items can be restricted for use only within the buildings of partner agencies for a specified period of time, or can be password protected so that only designated researchers can obtain access.

To date there is little commercial publishing on the web in Australia with most of the publications in the Collection being freely available. However, there are a growing number of commercial publications in the Collection.

When a commercial title is selected, the Library negotiates with the publisher to determine access conditions that will not undermine the publisher's commercial interest. The preferred model is for the publisher to allow use within reading rooms of the partner agencies for an agreed period of time, after which the title would become freely available to external users. Periods of restriction negotiated to date range from three months to five years. Agreements of this type have now been reached with publishers of about 80 commercial ebooks, ejournals and other publications.

The Digital Archiving System manages all of these restrictions and allows only those users in designated locations (based on IP address) or with the required password to gain access to archived versions. As time periods for restrictions expire, the system automatically updates the title entry pages to indicate the changed access conditions.

Preservation

The ultimate purpose of the National Collection is to ensure that Australians of the future will be able to have access to significant

Australian information resources currently being published on the web.

As mentioned above, a first step in managing an archive of online publications involves creating and managing a safe place where digital resources can be stored. The second and vital step is to ensure that the resources remain viable and accessible in the long term. Given the diverse collections and formats for which it is responsible, the Library will use a combination of preservation methods for the foreseeable future, including:

- some technology preservation, including maintenance of software and even some hardware;
- negotiating with publishers to supply stable source files of some streaming or dynamic formats;
- migration strategies for those file formats which correspond to compatible new formats, and which are amenable to mass conversion;
- use of emulators, if they can be found or developed, for some file formats; and
- simply keeping and refreshing some files, not amenable to migration or emulation, in the hope that a suitable access pathway will emerge.

The Library stores and manages at least two copies of archived files, maintaining the original copy unchanged in its native formats as the preservation copy and creating a second copy, which may have to be manipulated in some way, for access.

When preservation action is required, this will take place on yet another copy, which will be created for the purpose. This procedure will safeguard the Collection in the situation where, for example, a series of migrations leads to a dead end. We will always have the original files to go back to.

In 2001 a small trial migration of 127 files was successfully undertaken. In preparation for this, the Library had identified file formats held in the Collection, with a view to establishing an effective preservation path for each format. It had also identified dead and deprecated HTML tags in the Collection, which may not be recognised by later browsers. This analysis found:

- 127 tags dead in HTML 4.0;
- 7 million tags due to be made non-standard in later versions of HTML; and
- 14 million tags with deprecated attributes.

Clearly, our future migration tasks will be on a much greater scale than the first small trial!

A working group of staff involved in digital archiving is currently engaged in the task of identifying the 'significant properties' of various types of digital objects, including those stored in the PANDORA Archive. This group is attempting to answer the question in relation to a given digital object (or class of objects) 'What exactly is it that we want to preserve?'

The Cedars Project Team in the United Kingdom has also grappled with this matter, and defines 'significant properties' as 'the level of content and functionality retained' by the archiving and preservation process. The Cedars Project report notes that the '...Significant Properties of a digital object as they have been agreed...may alter the costs associated with preserving those specific properties....The preservation of an object's full functionality may prove more costly than just a bare-bones preservation of basic intellectual content. The question that has to be asked is whether the object's long-term value is worth the long-term expense of preserving the 'bells and whistles'.

Defining 'significant properties' of different kinds of digital objects in the Collection will help the Library to

- understand its preservation task better;
- set up quality control criteria for judging whether preservation action has been successful;
- allocate resources to preservation work that is really needed; and
- determine the level of metadata required to support the management of the digital objects.

Ultimately, decisions about significant properties will be implemented automatically to whole classes of material, in order to manage the Collection cost effectively. Defining the significant properties of classes of materials will be an important step forward.

Preservation Metadata

Significant properties are closely related to the next matter–preservation metadata – as determining the significant properties will dictate the amount of metadata that must be recorded and stored. A successful preservation process relies on an accurate record of the types of files to be preserved, the nature of any preservation activity carried out on them, and the result of such activity.

What information are we likely to need? In addressing this question, the Library in 1999 developed and published a draft set of digital preservation metadata requirements. In 2000, the Research Libraries Group (RLG) and the Online Computer Library Centre (OCLC) invited the Library and a number of others to join an international working group charged with the task of proposing a draft international standard for preservation metadata.

The working group has taken as its starting point the approaches to preservation metadata of the NEDLIB Project in Europe, the Cedars Project in the UK, and Harvard University Library's Data Repository Service, as well as the National Library of Australia's draft. A White Paper issued in January 2001 compared these approaches as a springboard for defining a comprehensive, structured preservation metadata framework, applicable to a broad range of digital object types, archival processes and institutions. The working group's recommendations for a preservation metadata standard are expected in early 2002.

Cooperation with Publishers

In the online environment, legal deposit legislation will not succeed without cooperation between libraries and publishers. Accordingly, the National Library has been working with the Australian Publishers Association to develop a Code of Practice for archiving, preserving and providing access to commercial publications. It has been important to establish mutual trust and overcome the suspicion that has existed between publishers and libraries in relation to access to electronic publications. Publishers feared that their control over their intellectual property would be lost and their livelihoods undermined. Libraries need to demonstrate to publishers that they can control access in agreed ways and that there are advantages to publishers in legal deposit through wider knowledge of their works and also long-term care and maintenance of them.

The Australian Publishers Association and the National Library have recently reached agreement on the Code and will now ask a small number of publishers to trial it. The Code recognises that safeguarding Australia's published cultural heritage is a concern shared by publishers and the National Library. It outlines the conditions and responsibilities that each partner agrees to observe in order to ensure Australian online publications remain available for use into the future.

Lessons Learned

In five years of digital archiving the National Library has learned a lot about the technical, legal and organisational aspects of the work and the kind of infrastructure needed to support it. We have reported on what we have learned in conference papers, journal articles, and documents on our web site. There are some other aspects that are not commonly discussed and I would like to share a few of these with you.

We have found that in the digital environment it is advantageous to liaise and cooperate with a wider range of parties than was necessary for print collection development. Active working relationships are required with publishers and indexing and abstracting agencies. Collaborative relationships with other libraries and collecting institutions, both in Australia and overseas, are beneficial for exchange of information and to share the high costs.

Taking a practical approach and 'learning by doing' worked well for us in the beginning and continues to do so as we investigate new aspects. Once we start work on a particular task, instead of just considering it theoretically, we sort out many issues as we go along and gain confidence in our ability to tackle the task at hand, no matter how hard. There are still sometimes problems that we can't solve immediately, but at least we know what they are.

A team-based approach to devising and implementing policy and procedures enables us to draw on the expertise of a wide range of staff within the Library and helps to motivate their commitment to the work.

Starting small also worked well for us. This approach kept the workload manageable while we built up efficiency and expertise. It also enabled us to address issues like quality control in detail and gave us time to learn.

Deciding not to exclude a web site or publication on the basis of its file formats meant that we learn a lot about web publications and what can be done with them, even the very complex ones. That does not mean we always succeed in gathering them, for example, we have not yet managed to archive databases.

Staff undertaking this work need certain qualities – willingness to learn, adaptability, persistence, initiative, ability to tolerate frustration and to think creatively.

Issues the National Library of Australia has Still to Resolve

Digital archiving is an area of work where the learning and development never stop. There are still a number of issues that the National Library has to solve and, given the nature of the digital environment, as soon as we find solutions for these, others will emerge.

As already mentioned, the National Library still lacks legal deposit for electronic publications and has to resolve many of the issues that go with that.

The Digital Archiving System does not yet deal adequately with a number of significant matters:

- gathering and storing the software and plug-ins that publications and web sites are dependent on for display;
- clearly indicating to users that they are viewing an archived object rather than a current version on the publisher's site; and
- other authenticity issues.

Although we know in theory what preservation metadata we want to record, at this stage we do not have a mechanism for recording all of it. (The Digital Archiving System keeps some.) This deficiency is being addressed through the development of a

Digital Object Management System which will contain, among other things, the data to support migration and other preservation activities aimed at providing long-term access to digital objects. The Library has developed a specification for its Digital Object Management System, and is currently developing part of this system, known as a 'Special Collections Manager' in-house, after failing to identify a sufficiently affordable and low risk solution in the market place. Completion of the Special Collections Manager, which will provide for preservation metadata, is planned for late 2002.

Another issue still requiring resolution relates to the archiving of databases. I noted earlier our plans to address this problem this year.

In adopting the selective approach to archiving, we are archiving only a very small proportion of the Australian domain. We would like to supplement the selective Collection with periodic snapshots of the entire Australian domain. A short-term consultancy during 2001 identified the associated issues for us.

While we have developed a system of persistent identification for the Library's digital objects, we see a need for a national system. A proposal for an Australian Digital Resource Identifier has been endorsed in principal by the Council of Australian State Libraries, but this initiative requires further practical development and the implementation of a national agency for allocation of identifiers.

RLG/OCLC are in the process of defining the attributes of a trusted digital repository with their report due out early this year. The Library will assess the PANDORA Archive against the attributes listed in this document and, where any deficiency exists in our system, work towards meeting the standard.

Like every other digital archive in the world, we still have a host of preservation issues to resolve. We will keep abreast of research, contribute a little of our own, and work in cooperation with others to find solutions.

Conclusion

As a national deposit library, the National Library of Australia has clear responsibilities for collecting and preserving the documentary heritage of Australia now appearing in digital formats. After five years experience with archiving web publications, building the National Collection of Australian Online Publications has become a routine part of the Library's collection management activities.

A SURVEY OF FOUR LIBRARIES IN KUNMING

Kunming, the capital of Yunnan Province, China incorporates industrial, commercial, and residential areas. It boasts not only rich and varied minority national cultures, but also a varied array of developing and surprisingly modern libraries. In 1998, Jianli and I had the opportunity to visit some of Kunming City's most treasured libraries, together. In 2000, we updated our findings, which follow.

Over the last fifteen years, in a major effort at modernization and with an increasing investment by the Chinese government, China established more than twenty national information systems. The libraries we visited were member of some of those national information systems. These national information systems have been charged with setting up the basic foundations of an information industry. They belong to, respectively, the Education System, the Cultural Ministry, the Science and Technology Committee System, and the Chinese Academy of Sciences.

Everything is relative, so they say. One must judge, then, how far library automation has progressed in China by understanding how far it has moved forward in the last five years. We wanted to see first hand how modernization of libraries in China had progressed to date. We felt strongly that viewing four Chinese libraries in a province far removed from the more sophisticated population centres of Beijing and Shanghai, would be a good test as to how far China has progressed in its automation and modernization efforts.

The survey was initiated by two Librarians, one a Director of an academic library in Kunming, and the other an American Reference Librarian visiting Yunnan for the first time.

The Education System library that we chose to survey was

Yunnan University library. Yunnan University, established in 1923, has a beautiful campus, along with a new 196,000 square foot library, the Yifu Building, named after its benefactor, Mr. Yifu Shao. Of the 1,160,000 volumes held, about 162,000 are deemed rare or ancient, and of the traditional thread binding of Chinese books. 4,217 volumes are listed in the Catalogue of Chinese Rare Editions collection. Additionally, there are also hundreds of rare Japanese and Korean block printed editions.

The Library, which serves almost 10,000 students and faculty, is divided into ten departments, including an information department for Science and Technology, computing and media departments, and comprehensive services.

Naturally, we were most interested in the state of the Library's technology, and were able to question Yang Yong, the Library's Deputy Director, on the subject. Yong explained to us that modern equipment is available in the form of microfiche duplicators, viewing equipment, and digital cameras. A computer management system, developed beginning in 1987, is connected to the campus network (YNUNET) for use by the Cataloguing, Circulation, and Acquisitions Departments. Also, computers connect the Yifu Library with CERNET, the China Education and Research Network. Currently, an electronic library and electronic reading room are being constructed on the network. Additionally, the Library hosts a world wide web home page at <http://www.lib.yni.edu.cn>.

Our expectations were that the Yifu Library would be one of the most automated libraries in Yunnan. Thus, we were curious to survey the state of technology in the Kunming Public Library, which is operated under the auspices of the Cultural Ministry System, and serves a population of 3.5 million in urban Kunming City.

Kunming Public Library was constructed in 1988 and houses 3,320,000 volumes. The pride of the Kunming Public Library is its Juvenile Department, which is built outside the main building on a garden. This design integrates literature and nature for the children of Kunming. We discovered that the Children's Reading Rooms are particularly popular. They are small, and arranged side by side, allowing the child to choose a book and a room in which to go and read.

Concerning automation management in Kunming Public Library, just before our visit in July, 1998, hardware and software had been installed. Network equipment, printers and other installations were also provided at the same time. The software used is called ILAS (Integrated Library Automation System). The copyright is reserved by the Shenzhen Library in Guangdong Province, which points out that China is not only buying technology from other countries, but also is intent on developing its own. Since, 1998, cataloguing has been done by computer. Public access to records is still done with a card catalogue, though. More study of the automation of Readers' Services is being done at the present time, and if the ILAS system is officially applied, Kunming's citizens will get high speed, quality, and efficient service.

Next, we visited the Information Institute of the Yannan Academy of Agricultural Sciences. The Information Institute is not as advanced in automation as the Yifu Library and the Kunming Public Library, but as its bright, young Librarian, Mr. Lianz Zhen Chen told us, preparations are currently being made. The Institute is located in the northern suburbs of Kunming, and belongs to the National Science and Technology Committee system.

A major task of the Institute is the publishing of two journals, the *Journal of Yunnan Agricultural Sciences* (Yunnan has a vastly rich agricultural region) and the *Journal of the Honeybee.*

The Library is one of the five departments in the Institute, along with the Information Department, Administration, and the two journal's editorial departments. Its collection, about 130.000 volumes, emphasizes Agriculture, Biology, and Chemistry.

Since 1988, the Library staff has been building databases, including a Chinese periodical contents database, a an English periodical contents database, a restricted publication database, and an archive of science and technology database. A CAB CD-ROM and three Chinese databases have also been constructed.

The Information Department of the Institute edits the "Bulletin of Agricultural Science and Technology," which mainly reports recent developments in agricultural research in the Academy or in Yunnan. They also investigate many general problems about agriculture.

The plan is for the Information Department to become a part of the YAAS network, and the Library will build its collection database using its own resources and those of the Information Department.

Choosing a Chinese Academy of Science library to visit was easy since Jianli, one of the co-authors of this article, is the Director of the Library at the Kunming Institute of Zoology (KIZ). She has long been interested in automation, in a strong service ethic, and modern service methods.

The Kunming Institute of Zoology library is noted for its distinctive collection features, as it must cover zoology, entomology, biochemistry, reproduction, neuroscience and the related conservation of resources.

It is noteworthy that the Institute has exchange relationships with 75 other institutes or colleges abroad, and 51 institutes in China.

In 1989, librarians at the Institute began to study automation management. Today, they are network based, and are able to make full use of the Internet, email, and their computerized catalogue.

Scientists at the KIZ contribute to journals worldwide, and the librarians must assist them by doing everything from copying articles, to collecting email addresses to journal presses, to providing a molecular biology database by email, as well as providing CD-ROMs and specialized databases. Among those specialized databases is a Chinese science periodical database, a Union Catalogue Database of Serials in Chinese and Western Languages, a Chinese Science Citation Database, and a book database.

After surveying these four libraries, from four different systems in an area of China that is much closer to Vietnam than it is to Beijing, our conclusions are as follows:

(1) Great progress has been made since 1988 in all types of

libraries in Kunming, China, no matter what subject matter the collection covers. As with much of the rest of the world, libraries in Yunnan province are attempting to introduce the benefits of electronic technology to their patrons.

(2) Librarians are learning new modes of work, which are necessary to deal with this new and emerging technology. Many librarians in China are studying automation with special attention given to its implications for library management. Automation and modernization has happened, relatively speaking, very fast in China, and with little historical preparation. As we witnessed in Kunming, library automation and modernization is working amazingly well.

(3) Training of librarians is of primary importance in Chinese libraries. The hope is, here, that librarians will move from their traditional role to network navigators.

ARE LIBRARIANS TOTALLY OBSOLETE?

1. Not everything is available on the internet

The amazing amount of useful information on the web has, for some, engendered the false assumption *everything* can be found online. It's simply not true.

Google Book Search recognizes this. That's why they're taking on the monolith task of digitizing millions of books from the World's largest libraries. But even if Google does successfully digitize the sum of human knowledge, it is unlikely that the sum of contemporary authors and publishers will not allow their works to be freely accessible over the internet.

It is already prohibited by law to make copyrighted books fully accessible through Google Book Search; only snippets. And it'll be a long time before that must-read New York Times bestseller gets put up for free on the internet: current copyright law protects works for 70 years beyond the death of the author.

Even some public domain works are off limits. If an out-of-copyright copy includes prefaces, introductions, or appendices that are still in copyright, the whole work falls under copyrighted status.

2. *Digital libraries are not the internet*

A fundamental understanding of what the internet is – and what it isn't – can help more clearly define what a library is, and why libraries are still extremely important.

The Elmer E. Rasmuson Library at the University of Alaska at Fairbanks clearly spells out the difference between "Online Collections" and the "Internet or Web Sources". The internet, this site explains, is a mass of largely unpublished materials produced by organizations, businesses, individuals, experimental projects, entrepreneurial webmasters, etc.

"Online Collections", however, are different. They are typically provided by libraries and include materials that have been published via rigorous editorial processes. Works selected for inclusion in a library catalogue undergo vetting from qualified staff. Types of materials include books, journals, documents, newspapers, magazines and reports which are digitized, stored and indexed through a limited-access database.

While one might use the internet or a search engine to find these databases, deeper access to them requires registration. You are still online, but you are no longer on the internet. You are in a library.

3. *The internet isn't free*

While Project Gutenberg boasts 20,000 free, downloadable eBooks on its homepage, we are promptly reminded that these books are only accessible because they are no longer in copyright.

And books are just the tip of the iceberg. Numerous academic research papers, journals and other important materials are virtually inaccessible to someone seeking to pull them off the web for free. Rather, access is restricted to expensive subscription accounts, which are typically paid for by libraries. Visiting the library in person, or logging in to the library through your member account, is therefore the only way to affordably access necessary archived resources.

4. The internet complements libraries, but it doesn't replace them

To guide people in finding information, the Long Island University provides a helpful explanation of what types of resources can be accessed through the library. These include news, journals, books and other resources.

Interestingly, the World Wide web is among these resources as yet another approach to finding information. But it's not a replacement. The page goes on to differentiate and explain the advantages of libraries over the internet for research. It does cite the benefits of the internet, including "sampling public opinion", gathering "quick facts" and "a wide range of ideas". Overall, the point is well made: libraries are completely different institutions from the web. In this light, to talk about one replacing the other begins to seem absurd.

5. School Libraries and Librarians Improve Student Test Scores

A 2005 study of the Illinois School Libraries shows that students who frequently visit well-stocked and well-staffed school libraries end up with higher ACT scores and perform better on reading and writing exams.

Interestingly, the study points out that access digital technology plays a strong role in test results, noting that "high schools with computers that connect to library catalogs and databases average 6.2% improvement on ACT scores".

6. Digitization Doesn't Mean Destruction

The eagerness with which libraries have jumped into partnership with Google Book Search is not the work of a lemming mentality. Libraries including Oxford University, University of Michigan, Harvard, the Complutense University in Madrid, the New York Public Library, the University of Texas, the University of California and many others have teamed up with the Google's project, not eschewed it.

In return for opening up their stacks, these libraries will have all their books electronically available for their own members. While it can be expected that fully out-of-copyright books will, on many occasions, be made fully accessible to the public, copyrighted materials – including subscription journals– will still be kept under restricted access. The reason for this is in part because Google Book Search's indemnity clauses don't reach that far; Google Book Search won't shield libraries from any liability that they might incur for overstepping the bounds of copyright. And there's a real cause for caution – Google Book Search is currently facing two major lawsuits from authors and publishers.

7. *In fact, digitization means survival*

Daniel Greenstein of the University of California cites a very practical reason for digitizing books: in electronic form, books aren't vulnerable to natural disasters or pulverization that comes with age. He even cites the libraries destroyed by Hurricane Katrina as an important reminder of the vulnerability of "cultural memory".

8. *Digitization is going to take a while. A long while.*

While book search has developed the air of an unstoppable movement rapidly breaking down library walls and exposing untouched treasure troves, it is breathtakingly far from reaching its goal. With an estimated 100 million books in print since the invention of movable type, the process has hardly made headway. Digitizing is expensive and complicated, and so far Google's million books digitized is just a drop in the bucket. "The majority of Information", said Jens Redmer, Google Book Search's European director, "lies outside the internet".

But how long will it take to index the world's knowledge? In 2002, Larry Page boasted that Google could digitize approximately seven million books in six years. Since 2004 Google Book Search has been plugging along through a series of fits and starts. By 2007, they have managed to index a million books. So, at the rate of approximately half a million books per year, digitizing 100 million books would take about...200 years. Assuming Google could shake off the legal and logistical challenges and crank out 7 million books every 6 years, the earliest possible completion date would still be 2092.

In the meantime, a larger user base will rely on local libraries, or online collections of what have been digitized. Dumping physical libraries before digitization is complete would leave library patrons in the lurch.

9. Libraries aren't just books

Technology is integrating itself into the library system, not bulldozing it. Pushing this trend to its logical extreme (although it's likely not to happen), we could eventually see libraries' entire stacks relegated to databases, and have books only accessible digitally. So where does that leave librarians? Are they being overtaken by technology, the timeless enemy of labour?

Technology is integrating itself into the library system, not bulldozing it. Pushing this trend to its logical extreme (although it's likely not go this far), we could eventually see libraries' entire stacks relegated to databases, and only be able to access books digitally.

So where does that leave librarians? Are they being overtaken by technology, the timeless enemy of labour?

Not this time. In fact, technology is revealing that the real work of librarians is not just placing books on bookshelves. Rather, their work involves guiding and educating visitors on how to find information, regardless of whether it is in book or digital form. Technology provides better access to information, but it is a more complex tool, often requiring specialized know-how. This is a librarian's specialty, as they dedicate themselves to learning the most advanced techniques to help visitors access information effectively. It's in their job description.

10. Mobile devices aren't the end of books, or libraries

Predictions of the End of the Book are a predictable response to digitization and other technologies, and the crystal ball of some in the pro-paper crowd seems to also reveal a concomitant crumbling of civilization.

One of the latest dark threats to paper (and society) seems to be Google's plan to make e-books downloadable to mobile devices. The iPod version of the novel is here. Google has already scanned a million books. Japanese train commuters are reading entire bestsellers on their cell phones. The end is near.

But if the mobile e-book is a hit and a lasting phenomenon, it's unlikely that they will be an all-consuming transition for readers. Radio lives on despite TV, film is still in high demand despite video, people still talk on the telephone despite email. People who like paper books will continue to read pàper books...even if mobile downloads prompt the majority of publishers to release e-books instead of paper. After all, an immense backlog of printed books will still be accessible to readers.

Where do libraries fit in supposing that mobile e-books actually do completely overtake printed books, the presence of the digital library will continue to be extremely important, whether it's paper or electronically based.

11. The hype might really just be hype

Paper books aren't exactly doomed, even years after the invention of the e-book. In fact, by contrasting the merits of the e-book to those of the paper book, one could argue that paper books are actually a better product.

It would be premature to write off libraries and their freely accessible books amidst predictions of e-books' impending prominence. Society could lose valuable access to a trusted medium – even if e-books do take off.

12. Library attendance isn't falling – it's just more virtual now

With approximately 50,000 visitors a year, attendance at the American History Archives at Wisconsin Historical Society has dropped 40% since 1987. This statistic, when set alone, may prove sufficient for anybody casually predicting the Collapse of the Library. But it is only half the story. The archives have also been digitized and placed online. Every year the library receives 85,000 unique online visitors. The number of online schools offering online degrees is constantly on the rise as well. Many of these schools are improving their virtual libraries by the day.

13. Like businesses, digital libraries still need human staffing

Even online businesses rely on quality support for better sales and customer satisfaction. The availability of email, phone and live chat services improve the experience of people seeking goods and services. The same goes for people seeking information.

In return for paying taxes or library fees packaged with University tuition, library members should expect reliable "customer support" in exchange for their dues. Librarians are indeed very important in servicing their visitors. And still today there is no equivalent replacement to the library, which provides access to mountains of content that is not available through search engines or even Google Books Search, which only provides snippets and links to retailers where books can be bought.

14. We just can't count on physical libraries disappearing

Physical libraries won't ever go away. Even as Google Book Search picks up the pace and libraries finance their own digitization projects, the future of physical library space continues to be necessary.

This is because many libraries aren't digitizing yet and many may never digitize. There's a good reason: it's expensive. At a low estimate of $10 per book (and probably much more for older, more delicate works), digitizing an entire library of, say, more than 10,000 books – well, it adds up. And for many library users, they still depend on this traditional, effective approach to pinpointing information with onsite computers or librarians available to assist them.

15. Google Book Search "don't work"

If a Google-style indexing of all the world's books were to mirror the company's well-known search service, one might have that much more fodder for the argument against keeping libraries around. After all, Google has great technology for searching the web, right? Couldn't we just bypass libraries?

But experts point out that Google Book Search is far off from such user-friendliness as experienced with the company's internet search service. The lofty ideals of information-for-everybody are hindered not only by copyright lawsuits, but by the Google's own desire to be top dog. They're not about to hand over their index to other competitors, like Microsoft, Yahoo!, Amazon and other non-partnered digitizing projects. The user loses out by not being able to access everything through his or her preferred book search service.

By not giving up digital archives to their competitors, companies that take this competitive, corporate approach to digitization risk veering off the map, away from the philosophy of the public library. In the meantime, libraries should remain in tact and available to the general public.

16. Physical libraries can adapt to cultural change

The U.S. National Commission on Libraries and Information Science (NCLIS) is just one among countless groups that study and debate the evolving role of the physical library in the digital age. In a 2006 symposium the NCLIS created a report that calls for a refining of what physical library space is. Less like "warehouses", was one of the conclusions, and more like "intellectual crossroads for working, learning, teaching, and new types of programmes."

17. Physical libraries are adapting to cultural change

Anyone subscribing to the theories of 20th century thinker Marshal McLuhan might say that along with changed life patterns brought on by electronic technology, knowledge that was once encased in books and compartmentalized by subject area is now being liberally disseminated in an explosion of democracy, rendering obsolete the austerity of the lonely, echoing corridors of the Library. Interestingly McLuhan, who died in 1980, once even said: "the future of the book is the blurb".

Indeed, this cultural change predates widespread use of the internet, as well as Google Book Search. For decades society has been seeking a more holistic understanding of the world, and increased access to information. The search for new methods of organizing educational structures (including libraries) has long been active. And while libraries might not be on many peoples' "Top Ten Cutting Edge List", they have been adapting.

Washington State University director of libraries Virginia Steel, for example, is a proponent of maximizing the social and interactive nature of physical library space. Group study, art exhibits, food and coffee – talking, not whispering; this is the new library. It's not obsolete, it's just changing.

18. Eliminating libraries would cut short an important process of cultural evolution

The library that we are most familiar with today – a public

or academic institution that lends out books for free – is a product of the democratization of knowledge. In the old days, books weren't always so affordable, and private libraries, or book clubs, were a privilege of the rich. This started changing during the 1800's, with more public libraries popping up and the invention of the Dewey Decimal Classification system to standardize the catalogues and indexes.

Libraries began blossoming under the watch of President Franklin Roosevelt, in part as a tool to differentiate the United States from book-burning Nazis. This increased interest in building a more perfect, liberal society culminated in 1956 with the Library Services Act, which introduced federal funding for the first time. Today there are tens of thousands public libraries in the United States. (More info on the history of libraries here).

19. The internet isn't DIY

It could be said that the internet has endowed society with a giddy sense of independence. Access to all the world's information – and free search engines to browse it with – calls into question the need for a librarians, moderators or other such middlemen; the web, it might seem, is a do-it-yourself medium.

But a quick look at the driving forces of today's internet shows us something different. The internet is intensely social and interactive, and has created communities of users that are often remarkably as tight-knit as they are large. The internet is serving as a tool for humans to fulfil their natural community building instincts – sharing, interacting and doing business.

The online economy is driven in large part by the web 2.0 philosophy of human interaction, peer review and the democratization of knowledge and analysis. Search engines rank web pages based on their popularity, social networking platforms pull in millions of visitors daily and the internet's most popular encyclopedia is written by the same people who read it.

Like Wikipedia, the most popular online meeting grounds are often the best moderated. Since riff-raff and spammers are an inevitable part of any society (whether physical or virtual), quality control helps contribute to the best online experiences. Good citizenship among online communities (intelligently contributing to the discussion, not spamming) is a surefire way to bolster your reputation as a helpful member of the group. In order to be fostered, this type of environment must be moderated.

Interestingly, the role of the moderator very much parallels the role of the librarian: to safeguard an environment in which knowledge can be accessed and ideas can be shared.

The notion that libraries are a thing of the past and that humankind has sprouted wings and flown into a new era of self-guided Truth is nothing short of farcical. Unfortunately, it's this same notion that could lead to the dismemberment of libraries as stuffy and out-of-date. In reality, the quality of the web depends on guidance from the academic, library model. While moderators do have brush to clear in the new and savage cyber-scape, librarians have trail blazed significant parts of the journey.

20. Wisdom of crowds is untrustworthy, because of the tipping point

The high visibility of certain viewpoints, analysis and even facts found online through social networking sites and wikis is engineered – ideally – to be the result of objective group consensus. Google's algorithm also hinges on this collective principle: rather than an in-house "expert" arbitrarily deciding what resource is the most authoritative, let the web decide. Sites with higher link popularity tend to rank higher in the search engines. The algorithm is based on the principle that group consensus reveals a better, more accurate analysis of reality than a single expert ever could. Writer James Surowiecki calls this phenomenon "the wisdom of crowds."

In a vacuum, crowds probably are very wise. But all too often we see the caveat to James Surowiecki's crowd wisdom in Malcom Gladwell's "tipping point", which, in this context, explains that groups are easily influenced by their vanguard – those who are the first to do something and who automatically have extra influence, even if what they are doing is not necessarily the best idea.

The highly social nature of the web therefore makes it highly susceptible to, for example, sensationalized, low-quality information with the sole merit of being popular. Libraries, in contrast, provide quality control in the form of a stopgap. Only information that is carefully vetted is allowed in. Libraries are likely to stay separate from the internet, even if they can be found online. Therefore, it is extremely important that libraries remain alive and well, as a counterpoint to the fragile populism of the web.

21. Librarians are the irreplaceable counterparts to web moderators

Individuals who voluntarily devote their time to moderating online forums and wikis are playing a similar role to librarians who oversee the stacks – and those who visit the stacks. The chief difference between librarians and moderators is that while the former guides users through a collection of highly authoritative, published works, the moderator is responsible for taking the helm as consensus is created. While the roles are distinct, each is evolving along with the fast paced growth of the internet and the evolving nature of libraries. Both moderators and librarians will have a lot to learn from each other, so it is important that they both stick around.

22. Unlike moderators, librarians must straddle the line between libraries and the internet

Admittedly, libraries are no longer both the beginning and ending point of all scholarly research. The internet is effectively pulling students away from the stacks and revealing a wealth of information, especially to one who is equipped with the tools to find it. Indeed, the dream of cutting out the middleman is possible to attain. But at what price?

Media literacy, although an extremely important asset for scholars and researchers, is far from universal. Who is going to teach media literacy? Many argue that librarians are the best fit to educate people about the web.

After all, web moderators are concerned primarily with the environment which they oversee and less so with teaching web skills to strangers. Teachers and professors are busy with their subjects and specializations. Librarians, therefore, must be the ones who cross over into the internet to make information more easily accessible. Instead of eliminating the need for librarians, technology is reinforcing their validity.

23. *The internet is a mess*

As one pro-librarian website puts it, "The internet in very few ways resembles a library. A library provides a clear, standardized set of easily retrievable resources".

Despite the slightly combative nature of this one-liner, its premise is essentially correct. Despite improvements in search technology and the creation of amazingly comprehensive sites like Wikipedia, the internet is still, in many ways, a free-for-all. Flooded with sites from all sorts of sources that inexplicably languish about or jockey for top positions in the rankings, the web is like an overpopulated Wild West. Many have taken confronted this chaos with grass-roots social networking sites or large, complex and highly successful efforts to organized information (Google, Wikipedia, et al). But despite these efforts, a morass of questionable pages still tends to be served up in many search results, and the credibility of each source accessed must inherently come into question.

Not that that's a bad thing. The oceans of information, uncertainty and spontaneity on the web can provide an exciting, enriching experience. But if you need to limit your search to logically indexed resources that have been published and then vetted by a professional staff, then the library is still your best bet.

24. *The internet is subject to manipulation*

As long as the bright minds behind Google are coming up with a better search algorithm, the bright minds of search engine optimizers will continue to crack it. This could involve conforming to Google's quality standards or, in many cases, skirting around them. It is important for the user to keep in mind the limitations of Google. In many cases the search giant succeeds in serving up good information. But in many cases it still falls short.

In contrast, it is extremely hard to enter into libraries' indexes. Books, journals and other resources must be nothing less than high caliber, published material. If they're not, they simply don't get in.

Furthermore, the economic incentive to manipulate library collections is much less fierce than on the internet. It is estimated that only 4% of book titles are being monetized.

Meanwhile, Google alone is experiencing incredible earnings through online advertising, not to mention everyone else positioning for a piece of the Internet pie.

But libraries simply aren't facing this kind of pressure. Their way of providing information, therefore, will inherently be less influenced by corporate interests.

25. Libraries' collections employ a well-formulated system of citation

Books and journals found in libraries will have been published under rigorous guidelines of citation and accuracy and are thereby allowed into libraries' collections.

These standards are simply not imposed on websites. They can show up in search results whether or not they provide citation. With enough research, the accuracy of web resources often *can* be determined. But it's very time consuming. Libraries make research much more efficient.

26. It can be hard to isolate concise information on the internet

Certain subject areas like medical conditions or financial advice are very well mapped on the web. Quality sites for more marginal subject areas, however, are less easy to find through web search. One would have to know which site to go to, and Google isn't necessarily going to serve you exactly what you are looking for.

Wikipedia, which ranks well for a wide variety of specialized subject areas, is improving web concision. But Wikepedia is just one site, that anyone can edit, and its veracity is not guaranteed. Libraries retain a much more comprehensive and concisely indexed collection off research materials.

27. Libraries can preserve the book experience

Consuming 900 pages on the intellectual history of Russia is an experience unique to the book. In general, the book provides a focused, yet comprehensive study that summarizes years of research by an author – or team of authors – who have devoted their academic to a particular subject area.

Through Google Book Search, the internet can be a tool to find where to buy a book. Normal search results also reveal a variety of book resellers, academic courses or upcoming web projects.

But even when the internet does provide actual content (as in a search for the history of Russia) the information is often snack-sized or the overall experience cursory – a sort of quick-reference browsing. Knowledge can be found, but the experience of delving into a book for hundreds of pages just doesn't happen online. The preservation of stacks, therefore, will help preserve access to this approach to learning and the more traditional form of scholarship can continue alongside the new.

28. Libraries are stable while the web is transient

In an effort to improve their service and shake out the spammers, search engines are constantly updating their algorithms. Often, however, collateral damage will knock out innocent sites including, perhaps, authoritative resources.

In addition, websites commonly go offline or their addresses change. Other sites that point to these resources (which were once good) could easily and unwittingly house a number of "broken links". These sites can remain unedited for years.

Libraries, on the other hand, have a well-accounted-for stock of available resources and a standard indexing system that will deliver stable, reliable results consistently.

29. Libraries can be surprisingly helpful for news collections and archives

In many ways, libraries fall short of the internet when it comes to aggregating news content. Online TV, radio and newspaper sources – not to mention an abundance of blogs referencing and commenting on daily events around the world – can often satiate anyone from the casual headline browser to the news junkie.

Meanwhile, libraries continue to subscribe and stock a certain list of newspapers, and archive the back issues. This effort may seem humble alongside the lengthy lists of online news aggregators and instantaneous access to articles published within the minute.

Nevertheless, a library's news cataloguing can provide a number of advantages. For starters, many publications continue to exist offline. For someone seeking a specific article by a specific journalist, a library could yield better results – even if the publication had to be tracked down through inter-library loan.

Libraries often provide freely accessible issues of major periodicals that would otherwise require online subscription, like many sections of the New York Times

In addition, archives often disappear offline, or become increasingly expensive online. (Try Google's news archive search). This can leave libraries with the only accessible copies.

30. Not everyone has access to the internet

In less developed nations or even poorer parts of the United States, library access is often the only clear-cut way for an individual to conduct serious research. There are at least two major reasons that the internet may not provide even an illusory alternative to libraries.

Firstly, online access may be much more difficult to attain than library access. A public library may have but one computer console, while other internet access points may charge someone who simply doesn't have the means to pay.

Secondly, even if internet access is obtained, the lack of technological education in poorer areas of the world will render the technology much less useful than it would be for the person who has more experience navigating the web.

31. Not everyone can afford books

Outside of developed nations, books are more rare and often more expensive than their first-world counterparts. Compounding the problem is an incredibly low minimum wage making the real cost of books astronomical. The public library, wherever it exists, therefore becomes much more crucial to democratizing information.

Since the United States tends to be a trend leader, especially technologically, it must underscore the importance of libraries even as technology moves forward. Touting a culture of BlackBerry devices over books may jeopardize the existence of traditional libraries, leaving poor people without books *or* BlackBerrys.

32. Libraries are a stopgap to anti-intellectualism

It's not that the internet is anti-intellectual; its academic roots and the immense quantity of scholarly sites certainly attest to it being a smart medium. It's not that the internet is anti-intellectual; its academic roots http://www.nap.edu/readingroom/books/far/ch7.html and the immense quantity of scholarly sites certainly attest to it being a smart medium.

But for some, the alluring immediacy of the internet can lead to the false impression that only immediate, interactive and on-the-spot online discussion is of value. Dusty books on tall shelves then seem to represent stagnant knowledge, and their curators (librarians), behind the times. Books and reading easily gets regarded as elitist and inactive, while blogging becomes the here-and-now.

But, as mentioned earlier, not everything is on the internet. Access to books and theories from hundreds of years of cultural history is essential to progress. Without this, technology could become the ironic tool of the sensational and retrograde cultural tendencies. Preserving libraries to store knowledge and teach the limitations of technology can help prevent the hubris and narcissism of technological novelty.

33. Old books are valuable

The idea of a library becoming a "book museum" in the age of digitization is sometimes tossed about as an apocalyptic figure of speech. It's a real scare for librarians. The term insinuates that, rather than become contemporary and useful, libraries could turn into historical fetishes like vinyl records or typewriters. And instead of continuing on as research professionals, librarians would be forced to become like museum curators – or, more likely, they would just lose their jobs.

But if the evolution of libraries grows to become an interactive meeting place for cultural events and the exchange of ideas, the preservation and exhibition of archival literary relics could be yet another facet to their importance (and, yes, intrigue). Indeed, old books are not only monetarily valuable, but they are part of cultural, historical memory that mustn't be lost to digitization.

Conclusion

Society is not ready to abandon the library, and it probably won't ever be. Libraries can adapt to social and technological changes, but they can't be replaced. While libraries are distinct from the internet, librarians are the most suited professionals to guide scholars and citizens toward a better understanding of how to find valuable information online. Indeed, a lot of information is online.

But a lot is still on paper. Instead of regarding libraries as obsolete, state and federal governments should increase funding for improved staffing and technology. Rather than lope blindly through the digital age, guided only by the corporate interests of web economics, society should foster a culture of guides and guideposts. Today, more than ever, libraries and librarians are extremely important for the preservation and improvement of our culture.

Library legislation and free access to information as new topics in library and information science education.

The Undergraduate Programme

Up to 1998 the only LIS programme in Croatia leading to the Bachelor's degree was organised at the Department of Information Sciences, Faculty of Philosophy, University of Zagreb. In spite of its restrictive name the Faculty of Philosophy offers programmes for students of the humanities and a number of social sciences disciplines and with its 5.500 students is in fact a small university in itself. LIS studies were first introduced in 1976 as a two-year basic professional programme offered to the students enrolled in another major programme at any faculty in Croatia.

Ten years later, in 1986, a new four-year programme of information sciences was introduced for students of librarianship, archival studies, museum studies, and information science. Courses offered in the first two years were obligatory for all students, and in the third year students had to opt for a stream of their choice. In other words it was only in their third year that students decided whether they were going to take librarianship, archival, museum or information science group of subjects.

The librarianship programme offered traditional core subjects, such as library management, bibliographic organisation and control, classification and subject indexing, information sources and services and history of libraries, and a number of electives, such as sociology of the book and reading, introduction to thesauri, slavic paleography, special or public or school libraries, etc. In the beginning of the nineties a revised four-year programme for students of librarianship, archival studies, museum studies and information science was submitted to the educational authorities.

The programme was made up of four separate programmes for four distinctive streams taught at the department.

However, a number of subjects was to be taken by students of all four streams. The referees who evaluated the programme were nominated by the educational authorities. In their report they emphasized the importance of LIS studies, but their appraisal of the museum studies and archival studies programmes was not quite favourable. A heated debate among the faculty followed.

In the meantime we have all become aware of the tremendous changes introduced by the new information and telecommunication technology and the new opportunities the technology offers to educational institutions. Therefore we decided to take into consideration all external changes taking place in the education field and make a thorough revision of all our programmes. The revised programme was submitted to the authorities in the early summer of 1999 and we have been expecting their response.

The Postgraduate Programme

A two-year postgraduate programme leading to an academic master's degree was first introduced in 1993 and opened to students who had graduated in LIS, but also to applicants without degrees in LIS sciences. These applicants must be employed in a library or have some practical experience in it, and prior to admittance are required to pass an entrance examination. The aim of the postgraduate programme is to prepare students for research in the LIS field. A number of library directors and heads of library departments were among the first candidates enrolled in this programme.

The Doctoral Programme

Although there is no doctoral programme offered at present, it is possible to submit and defend a dissertation. Doctoral degree is considered to be the highest academic degree and top managers in libraries are most likely to have it. It is normally required for university teachers as well. The university authorities have recently decided that doctoral programme must be a component part of postgraduate programme. Thus, students who finish their two-year postgraduate studies and earn their master's degree, will be able, but not obliged, to continue their studies for one more year and submit their dissertation.

Factors Affecting Curriculum Review

At present the faculty of the Department of Information Sciences are confronted with a number of questions and dilemmas. It is quite obvious that the curriculum has to be changed and adapted to new needs. We have been avid readers of new Council of Europe documents regarding the information society and the changes it brings about. New professional profiles and new competencies required to perform new jobs are well-understood (Council of Europe, 1998c). But the real environment in which our students come to live and work has not yet much changed. Libraries are still struggling with automation of basic library functions, relying mainly on the home-made computer applications. A number of public, academic and school libraries have not yet been touched by automation.

Electronic publications are scarce and libraries have not yet started processing them like other library materials. Librarians are not autonomous in the selection of library materials, because of the state policy of subsidising publishers by selecting the titles and buying them for libraries. Financial constraints are great and it is difficult for libraries to buy equipment, train staff and acquire materials.

Librarians' salaries are low and at present no trade union takes proper care of them. The reorganisation of a number of public libraries which at present function as departments of Public Universities or Houses of Culture but which, according to the Law on Libraries enacted in 1997, have to become independent institutions is still pending. The internal reorganisation of many large libraries, the National and University Library in Zagreb included, is expected to improve the number and quality of the services offered to users.

Reasons for the Introduction of a New Course

The present situation in libraries makes a great impact on our students. For quite some time now we have been aware that our students, although some of them have gradually advanced to posts of library directors or heads of departments, have difficulties in instigating changes to the traditional practice in libraries. There is no doubt that some of our students have succeeded in improving their working environment. But we have also noticed the counter influence that traditional library environment makes upon a number of our students.

Once they get the job in a library many of them seem not only to adapt themselves quickly to the poor conditions, but they also accept without questioning the practice set in the library, which has not always been harmonised with professional standards they learn about during their studies. Since I have been teaching cataloguing standards I know how much care I put into the interpretation of the standards and establishing the rationale for them.

But during my occasional visits to libraries and talks with my former students I came to realise how difficult it is to make a real change. I also understood that something important must have been missing from my lectures. I told my students what they had to do and why; I did not tell them *how* they could implement what they had learned in the surroundings they had to live and work in.

The idea that a new course in the curriculum, which would include the basics of library legislation and professional ethics, might be useful to students and make them more aware of their rights and responsibilities as well as of the rights and responsibilities of their users, occurred to me some time ago. The real impetus came two years ago from a student who prepared her final thesis. In the thesis she described automated book lending system used in a public library network in Zagreb. In her paper the student enclosed a facsimile of a list of borrowers and the titles they borrowed. The list contained names of real users along with the book titles they borrowed, and the notes about the overdue books and fines they had to pay. I expressed my wonder that the student was allowed to copy such a document. Then I realised that she did not quite understand my reproach. The idea that data about the books one reads might belong to a sphere of privacy and should be protected never occurred to her. I realised that it was not enough to impart technical knowledge and that it takes more to make a professional.

Courses on Library Ethics in the Curricula of the Nineties

The issue of users' privacy belongs to the professional ethics domain. In the early nineties, when we were discussing our present curriculum, a number of library schools offered a separate course on library ethics. Our departmental library still keeps several printed booklets issued in the beginning of the nineties by LIS schools. A course entitled *Information ethics* was taught at the University of Maryland College of Library and Information Services (1992). The University of New South Wales Faculty of Professional Studies (1992?) offered the course of the same name.

In some schools, however, professional ethics was taught as a part of a broader course. For instance, the School of Library and Information Science of the Catholic University of America offered to its students a course on *Libraries and information in society* (1992). The short description of the course included a discussion of the role of library and information professionals and institutions in the past and present, discussion of standards governing ethical professional conduct, exploration of the various aspects of access to information, and discussion of funding patterns. An interesting course was offered by the University of Toronto Faculty of Library and Information Science to its PhD students.

The course entitled *The Library in the Political Process* included an investigation of the nature and importance of political forces in the governance of libraries and in the behaviour of librarians, and an examination of the activities of various pressure groups, such as library associations, book publishers and book sellers (University of Toronto, 1990; 26).

In the beginning of the nineties, however, legal and ethical issues related to the library environment in Croatia were regarded as supplementary to the core and they were incorporated in the course in library management. It should be added here that it was only in 1992 that the Croatian Library Association adopted its first Code of Ethics (Croatian Library Association, 1992)

A Course in Library Legislation and Standards

Since at the time when I first started thinking about the new course, the reshaping of the curriculum was out of question, I used the opportunity allowed to the faculty to introduce a new course. In order to do this I had to give up teaching one of my previous courses, because the total number of hours approved for the whole programme had to be respected. The course could not consist of more than 30 hours in order to be considered 'a slight change' to the curriculum, for which no special administrative procedure is required apart from the agreement of the faculty. I had to write an outline of the proposed course and explain its aim.

A random search of the LIS schools' curricula on the Internet revealed that a number of schools had introduced at least one course related to societal and/or legal aspects of information. (Catholic University of America, 1999; City University London, 1999; Université Libre de Bruxelles, 1999; University of Central England, 1999; University of Loughborough, 1999; University of Sheffield, 1999; University of Toronto, 1999).

The titles of courses such as *Libraries and information in the society, Information systems and the information society, Libraries, information and society, Information and its social contexts, Media law, Legal and professional issues* point to the relation between the LIS field and its wider environment. The content of the courses normally includes elements of professional ethics, but the courses typically cover a wide range of societal and legal issues relevant to library and information institutions and professionals.

The Internet search encouraged me to broaden the scope of the new course and make it cover a variety of relatively recent issues relevant for the LIS field. I chose the name *Library legislation and standards.*

First I wanted the students to become aware of the fact that apart from the *Law on Libraries* (1997) there are other laws and legal regulations which shape the library environment. I wanted to make them attentive to any part of legislation related to libraries in any possible way.

I also wanted to introduce to them a few relevant documents adopted by various international bodies. My main aim was to try to induce students to think about the role of libraries in a larger context and appraise critically library legislation and standards.

Structure of the Course

I decided to structure the course as a series of seven sessions of four hours each. Two hours in each session would be used for lectures and another two hours for students' presentations of assignments. Each of the seven sessions was to be centred on one topic.

A lecture would start with relevant international documents covering the topic, followed by a description of the institutional practice abroad and then the Croatian Constitution and the respective national law(s) would be interpreted as well as the national practice.

Assignments would be given to students to investigate particular issues and they would be required to have 10-15 minutes presentations in the classroom.

The seven sessions would cover the following topics, not necessarily in this order.

1. Organisation of libraries, their mission and functions as presented in legislation and internal library regulations

In this session the relevant text describing international trends is UNESCO Manifesto for Public Libraries (1994). The emphasis is on need to organise services for various categories of users, including blind and physically impaired people, prisoners, hospital patients, people living in isolated rural areas, as well as ethnic minorities. Students have to find out how the new Law on Libraries of Croatia (1997) deals with this issue. Council of Europe

Recommendation on Library legislation in Europe (1999) is presented as another document of potential significance for all European libraries. Since the *Recommendation* covers a number of topics that are discussed in other sessions, such as copyright, freedom of access to information, etc., it is referred to in other sessions as well. M.

Ryynänen's report on the Role of libraries in the modern world (1998), that gave impetus to the drafting of the Recommendation is also mentioned.

The Law on High Education (1993) and the *Law on Scientific Research* (1993) contain stipulations on libraries and librarians that are discussed. Available library statutes and rules of proceeding are examined and interpreted in order to find out how libraries serve the public. Lack of written selection policies in libraries is pointed out.

2. *Freedom of expression and freedom of access to information in libraries and archives*

UN Universal Declaration of Human Rights (1948) ánd *European Convention on Human Rights* (1950)>are the two principal international documents students have to know about. The articles of the *Constitution of the Republic of Croatia* (1991), which guarantee freedom of expression, freedom of press and other means of communication and freedom of speech, are interpreted.

The abstract issue of human rights must be connected to the specific library world. An assignment is given to a student to trace in what form these rights are introduced in the Library Law. The *Croatian Library Association Statute* (1992)and its *Code of Ethics* (1992) are introduced as texts relevant to the profession. They are compared to codes of conduct of other professions and/or other library associations. The work of IFLA/FAIFE (1999) in this field is described.

3. *Freedom of expression and freedom of access to information in the digital world*

Are the rules on freedom of expression in the book world applicable to the digital world? Excerpts from a report prepared for the Council of Europe (1998b) on freedom of expression and public access points are used for discussion. The use of filters on the Internet is explained and discussed. The local situation is investigated.

The state *Regulation on the Foundation of the Croatian Academic and Research Network (CARNet)* (1995) is presented to students. The lack of national legislation covering digital world is discussed. An assignment is given to a student to find the *CARNet Rules of conduct* (1995) on Internet.

Netiquette guidelines as an informal standard of behaving on the network is a good enticement to discuss the style of written messages, indicate differences between style of written letters and e-mail messages, and emphasise ethical issues related to the communication in the digital world.

4. *Censorship*

The *Constitution of the Republic of Croatia* (1991) and the *Law on Public Communication* (1996) are both relevant to the issue of freedom of expression and can be good starting points to discuss censorship. Censorship in libraries has a long history and in this course only those aspects of it which are relevant to present-day libraries are dealt with. Recommended literature includes works of Rauch (1993) and Malley (1993).

5. *Privacy*

Privacy as a constitutional right is discussed. It is pointed out that the right to privacy is confirmed in the *European Convention on Human Rights*. The Council of Europe (1981) *Convention concerning protection of individuals with regard to automatic processing of personal data* and the EU *Directive on the protection of personal data* (1998) are mentioned. The national *Law on protection of confidential data* (1996) is interpreted. Professional, state and military secret is defined as it appears in the national legislation.

The treatment of personal data kept in government databases, databases of large firms, and archives although not directly connected to libraries are considered important and explained. Selected excerpts from works of McLeod & Cooling (1990) and Marett (1991) are offered to students who have to prepare their assignments.

6. Copyright

Protection of authors' works guaranteed in the Constitution is another topic for discussion. International conventions like *Berne Convention* and *Universal Convention* are introduced and the relevant articles of the Croatian *Copyright Law* (1998) presented. The concept of lending right, not known in Croatia, is explained. Possible reasons for limiting photocopying in libraries are put forward.

The rights of producers and reproductive artists are interpreted because they are relevant for public libraries, which hold collections of sound recordings. The need to establish a balance between author's rights to remuneration and users' right to free access is emphasised. Selected chapters from Marett (1991) are used in preparing the lecture.

7. Protection of cultural heritage

The fact that libraries hold a part of the country's cultural heritage is explained. The activities and some documents of the Council of Europe (1998a) in this field are outlined. Legal deposit is shown to be a means to protect the written heritage. Problems related to the legal deposit of electronic materials are discussed.

Relevant parts of the *Law on Libraries* are examined. *Law on protection and preservation of cultural heritage* (1999) and various professional texts on preservation and conservation in libraries and archives are examined and interpreted. Relevant parts of the *Criminal Law* (1997) concerning illegal export of cultural heritage are interpreted.

Conclusion

It should be kept in mind that a number of issues dealt with in this course are by no means new to students. Issues like organisation of libraries, legal deposit or preservation of cultural heritage appear as topics in other courses as well. In this course, however, technical aspects have intentionally been put aside and legal and ethical aspects only have been considered. The intention has been to make students aware of the existence of international documents of relevance to the library community and to show how the international trends and attitudes have been followed at the national level.

The existence or lack of adequate national legislation has been investigated and possible differences in the international and national treatment of particular issues explained. Ethical aspects have also been underlined. It is hoped that the course might help students to improve their understanding of the legal context in which they are going to work and teach them to appreciate the importance of good legislation.

It is also hoped that students will be able to recognise basic moral principles of the profession and could rely on them in their future work.

5

Libraries and Literacy : A Preliminary Survey

Background

A search of two major English language databases, Library Literature (U.S.) and LISA (Library and Information Science Abstracts, U.K.) for the dates, 1990-2000, was undertaken for the latest reports pertaining to literacy including: major surveys, evaluation studies, manuals on libraries and literacy, plus recent major national or regional literacy movements that involved libraries.

The search could only be characterized as cursory, mainly English-language based, and selective for materials available from a local research library or from interlibrary loans. Though an attempt was made to secure materials on literacy and libraries in other countries, mainly documents from the International Federation of Library Associations (IFLA) and the United Nations Educational, Scientific, and Cultural Organization (UNESCO) were located. Published reports from the U.S., the U.K, and Canada dominated this literature. Several documents were found only on the worldwide web through web home pages of literacy agencies or governmental organizations.

Though no attempt was made to define literacy for this search, almost all the publications included some type of definition. Historically, in the U.S., literacy has been defined in terms of years of schooling which has constantly increased, from three or more years of schooling in 1930 to having completed eighth grade in 1960. By 1992, the definition used in the U.S. National Adult literacy Survey included: "...using printed and written information to function in society, to achieve one's goals, and to develop one's knowledge and potential." An increasingly sophisticated and differentiated scale of literacy skills have been identified in several major studies.

In these recent studies, adult literacy was broken down into three scales including; prose literacy, document literacy, and quantitative literacy; these scales have a 500 point basis which allows five major breakdowns of levels of literacy (Adult Literacy, 1993; Literacy, Economy and Society, 1995). Types of literacy have been expanded to include family literacy (or intergenerational literacy), and information literacy-often including computer literacy (much of which was not considered relevant to the current search). Literacy among specific groups of people has sometimes been the focus, such as that of the language minority community (Constantino, 1997, IFLA, 1999), the blind (Leach, 1992), the poor (Ventruelle, 1998), the labour force (Sum, 1999) and families (Thomas and Fisher, 1996).

However, most of the studies and reports focus on the adult illiterate which usually includes those 15 or 16 years of age and older. Some interesting trends in the 1990s has been the movement toward family literacy and special consideration of women in literacy programmes in recognition of gender inequity in literacy rates. Another trend in literacy activities has been an increased focus on the learners' needs and preferences through establishment of New Reader (learners) Advisory Groups, inclusion of learners on Literacy Advisory Groups and in local and regional forums on literacy activities, providing a voice for the learners themselves especially in community-based programmes.

Several centres of literacy have been established, such as the National Literacy Secretariat of Canada and the Literacy Resource Centre in Ottawa, Canada, the National Literacy Institute (U.S.), the International Literacy Institute at the University of Pennsylvania in the U.S. sponsored by UNESCO; and the National Centre for Family Literacy in Louisville, Kentucky (U.S.); and many web sites of these centres and other literacy-related organizations were found. Several manuals and workbooks which describe library literacy programmes have been written. Though before 1990, there had not been many country-wide surveys of literacy in general, nor much attention to evaluation and research studies relating to literacy, that has begun to change as will be noted later in this paper.

Several books discuss the role of libraries in literacy including Salter (1991) and Weibel (1992) in the U.S., and Scheel (1989) in Canada. There are several manuals for developing literacy programmes in libraries such as Quezada's guide for small and medium-sized libraries (American Library Association, 1996) and the Literacy Tool kit: A Resource for Libraries (Regina Public Library and the Saskatchewan Library Association, 1996). National efforts at establishing policy for literacy programmes and libraries are found in Quigley, developed for the Canadian Library Association (1995) as a result of a summit on libraries and literacy.

Most of the journal articles centred on national or local literacy and reading initiatives, and campaigns such as the U.K.'s National Year of Reading (Attenborough, 1998, 1999) and their Reading Is Fundamental project, with a focus on access to books for school children.

Many efforts in the U.S. have focused on youth, reading, and book access including: Reading Is Fundamental, and a series of family literacy projects such as Born to Read, a programme for babies and their parents; the Bell-Atlantic/ALA Family Literacy projects starting in 1989, and California's Families for Literacy programme begun in 1988 (Monsour, 1993). More on some of these projects will be found in a later section, and much more can be found in the items in the attached bibliography. Articles on literacy covered many parts of the world: most of the English-speaking countries, France, and several developing countries such as India, Malaysia, Peru, islands in the South Pacific, and several African countries and regions. Most of that information is not reviewed in this paper.

A Brief History of Literacy

According to Kaestle (1991), "very little evidence is available about the extent of literacy before 1850 except that provided by people's ability to sign such documents as marriage registers, army rolls, and wills. " In Europe, the literacy rise between 1850-1900 was rapid, for both men and women due to national consolidation, state intervention, and wider male suffrage along with expanding capitalism and establishment of school systems. In the U.S., literacy rates in colonial British America were quite high, and America's rise to nearly universal white literacy was earlier than Europe's.

By 1850, the rudimentary literacy rates of white men and women, self-reported to the U.S. Census, were nearly equal. In 1979, only .6 percent of all persons fourteen years of age and older reported that they were illiterate, but this equalled nearly one million people (Kaestle). As early as 1930, the term, functional literacy gained popularity, usually defined as the ability to read at the fourth or fifth grade level. As the definitions of literacy have changed, there have been few studies of literacy on a national level until the 1992/93 Adult Literacy Survey in the U.S.

Bramley (1991) commented that during the 1960s it became very apparent that, in both Britain and the U.S., there were adults in society with severe literacy problems. What followed were the literacy campaigns of the 1970s and the 1980s. The adult education movement and the term adult basic education (ABE) has tried to focus on the academic skills needed to function in society (reading, writing, spelling and handwriting, and basic numeracy). Later, the concepts of social and life skills (coping or survival skills) became part of ABE. Educational opportunities centred around these concepts. Bramley presents the role of public libraries in Britain and the U.S. in both the early literacy and the later adult basic education programmes. He believes that these literacy campaigns sparked the incentive for the emergence of public library services to ABE students and also to the educationally disadvantaged.

Literacy needs and services through public libraries are presented not only for ABE programmes but for those with special educational needs including racial and ethnic groups (African Americans in both the U.S. and Britain, the Hispanic communities in the U.S., Asian communities in Britain, and groups with physical disabilities). In the 1970s the U.S. Office of Education commissioned the Adult Performance Level study, to establish what was meant by functional literacy, including relating levels of academic competence to economic achievement.

Three levels were established with only one level being established as less than functionally literate. Until the 1960s it was assumed that the introduction of compulsory, full-time education had led to the elimination of illiteracy. Suddenly it was recognized that this was not true, first in the U.S., and then later in Britain.

This led to several waves of literacy campaigns and advocacy. Also in 1973, the Russell Report in Britain concerned itself with adult education and adult literacy. In May 1974, the British Association of Settlement and Social Action Centres (BAS) published a document, A Right to Read: Action for a Literate Britain after two million adults were identified with literacy problems. A series of TV programmes were introduced by the BBC for adults with reading problems. An Adult Literacy Resource agency was established in 1975, to allocate funds to local bodies for literacy purposes. Later the Adult Literacy Unit was established with Education and Science. Britain has in the 1990s established a National Curriculum, trying to ensure all would have a "good basic education."

In the U.S. a similar pattern can be found but occurring a bit earlier. Evidence of a large number of illiterates was found due to the large number of non-English speaking immigrants in the 19th and 20th centuries; and later, during the two world wars, an alarming number of registrants in the armed forces were found to be lacking literacy skills.

As part of the literacy movement in the U.S., voluntary organizations continue to make a substantial contribution to teaching literacy skills, especially Lauback Literacy International (LLI) and the Literacy Volunteers of America (LVA). Lauback, a one-on-one teaching method for adults, began in the 1930's in the Philippines (though established as a formal organization by Frank C. Lauback in Syracuse (NY) in 1968; while LVA began in Syracuse (NY) in 1962 through the Church Women United. The role of federal and regional governments in each country is very important in literacy efforts. Early on in the U.S,, efforts were tied to employment issues such as with the Economic Opportunity Act in 1964. In 1966 the Adult Basic Education Act (ABE) was approved as part of the Elementary and Secondary Education Act, and the establishment of a National Advisory Committee on ABE.

In 1969, the Right to Read Campaign was started; and in 1974, the National Reading Improvement Programme.

The general population was startled and perhaps stimulated to action by the stark picture of illiteracy in the U.S. presented by the well-known writer and educator, Jonathan Kozol, in 1985 by his book, Illiterate America. Consequently, Congress authorized the Department of Education in 1988 to address the need for information on the extent of adult literacy. Finally through many efforts, the National Adult Literacy Survey (NALS) was designed and conducted in 1992 (Adult Literacy, 1993).

The 1990s have seen a major response by the U.S. government concerning the literacy problem. For example, at the 1989 National Governors' Association, one of the six national education goals listed was the following:

By the year 2000, every adult American will be literate and will possess the knowledge and skills necessary to compete in a global economy and exercise the rights and responsibilities of citizenship.

Congress passed the National Literacy Act of 1991, "to enhance the literacy and basic skills of adults, to ensure that all adults in the U.S. acquire the basic skills necessary to function effectively and achieve the greatest possible opportunity in their work and in their lives, and to strengthen and coordinate adult literacy programmes." In 1993, a report from the U.S. Office of Technology Assessment described the current patchwork of programmes that provide adult literacy education, suggesting that even the governmental programmes had led to greater fragmentation of efforts.

This report analyzed the ways technology (computer software, interactive video, and multimedia) can expedite in an efficient way literacy training. Though the authors felt the technology had great potential, they found only about 15% of programmes utilizing such technology. Some advantages of the use of technology included:

- reaching learners outside of the institutional setting both in recruiting and retaining learners through sustaining motivation
- using learning time efficiently through improved curriculum and individualizing instruction
- meeting staff development challenges
- enhancing assessment and evaluation
- streamlining administration and management
- augmenting funding and coordination

Though libraries are listed in the report as one of nine providers of literacy, only one example of a specific library literacy programme was noted. The report strongly recommends more funding to encourage public and private partnerships to bring technology to literacy training.

The book trade has been closely associated with campaigns for national literacy, including an intensive effort with the Coalition for Literacy which was mainly an informational and marketing campaign to expedite literacy training. The Coalition was administered by the American Library Association. Private foundation monies have been and continue to be important. Workforce literacy needs have brought the business community into the various efforts and coalitions.

Major National and International Studies of Adult Literacy

A study of literacy was conducted in the U.S. in 1992, the National Adult Literacy Survey (NALS), sponsored by the National Centre for Educational Statistics in the U.S. Department of Education (Adult Literacy in America, 1993; also see Kirsch in Smith, 1998). This was a very major study in terms of methodology and population studied. Trained staff interviewed nearly 13,600 individuals aged 16 and older during the first eight months of 1992. All had been randomly selected to represent the adult population. Another 1000 adults were surveyed in each of 12 states to look at state-level results comparable to the national data.

Also, 1100 inmates from prisons were interviewed to ascertain information on the literacy of the prison population. Over 26,000 individuals were surveyed.

This study developed the methodology later used in the international literacy survey; with the three scales (prose, document, quantitative) used to define levels of literacy.

The study made connections between literacy skills and social, educational and economic variables. For example, "where one is in the literacy distribution is strongly associated with the likelihood of living in or near poverty" (Kirsch). It was found that there was a relationship between literacy and employment status: individuals with more limited literacy skills are less likely to be employed, less likely to work full-time, less likely to be professionals, managers, and technicians but more likely to be "labourer, assembler, or involved in fishing and farming," or in "craft, or service jobs."

In general, a clearer view of why so many U.S. adults demonstrated limited English literacy skills was presented including the following profile of those with lower literacy skills:

- 25% who performed at the lowest level were immigrants
- nearly 2/3rds of those at the lowest level did not complete high school
- 1/3 of those at the lowest level were over the age of 65
- 19% had some visual difficulty
- 12% had some type of health condition that kept them from participating fully in daily activities.

African-American and Hispanic adults were disproportionately represented in the lowest two levels of the NALS. Yet, perhaps the most interesting results included these:

- ½ of American adults performed at the two lowest levels of literacy proficiency
- 21-23% (40 to 44 million of the 191 million adults) were at the lowest of five levels of literacy.
- 25-28% (50 million people) were in the next higher level of literacy.

- educational attainment was associated with literacy proficiency

Many of the definitions and levels of literacy in this study were used as the basis for a series of international literacy surveys. Internationally, a series of studies of adult literacy in countries of the Organisation for Economic Cooperation and Development (OECD) were conducted between 1994 and 1999. The first International Adult Literacy Survey (IALS) was published by the OECD and Statistics Canada (Literacy, Economy and Society, 1995). The survey included interviews and tests of representative samples of adults aged 16 to 65 in the following countries: Canada, Germany, the Netherlands, Poland, Sweden, Switzerland, and the United States. For the first time, the literacy and numeracy of adults in different countries can be profiled and compared.

The survey provided pertinent information on the economic performance and strength of each country, and the information needed to improve literacy. The survey used large samples of adults (ranging from 1500 to 8000 per country) in Europe and North America during 1994 in a uniform test of their literacy skills using the same methodology and scales of the National U.S. Adult Literacy Survey. The IALS also followed the procedures of the 1989 study by Statistics Canada, another national assessment of adult literacy, which was the first study to assess literacy in a valid and reliable way across language and culture (English and French).

Building on these two major studies of the U.S. and Canada, the Educational Testing Service on behalf of the U.S. Department of Education and Statistics Canada joined with the OECD, the UNESCO Institute for Education in Hamburg, and the Commission of the European Communities to encourage national governments to participate in the study. The Canadian results were published also separately in Reading the Future: A Portrait of Literacy in Canada (1996). Warren Clark has issued a report comparing three of the countries: Canada, the United States, and Germany (Clark, web report).

The first IALS study included data from the seven countries listed above. A second study included data collected from the following countries: Australia, New Zealand, Great Britain, Ireland

and Flemish Belgium and the report presents comparative data from all twelve countries (Literacy Skills for the Knowledge Society, 1997).

A third study included an additional eight countries: Chile, the Czech Republic, Denmark, Finland, Hungary, Norway, Portugal, and Slovenia (Literacy in the Information Age, June 2000). There are now 20 countries in this international database with comparative data on literacy levels. According to a press release on the worldwide web regarding the final report (newly released, not available to the writer), the following conclusions were noted:

- The higher a nation's literacy skills, the more likely its population will work in better quality jobs, earn more and have healthier habits and lifestyles.
- There is a measurable, net return to literacy skills.
- Literacy proficiency has a substantial impact on earnings when other aspects of human capital, specifically educational attainment and experience, are taken into account. The higher a nation's literacy skills, the higher its economic output measured in gross domestic product per capita. For example, Canada ranked among the top countries on both gross domestic product per capita and prose literacy.
- No nation did so well in literacy attainment that it could be said to have no literacy problems.

Additional information on countries can be found in the UNESCO work on illiteracy gleaned from national reports done for Education for All Year 2000 (EFA), which provides data on 167 country reports.

The UNESCO Institute for Statistics prepared the report based on these country and regional reports enhanced by the Institute's global estimates and trends (Education for All 2000 Assessment, 2000). Two groups of persons have been used in the study: young adults (aged 15-24 years of age) and adults (aged 15 years and over). Because countries collected data in different ways (household surveys, school surveys, population censuses), resulting in differences in samples and frequency/recency of data collection, the report suggests caution in interpreting reported literacy rates, especially the very high literacy rates. Some of the findings and projections include the following:

- Four out of every five adults (aged 15 years and over) in the world are literate.
- Literacy rates have risen over the past thirty years, to approximately 79 percent in 1998.
- There were still some 880 million illiterate adults in the world in 1998 and:
    - o two-thirds of them were women
    - o more than 98 percent live in less developed regions
    - o includes one in seven young adults.
- The adult literacy rate is the lowest in sub-Saharan Africa and South and West Asia (median rates of 57 and 58 percent respectively).
- Latin America, the Caribbean, the Arab States and North Africa have intermediate rates of 88 percent and 80 percent.
- The highest adult literacy rates are in East Asia and the Pacific (94 percent), and in Central Asia and Central and Eastern Europe (98 percent).

The report also points out the considerable inter-country disparities within each region. Significantly, for the majority of reporting countries, substantial progress was made in raising adult literacy rates over the decade, for example, a reported 21 percentage points in Bangladesh. Yet in some regions adult literacy rates dropped as in Honduras (from 27 percent in 1990 to 21 percent in 1998).

Gender disparities in literacy only improved slightly over the decade though where the literacy rates are the highest, disparities are the lowest. Gender disparities remain high in South and West Asia, in the Arab States and North Africa, and in sub-Saharan Africa. It is important to point out that the statistical report not only included findings on young adult and adult literacy levels (and gender disparities) but also examined several core indicators that assess education overall but which are obviously related to literacy over the long-term such as enrolment in early childhood programmes, educational levels completed plus expenditures and trained personnel related to the educational systems.

This assessment effort is a follow-up on the UNESCO 1990 World Conference on Education held in Thailand in 1990, entitled Education for All (EFA) which set a global agenda for education and literacy with several goals including the reduction of adult illiteracy. This global agenda was part of the World Declaration on Education for All adopted at the Conference which was also part of the International Literacy Year of 1990.

For Asia and the Pacific, the task was assigned to the Asia-Pacific Programme of Education for All (APPEAL). Progress has been made in the Asia and Pacific area according to a UNESCO assessment of the region; from a literacy rate in 1960 of almost 40% to close to 69%, with the projected raise to 77% by 2000. Whether this has been met has not been ascertained. Yet, southern Asia has a rising number of illiterates in terms of absolute numbers even though the percentage has declined. Countries included in these studies included: Bangladesh, China, India, Indonesia, Laos, Malaysia, Nepal, Pakistan, Philippines, Thailand, Vietnam as part of the Asia-Pacific Programme of Education for All.

According to a UNESCO Education News in Brief (UNESCO web site), a recent survey carried out in India, Nepal, Philippines and Thailand reveals their [adult education programmes] positive impact on personal development, women's empowerment and the economy. A UNESCO-E-9 initiative which began in 1993 included nine of the world's most populous countries (Bangladesh, China, Indonesia, India, Pakistan, Brazil, Egypt, Mexico, and Nigeria) and involved planning and management of literacy campaigns and efforts. A UNESCO News in Brief item (UNESCO web site) outlined some findings of "What Works in Asia in Literacy Campaigns" including:

- the need to involve the future learners and sensitize them to the usefulness of literacy
- that literacy classes be community-based and designed to improve daily lives
- NGOs have the know-how in mobilizing the community

- the need for attractive, relevant, and accessible literacy and post-literacy materials
- the need for libraries and resource centres
- sustained commitment and perseverance even as governments change

Role of International Agencies

Several international agencies have been vitally involved in advocating for life-long learning and the acceptance that literacy is a human right. According to Rogers and McChesney in 1984, UNESCO "has played a key role in the promotion of books and libraries... (their) book development programme... Starting out primarily as a promotional programme to emphasize the importance of books and reading, it has since laid even greater emphasis on action designed to provide technical advice, equipment, and materials, and professional training, and has above all stressed the need to develop national book policies."(p. 270).

The International Book Year stimulated activities in the world community for book promotion and UNESCO with a plan of action called Books for All. In 1980, UNESCO convened a World Congress on Books in London, with the theme, Towards a Reading Society, for the purpose of assessing progress in book promotion since the International Book Year,

UNESCO declared 1990 the International Literacy Year to continue public awareness of illiteracy and to encourage cooperation among countries in combatting illiteracy. In 1993, UNESCO published "Guidelines for Public Libraries Promoting Literacy," a project contracted through IFLA and its Section of Public Libraries. In 1994, UNESCO, in cooperation with the University of Pennsylvania's Graduate School of Education, established an International Literacy Institute in the U.S. for the purpose of providing leadership in research, development, and training in the broad field of literacy at the international level, with an emphasis on developing countries. They have published a CD-ROM and web site which provides an overview of literacy issues and practices, statistics, and innovative projects.

The International Federation of Library Associations (IFLA)

has had several workshops and preconferences on illiteracy: including work by the Section of Public Libraries in 1989 and 1990. Other sections have had workshops such as the combined efforts of the Sections of Children's Libraries, the Blind, Multicultural, and Public Libraries during the India IFLA Conference in 1992. IFLA continues to have an important role in connecting libraries with literacy.

In 1994, a proposal was made for a new core programme for literacy and reading promotion; in 1995, that recommendation was rejected but a working group on literacy was formed to study the feasibility of such an initiative by IFLA. In 1999, the Final Report of the Working Group on Literacy was submitted to the IFLA Professional Board. The current work of the Section on Reading, including the papers at this programme, are a follow-up to that work. The Section also sponsored a workshop at the 1998 IFLA Conference on Literacy and Reading Services to Cultural and Linguistic Minorities. The work of the International Reading Association is important to the field of reading and literacy also.

National and International Literacy and Reading Campaigns

In both developed and developing countries there have been major attempts to promote reading and literacy through publicity campaigns which have involved libraries, library associations, the book industry, business, foundations, the media, and governments. Internationally there has been UNESCO efforts with both World Book Day (April) and International Literacy Day (September). Several countries have used these campaigns as the basis for their own national efforts such as Great Britain's free book vouchers in 1998 to children between 4 and 18 years of age still in school. These efforts are often well-funded and generate not only promotional materials but specific programmes and activities in many school and public libraries.

In the U.K., their National Year of Reading (September 1998-August 1999), was a major effort administered by the National Literacy Trust which distributed funds for innovative projects that stimulate reading. Several pilot literacy projects were included and several book give-away programmes were part of the efforts. Their theme of Read Me was extended to one of Read On as the project continues for three years. One of the main strengths of such campaigns is the networking that is involved and hopefully continues. Since 1989, the Canada Post has devoted some attention to literacy including the release of three literacy-oriented stamps and stamp sets, with proceeds going to literacy organizations.

In the U.S. there are two specially-designated weeks a year, Children's Book Week in the Fall and National Library Week in the Spring. National Library Week (NLW) has been strengthened in the last few years due to a great deal of promotion by the American Library Association with special activities such as the Night of a Thousand Stars (celebrity involvement in reading in each community). In 1991, the Year of the Lifetime Reader was sponsored by the Centre for the Book at the Library of Congress, and funded by donations, with then First Lady Barbara Bush as honorary chair.

In Nigeria, since 1981, a Library Week is sponsored by the National Library and with help from the International Reading Association (Loho, 1991). In South Africa, the USIA, the READ Educational Trust (a 20 year old private NGO which tries to improve education, and provides access to books and libraries in the townships), and local organizations worked with ALA's Peggy Barber to establish a major reading campaign as a five year project beginning in 1995. These are simply examples in an area where almost all parts of the world have similar campaigns or join those of the international organizations such as World Book Day or the International Literacy Day.

Book Access and Funded Projects

Though many of these projects become a part of the reading and literacy campaigns described above, they also have a life of their own in some instances. Several developed countries have established book donation programmes usually targeted at developing countries, such as Book Aid International in the U.K. (until 1994 known as the Ranfurly Library Service) which sends donated books by publishers and charities to more than 60 countries worldwide and especially targets sub-Saharan Africa.

They also helped set up the Intra-African Book Support Scheme along with the African Books Collective to distribute African books overseas, to encourage African writers and publishers, and to work closely with World Book Day. The Canadian Organization for Development through Education (CODE) sponsors several projects as well as formerly served as chiefly a book donation programme. Their projects have been predominantly in rural, isolated areas of Africa, usually with partners with other overseas organizations along with those in local communities. Their current target audiences include: children up to the age of fifteen, and adults with six or fewer years of schooling.

For example, they initiated the Children's Book Project in 1991 to support the production and distribution of Tanzanian books especially books in indigenous languages. Most of their work has been in Africa and the Caribbean. Many other countries have similar international aid organizations, either private or governmental, such as the Danish International Development Agency (DANIDA) and the Swedish International Development Agency (SIDA). Though Japan has also had similar projects, descriptions of their work was not found in the current literature search. The World Bank has made major contributions in many developing countries in the area of literacy and education.

The U.K. and the U.S. have the most documented reading and literacy initiatives in the 1990s, and many are governmental projects. For example, Reading Is Fundamental (RIF), backed by donations and started in the U.S. in 1966, is a project that provides free books to children through schools and grassroots community organizations. Today RIF cooperates with several other national initiatives including some of the following. The Prescription for Reading programme has, since 1997, provided free books through health care providers at each child's health check-up until age 6 and has given away over 1 million books. Similar in purpose is the Born to Read programmes, and Reach Out and Read, another book give-away programme now in 43 states.

Most of these projects were expanded when the America Reads Challenge was announced by President Clinton in 1997 for the purpose of having every child in the U.S. reading independently by the end of grade three, a programme administered by the U.S. Department of Education. Several of the projects are partners with the National Centre for Family Literacy and Head Start organizations. Most of the projects work with the American Library Association as well as with public and school libraries.

Examples of projects initiated by the book trade include: a project called All Books for Children, sponsored by three publishers (Disney, Harper Collins, and Scholastic) in cooperation with Starbucks Coffee Shops, to provide free books to Boys and Girls Clubs of America; another called First Book started in 1992, through a national non-profit organization with donations from several publishers and bookstores, giving "first" books to disadvantaged children; a national donation project called the Book Bank based on publisher donations and with foundation support; the Books for Kids Foundation, which provides books to day cares, shelters, and hospitals; and the National Children's Book and Literacy Alliance (organized by children's authors and illustrators).

Every Child a Reader is a 1999 pilot project to distribute remaindered books to literacy groups and children's agencies. The National Education Association (a teachers group) sponsors an annual event to promote literature, Read Across America. The Newspapers in Education project, supported by local newspapers, the United Way, and other corporations, provides newspapers to classrooms at certain grade levels. Beginning in 2000 a PBS television series, Between the Lions, will promote children's reading.

Reading Is Fundamental began in the U.K. in 1996, backed by corporate funding, and organized by the National Literacy Trust in London. Again RIF provides free books for young children to choose and own, to motivate reading. According to Blunkett (1998), U.K.'s Education and Employment Secretary, the country's National Year of Reading is part of a National Literacy Strategy to ensure that 80% of eleven-year olds reach the standard in English by 2002. Also, as part of the NYR, the National Literacy Trust was established including several literacy components. The Royal Mail along with television channels promoted the 40,000 adult literacy classes and development of information packs to help in literacy. The BBC television led a Books for Babies campaign. A BookStart project works through health visitors to deliver books and book information into the homes of nine-month old babies.

These are only a few examples from the literature of literacy and reading promotion initiatives but it does appear that book promotion for children and family literacy projects have been the focus of the 1990s in the U.S. and the U.K. Some apology should be made again for the many examples from the U.S., Canada, and the U.K. mainly because they appear to be more documented in the English language publications available to the writer.

Libraries and Literacy-Historically and Currently

Libraries did become involved quite early in the adult literacy campaigns and activities though many were (and some still are) reluctant to do so. Both the Library Association in Britain and the American Library Association in the U.S. have played important roles-especially with school and public library involvement in literacy and reading. The access to adult literacy reading materials, the need for library education to include literacy programme information, the need for studies and reports-all were major challenges that brought forth efforts and collaboration from the professional societies. Some early efforts included the establishment in 1924 of the ALA Commission on Library and Adult Education (Lyman, 1977).

The public library in the U.S. responded as early as the 1890s to the language and literacy needs of a large influx of immigrants, providing English and citizenship classes in many urban libraries. Lyman reported on a Reading Improvement Programme begun at the Brooklyn Public Library in 1955 which was financed by a grant from the Carnegie Corporation of New York. Public libraries initially provided print materials to help in literacy activities. A focus on social responsibility and outreach was clearly delineated for public libraries during the 1960s and 1970s; literacy activities and an activist approach to users falls easily into the outreach focus.

Throughout the 1960s and 1970s, major efforts were made by a few libraries. Several efforts at federal intervention and federal aid mainly through the Library Services and Construction Act (LSCA) and the Title IIB of the Higher Education Act encouraged these efforts at the state level especially in public libraries. These efforts also showed the need for literacy training through state libraries, networks, and schools of library science. ALA was influential in promoting, and providing advocacy and training for literacy activities in libraries. In 1978, ALA's Office for Library Outreach Services (OLOS), the office charged with literacy activities, with a grant from the Lilly Foundation, conducted a series of workshops to train librarians in the techniques of establishing literacy programmes

Public libraries realized the need for better easy-to-read print materials, the importance of providing space and resources, and sometimes even access to literacy training. Helen Lyman, a pioneer in literacy activities sponsored by public libraries, published two important books, Library Materials in Service to the Adult New Reader (1974), and Literacy and the Nation's Libraries (1977). By 1980, many libraries were providing the easy-to-read materials, accommodating literacy activities, encouraging staff involvement, providing referral services, and even financial resources. In the 1980s, ALA's activity and the stimulus of federal funding brought literacy and public libraries more to the forefront. ALA's work with the Coalition for Literacy beginning in 1981 allowed the combination of efforts by associations, advertising, the book industry, and literacy organizations, all coordinated by ALA's Office for Library Outreach Services and with the expertise of the Advertising Council Incorporated.

This three year literacy promotion campaign highlighted the existence of widespread illiteracy, the resulting problems in society, and stimulated local efforts with recruitment and involvement including libraries. Statewide and local coalitions were formed; and a great deal of information and networking resulted. In 1984, the federal programme of funding libraries, LSCA, was amended with a new title, the Library Literacy Programme which gave more substantial monies to state and public libraries for their literacy efforts. Several states such as California, were especially successful in their efforts, with state-wide planning and major literacy grants from these monies.

In 1986, a major study funded by the U.S. Department of Education, and conducted by the University of Wisconsin-Madison's School of Librarianship, examined the literacy programmes of publicly funded libraries (Johnson, Robbins, and

Zweizig, 1990; Bramley, 1991). Johnson (1987) produced a planning manual for the American Library Association which examined the public library's role in literacy activities and recommended the process of planning such services.

The study found that though libraries are active partners in the national literacy effort, public libraries report the greatest involvement in all three literacy roles-collections, instruction, and support services. Over 25 percent of the libraries provided direct literacy instruction. Through a major literature search and questionnaire results they confirmed that public library literacy programmes have the longest history.

As early as 1963 public libraries were offering literacy services. In many of these libraries, the programmes had become a part of "traditional public library services." Nearly 50 percent of the libraries reported involvement in literacy coalitions. State library agencies have the most consistent profile of literacy services than any other type of library in a "supporting role;" they are a key information source in literacy providers and the problem of illiteracy; they provide advice and guidance on the use of materials and development of services; and they offer continuing education on the topic of literacy and libraries. Historically, as a fiscal agent for the national LSCA funds, they administer monies for local literacy projects; and sometimes provide state-level funding as well for literacy.

This study called for more research on the impact of literacy services and activities at the local and state levels including inclusion of some of the variables they identified as a set of community variables: percent for whom English is a second language, ethnicity, educational levels, and poverty levels. Despite not finding a direct relationship between level of literacy and these community variables, the researchers felt they should be explored further. The main relationship they did find was that between the level of literacy activity and the managers' attitudes toward library literacy services.

They found that materials to evaluate literacy programmes in public libraries were not available; this led to a major effort in that area, with the publication of the manual, Evaluation of Adult

Library Literacy Programmes (Zweizig, Johnson, and Robbins, 1990).

Salter (1991) provided a discussion of all literacy efforts in the U.S., in libraries and beyond libraries. This historical and descriptive overview of literacy efforts is still useful today. The White House Conference on Library and Information Services held in the U.S. in 1991 included literacy as one of three major issues, along with democracy and productivity, for discussion during the conference.

Though this brief review of literacy and libraries is primarily based on the U.S., similar efforts have been made by the U.K., Canada, Australia, and New Zealand according to much of the literature found.

Evaluation Reports

Beder (1991) has synthesized many fragmentary articles and research which provide information about literacy and influenced both policy and practice. His book is helpful as a prelude to the work cited in this paper which is predominately post-1990. His chapter on "Outcomes and Impact" is useful for thinking about evaluation and assessment of literacy programmes. His recommendations are based on theoretical principles which have been tested in several studies. Most importantly, he recommends:

- It is more useful to conceive adult illiteracy as being a social construction maintained by social forces than to view illiteracy as being a collection of individual deficits spawned by personal failure (stop blaming the victims).
- Because the great majority of those who are eligible for the federal adult literacy programme do not participate, we need to differentiate service to meet the multiplicity of individual needs and provide new models of education to appeal to nonparticipants.
- The adult literacy programme which adapts to local needs and conditions has been successful and should not be limited but rather maintain adaptive, pluralistic orientations.
- Though the social justification for federal involvement may be dictated by human capital outcomes, limiting

literacy goals to this is not useful, but rather should include attention to individual goals and needs.

Some evaluation efforts of specific library literacy projects provide useful information on the issues and processes of evaluation such as Quigley's 1994 publication on the Vancouver Public Library (Canada) project. Other manuals on evaluation of library literacy projects were found: one by the New York State Library (Evaluating Library Literacy Programmes, 1991).

Evans (1998) describes an evaluation process used for evaluating CODE's activities in Africa, a process developed by Gwynneth Evans and Raymond Genesse in the 1990s as a framework for identifying basic benchmarks and measuring progress. As noted before, CODE projects have been predominantly in rural, isolated areas of Africa, and include partnerships with overseas organizations and those in local communities. Retrenchment of funding from the Canadian International Development Agency in the early 1990s required CODE to close regional offices and form even stronger partnerships with local agencies. This necessitated the need for more results-based management and a framework of monitoring and evaluation.

The process consisted of surveys at local sites of management committees and target audiences both as baseline data and outcome data. This helped establish profiles of library services in each community and provided information on the program's impact on reading behaviour. All types of data were used: interview, quantitative (census data), use of libraries, reading habits, and level of satisfaction with library services. Consultants travelled to local communities and collected the data including observational and anecdotal data. Using the benchmark data and information from many international studies of literacy, six key assumptions were used as the organizational and analytical framework:

- Literacy is a concept, a process, and a skill that has meaning in relation to the demand of the economy and society or individuals and communities.
- Literacy is a mode of behaviour, which enables individuals and groups to gather, analyze and apply written information to function in society.

- Communities have a responsibility for creating a culture of literacy for their members, if they value development.
- If literacy is to culminate in a print mentality, the importance of the oral tradition and the communal nature of learning in African society must be understood and integrated into the approaches and programmes of local groups.
- If libraries are to support the reading habits of their citizens, they must understand the information needs of their communities.
- Literacy assists citizens in taking advantage of the changes affecting all societies, as well as allowing them to safeguard their traditions and values.

According to Evans, the rationale for evaluation was the need to develop indicators which would allow the programmes to assess their own performance. They also wanted to involve each project's African and Caribbean partners. This allows the communities to both know their own communities and to assess their own effectiveness. This allows them to plan and manage their programmes, and also puts them in a position to make their needs and successes known beyond their communities-perhaps for future funding.

Their evaluation efforts made it very clear that community members are rarely involved in identifying their own needs, and one of the strongest needs is providing appropriate materials (*i.e.* information related to agriculture, health, and community development) in languages used by the people.

Evans and Genesse applied this mode of evaluation and these assumptions to a literacy and libraries project in Peru, and found that several of the assumptions proved applicable. The Peruvian project dates from the early '70s with recognition of community needs-common languages, and cultural commonalities. CODE's aim and motto throughout the 1990s, "self sufficiency through literacy in the developing world" is at the core of their evaluation processes.

Several case studies of rural communities in Zimbabwe are presented by Moyo (1995) of projects sponsored by the Rural

Libraries and Resources Development Programme (RLRDP) in establishing 42 rural school/community libraries (some in storerooms or unoccupied classrooms). Their emphasis on community involvement is obvious even though several organizations within Zimbabwe (Book Development Council, Library Association, National Library) serve as partners as do some international organizations including CODE (Canada).

Specific outcomes of these efforts included: progress in academic examination passes, income-generating projects, and community-based meetings. Here, as in most of the projects in developing countries, one of the greatest constraints is the lack of reading materials; another is the need for more training on the part of library or literacy managers.

The work of Zweizig et al (1990) is the major evaluation tool developed in the U.S. for libraries and literacy. The manual introduces an overall process for evaluation and specific measures of relevance for literacy programmes, beyond measures of student progress alone. The manual drew from previous work on public library planning and evaluation models commissioned by the American Library Association. Seven steps in the process include the following:

- Determine the target area (specific goal(s): what you want to accomplish (effectiveness) and/or how well you want to do it (efficiency)
- Set the target (measurable objectives)
- How will you know? (Types of measurement, assessment)
- Take a look (gather the evidence)
- How close are you? (Comparison with target and actual figures)
- So what? (Is it good enough? Should you reasses the targets? Analyze the reasons for not achieving targets)
- Rethink (need to refine the target, involve other constituents)

They recommend that a sample programme profile should be developed with the kinds of information needed to understand the literacy level of the community, the current literacy efforts beyond the library, and the resources available to the library, such as space, personnel, collections, and equipment. Specific literacy programme measures are suggested along with specific criteria for three areas of measurement: collections, support services, and instruction.

In addition to these quantitative measures, some suggestions for other evaluation approaches are described including qualitative measures such as the degree of cooperation between the library and other service providers, and information from both tutors and learners. This work reflects current thinking on evaluation, the importance of outcomes especially to end users. Johnson (1987) pointed out the critical area of a need for evaluation of literacy programmes-what differences do these programmes make? This highlights the need for well-specified objectives for literacy programmes so that they can be adequately evaluated including all aspects of the library's role in literacy, rather than limited to only the learner's progress, such as: collection development, support services, and adequacy of funding and resources.

More recently, much has been written about the need to break the cycle of illiteracy through generations, mainly through family and inter-generational literacy programmes. Much of the literature has been devoted to family literacy projects including Library-based Family Literacy Projects (Monsour and Talan, 1993). These projects have been suggested as models for public libraries nationwide in cooperative work between libraries and other community agencies. The concept of partnerships in the joint coordination of each organization's resources and expertise led to the most successful projects. The authors feature these projects as ones that should be replicated and they tried to identify components of such projects that have led to their success.

All of the projects developed individual evaluation plans for their libraries based on the specific goals for the project in the community. Included in the "lessons learned" are: team building, the difficulty and importance of recruitment, the need to plan for the different age groups of children including child care during tutoring sessions for parents, the importance of quality literature for sharing, the need for coalition building with other community agencies including marketing and publicity, the need for personal contact and follow-up, and the recognition of the public stake in family literacy including information and feed-back to community leaders. Outside the library field, there is a great deal of work on both establishing and evaluating literacy programmes such as the work by Bhola (1990).

These are especially useful as librarians work with those in educational systems and community-based organizations who often do not see the literacy role and activities as part of public libraries. Also, in many developing countries, the lack of a strong public library system and the lack of books and reading materials especially in the indigenous languages means that some literacy projects must work without the institutional structure of libraries.

Guidelines for Libraries Involved in Literacy

Several countries and organizations have worked on guidelines, some for establishing literacy programmes in libraries, especially public libraries, others for a specific type of programme, such as family literacy programmes, and some for developing training guidelines for library workers (Scott, 1995).

The most extensive ones to date appear to be those by UNESCO in 1993 under contract with IFLA and under the direction of Barbro Thomas: Guidelines for Public Libraries Promoting Literacy. This follows extensive meetings organized by IFLA concerning the role of public libraries in literacy work, and follows UNESCO's 1990 International Literacy Year. Following this work, a third revision of the UNESCO Public Library Manifesto was issued in 1994 after a long period of work. This Manifesto addresses functional literacy and the principle of human rights with open access for all.

Now that there are more studies of illiteracy around the world, more recognition of the need for individualized community programmes based on local needs, as well as new models for literacy programmes-including adult literacy, family literacy and workplace literacy projects-perhaps it is time for another try at guidelines for libraries and literacy efforts. There also appears to be a need for more international coordination of library and literacy efforts, as a clearinghouse of information and as a coordinator of potential funding sources, among other functions.

LIBRARIES FACILITATING SELF-PUBLISHING

Electronic Journals: why Libraries should be Involved

Two years ago my presentation for the 1996 Summer School on the Digital Library [Roes, 1996] started with the question "What is a library without journals?" and its corollary "What is a digital library without electronic journals?" The answer is obvious: it is hard to imagine a digital library without electronic journals.

If electronic journals are defined as scholarly, refereed journals which are only published electronically-that is, are not electronic versions of printed journals as delivered by major publishing companies like Elsevier and Springer-than recent history shows that electronic journals are one of the two main vehicles for self-publishing by scholars, the other being electronic preprint archives. Especially with the advent of the World Wide Web, it has become relatively easy, at least in a technical sense, to publish electronic journals.

A study of the phenomenon also gives the main reasons why (digital) libraries ought to be involved in the development of this new medium [see also Roes, 1995].

The first reason which comes to mind is the well-known *serials pricing crisis*. The rate at which the volume of scholarly publishing is expanding-sometimes estimated to double every ten years-is pushing the current print system to its limits. With prices of printed journals also doubling roughly every seven to ten years, most libraries are no longer trying to develop collections but are more concerned with the question which journals next to cancel. Information and communication technology traditionally promises faster, cheaper and better services. Not so in the publishing industry, for a quick glance at electronic versions of printed journals offered by the major publishing companies shows that:

- electronic versions are usually delivered weeks after the print versions, not surprisingly since often these electronic versions are derived by scanning the printed journal
- electronic versions are mostly only available in conjunction with printed versions, implying a higher price-libraries are forced to pay for the extra

- the use of electronic versions is often limited through strict licensing terms to on-campus use only

So, if we leave the matter to publishers what we seem to get is slow delivery of electronic versions, more expensive journals, and only debatable improvement in service to a limited audience. This can hardly be considered a contribution to the solution of the serials pricing crisis.

Instead of merely substituting parts of the information chain, electronic only journals are a true innovation of the information chain. Since their whole production process is electronic only, a well organized use of today's technology offers fast communication between authors, editors and referees, resulting in a potentially far more faster medium than the present printed system which is characterized by publication lags varying from three months up to, sometimes, several years. Faster and more efficient scholarly communication is the result.

By using existing tools and infrastructure, the costs of printing and distributing almost vanish, resulting in dramatically lower costs. Some observers claim that cost reductions of up to 70 percent are possible. Cost reductions for libraries are also possible since processing can be more efficiently organized and physical shelving costs are traded for electronic storage. Where costs of buildings will only go up, electronic storage becomes cheaper and cheaper every month, and, anyway, one copy of an electronic journal on the entire global network is enough to service libraries and scholars worldwide.

The first reason for libraries to be involved in the development of electronic journals is therefore their promise in solving the serials pricing crisis which at the present is seriously eroding their position in the information chain. Printed journals are under serious threat and libraries need to be involved in the development of cheaper and faster successors-which are likely to be electronic journals.

Other promises for innovation have to do with overcoming the limits of paper. Contributions can be longer, source material, experimental data, computer programmes, animations and audio can be linked, and of course, electronic articles can be linked to other electronic articles. Also, the process of peer review could become more open by organizing discussions of peers around a contribution. In practice these advantages have hardly materialized yet in existing electronic journals. So as a second reason, libraries, which have traditionally been involved in the *organization* of information, should want to be involved in shaping these aspects of the information cycle in the twenty-first century.

An important third factor is that developing electronic journals offers a unique opportunity for close cooperation between library staff and their most important patrons, faculty. In the end, (university) libraries exist only to support the (educational and research) processes of their parent institutions. If you want to be good at that, you have to know what your customers want. Cooperation is an excellent way to find out what your patrons need.

A final, and perhaps more personal reason, is that developing an electronic journal is *fun*. It is challenging because it requires the organization and coordination of many skills, many of which are yet foreign to librarians, but which lead to a better understanding of the scholarly communication process and, by implication, the evolving position of libraries in today's information chain.

Case-study: Electronic Journal of Comparative Law (EJCL)

An important factor in developing a project proposal for an electronic journal were intensive discussions library staff and faculty had with the board of Tilburg University early 1995 about reshaping the budgeting of the collection development process. Given the ever increasing prices of journals and the not-always increasing university budget it was clear that, although we could at least stabilize collection development in the short run, in the long run we would-and will-inevitably face ever deteriorating journals' collections. So why not try and find out how difficult self-publishing would be? To see whether we could do the job at lower cost. To gain control over-after all-our own work again and to introduce some *countervailing power* in the publishing industry.

This idea met response in the Faculty of Law and by the end of 1995 a first project proposal was submitted to IWI, the Dutch platform for the innovation of the supply of scientific information. This first proposal was rejected by IWI, the organization not yet being familiar with the idea and possibility of self-publishing. But, in retrospect we were fortunate because the rejection made us rethink the whole proposal and come up with a better document [Controlling Document] at next year's call for proposals, when self-publishing was in fact one of the main themes for which IWI invited project proposals.

Notable improvements were a cooperation with Utrecht University and the explicit aim for an international editorial board-both factors which considerably broadened the scope of the project. Also it was decided to limit the journal's scope to comparative law, one of the important research themes of the Tilburg Faculty of Law. A project team, consisting of staff from Tilburg University and Utrecht University libraries and computer centres, and a preliminary editorial board, consisting of legal scholars from the Tilburg and Utrecht Faculties of Law, were put together.

Aim of the Project, Work Packages and Results

The project's aim was to: "[Develop] an editorial, technical and organizational concept for an electronic review of comparative law which publishes articles of high quality in the English language contributed by Dutch and foreign scholars, as well as producing two issues of this journal." [ibid.]

An important indirect aim is to give scholars and universities more control over their scientific output. Copyright remains with authors, but articles may be downloaded, printed and circulated for scientific and educational purposes as long as the article including the copyright notice which asserts the moral right of authors remains intact.

To this end the project was divided in seven work packages. Work package one set out to make an inventory of the existing printed journals in the field of comparative law. The twofold purpose of this exercise was (i) to gain insight into the market in terms of potential readers and authors, and (ii) to get an overview of existing editorial policies which could be helpful in the design of the EJCL procedures. The report on this section [Tims, van Waelsden, 1997] led to the conclusion that there was room for a journal specifically geared toward comparative private law and the methodological issues of comparative law in general. A closer look at five of the 60 journals contained in the sample revealed that aim and scope are usually quite broadly defined.

Another major finding was that guidelines for authors are rarely given and in none of the five journals refereeing policies were mentioned. Legal journals seem to operate in a sort of 'black box' mode from the viewpoint of (especially young) legal scholars. This is a result which might come as a surprise to those outside the legal profession, it stresses though that each discipline has its own culture of publishing.

Work package two was similar to the first in that it also was mainly about reconnaissance, this time regarding existing electronic law journals, again to gain insight in how these journals were set up, with a specific interest in technical models. An important secondary goal was that while surfing the Web channels for promotion and distribution of EJCL were identified [covered in Tims, van Waelsden, 1997]. Findings [Roes, 1997] were rather diverse but instructive. The Journal of Information Law and Technology was chosen to serve as an example in the development of the EJCL site.

The goal of work package three was to develop an editorial policy, guidelines for submissions, and a style-guide for contributions. Other important tasks for the editorial board in this work package were the expansion of the editorial board with distinguished foreign scholars, and the recruitment of a panel of independent referees which would be able to judge contributions, and of course soliciting publications for the first issues.

The input of work packages one and two proved, of course, to be of considerable value. The result of this work is clear from the journal's site: http://www.ejcl.org/general/about.html. Furthermore the editorial board was expanded with scholars from Sweden, Germany and the UK. What proved to be far more difficult was the implementation of proper refereeing procedures, a task so far carried out by the editorial board itself. Also soliciting publications proved to be a difficult task, although it should be mentioned that this was predicted in the project proposal since an electronic journal not only suffers from the fact that is a *new* journal which has yet to prove itself, but also because it is a relatively *new medium*, introduced in a culture still governed by print.

Work package four, using the results of work package two, involved the development of the journal's Website as well as the supply of tools necessary for the editorial board to cooperate in an internationally distributed context. With the help of an external graphics designer, the project team designed a dummy site which was demonstrated to the editorial board, adapted, ergonomically tested to see whether the site was easy to navigate, and again adapted after which the editorial board finally approved. The issue of tools seemed difficult at first, then easy and, in the end, again difficult.

Difficult at first because the presumption was that editors would also be responsible for the actual production, which meant a lot of effort would need to be put in the development of HTML-templates and instruction. After the Tilburg Faculty of Law decided to appoint an assistant editor (0.2 full time equivalent, two years) to take care of the technical tasks, matters seemed much easier. Now the presumption was that editors could rely mainly on electronic mail with attached manuscripts to support the editorial process.

The use of different, and differently aged, mail packages made this presumption illusory. At the time of writing of this paper, a WWW-based groupware tool, BSCW-Basic Support for Cooperative work is being implemented to better support the exchange of manuscripts as well as the editorial workflow. The choice of BSCW illustrates the preference for existing public domain tools where possible, another example being the use of standard list server software for the notification of subscribers to the list of newly published issues.

Work package five concerned the actual production of two issues. Of course this also implied the actual test of the design work and the procedures, which both turned out to be robust, except for the support of editorial workflow described above. Because of this, and because soliciting manuscripts proved to be more difficult than expected, the project cycle was extended with three months, now covering March 1997 till June 1998.

The first issue was published in November 1997, the second issue was planned for late March 1998 but was published in May. Both issues carried two extensive articles which would have been difficult to publish in printed journals. In this way, one of the goals of the EJCL project, namely to provide a much wanted outlet for more extensive publications, was met. The third issue is, at the time of writing, scheduled to appear late June 1998, after which the project will end and the editorial board supported by the assistant editor will carry on.

The final two work packages are of a supportive nature. Work package six is concerned with costs. The issue of the cost of electronic journals is widely debated in the literature. Work package six/a set out to contribute to this discussion by asking an independent accountant to develop a general costing model for publishing an electronic journal.

This model, developed by Coopers & Lybrand, will be tested by using the actual costs incurred in developing and maintaining EJCL. At the moment of writing of this paper this latter exercise still needs to be carried out. Work package six/b explored the technical possibilities for selective exclusion of non academic users, or, stated otherwise, the effective possibilities for price differentiation between academic and non academic users. At the time of writing of this paper it is unlikely that any barriers will be raised for non academic users since (i) marginal costs might well exceed marginal revenues as the expected interest in non academic circles is not high and (ii) these barriers might also well be a nuisance to academic users.

Work package seven, finally, was concerned with dissemination. This involved publications, presentations and the organization of a seminar on self-publishing by legal scholars in Tilburg, early May 1998. Promotion of the journal was carried out through the network through the channels identified in work package two. This proved to be more difficult than expected, so it was decided to design a printed leaflet which was sent along with correspondence, a print journal, and was handed out at seminars and conferences. The interest of legal scholars for the journal can be measured by the number of people who have subscribed to the list server which notifies of newly published issues.

Just prior to the publication of the second issue, a little less than a hundred legal scholars had subscribed worldwide: 33 from the Netherlands, 23 from the USA, 12 from Germany, the rest coming from such remote places as Argentina, India, Singapore and China. These numbers are still too low to conclude the journal is successful. On the other hand, establishing a new journal takes time, in the publishing industry it is not abnormal for a new journal to reach break even in five years. Analysis of the log files of the journal's Website still needed to be carried out at the time of writing of this paper.

Lessons and Discussion

Don't get frustrated if a project proposal is turned down. Reconsider it and if you still think your project is worth pursuing, redraft it, chances are you might still find resources.

In order to facilitate the transition for authors and readers from print to electronic and also to keep the maintenance effort to a minimum, an explicit choice was made to keep the site as simple and effective as possible. The journal's site is easy to maintain by the assistant editor who had no prior background in WWW-publishing. Manuscripts, which can be in English, German or French (notice the difference with the original project's aim), are received in either Word or WordPerfect formats with relatively little markup as required in the Guidelines for Authors.

From these originals, after copy-editing, HTML, ASCII and Word and WordPerfect versions are created. In a sense the journal's site is not so much designed for reading, it is rather a medium for distribution. Most readers will probably choose to print out an article after a quick scan of the abstract and the article. Also the choice of public domain solutions again stresses the idea to make the most efficient use of what is available. The Internet is full of building blocks and ideas, don't try to reinvent a wheel others have invented before you. Always keep in mind the specific group you are working for.

The most difficult factor, as rightly foreseen in the project proposal, proves to be the attraction of high quality manuscripts. Three factors are at work here which make this task not easy: (i) a new journal is being published and has to attract authors which would rather publish in well known printed journals with well-known prestige, a new journal has yet to establish its prestige, this can take up to several years to achieve, (ii) not only the journal is new, but there is also a new medium involved, one with whom most authors, and especially established authors, are not yet familiar, (iii) the journal introduces refereeing, a practice not yet too common among legal scholars, and a possible threat for again, especially, established authors.

The only possible way to overcome these hurdles are enthusiastic editors who believe in this new medium and can persuade their peers of the necessity to make this new venture a success because it is in the interest of the profession as a whole, since the existing print information cycle is under threat. Since we are dealing mainly with cultural issues here, editors need in effect to be *change agents,* willing to make use of their professional networks.

In the EJCL project it seems necessary to enhance the editorial board so as to divide this task among more scholars. The focus will be on North American scholars, expected to be more accustomed to self-publishing, and Eastern European scholars, since the outlets for publications are limited in Eastern Europe. Physical contact between editors at least once a year seems also of importance here since the asynchronous communication via mail and WWW is probably not enough to generate the necessary commitment in this culture at this moment. International conferences provide a good and efficient venue for these meetings.

The main discussion point here seems to be whether scholars, whether or not aided by libraries, should become publishers, or that publishing is a trade best left to publishers.

Another discussion point is whether we are able to confront scholars with the consequences of the present system of tenure track decisions. This system is becoming more and more centred around publications in well-established journals with preferably high impact factors. More and more of these publications are in the hands of publishers which to date have done little to alleviate the serials pricing crisis. The logical consequence of this development is the paradox that in a world where more and more knowledge is being produced every day, this knowledge is becoming more and more inaccessible.

Accessibility of knowledge leads us, finally, to the role of libraries. As stated before, cooperation with scholars is a major reason for getting involved in these kinds of projects. Not only to get to know your patrons better, the corollary is that your patrons also get to know the library better and become aware of accessibility issues. Not only librarians, but also scholars will be in a better position to judge their position in the information chain in which they are the beginning (as authors) and the end (as readers). Whether libraries will stay involved in facilitating self-publishing remains to be seen with technology still evolving. Important tasks remain though in the organization and preservation of scholarly information. And in stimulating and facilitating self-publishing in the meantime.

LIBRARY AID TO DEVELOPING COUNTRIES IN TIMES OF GLOBALIZATION

is emerging as a major issue in the world today, affecting both "have" and "have-not" countries in many significant ways. In the library world, interactions between libraries in developing countries and organizations assisting libraries are not new: provision of information, resources, and expertise has been ongoing for much of the second half of the last century. Some of the issues raised by renewed concerns about globalization, however, stimulate inquiry into the efforts of developed countries assisting libraries in developing nations. Despite questions being raised in the literature of other disciplines about the impacts of globalization, it appears that very little research has appeared in the library literature that examines the impact of this phenomenon on the practice of library aid. The concept of "globalization" carries considerable political baggage: whether one views the term positively or negatively depends on one's social and economic view of the world.

For Held and McGrew, globalization is a "re-articulation of international space, in which the notions of sovereignty and democracy are being prised away from the traditional rootedness in the national community and the territorially bounded nation-state." North American information-related companies view this "re-articulation" as an opportunity to expand their customer base into developing countries with technology-driven products, and most articles on globalization reflect this commercially-oriented, North American focus.

Peter Evans, in "Trends, Pressures, and Realities in the Library Systems Marketplace," speaks of the need for LIS companies to develop a different "corporate, cultural, and design philosophy" so they can compete and survive in countries with different languages and cultures. David Dorman, in "Taking Library Services around the World," reports on library service companies such as OCLC, Blackwell, and EBSCO, whose globalization strategies are designed to increase their share of the international customer marketplace and place their products in developing countries.

Some librarians note that globalization can be a "very positive force for cultural and social and economic development... provid[ing] the opportunity for a much greater understanding and interaction among the various peoples of the world." But this view, also expressed by Dorman, relates primarily to the opportunities and advantages realized by North American libraries whose access to information becomes more global as national barriers fall.

David Korten, former faculty member at the Harvard Business School, expresses a more pessimistic view of globalization. He gives evidence of increasing social and environmental disintegration in developing countries, and documents the negative human and environmental consequences of the successful efforts of international corporations to reconstruct values and institutions in developing countries to serve the company's own narrow ends. According to Korten, the convergence of ideological, political, and technological forces behind this process of economic globalization shifts power away from the local governments who should be responsible for the public good (including funding for libraries) and shifts that power toward a handful of corporations and financial institutions driven by the quest for short-term financial gain.

A negative view of globalization is also voiced by Alan Scott, who notes that increasing cross-national flows of information tend to make "nations, nationality, and national boundaries less important to people's lives," resulting in a loss of local identity, control, and responsibility.

This review of literature pertaining to library aid and globalization was prompted by the authors' vacation visits to libraries in various countries, conversations with librarians in developing countries about the "double-edged sword" of donations, and by the authors' admiration for those librarians who continue to deliver very important services in developing countries despite limited resources.

The review will focus on two questions: what are the major needs of libraries in the developing countries? And, what are some of the ways those needs are – or are not – being met? Despite anecdotal evidence gathered by the authors during visits to developing countries that globalization has affected the type of library aid now needed, no research could be found that linked these two phenomena. It is the contention of the authors, however, that lessons learned from the existing research about more traditional "book" aid remain very relevant to library aid relationships affected by globalization, and that these lessons should be used as the basis for further research that incorporates this new phenomenon of internationalization.

The phrases "Third World" and "developing countries" are essentially Western in origin and use; they are used to describe less affluent countries in Latin America, the Caribbean, the Middle East, Africa, Asia, and the Pacific. These descriptions are considered to be ethnocentric by most outside the Western world who do not characterize themselves in this way, nor divide the world into two camps – developed and developing. However, in the context of the literature to be discussed, these terms will be used as they are in the literature.

"The phrases 'Third World' and 'developing countries' are essentially Western in origin and use; they are used to describe less affluent countries in Latin America, the Caribbean, the Middle East, Africa, Asia, and the Pacific."

Because a wide diversity of political, economic, cultural, historical, and geographic factors affect libraries in different countries, it is impossible for a single document, or even a suite of documents describing specific needs, to serve as a detailed blueprint for all. As a result, the literature chosen for Part One of this review was selected for its ability to provide general overviews of library needs in developing countries. Essays and books are included that provide a philosophical overview of issues and attitudes for both "givers" and "receivers," an understanding of which is essential in developing successful programmes. Although published in 1966, Lester Asheim's classic, Librarianship in Developing Countries, remains an excellent explanation of the philosophical underpinnings of culture and libraries, knowledge of which is central to developing successful aid programmes. Asheim's book will form the starting point for Part One of the review.

In Part Two, the focus is on articles that describe an array of different programmes that have assisted Third World countries with library development. There are many different past and present aid programmes to libraries all over the world; it is impossible to review all of them. Therefore, we have selected articles that represent both positive and negative examples of different types of projects, while also highlighting a variety of donor and recipient countries.

One further point regarding literature selected: not surprisingly, much of the literature written in recent years about both the needs of libraries in developing countries and the projects in place concerns technology. While not discounting the importance of technology in this field, we have chosen to focus our attention upon more traditional areas of need, such as collection development and preservation, literacy, indigenous book publishing, and staff training initiatives. Despite the attention being diverted to automating and connecting libraries in both developed and developing countries, traditional areas of need still exist and, perhaps, are in danger of being overshadowed. As Lucinda Zoe explains in her thesis on women's information centres in developing countries: While library scientists and information specialists praise the abilities of the new technologies developed for information management – computerized online catalogs, commercial online database services, CD-ROMs, laser printers, FAX machines, and electronic networking to name a few – the small information centres in the developing nations of Asia, Africa, and Latin America struggle with fugitive materials that do into fit neatly into traditional classification schemes. ... Furthermore, however impressive the new information technologies and communication systems appear, use is difficult, if not impossible in areas where the infrastructure is not solid: the telephone system is unreliable or erratic; power supplies are often interrupted or non-existent for days, if not weeks; equipment, maintenance costs and access to continued materials (disks, paper, ribbons, etc.) are beyond the financial resources of organizations; and privacy, confidentiality, and protection of information is difficult...

PART ONE: LIBRARY NEEDS IN DEVELOPING COUNTRIES

Lester Asheim wrote his brief but compelling book, quoted from below, after he spent five years (1961-1966) visiting libraries in Africa, Latin America and Asia as Director of the American Library Association International Relations Office. The quotation provides his basic premise for appropriately serving the cause of librarianship around the world. Although written nearly four decades ago, many of Asheim's observations about library operations in North America and developing countries still hold true, but his opinions must, of course, be taken in the context of the times – the early 1960s.

You may remember that I began with a reference to Culture Shock, which I said occurred whenever the system of logic in which we believe is challenged by a logical system to which we do not yet possess the key. It is not the other system that must be corrected, but the absence of the key. There are usually reasons for what people do, even if they are not our reasons. Before we condemn out of hand a pattern of behaviour which happens not to fit our preconceptions, we should try to find out what the reasons were that led to it. We may still not accept the reasons as valid for us, but we may discover a different context of validity for evaluating the behaviour pattern and its use by others.

Lester Asheim, Librarianship in Developing Countries

Closed shelves, lack of extensive reference or circulating services, differing or absence of classification schemes, limited children's service and, above all, an emphasis on the primacy of the book over the reader are characteristics of Third World libraries as observed by Asheim. These characteristics are still prevalent today. In his book, Asheim looks for the "key" he mentions above.

He describes how economics, education, societal structure, attitudes towards authority, the impact of colonization and its (supposed) overthrow, the predominance of the English language worldwide, religious beliefs, attitude towards work, low prestige assigned to librarianship, and even climate have affected the development of libraries in these countries, and have resulted in libraries which, to Western standards, may appear to be below the mark. Asheim urges us, however, to avoid making that evaluation because:

> ... the difference between two concepts of a service, an objective, or a procedure can be measured by the gap that exists between what each faction sees as the essentials. The essentials are determined by the goals each side wishes to attain, whether overtly stated or not. And the goals reflect the system of values each party holds, determined by its history, its tradition, its culture. We are as much victims of our heredity and environment as they are of theirs...

Despite the "chasm" between cultures Asheim describes, he believes librarians can establish bridges. According to Asheim, the first question to answer is the hardest: "Does anyone really want the help we offer?"

To provide background for one's decision, Asheim then discusses many of the negative ways that Americans and Europeans have used libraries as propaganda agencies for political reasons (for example, donating books reflecting an anti-communism ideology) that in some cases led to the retardation of local development, an opinion shared by others: "[In the past,] ... the establishment, growth and decline of donation programmes were more closely related to changing American foreign policy objectives than to the success or failure of... [the programmes themselves]." Despite possible negative elements, Asheim concludes that six characteristics of American librarianship are worthy of export:

1. the conception of the library as an organization of books,
2. the evolution of a library profession,
3. the attitude of service,
4. the function of the library as an education institution,
5. the role of the library in the advancement of intellectual freedom, and
6. the conception of organized information as a public resource and responsibility.

Simply put, aid programmes that support one or more of these functions and have the support and cooperation of local authorities are desirable. Attitude is everything, according to Asheim: "...we must begin to see ourselves as an equal partner in an exchange rather than as a condescending Lady Bountiful. We must... develop an Ear of America as well as a Voice.

We must listen as well as tell, learn as well as teach, receive as well as give." To further this interactive rather than autocratic viewpoint, Asheim favours programmes that acknowledge the need "...to adapt rather than to adopt the methods and procedures that we happen to favour for our own purposes." Finally, quoting "an old India hand" [Ranganathan], Asheim encourages those wishing to advance librarianship in developing countries – "a daunting task" – to substitute the word "problem" with "opportunity."

"Despite the 'chasm' between cultures Asheim describes, he believes librarians can establish bridges."

Donor Objectives

A thorough search for reports or theses reporting research results focused specifically on library aid revealed little scholarship in this area. The research of Jesus Lau, however, provides excellent information necessary for understanding the economic and political complexity of well-intentioned but sometimes ill-advised donor objectives. His assessment of the relationship between information growth and social development in 31 countries from 1960 to 1977 revealed that the information gap between developing and highly developed countries is widening faster than the social gap (life expectancy, food consumption). His results also suggested that increased information development as shown through library indicators is associated with positive change in social development.

D.E.K. Wijasuriya, International Federation of Library Associations (IFLA) Representative for Asia and Oceania in the 1990s, echoes Asheim's and Lau's recommendations in a framework for development adopted by IFLA and described in "The Advancement of Librarianship (ALP): IFLA's Core Programme Orientation to the Third World." Much of this document concentrates on facts about developing countries, terms of reference, and time tables, but the author also outlines general objectives and programme areas:

> The main objectives of the ALP Core Programme are to contribute, within the framework of IFLA's programme structure, to the progressive improvement of library and information services within the developing countries so as to enable them to contribute significantly to national development. At the same time, programme objectives shall place special emphasis on the creation of conditions likely to contribute towards national initiatives and a systematic progression towards self-sufficiency.

Wijasuriya acknowledges that the advancement of librarianship (ALP) "can be conceived in the most infinite terms," but maintains that for practical purposes, the primary goals in 1990 were:

1. the establishment and development of public library systems with particular attention to the needs of rural and urban marginal areas,
2. greater identification of libraries with literacy programmes, and
3. greater attention to education and training.

According to Irene Norlund, Scandinavian aid agencies (SIDA, NORAD and DANIDA) have specified support of culture through library/archival aid as a primary objective since the early 1980s. In "Culture and Institution-building," Norlund outlines both the problems and benefits of aid programmes designed to support cultural heritage. Major obstacles include the reticence of aid organizations to support such programmes, combined with the ambiguous attitude to cultural aid funds held by governments in some recipient countries, who may favour programmes that show a direct economic benefit. She promotes providing assistance to 1) set up new archives and libraries, 2) collect and organize documents, and 3) train librarians to maintain access to historical materials as the key components in preserving of indigenous cultures. "Support to culture will also lead to the building up of enriched and renewed institutions and by that means increased capacity," observes Norlund.

The fragile nature of important cultural and religious documents in developing countries makes more compelling the need for collection and preservation. Many are held in private collections and religious temples or monasteries, where maintenance is not secure. "There is limited time to save these irreplaceable heritages, which are a key both to enlarging knowledge and self-confidence and to building institutions which can link up to the world at large," concludes Norlund.

Carolina L. Afan, Library Director-Cultural Centre of the Philippines, agrees with Norlund's point of view about the importance of preservation, but from the perspective of an aid recipient, not a donor. She sees a need for support beyond written forms of communication: "The librarian and other cultural workers should have the skills and knowledge in documenting prints, tapes, photographs, films, videos and others."

Expertise in preservation regarding these different media is necessary as audiotape, video, film, etc. are more "natural" media for oral cultures to record their stories, history, etc., rather than in the Western tradition of print. Afan speaks strongly and persuasively in favour of repatriating rare historical and cultural materials that are in European and American archives since "colonizers had their share in looting and taking away the resources of their former colonies." In the same vein, she cautions her colleagues:

[Developing] countries should guard against the intellectual and cultural exploitation being done by some foreigners who in the guise of doing research are actually taking advantage of our natural and human resources for their own use and interest. Cultural agreements, donor contracts and exchanges should be carefully studied and analyzed before going into them. Any agreement should benefit both countries and must not be a one-sided affair.

Other librarians and educators have voiced the same concern – that aid to libraries not be a form of "neocolonialism...to perpetuate cultural and economic dependency" on donor countries. Mary Niles-Maack believes that donors' goals must be examined closely: initiatives based on the aim of spreading Western culture have caused "intellectual consequences" for developing countries, as a dependence on foreign books prevents the promotion of local publishing initiatives.

As well, donor objectives may be tied to larger global alliances – for political and strategic reasons the donor country may want to strengthen ties with the recipient country. Afan concludes her report by noting that the central government of the Philippines has embarked on a decentralization process for both cultural centres and libraries, which she describes as "the democratization of access to libraries and other learning centres, insuring the provinces and regions that their cultural treasures will be left to them to be utilized, conserved and appreciated."

Rosario Gassol de Horowitz also writes about donor objectives from "a Third World perspective" (the sub-title of her book *Librarianship*). Like Asheim, she observes that library development has taken place from "the Anglo-Saxon tradition" and has been "propagated, consciously or unconsciously, by Western librarians travelling abroad on consultant missions and through library literature, much of which has been produced in the United States." Paraphrasing Ivan Illich, she states that "the nations of the West are packaging their services to contain their views of the world." Rather than rejecting the contributions of the West, Horowitz (in terms she herself identifies as more closely related to liberation than development), calls instead for innovative leadership from librarians in developed countries and an enhanced communication process to assist those countries in breaking free from their inherited mantle of dependency and oppression.

"The new orientations confirm the calls for a new type of professional and for a bold and non-traditional library service which cuts across the compartmentalization imposed by tradition and organizations, to meet the circumstances and conditions in which people find themselves." She urges that isolated library workers in developing countries seek support through strengthened ties with other workers throughout the country—as well as the continent—by creating active and cohesive professional associations.

Language Challenges

Language issues are problematic for many developing countries—as well as for donor agencies. In *The Bookseller* (11 April 1997), Caroline Horn notes that South Africa and Ethiopia each have eleven language groups, and she identifies language as a prominent concern for library/literacy projects in these countries and others. Her article also supports the fact, often mentioned in the literature, that libraries are foreign to the way of life for many traditional, oral societies in Africa. As a consequence, governments may be unaware of the purpose and benefits of libraries and reluctant to support them financially.

The issue of language and library development also surfaces in Asian countries where oral traditions have predominated. From a Malaysian perspective, Diljit Singh notes that the "...reading habit is still not fully ingrained in the Malaysian public." He attributes this partially to the fact that Malaysians (East and West) speak many different dialects, creating difficulties for library clients seeking service and materials in their local language. This problem highlights the need for support of local publishing initiatives so people can have access to literacy programmes and to relevant materials in local libraries and bookstores-in their own language.

Need for a Cooperative Approach

With its long history of apartheid, South Africa serves as an interesting example of "have" and "have-not" communities within one country. *The Use of Libraries for the Development of South Africa;*

Final Report on an Investigation for the South African Institute of Librarianship and Information Science proposes a plan for development consistent with the views expressed by Asheim. The report states: "Librarians should familiarize themselves with the psychology and the sociology of the underdeveloped.

In particular they should not expect persons bred in the culture of the subordinate to act according to the cultural and psychological patterns of the dominant." The report is also reminiscent of Asheim's observations regarding assumptions about the "apathy of the underdeveloped," a phenomenon that Zaaiman describes as a psychological state induced by subordination and a dependence on "the dominant group" as well as the overwhelming battery of problems that disadvantaged individuals face. Skepticism on the part of recipients and frustration and discouragement on the part of librarians from donor countries can result. This report says that a cooperative approach to development is absolutely necessary to counteract creation of a cycle of apathy and donor disappointment:

> Developing communities should always be fully involved in the planning, development and execution of development projects that concern them... Community involvement means exploring the people's basic needs with them, and designing and developing methods with them to fulfil those needs. It should be remembered that the underdeveloped cannot relate to a concept such as "libraries" of which they have had no experience... Key groups of opinion makers within the developing community should be identified and their views and approval sought at all stages of the investigation, design and implementation of library services... Librarians, should, however, guard against the danger of accepting the views of elites in developing communities as representative of all the needs of that community.

One of the strongest supporters of this cooperative approach is Carol Mills, librarian from the University of the South Pacific in Fiji. In "Aid for Libraries: Should One Look the Proverbial Gift Horse in the Mouth?" she criticizes blanket donations given without prior collection management assessment work done by recipients, saying that this lack of joint responsibility institutionalizes aid and causes an "aid dependent mentality."

Special Needs of University/Research Libraries

In her article "Filling Bare Shelves," Carolyn Sharples laments the fact that as aid organizations and governments of developing nations have focused on literacy and books for children, academic institutions have suffered. Cancellation of journal subscriptions has been common as prices have increased, mostly in the area of medicine. Specifically, she notes that books on "tropical medicine, primary health care, women in development, and intermediate technology are...priorities" for her agency, Book Aid International.

Sharples also discusses the difficulties that academic librarians in developing countries encounter when they try to obtain information about newly published material. It is a "Catch 22" situation if library staff are expected to indicate what they need when they do not know what is available. This situation makes bibliographic and selection tools high on the list of desirable materials. These concerns are reinforced by Yogendra P. Dubey, Professor in Library and Information Science at Banaras Hindu University in India, who describes in his 1986 conference presentation the problems that Indian librarians encounter when they try to meet professors' and scientists' demands for scientific and technological information.

Although widespread use of the Internet now makes some of Dubey's observations about information needs outdated, many of the problems he mentions still exist in academic libraries. These include heavy reliance by developing countries on scientific books and journals from the West, in the absence of "home-grown" publishing; supply and currency problems; high prices for subscriptions; copyright restrictions that limit the free-flow of information; constraints of multiple indigenous languages; educational systems that foster rote learning and do not promote individual research; low demand for library services due in part to lack of awareness of their role; and passive attitudes of librarians.

Dubey confirms Asheim's observation that when resources are very scarce, service may not be a priority, and "the book" is more important than the person: "they [librarians] are more product than service oriented, *i.e.*, more toward production of bibliographies, catalogues, etc. than toward services directly oriented to users (such as question-answering)." He concludes with a recommended strategy to alleviate these problems that will result in the development of information distribution industries (publishing, libraries, scientific and technical services), knowledge production industries (research and development, education) and information technology industries.

Importance of Local Publishing

Mills and Priestley both emphasize the key role played by aid or assistance to support indigenous publishing: they maintain that such help is essential if developing nations are to gain true autonomy and supply relevant materials to their citizens. Priestley breaks down the book needs of Third World African countries into six categories: capital funding; the need for textbooks to support education; distribution and marketing knowledge; paper; the need for local language translation, co-publishing, and licensing; and training.

Her support for local publishing is strong, but she cautions that poverty and inexperience may be the catalysts for corruption within projects: misappropriation of paper stock and "mismanagement by cumbersome, bureaucratic procedures and unqualified officials" are often significant issues to consider. She concludes that for local publishing to succeed, business management training in areas specific to publishing is crucial, to ensure that grant monies are better managed, overhead costs are considered, and marketing plans are developed. Donor countries need to shift from facilitating the dumping of unwanted materials, such as surplus print runs, to supporting indigenous publishing.

PART TWO: SPECIFIC AID PROJECTS

Research Reports

Investigations on the efficacy of library aid projects in specific countries or to particular institutions appear to be very scarce: no research case studies or analyses were located. However, studies that focus generally on library services in one developing country or to one client group in such countries provide informative contextual background. The most relevant research projects that discuss some aspect of library aid are those of Al-Hanari, Bouri, Stander, Floren-Romero, and Zoe.

Abdulaziz Mohamed Al-Hanari's Ph.D. survey research revealed the important roles that national libraries play in developing countries, and resulted in a list of recommended functions for a proposed Saudi Arabian national library. Elizabeth Bouri examined Egyptian public library development in her doctoral research, revealing the positive influence of international agencies such as UNESCO in the 1960s and subsequent public policy choices of the Egyptian government that led to the decline of public libraries.

How to formulate standards and guidelines for school libraries in developing countries was the central question in Cecilia Stander's research, based in South Africa. Stander concluded that basic school library principles can be applied, but that the diverse perspectives of users make adherence to universal standards problematic. Two theses focused on information needs/services of special groups within developing countries: Maria Floren-Romero examined the difficulties that pharmaceutical researchers in the Dominican Republic encounter when trying to obtain information, and their reliance on colleagues' resources outside the Republic, while Lucinda Zoe explored the growth of women's information centres in developing countries – their relationship with and reliance on the international library community.

Book Donations, Publishing and Distributing

In many cases in the past hundred years, libraries and publishing companies shipped off surplus materials to well-intentioned organizations that "dumped" those items in developing countries, notably those in Africa. As described by Mills:

> First came the missionaries who propagated their faith by direct action, religious and social; their return being souls and the pacification of the area. In more recent times, governments have largely replaced the churches, aiming to spread the word of their friendly intentions. At times, aid to libraries has had little to distinguish it from the 19th century 'books for heathens' syndrome.

Donors paid little attention to the language, currency, or context of the material, and the recipient countries were rarely, if ever, able to choose their own books. And even if the recipients could choose, they had little knowledge of what to request. In her article for *The Bookseller*, Seaton gives a list of "unhelpful books donated" to Book Aid International's Africa book drive, which includes the *AA Road Map of Bristol*, and *The Garth Brooks Scrapbook*. This problem of inappropriate giving is frequently noted in both research articles and opinion pieces on library aid, with poor communication between donor and recipient cited as the primary cause.

According to Margaret Bywater, libraries in Cambodia receive some material from overseas that is useful, but they have also received material "which is totally irrelevant to [their] needs now or in the future." Filling library shelves with this irrelevant material discourages rather than encourages use, thereby thwarting the donors' intentions.

As an alternative, Bywater recommends the donors consider giving monetary grants that allow staff in libraries to select their own books: this will ensure relevancy and support local publishing. Carolyn Sharples agrees with Bywater regarding "problem" donations and the need to support local publishers. She notes that since 1990, Book Aid International (BAI) has been "refining [their] work to become far more targeted and responsive to the needs of partners overseas." This resulted in project development that specifically targets subject areas where materials are scarce. One project – BAI's Africa Book Collective – purchases African books published locally and then distributes those materials throughout the region, thereby helping to establish a local book market. Sharples acknowledges, however, that despite the increasing output of small local publishers, sufficient "suitable" material is difficult to find, especially children's books, which are in high demand.

"Bywater recommends the donors consider giving monetary grants that allow staff in libraries to select their own books; this will ensure relevancy and support local publishing."

E.A. Mwinyimvua of the Tanzania Library Services Board also discusses the measures that Book Aid International has taken in his country to provide suitable books, promote local book production, and ease the administrative burden on recipients.

Three members representing recipient libraries now sit on the BAI Council, facilitating information flow and influencing policy regarding donations to Tanzania and other African nations.

As well, all recipients fill out detailed evaluation forms each year, which enables BAI to select books according to library requirements. BAI also invites librarians from recipient countries to spend three months at BAI Headquarters in England selecting books. To stimulate local book production, BAI provides funds for Tanzanian librarians to purchase books published in other African countries. Mwinyimvua believes that Tanzania will continue to need book aid for many years as currency devaluations make purchase of expensive foreign books even more difficult and as rising literacy rates cause demand for books to outstrip the supply, even with increased local publishing efforts.

The IFLA/UNESCO "Books for All" initiative is another international library project. As project coordinator Lioba Betten explains in "Foreign Aid for Children's Libraries: 25 Years," its aim is to fight illiteracy through providing children in developing countries with books. Betten notes that Books for All seeks to provide long-term aid to libraries and to local booksellers, authors, and publishers by purchasing books in local languages.

Caroline Horn also is critical of those overseas publishers who donate irrelevant materials and encourage "librarians in developing nations to send their orders outside the country." Speaking specifically of African aid projects, she reports that in Senegal "some 80% of books are imported, but are too expensive for the indigenous population. Once students leave school, they are unlikely to pick up a book again." Local efforts are the best means to ensure literacy and relevancy. In her opinion, "book aid programmes can, where properly targeted, help to overcome some of the shortages [of materials], but while libraries remain dependent on aid they are not supporting local publishing initiatives."

S.M. Made, speaking of African aid projects in the early 1980s and Zimbabwe in particular, notes that "low literacy and purchasing power and high unit costs necessitate small editions [of locally produced material], which in turn necessitate small markets and limited distribution." Local printers in developing countries may lack the capital required to purchase paper stock, which often needs to be paid for in advance. Made adds that various local languages and dialects can pose challenges as they may not translate well into the Latin alphabet required for printing. Aid organizations may assist local publishers to solve these problems by encouraging and funding regional associations or consortia of publishers: combined purchasing power to buy bulk paper stock and combined expertise may help to overcome difficulties.

Carol Mills from Fiji is one of the few voices in the literature with a "recipient" perspective. She examines the reasons why developing countries in the South Pacific are not getting what they need from donors:

> Donor agencies tend not to set explicit targets, fail to evaluate their donations, and do not properly manage their aid. Books sent at cost may simply sit there if they are not appropriate, making the uninformed donor feel good while creating a burden for the recipient. Sometimes the recipient accepts simply to avoid giving offence and to keep communications open, or else accepts donations with a peripheral value because they are better than nothing.

Mills' comment is crucial to understanding the complexity of library aid in specific countries because her words concern the power relationship that exists with donor/recipient relationships. Many recipient libraries and information centres are reluctant to express their needs firmly for fear of being cut off entirely. This fear, in turn, is reflected in the collections, as it causes library staff in developing countries to be hesitant about weeding irrelevant material. They do not wish to offend donors by throwing out "gifts" and they are anxious that little would remain in their library if they culled all irrelevant material – collection "starvation rather than poverty."

As Margaret Bywater notes in her article on Cambodia: "[there is] a reluctance to dispose of anything... because people still feel strongly the loss of personal possessions during the Pol Pot period." Peter Brush, a consultant at the National Polytechnic Institute in Laos, also writes about the reluctance to weed. He observed that many titles in the Laotian collection were in foreign languages—Russian, English, French and Vietnamese—which presented a cataloguing dilemma because no translation services were available. The library could offer little material in Lao, as Laos has a small population and a very small publishing industry. The Institute had no collection development (or weeding) policy, and the Institute Director was reluctant to dispose of any books, even those outdated, irrelevant, and uncataloged because all had been donated.

Scandinavian countries have a laudable history of providing aid to libraries and other cultural institutions in developing countries. This support is documented in a 1995 issue of Scandinavian Public Library Quarterly that focused entirely on Nordic aid initiatives. The articles report on the purpose and progress of projects in Tanzania, Kenya, Uganda, Botswana, South Africa, Nicaragua, Vietnam, Laos, and Cuba. A typical project is one focused on Africa and funded by SIDA, the Swedish International Development Authority:

The SIDA project "Words-Books-Democracy" is one example of an attempt to get a holistic perspective within the literature area. The objective is to create and maintain a literate and reading environment and to protect freedom of expression. This requires access to books, newspapers, magazines and so on. The development cooperation shall strengthen the documentation of oral storytelling traditions, author organisations, independent indigenous publishing, the printing industry, distribution channels, libraries, and so on—all links in the complete chain.

An annotated list of current and recently completed library aid projects where Nordic funders are involved concludes the issue.

Children's books are in great demand in most developing countries, particularly in Africa, but the cost of a book, even one locally published, is beyond the price range for most people. Rebecca Knuth in an *IFLA Journal* article revealed how five international organizations are seeking to redress this situation. An innovative joint project by the International Board on Books for Young People (IBBY) and UNESCO involved the production of 2000 kangas (Kenyan cloth pieces used as clothing or baby carriers) that were "imprinted with words and pictures as a child's first text book." In another project, the International Youth Library

(IYL) supported "cross national publication and translation" of books from Africa and Europe, while the IASL (International Association of School Librarianship) and UNESCO cooperated to provide books for school libraries that focus on "local needs" in their collections. Citing a UNESCO project in Croatia as an example, Knuth stresses the special need for children's libraries in war-torn or famine-stricken countries as these libraries help refugee children who are "coping with stress and trauma."

Carol Mills provides the best overall assessment of different aid programmes, based on her experience at the University of the South Pacific (Fiji) where donations form the basis of the collection. Her evaluation includes the book aid models of 1) clearinghouses, 2) twinning (mentor/sister-city programmes) relationships, 3) interest groups, and 4) unsolicited donations. She concludes that clearinghouses have varying degrees of success, providing "unbalanced donations of discarded surplus materials," and indeed may impose a burden beyond useless books, as recipients may have to pay some or all of the freight costs in shipping materials. She is more supportive of twinning relationships because of the personal element involved, but cautions that these arrangements often cannot be sustained.

Academic Libraries and Archives

Academic libraries and archives in developing countries have garnered less attention in the past decades as aid organizations focused on literacy and books for children; however, several important initiatives are mentioned in the literature. The International Campus Book Link Project (ICBL) was created in 1992 by Book Aid International to support African university libraries through donations of current and back issues of academic journals, particularly in the area of medicine where the shortage is acute. In describing this project, Sharples notes that journals are particularly difficult materials to supply because of sustainability problems: many aid programmes are short term—three years at the most—and are dependent on fluctuating donations from institutions, not an ideal way to build a journal collection.

The Overseas Library Committee at the University of Calgary, Alberta was very active in the 1980s and early 1990s coordinating shipments of donated materials. As detailed in the *Canadian Library Journal* by King and Matheson, volunteer librarians gathered, sorted, boxed, and shipped scholarly and professional books and journals to universities, colleges and research corporations in China, Central America, Yemen, Bhutan, the West Indies and Africa. These volunteers clearly recognized the importance of communication between donor and recipient institutions. In this case, as in others identified in the literature, the motivating force for the volunteer librarians was a "feeling of professional solidarity, such as from one library to another." Books were not sent "on spec" to libraries in developing countries.

Instead, "inventory lists of donated materials [were] maintained and circulated to interested libraries, where selections were made by librarians. Only those items selected from the inventory list were sent." The project relied on the generosity of the Calgary corporate community, which provided free storage and sorting space, and arranged for free shipping of boxes. However, an economic downturn in the 1990s jeopardized corporate sponsorship, resulting in cancellation of the project.

Jan Lyall focuses on the preservation crisis in research archives and libraries in her *IFLA Journal* article. She cites the need for funding projects to preserve the audiotape and film that historians used to record the oral traditions of many South Pacific nations. Given the general lack of written cultures in this area, these media were very appropriate for information gathering, but their short life span in a tropical climate makes them an archival/library nightmare. Palm leaf manuscripts are another medium of concern in Southeast Asian countries: the leaves themselves are disintegrating, along with the disappearance of the skill to write and read the traditional script of most of the manuscripts. Lyall notes further that the political climate, as well as the physical, is an important factor in this crisis.

Governments in many developing countries are coping with cash shortages, health emergencies, and political strife and instability. As a consequence, they allocate a very low or non-existent priority to libraries, making the largesse of donors to fill this gap crucial. An example of such assistance is the "Preservation of Lao Manuscripts" project, funded entirely by the German government through the "Memory of the World Programme" launched by UNESCO. Its purpose is "to focus world attention on the need to safeguard endangered and unique library and archives collections, and to improve their accessibility to people of the world."

Expertise, Education, and Training

The practice of importing of experts from afar is also discussed in the literature, with most authors stressing that this approach neglects to address the problem of self-sufficiency, and does not promote long-term commitment and sustainability. Kari Gulbraar in the *Scandinavian Library Quarterly* emphasizes the importance of high caliber and accessible library education programmes within developing countries as the alternative to the visiting expert.. She relates the story of the Grace Lema Foundation, started in Tanzania by the Norwegian Library Association, and named after an untrained but experienced library assistant who was unable to enroll at the University of Botswana because she lacked financial resources. A member of the Norwegian Library Association International Committee supported her cause and through donations financed Lema's two-year programme.

Building on this initial success, the Association established a continuing fund to support library training within a developing country. This initiative was recognized as a model for library education aid at a 1994 IFLA Conference. Gulbraar also explains the other methods by which Scandinavian library agencies support education: supporting in-service training courses in Asia and the Pacific, funding scholarships to African, Asian and Latin American librarians for short-term visits to Swedish libraries and cultural institutions, and subsidizing librarians from developing countries to attend international workshops and conferences.

Brush reiterates the importance of indigenous training programmes geared to specific situations and the use of locally relevant methodologies when he relates his experiences as a library consultant in Laos. He attributes most errors in the bibliographic records to cultural and language misinterpretations caused by the librarians' attempts to apply cataloguing systems that are rooted in American culture – Dewey Decimal Classification and Library of Congress Subject Headings – to radically different situations. Brush believes that "visiting experts" would be well advised to promote British librarian Ronald Benge's philosophy expressed in his Cultural Crisis and Libraries in the Third World: "Librarians in developing countries would be better advised to follow the spirit of our librarianship, rather than our cataloguing rules..."

Recommendations for Further Study

This review has highlighted research reports and descriptive articles that address two questions: what are the major needs of libraries in developing countries and, how effectively are those needs being met?

It is apparent from these reports and articles that there are varying degrees of success regarding library aid projects: some address the problems and issues inherent within library aid initiatives and the general donor-recipient relationship, while the effectiveness of others is questionable. The literature indicates that when donors place a high priority on good communication; seek to understand and respect the indigenous culture, language and customs; and learn about the climatic, economic and political challenges that local librarians and publishers face, projects are more likely to succeed. Reports by those in the field show that when donor agencies follow Book Aid International's new slogan: "Give us what we need, not what you don't want" when providing demand-led services to developing countries, the match between donor largesse and library need is much closer.

Another recurring theme in the literature is the problem of short-term aid. Too often, financial and materials aid is "single-event," with no prior communication, no follow-up, and no opportunity for the recipient librarian to do long-term (or even 2-year!) collection management. To ensure that developing countries really benefit from assistance, commitment for long-term support is necessary.

This literature review reveals that globalization of information has created a double-hook for developing countries: library clients are aware of cultural sources from around the world, but these resources are often less relevant than indigenous ones. Continuing reliance on donated international resources hampers creation of a local publishing industry and precipitates loss of the local culture. There appears to be a gap in the literature regarding the impact of burgeoning globalization on library aid – how has this phenomenon affected the relevance of donations? How has it affected communication between donors and recipients, a crucial factor in the success of library aid projects? How can the negative aspects of globalization be minimized and the positive aspects increased within the donor/recipient relationship?

What is most lacking in the literature, however, is a corpus of in-depth research on this topic. As evident from this review, a wealth of articles exists describing Third World library needs from the point of view of the recipient and the objectives. Many articles also detail individual projects and the fund-raising efforts behind them. Missing are the research surveys and case studies that evaluate library aid in terms of a set of identified needs, and research that examines the changing needs of libraries as cultural and economic globalization advances.

The forces of globalization that move us ever closer to a single world society – mass communications, increased ease of travel, commerce, the Internet, popular culture, and the increasingly widespread use of English as an international language – must be included as variables in future research projects. Without these projects, we will not move knowledge in this area beyond opinion pieces to the reliable research results that will better inform the relations of donors and recipients. According to Lester Asheim (whose words introduced this review), "foreign relations are, after all, only human relations complicated by some geographical and some psychological distances. I think, with patience and understanding, we are equal to the challenge – and the opportunity – they present." Clearly, in order to develop effective programmes that make a difference within the new global economy and information world, further research on the challenges and opportunities of library aid is needed.

6

Modern Libraries

INTRODUCTION

The information age is here with many challenges and risks for the information generator and the information disseminator. The challenges before libraries and information centres are manifold. The main challenge will emerge from the expected change in the very nature of future libraries and information centres.

Library Scenario in India

The diversity of the Indian library scenario is an important aspect for consideration while speaking about a vision for the 3rd millennium, since different library sectors in India are in various stages of development and no single solution or approach will be relevant in the Indian situation.

Indian library and information sector can be divided into five major areas: the National Library sector; Academic library sector; the Special and Scientific library sector, Government library sector; and the Public library sector due to various factors the scientific and special library sector is much more developed and modernized than the other four sectors.

The challenges which Indian libraries and librarians will encounter in the 3rd millennium are manifold but the most important challenge will be the change in the very nature of libraries and librarians *i.e.*, the libraries must change from collection oriented institutions to service oriented organisations and librarians have to change from custodians of books and documents to information managers and disseminators. In this changing scenario IT will play the most important role. While taking advantage of the different components of information technology the libraries of each sector will have to ensure the following:

1. take stock of the actual need of the library and its users;
2. bring about change in the functions of the library to make it service oriented rather than collection oriented;
3. resource sharing and networking of libraries;
4. consider both preservation and access as vital components of library service;
5. marketing of information and library services;
6. development of library professionals to cope with the new environment;
7. utilization of management techniques for dealing with the new objectives.

At the decision-making level India will need a National Policy for libraries and information centres within the changed socio-economic environment keeping in mind the new requirements of the different sectors within the field of librarianship. It will now be worthwhile to analyze the present Library and Information scenario before preparing a vision for the 3rd millennium in each sector of librarianship in India.

The National Library Sector

The National Library sector in India can be divided into two types of libraries. The first one comprises the National Library, Calcutta and the recipient Public libraries under the Delivery of Books Act *i.e.,* Delhi Public Library (DPL), Connemara Public Library, Chennai and the State Central Library, Mumbai. These are the depositories of the printed cultural heritage of India under the Delivery of Books Act.

The depository libraries are a very important part of the National Library sector because India is a very vast and multi-lingual country with rich linguistic heritage. The 3rd millennium will have to see the cooperation between all these four libraries with the National Library at the apex. This can only be implemented if all these libraries are modernized at the same scale and have compatible systems to ensure resource sharing and networking. As these are financed by the Department of Culture (DoC) of the Government of India (GoI), the standards for modernization laid down by the DoC will be applicable to all these libraries.

The other part comprises the National level subject specific libraries such as National Science Library, National Medical Library, etc. In both these parts the National Library stands out as the largest single library which acts as the depository as well as the repository of all published material of India.

The 20th century saw the development of all these national level libraries in isolation. The main challenge in the 3rd millennium in the national library sector would be to bring about close coordination between all these national level subject libraries and the National Library of India.

Academic Library Sector

The Academic library sector comprises school and college and the university libraries. While evolving a vision for university libraries for the millennium, the main focus should be on the role of the existing university library in addressing the national issues. Since most university libraries in India work in isolation some information need to be collected and collated before preparing such a perspective plan.

1. Data regarding the actual functioning of the library, its collection, user approach, library facilities, IT application status, library manpower status, etc.
2. A national agency may be identified for undertaking this work.

A major aspect of the new millennium will be cooperation at all levels starting from the local to the global level. Cooperation is a pre-requisite for all types of networking for resource sharing. Therefore, the following must be ensured before preparing the plan for linkages between university libraries.

1. Institutional commitment to accept the given measures.
2. Fund and support resource sharing solution.

3. Attitudinal changes in library staff to undertake additional responsibility in resource sharing environment.
4. Training of library staff to understand and appreciate the changed situation.

If these pre-requisites are made available the university libraries could plan for resource sharing programmes, apprenticeship in libraries for learning new skills and IT training programmes, consultancy in retro-conversion and in developing IT infrastructure. All these put together will be the basis of preparing a perspective plan and evolve a vision for university libraries in the country.

School and College Libraries

Excepting very high brow private schools, most schools in India do not have a library per se in the present situation. This area of librarianship is very neglected and needs immediate and continuous attention. As regards college libraries, most colleges have libraries but other than very well known colleges in each state, the ordinary colleges do not run libraries of any consequence. Therefore, India faces the challenges of actually preparing a perspective plan from scratch *i.e.*, from collection development to networking through IT solutions, and will need a complete blueprint to develop these two types of libraries during the coming centuries.

India has set up the Information and Library Network (INFLIBNET) under the University Grants Commission (UGC) as the inter-university agency on library modernization to take the initiative and address the issues required to implement the perspective plan for the Academic sector. Each university and its affiliated college libraries also should be part of the overall scheme of development.

Distance Education

India has developed a well organized distance learning system through the Indira Gandhi National Open University (IGNOU) to achieve a high percentage of educated citizens as a prelude to an ultimate knowledge based society. The diversity and geographical distance of India need a strong, well-planned distance learning system for all citizens of the country. To make distance learning worthwhile the information base of the library sector will be equally responsible to be able to cater to the information need of Indians different societal levels. IGNOU has started some unique services for students with the help of IT but unless the rich collection of reading material available in different libraries in India are accessible to the younger generation the aim of distance learning gets nullified. Therefore, the academic sector has to be so inter-connected that it will also cater to distance learners.

Public Library Sector

The Public library system in India has developed over the years for more than a century, initially under the patronage of the aristocracy. However, the new independent India which developed a democratic society, recognised the need for public libraries which will work for the common good and will build a strong foundation for a democratic set up.

According to the Constitution of India, Public library development is a State responsibility. Therefore, all states are vested with the mandate to set up libraries within the state at different levels. But due to the diversity in the level of state-wise development, the Department of Culture, Government of India has set up Raja Rammohun Roy Library Foundation (RRRLF) to act as a nodal agency for development of public libraries in India.

Though library legislation is almost a pre-requisite, all the Indian states have not yet passed the library legislation. Therefore, RRRLF is also working towards a model Public Library Bill which may be able to encompass all the facets needed for development of public libraries to suit the new changing environment. Moreover, in the rural sector the local governments have been made responsible and accountable for the development of public library facilities through new constitutional amendments. Also, the Central Government is taking well-considered steps to make dissemination of information the main activity in all sectors which deal with rural and social development.

The 3rd millennium will see a drastic change which will ensure cooperation and collaborative efforts between the information generating agencies (whether government or NGOs) and the libraries and the information dissemination sector. The government is seriously considering to bring about conceptual change in the rural library sector by coordinating its activities along with the continuing education schemes of the National Literacy Mission (NLM).

The RRRLF has also been given the responsibility of resource mobilization for modernisation of the state and district central libraries, the development of infrastructure and training of personnel. The Department of Culture through the Central Secretariat Library (CSL) has laid down standards for library development software and networking as well as for bibliographic description to ensure standardization both in infrastructural development as well as retro-conversion of library catalogue in machine readable format.

Government Libraries

Government libraries in India were developed mainly during the British period to cater to the needs of the decision-makers and the bureaucrats. These libraries have always been institutionalised within the departments of the government. All these departmental and ministerial libraries have collected government documents mainly of their respective department/ministry and have restricted their acquisition to the need of the departmental staff alone. The Central Secretariat Library (CSL) has, however, worked within a broader spectrum being the main library in the ministerial and bureaucratic set up.

During the last 50 years some of the government libraries have been developed into well-organised collections which can cater to an informed clientele. Since government information started being handled by the National Informatics Centre (NIC), the use of information technology became the key word in the government sector. The Department of Culture, which is the nodal agency for library development in India, has taken viable steps towards resource sharing and networking of the libraries under its supervision. This includes the National Library, Calcutta, Central Secretariat Library and National Archives of India library, libraries under the Archaeological Survey of India and the Anthropological Survey of India, etc.

Special and Scientific Libraries

The special libraries and the libraries under Science and Technology group are in a much better developmental stage compared to the other four sectors. A good number of these libraries use current IT products and systems like computers, email, CD.ROMs and online storing and retrieval. Libraries and information centres of research institutions such as those under Council of Scientific and Industrial Research (CSIR), Defence Research and Development Organisation (DRDO), Indian Council of Agricultural Research (ICAR), Indian Council of Medical Research (ICMR), Department of Atomic Energy (DAE), Indian Space and Research Organisation (ISRO), Department of Science & Technology (DST) and Institutes of higher learning like the Indian Institutes of Technology (IITs), Indian Institute of Science (IIS), Indian National Science Academy (INSA), Indian Institutes of Management (IIMs), are modernized and have been given the necessary resources for development.

Library Networks

Other than INFLIBNET, there are a number of networks which have developed in the past decade. These are either city networks or activity subject specific networks. Developing Libraries Network (DELNET), Calcutta Library Network (CALIBNET), Madras Library Network (MALIBNET), Management Library Network, etc., are important and useful ventures for networking and resource sharing. Future of Library Development and the Challenges in the 3rd Millennium The details given above actually picturizes the latest situation encountered by Indian librarianship till the end of the last millennium.

The main challenge in the Indian situation is to visualise the present situation and bring about changes so as to nullify the observations made in the World Information Report, 1997-98, which are as follows:

- The bulk of the population is not information-dependent in day-to-day work and living.
- A large proportion of the population cannot consume information, especially if it is delivered in written form.

- The vast majority of the population does not have the means to access information.
- People in general are not accustomed to pay, cannot pay or are unwilling to pay for information. In fact, information does not even figure in their list of wants.
- The existing pattern of economic activities does not favour a growth in information consumption.
- The countries do not have sufficient capacity to invest in infrastructural development

Therefore, the future of Indian librarianship lies in descending from its ivory tower of catering to only a select few and the literate minority and to create a system which will penetrate into the actual information need of the majority of Indian people. So, there has to be a major paradigm shift to deal with the information needs of the vast majority of the population who at present do not have means to access information. Specially, the public library system in the country needs to be rejuvenated and re-modelled to cope with the present situation and the future trends.

There will be need to change the following on a broad-based basis in all types of libraries:

a. Library environment

b. Fragmented and isolated services

c. Organisational structure

d. Library collection

e. Information based infrastructure

f. Information and knowledge management

The first step towards this direction has been taken to a certain extent as the Report of the Working Group of the Planning Commission on Libraries and Informatics for the 9th Five Year Plan 1997-2002 addresses some of the challenges which confront Indian librarianship The Challenges and Risks for Librarians and Information Specialists in the 3rd Millennium The biggest challenge for Indian librarianship is to bring about attitudinal change among both library staff and users. Libraries and librarians are still the lowest priority in the decision making process and the librarians are the least visible persons. If this main challenge is confronted by librarians and libraries in real earnest it is only then that one can expect all the necessary changes within the system itself.

Libraries will also have to cope with the initiatives developed in the society in the changed IT environment. Libraries can no longer afford to remain institutionalized passive spectators. All the activities will now have to be tailored to give long distance and often home delivered information.

Opportunities and Risks

The new millennium will open up unprecedented opportunities for information professionals. Employers will no longer look for the traditional career requirements but a flexible work force which can take on different roles and responsibilities as and when required. In this context the following changes are to be brought about in India:

1. Change the teaching curricula in the field of library and information science.
2. Utilize the traditional expertise and apply them effectively in the new situations by understanding the actual requirements and applying these skills.
3. Content generation to suit the new fields of study with the help of IT.
4. Play the role of information managers by utilizing the new technology to give access to the rich resources available in libraries.

Tomorrows information professionals will be knowledge navigators instead of information collectors. In the Indian situation the new generation of librarians will have to face these challenges and risks to remain in the information business in all the sectors. Inter-changeability and capabilities to adjust from one sector to the other will be the biggest challenge for Indian librarians.

National Policy for the New Millennium

To fructify all that has been stated above there is a felt need to frame a National Policy of Libraries and Information Systems and Services, suited to the new environment. The DoC had framed a National Policy on Library and Information System (NAPLIS) during the late 1980s which is a very good foundation for preparing a new policy which will encompass the futuristic viewpoints for the library sector as a whole. It has to spell out all relevant issues, challenges, threats and opportunities which are envisioned for the new millennium.

India is on the threshold of major changes which will be possible only if a worthwhile and modern information system is set up at the right time, with the help of right infrastructure and is administered by the right type of qualified people.

Glossary

Accession: The act and procedures involved in taking records or papers into physical and legal custody by an archival agency or manuscript repository. The purpose is to extend basic control over a collection as quickly as possible to prevent its being confused or mixed with other material in custody. 2. The materials involved in such a transfer of custody.

Acid: A substance capable of forming hydrogen ions when dissolved in water. Acids can weaken cellulose in paper, board, and cloth, leading to embrittlement. Acids may be introduced in the manufacture of library or archival material. Acids may also be introduced by migration from other materials or from atmospheric pollution.

Address: An identifier that specifies the source or destination of IP packets and that is assigned at the IP layer to an interface or set of interfaces.

Alkaline Buffer: Alkaline substances, which have a pH of over 7.0, may be added to materials to neutralize acids or as an alkaline reserve or buffer for the purpose of counteracting acids that may form in the future. A buffer may be added during manufacture or during the process of deacidification. A number of chemicals may be used as buffers, but the most common are magnesium carbonate and calcium carbonate.

APIPA : See Automatic Private IP Addressing.

Archives: The noncurrent records of an organization or institution preserved because of their continuing value; also referred to, in this sense, as archival materials or archival holdings. Or to use David B. Gracy's definition: Archives are the records, organically related, of an entity systematically maintained because they contain information of continuing value.

ARP : See Address Resolution Protocol.

ARP Cache : A table for each interface of static or dynamically resolved IPv4 addresses and their corresponding MAC addresses.

ASCII (American Standard Code for Information Interchange): A standard code designed by the American National Standards Institute (ANSI) to facilitate information interchange between unstandardized data processing and communications equipment. The code, consisting of eight bits including a parity bit, can represent a character set of 128 alphabetic, numeric, and special symbols.

Automatic Private IP Addressing : A feature in Windows Server 2003 and Windows XP that automatically configures a unique IPv4 address from the range 169.254.0.1 through 169.254.255.254 and a subnet mask of 255.255.0.0. APIPA is used when the Internet Protocol (TCP/IP) component is configured for automatic addressing, no DHCP server is available, and the Automatic Private IP Address alternate configuration option is chosen.

Calendar: A chronological arrangement or list with description for each document in a collection.

Classless Inter-Domain Routing (CIDR) : A technique for aggregating routes and assigning IPv4 addresses on the modern-day Internet. CIDR expresses address prefixes in the form of an address prefix and a prefix length, rather than in terms of the address classes that CIDR replaces.

Coalition for Networked Information (CNI): Formed by ARL, CAUSE, and EDUCOM in March 1990 to "advance scholarship and intellectual productivity" by promoting the provision of information resources on existing and future telecommunications networks and the linkage of research libraries to these networks and their respective constituencies.

Colon Hexadecimal Notation : The notation used to express IPv6 addresses. The 128-bit IPv6 address is divided into eight 16-bit blocks. Each block is expressed as a hexadecimal number, and adjacent blocks are separated by colons. Within each block, leading zeros are suppressed. An example of an IPv6 unicast address in colon hexadecimal notation is 2001:DB8:2A1D:48C:2AA:3CFF:FE21:81F9.

Commission on Preservation and Access (CPA): A non-profit organization incorporated in 1988 for the purpose of fostering development and supporting systematic and purposeful collaboration in order to ensure the preservation of the public and documentary universe in all formats and to provide equitable access to that information.

Conservation: The treatment of library or archival materials, works of art, or museum objects to stabilize them chemically or strengthen them physically, sustaining their survival as long as possible in their original form. Conservation implies the restoration of an item to a state close to the original by means of physical treatment. See also preservation.

Correspondence: Letters, postcards, memoranda, notes, printed e-mail, and any other form of addressed, written communications sent and received.

Council on Library Resources (CLR): A private operating foundation based in Washington, DC, which aims to assist libraries, especially academic and research libraries, to take advantage of emerging technologies to improve operational efficiencies and services for library users.

Cubic Foot: An archival term used to describe the quantity of a collection. A bankers box, or records centre carton, holds one cubic foot.

Deaccession: The process of removing material from the care and custody of an archives, either because the material has been reappraised and found to be unsuitable for the archives, or because the legal owner has requested its return, or because it has been agreed to transfer it to another repository. Deaccessioning is a serious matter which requires careful consideration and documentation because of legal ramifications and possible donor reaction.

Default Gateway : A configuration parameter for the Internet Protocol (TCP/IP) component that is the IPv4 address of a neighbouring IPv4 router. Configuring a default gateway creates a default route in the IPv4 routing table.

Default Route : A route that summarizes all possible destinations and is used for forwarding when the routing table does not contain any other more specific routes for the destination. For example, if a router or sending host cannot find a subnet route, a summarized route, or a host route for the destination, IP selects the default route. The default route is used to simplify the configuration of hosts and routers. For IPv4 routing tables, the default route is the route with the network destination of 0.0.0.0 and netmask of 0.0.0.0. For IPv6 routing tables, the default route has the address prefix::/0.

Deposit Agreement and Instrument of Transmittal: A legal document that designates The University of Texas at Arlington Libraries as official depository for the records of a labour union, which are to be donated at scheduled intervals. The agreement permits the union to retain ownership of its records or to transfer ownership to the university. The agreement may be amended or terminated at any time by mutual consent. Both the union representative and a university representative must sign and date the agreement.

Description: The process of establishing intellectual control over holdings through the preparation of finding aids.

Direct Delivery : The delivery of an IP packet by an IP node to the final destination on a directly attached subnet.

Disposal: Removal of an item, or items, in a collection following the appraisal process.

Distance Vector : A routing protocol technology that propagates routing information in the form of an address prefix and its "distance" (hop count).

Donation: A voluntary deposit of records involving the transfer of legal ownership, as well as custody, to the archives.

Dotted Decimal Notation : The notation most commonly used to express IPv4 addresses. The 32-bit IPv4 address is divided into four 8-bit blocks. Each block is expressed as a decimal number, and adjacent blocks are separated by periods. An example of an IPv4 unicast address in dotted decimal notation is 131.107.199.45.

Double Colon : The practice of compressing a single contiguous series of zero blocks of an IPv6 address to "::". For example, the multicast address FF02:0:0:0:0:0:0:2 is expressed as FF02::2.

Ead: Encoded archival description.. EAD is a nonproprietary encoding standard for machine-readable finding aids.

Educational and General Expenditures (E&G): The sum of total institutional expenditures for instruction, research, public service, academic support, student services, institutional support, operation and maintenance of plant, scholarships and fellowships, mandatory transfers, and (in recent years) non-mandatory transfers.

Encapsulation; Polyester Encapsulation: A protective enclosure for papers and other flat materials that involves placing the item between two sheets of transparent polyester film that are then sealed around all the edges. The object is physically supported and protected from the atmosphere, although it may continue to deteriorate within the capsule. It can be removed easily from the capsule by cutting one or more of the edges of the polyester. Ideally an item should be deacidified before it is encapsulated.

EUI-64 Address : A 64-bit link-layer address that is used as a basis for an IPv6 interface identifier.

Extended Unique Identifier : A link-layer address defined by the Institute of Electrical and Electronics Engineers (IEEE).

Finding Aids: The descriptive media, published and unpublished, created by establishing physical, administrative, and intellectual control over records, papers, and collections.

Global Unicast Address : An IPv6 unicast address that is globally routable and reachable on the IPv6 portion of the Internet. IPv6 global addresses are equivalent to public IPv4 addresses.

GNP Deflator: An updated version of the general price index used to adjust the U.S. gross national product (GNP) for inflation.

Guide: A descriptive list of a repository's holdings.

Higher Education General Information Survey (HEGIS): The predecessor of the IPEDS surveys of post-secondary education institutions by the National Centre for Education Statistics, U.S. Department of Education.

Host : A node that is typically the source and a destination of IP traffic. Hosts silently discard received packets that are not addressed to an IP address of the host.

Host Route : A route to a specific IP address. Host routes allow packets to be routed on a per-IP address basis. For IPv4 host routes, the route prefix is a specific IPv4 address with a 32-bit prefix length. For IPv6 host routes, the route prefix is a specific IPv6 address with a 128-bit prefix length.

ICMP : See Internet Control Message Protocol.

IEEE : Institute of Electrical and Electronics Engineers.

IEEE 802 Address : A 48-bit link-layer address defined by the IEEE. Ethernet and Token Ring network adapters use IEEE 802 addresses.

IGMP : See Internet Group Management Protocol.

Illegal Address : A duplicate address that conflicts with a public IPv4 address that the ICANN has already assigned to another organization.

Indirect Delivery : The delivery of an IP packet by an IP node to an intermediate router.

Interface : The representation of a physical or logical attachment of a node to a subnet. An example of a physical interface is a network adapter. An example of a logical interface is a tunnel interface that is used to send IPv6 packets across an IPv4 network.

Internet Control Message Protocol (ICMP) : A protocol in the IPv4 Internet layer that reports errors and provides troubleshooting facilities.

Internet Control Message Protocol for IPv6 (ICMPv6): A protocol in the IPv6 Internet layer that reports errors, provides troubleshooting facilities, and hosts ND and MLD messages.

Internet Group Management Protocol (IGMP) : A protocol in the IPv4 Internet layer that manages multicast group membership on a subnet.

Internet Protocol (IP) : For IPv4, a routable protocol in the IPv4 Internet layer that addresses, routes, fragments, and reassembles IPv4 packets. Also used to denote both IPv4 and IPv6 sets of protocols.

IP : Features or attributes that apply to both IPv4 and IPv6. For example, an IP address is either an IPv4 address or an IPv6 address.

IPv4 **:** The Internet layer in widespread use on the Internet and on private intranets. Another term for IP.

IPv6 **:** The Internet layer protocols of the TCP/IP protocol suite as defined in RFC 2460. IPv6 is gaining acceptance today.

LAN segment **:** A portion of a subnet that consists of a single medium that is bounded by bridges or Layer 2 switches.

Lignin: A component of the cell walls of plants that occurs naturally, along with cellulose. It is largely responsible for the strength and rigidity of plants, but its presence in paper and board is believed to contribute to chemical degradation. It can be, to a large extent, removed during manufacture. No standards exist for the term "lignin free," and additional research is needed to determine the precise role of lignin in the durability and permanence of paper.

Linear Feet: 1. A measurement for descriptive and control purposes of shelf space occupied by archives, records, or manuscripts. For vertical files (records filed on edge), the total length of drawers, shelves, or other equipment occupied is calculated; in the case of material filed horizontally (flat or piled up), the total vertical thickness is used. Linear feet, except for card indexes, may be equated with cubic feet on a one-to-one basis for descriptions of textual records. 2. A measurement for descriptive and control purposes of length of film, tape, or microfilm. (Usually expressed as feet.)

Link State **:** A routing protocol technology that exchanges routing information consisting of a router's attached subnet prefixes and their assigned costs. Link state information is advertised upon startup and when changes in the network topology are detected.

Link-local Address **:** A local-use address with the prefix of FE80::/64 and whose scope is the local link. Nodes use link-local addresses to communicate with neighbouring nodes on the same link. Link-local addresses are equivalent to Automatic Private IP Addressing (APIPA) IPv4 addresses.

Local Address **:** An IPv6 address identified by the prefix FC00::/7. The scope of a Local address is an organization. Local addresses are reachable from other sites in an organization, but not from the IPv6 Internet.

Longest Matching Route : The algorithm used to select the routes in the routing table that most closely match the destination address of the packet being sent or forwarded.

Loopback Address : For IPv4, the address 127.0.0.1. For IPv6, the address 0:0:0:0:0:0:0:1 (or::1). Nodes use the loopback address to send packets to themselves.

Manuscript: A handwritten, typed, or electronically reproduced document or communication.

Marc Formats: The Library of Congress developed the MARC formats in the late 1960s for communication of bibliographic information in machine-readable form. These MARC (for Machine-Readable cataloging) formats identify bibliographic data for computer recognition and manipulation. In the mid-1970s as variations were developed, the formats used by the Library of Congress became known as "LC-MARC formats." Since the early 1980s, however, LC-MARC formats have come to be referred to as "USMARC formats" because they are standards for MARC records in the United States.

MARC: Derived from "machine-readable cataloguing," U.S. MARC is a standard for representation and communication of bibliographical and related information in machine-readable form.

Materials and Binding: Materials are expenditures for items purchased in a given time period, usually a fiscal year, to be added to a library's collections, including books (monographs), periodicals and other serials, microforms, audiovisual materials, and other library materials; also sometimes includes expenditures for electronic searching and other modes of access to information that is not added to library collections in traditional ways. Binding is expenditures for contract binding, usually by commercial binders.

Multicast Address : An address that identifies zero or multiple interfaces and is used to deliver packets from one source to many destinations. With the appropriate multicast routing topology, packets addressed to a multicast address are delivered to all interfaces identified by the address.

Multicast Listener Discovery (MLD) : A set of three ICMPv6 messages that hosts and routers use to manage multicast group membership on a subnet.

***Name Resolution* :** The process of resolving a name to an address.

***Neighbour* :** A node that is connected to the same subnet as another node.

***Neighbour Cache* :** A cache maintained by every IPv6 node that stores the IPv6 address of a neighbour and its corresponding MAC address. The neighbour cache is equivalent to the ARP cache in IPv4.

***Neighbour Discovery (ND)* :** A set of ICMPv6 messages and processes that determine relationships between neighbouring nodes. Neighbour Discovery replaces ARP, ICMP router discovery, and the ICMP Redirect message used in IPv4.

***NetBIOS* :** See Network Basic Input/Output System.

***Network* :** Two or more subnets that are connected by routers. Another term for network is internetwork.

***Network Address Translator (NAT)* :** An IPv4 router that translates addresses and ports when forwarding packets between a privately addressed network and the Internet.

***Network Basic Input/Output System (NetBIOS)* :** A standard API for user applications to manage NetBIOS names and access NetBIOS datagram and session services.

Neutral: Having a pH of 7; neither acid nor alkaline.

***Next-hop Determination* :** The process of determining the next-hop address and interface for sending or forwarding a packet, based on the contents of the routing table.

***Node* :** Any device, including routers and hosts, which runs an implementation of IP.

Online Computer Library Centre (OCLC): A not-for-profit organization serving over 15,000 member libraries worldwide, OCLC provides services such as cataloguing copy, interlibrary loan transactions, and retrospective conversion of bibliographic records. It has a bibliographic database currently in excess of 24 million unique bibliographic titles and 500 million items. It has expanded its services into reference, public services, and publishing.

Open Shortest Path First (OSPF) : A link state-based routing protocol for use within a single autonomous system. An autonomous system is a portion of the network under the same administrative authority.

Oral History Deed of Gift: A legal document transferring ownership of a taped interview from the interviewee to The University of Texas at Arlington Libraries, Special Collections Division. The deed of gift must be signed and dated by both the donor (interviewee) and the interviewer and by a university representative. Restrictions may be placed by the donor on the use of the interview.

Original Order: The order in which records and archives were kept when in active use. The principle of original order requires that this order be preserved or reconstructed, unless it is clear that there was no order or that the records had been accumulated haphazardly.

OSPF : See Open Shortest Path First (OSPF).

Other Operating Expenditures: Any expenditures other than those for materials, binding, and salaries and wages, from a library's budget during a given time period.

Packet : The protocol data unit (PDU) that exists at the Internet layer and comprises an IP header and payload.

Path Vector : A routing protocol technology that exchanges sequences of hop information that indicate the path for a route. For example, BGP-4 exchanges sequences of autonomous system numbers.

Permanent/Durable Paper: A term generally applied to pH neutral papers.

Personal Papers: The documents accumulated by an individual or a family.

Polyester: A common name for the plastic polyethylene terephthalate. Its characteristics include transparency, colorlessness, and high tensile strength. Polyester is useful in preservation because it is chemically stable. Commonly used in sheet or roll form to make folders, encapsulations, and book jackets. Its thickness is measured in mils. Common trade names are Mylar by DuPont and Mellinex by ICI.

Prefix Length Notation : The practice of expressing address prefixes as *StartingAddress/PrefixLength*, in which *PrefixLength* is the number of high-order bits in the address that are fixed.

Preservation: Activities associated with maintaining library, archival, or museum materials for use, either in their original physical form or in some other format. Preservation is considered a broader term than conservation. See also conservation.

Private Addresses : IPv4 addresses that organizations use for private intranet addressing within one of the following address prefixes: 10.0.0.0/8, 172.16.0.0/12, 192.168.0.0/16.

Processing: The operations performed on materials to make a collection available for use.

Public Addresses : IPv4 addresses that are assigned by the ICANN and that are guaranteed to be globally unique and reachable on the IPv4 Internet.

Records: All recorded information, regardless of media or characteristics, made or received and maintained by an organization or institution in pursuance of it legal obligations or in the transaction of its business.

Request for Comments (RFC): An official document that specifies the details for protocols included in the TCP/IP protocol suite. The Internet Engineering Task Force (IETF) creates and maintains RFCs for TCP/IP.

Research Libraries Group (RLG): A not-for-profit membership corporation of over 120 libraries, archives, historical societies, museums and other institutions devoted to improving access to information that supports research and learning.

Research Libraries Information Network (RLIN): Owned and operated by RLG, RLIN serves the information access and management needs of its member institutions as well as individuals worldwide. It contains over 55 million bibliographic records.

Retrospective Conversion: The process of converting bibliographic records from print to a machine-readable format.

RFC : See Request for Comments (RFC).

RIP : See Routing Information Protocol (RIP).

Route Determination Process : The process of determining which single route in the routing table to use for forwarding a packet.

Route Summarization : The practice of using address prefixes to summarize the address spaces of regions of a network, rather than using the routes for individual subnets.

Router : A node that can be a source and destination for IP traffic and can also forward IP packets that are not addressed to an IP address of the router. On an IPv6 network, a router also typically advertises its presence and host configuration information.

Router Advertisement : For IPv4, a message sent by a router that supports ICMP router discovery. For IPv6, an IPv6 Neighbour Discovery message sent by a router that typically contains at least one Prefix Information option, from which hosts create stateless autoconfigured unicast IPv6 addresses and routes.

Router Discovery : A Neighbour Discovery process in which a host discovers the local routers on an attached subnet.

Routing Information Protocol (RIP) : A distance vector-based routing protocol used in small and medium sized networks.

Routing Protocols : A series of periodic or on-demand messages that contain routing information that is exchanged between dynamic routers.

Routing Table : The set of routes used to determine the next-hop address and interface for IP traffic sent by a host or forwarded by a router.

Salaries and Wages: All monies paid in salaries and wages from the library's budget during a given period of time before deductions for all staff paid.

Series: File units or documents arranged in accordance with a filing system or maintained as a unit because they relate to a particular subject or function, result from the same activity, have a particular form, or because of some other relationship arising out of their creation, receipt, or use. Also known as a record series.

Site-local Address : A local-use IPv6 address identified by the prefix FEC0::/10. The scope of a site-local address is a site. Site-local addresses are equivalent to the IPv4 private address space. Site-local addresses are not reachable from other sites, and routers must not forward site-local traffic outside the site.

Solicited-node Multicast Address : An IPv6 multicast address that nodes use to resolve addresses. The solicited-node multicast address is constructed from the prefix FF02::1:FF00:0/104 and the last 24 bits of a unicast IPv6 address. The solicited-node multicast address acts as a pseudo-unicast address to efficiently resolve addresses on IPv6 links.

Sorting: The process by which manuscripts are physically divided into appropriate alphabetical, chronological, numerical, subject, or other groups. Less frequently used with archives, except when restoring them to their original or intended order.

Static Routing : The use of manually configured routes in the routing tables of routers.

Subnet : One or more LAN segments that are bounded by routers and that use the same IP address prefix. Other terms for subnet are network segment and link.

Subnet Mask : The expression of the length of an address prefix for IPv4 address ranges in dotted decimal notation. For example, the address prefix 131.107.0.0/16 in subnet mask notation is 131.107.0.0, 255.255.0.0.

Subnetted Address Prefix : Either a new IPv4 address prefix that is the result of subnetting an IPv4 address prefix or a new IPv6 address prefix that is the result of subnetting an IPv6 address prefix.

Subnetting : The act of subdividing the address space of an IPv4 or IPv6 address prefix.

Subseries: An aggregate of file units within a record series readily separable in terms of physical class, type, form, subject, or filing arrangement.

Supernetting : The obsolete use of route summarization to assign blocks of Class C address prefixes on the Internet.

TCP : See Transmission Control Protocol.

TCP/IP : See Transmission Control Protocol/Internet Protocol (TCP/IP).

Textual Records: The term usually applied to manuscript or typescript, as distinct from cartographic, audiovisual, and machine-readable records and archives.

Total Library Expenditures (TLE): The sum of expenditures for materials, binding, salaries and wages, and other operating expenditures during a given period of time.

Transfer of Title: A legal document transferring ownership of a body of papers from one entity to another. The transfer of title must be signed and dated by the donor and by a university representative.

Transmission Control Protocol/Internet Protocol (TCP/IP) : A suite of networking protocols, including both IPv4 and IPv6, that are widely used on the Internet and that provide communication across interconnected networks of computers with diverse hardware architectures and various operating systems.

Unicast Address : An address that identifies a single interface and is used for delivering packets from one source to a single destination. With the appropriate unicast routing topology, packets addressed to a unicast address are delivered to a single interface.

Unspecified Address : For IPv4, the address 0.0.0.0. For IPv6, the address 0:0:0:0:0:0:0:0 (or::). The unspecified address indicates the absence of an address.

Upper-layer Protocol : A protocol above IP that uses IP as its transport. Examples of upper-layer protocols include Internet layer protocols such as the Internet Control Message Protocol (ICMP) and Transport layer protocols such as the Transmission Control Protocol (TCP) and User Datagram Protocol (UDP).

User Datagram Protocol (UDP) : An unreliable, connectionless Transport layer protocol that runs on top of IP.

UV Filter: A material used to filter the ultraviolet (UV) rays out of visible light. Ultraviolet radiation is potentially damaging to library, archival, and museum objects. More UV is present in sunlght and fluorescent light than in incandescent light. Removing UV radiation from storage, use, and exhibition spaces will reduce the rate of deterioration of library materials stored there.

Variable Length Subnet Masks (VLSMs) : The use of different subnet masks to produce subnets of different sizes.

Variable Length Subnetting : The practice of using variable length subnet masks.

Volume: A physical unit of any printed, typewritten, handwritten, mimeographed, or processed work, contained in one binding or portfolio, hardbound or paperbound, which has been catalogued, classified, and made ready for use. (The study follows the definition used by ARL.)

Volumes Added Gross: The volumes catalogued by a library during a given period, usually a fiscal year. Not to be confused with acquisitions, although sometimes considered a surrogate for them.

Windows Sockets : A commonly used application programming interface (API) that Windows applications use to transfer data using TCP/IP.

Zone ID : An integer that specifies the zone of the destination for IPv6 traffic. In the Ping, Tracert, and Pathping commands, the syntax for specifying a zone ID is *IPv6Address%ZoneID*. Typically, the *ZoneID* value for link-local addresses is equal to the interface index. For site-local addresses, *ZoneID* is equal to the site number. The *ZoneID* parameter is not needed when the destination is a global address or a Local address and when multiple sites are not being used.

Bibliography

Aparac-Gazivoda, T & K, Dragutin: *Wounded Libraries in Croatia*, Zagreb, Croatian Library Association, 1993.

Brichford, Maynard J.: *Archives and Manuscripts: Appraisal and Accessioning*, Chicago, Society of American Archivists, 1977.

Chan, L.M.: *Library of Congress Subject Headings: Principles and Application*, Colo, Libraries Unlimited, 1995.

Kearfott, R.B.: *Rigorous Global Search: Continuous Problems*, Dordrecht, Kluwer, 1996.

Khanna, J.K.: *Colon Classification*, New Delhi, Ess Ess Publications, 1986.

Lesly, Philip: *Lesly's Handbook of Public Relations and Communications*, AMACOM, 1991.

Neumaier, A.: *Interval Methods for Systems of Equations*, Cambridge, Cambridge University Press, 1990.

Saraswathi, T.S., and Baljit Kaur: *Human Development and Family Studies in India: An Agenda for Research and Policy*, New Delhi, Sage, 1993.

Seitel, Fraser P.: *The Practice of Public Relations*, Macmillan, 1994.

Taylor, Arlene G.: *The Organization of Information*, Englewood, Libraries Unlimited, 1999.

Taylor, Arlene G.: *Wynar's Introduction to Cataloging and Classification*, Westport, Libraries Unlimited, 2000.

Vatuk, Sylvia: *American Studies in the Anthropology of India*, New Delhi, Manohar, 1978.

Wynar, B.S.: *Introduction to Cataloguing and Classification*, Englewood, Libraries Unlimited, 1992.

Index

□□□

Art as Dialogue

Essays in Phenomenology of Aesthetic Experience

Goutam Biswas

Indira Gandhi National Centre for the Arts
New Delhi

D. K. Printworld (P) Ltd.
New Delhi

Cataloging in Publication Data — DK

Goutam Biswas.
Art as dialogue.
Includes bibliographical references.
Includes Index.

1. Phenomenology and art. 2. Aesthetics. 3. Philosophical Anthropology. 4. Art — Philosophy. I. Title.

ISBN 81-246-0043-0

First Published in India in 1995

Publishers :
Indira Gandhi National Centre for the Arts
Central Vista Mess, Janpath, New Delhi - 110001

D.K. Printworld (P) Ltd.
Regd. office : 'Sri Kunj', F-52, Bali Nagar, New Delhi-110015

Printed at: D.K. Fine Art Press (P) Ltd., Delhi

For

RANJU

and

RUNIMA

Foreword

Dr. Goutam Biswas's monograph is a companion volume to the earlier one entitled *Inter-Cultural Dialogue and the Human Image* based on the four lectures delivered and the discussion-seminar co-ordinated by Prof. Maurice Friedman focusing on Dialogue; the 'I-Thou' and the 'I-It' relationship. Time and again, Prof. Friedman draws attention to art and dialogue, and the relationship between the artist, the critic and the beholder on the one hand, and the art object, on the other. Dr. Goutam Biswas picks up the threads of this discussion and devotes a full volume to Art as Dialogue. These essays, although written independently as part of a Fellowship at the Indian Institute of Advanced Study, Shimla, have a very close and intrinsic relationship with the nature of discourse which took place during Prof. Friedman's visit to the Indira Gandhi National Centre for the Arts. Therefore it was only logical to include this monograph in the publication programme of Indira Gandhi National Centre for the Arts, since it is both relevant in its programme on cross-cultural studies as also in the Kalāsamālocana series where critical writings on the Arts is the focus of attention.

'Aesthetics' and artistic experience as a subject of enquiry has a long history, both in the East and the West. In India the discussion on the nature of the aesthetic experience from the point of view of the creator as also the receiver and relationships so established can be traced back to *Bhārata* and the *Nātyaśāstra*. The discourse has its inception in many ideas expounded in earlier literature but especially the *Upaniṣads* and the *Āraṇyakas*. From the sixth century onwards there was vibrant and complex debate on subject, object, name and form (*nāma* and *rūpa*). Also, the nature of the 'artistic creation' was minutely analysed. Many interpreters applied the basic tenets of the *darśanas* (philosophic schools) to comprehend the nature of experience, cognition, the art object, the resonance and the response in the spectator or the hearer. The exploration was on the totality of the relational dialogue between and amongst the creator, the created object and the beholder. However, all this emerged from a unified vision, a holistic perspective which saw all phenomenon as fundamentally inter-connected and inter-webbed. While differentiation was recognised, dichotomy was eschewed.

Against the background of a highly sophisticated tradition of dialogue in India, it is interesting and rewarding to find a different but equally relevant perspective on the subject in Dr. Goutam Biswas's volume. His concern is not to identify the commonalities or to emphasize the universals underlying different art forms. He also does not critically examine different theories of aesthetics and art experience. Instead, his concern centres around Martin Buber's concept of Art as Dialogue. As I have observed in the Foreword to the volume *Inter-Cultural Dialogue and the Human Image* the concern with Art as Dialogue was part of the larger and more fundamental exploration of the 'I-It' and 'I-Thou' dialogue. Moreover, both Martin Buber's reflection and now Dr. Goutam Biswas's work have to be juxtaposed against the immediately preceding postivistic discourse and notions of both 'objectivity' and the role of intellect and reason. The need to recognise relational values and even relational reality arose because of the unbridgeable chasm which has been created by the total dissociation of man from nature, of thing from person, of the inanimate from the animate and of the body from soul. The intrinsic relationship of the senses, emotion, intellect and consciousness was replaced by a paradigm of dualities and binary opposites. Resultantly in the realm of art, a-causal experience, process of artistic expression, the artistic product and communication were no longer seen within a continuum, or in dialogue. There was fragmentation. Art was not related to life and functionality. The artist became autonomous, and art a product. But art emerges from a unified state of experience where dualities and specificities are dissolved and transformed into a new whole. Understandably there were major attempts to re-establish these relationships and re-evoke wholeness. 'Dialogue and the Dialogical' was and is one such approach amongst others to refocus on the importance of process, of the in-between and the relational. The emphasis is on the 'I-Thou' rather than the 'I-It'. Such an approach echoes many concepts in Indian theories of art. As is well-known, according to some Indian theories the artistic experience arises in the consciousness of the 'artist' and is given form through artistic expression, that blossoms in the heart of the spectator.

Dr. Goutam Biswas takes us through an engaging journey on the nature of the discourse in the West, especially in modern philosophy — Sartre, Heidegger, Roman Ingarden and Mikel Dufrene — always keeping Martin Buber's work as the centrepiece. He also takes into account the work of scientist-philosophers like Maurice Merleau Ponty. He continues by exploring Rabindranath Tagore's philosophy of Art from a dialogical point of view especially his views on Personal Man and Artistic Truth. The journey concludes by examining Sarvepalli Radhakrishnan's phenomenology of Art and his notions on what constitutes artistic knowledge.

The guiding principles of the explorations of this universe of dialogue and the in-between is the dynamics of dialogue between the artistic experience and expression in language; and, dialogue preceding and surpassing language. However, dialogue cannot be restricted to language and is, without doubt, more encompassing. Dr. Goutam Biswas endeavours to comprehend art experience as dialogic in the sense of the pre-linguistic, linguistic and trans-linguistic aspects. Pertinently no closed theory of art is being propounded. Only the ideas of modern philosophers as also of Tagore and Radhakrishnan are being examined within the frame-work of phenomenology of dialogue. The five essays on the phenomenology of the aesthetic from diverse but interconnected points of view, provide very refreshing insights into the nature of the modern discourse on these perennial concerns. They also re-illuminate the discussions on the distinctions between the factual and the real, the specific and the universal, the speculative and scientific theories of truth; these facilitate re-thinking on the notion of intuition, intellect and knowledge. The two essays on Rabindranath Tagore and Radhakrishnan clearly demonstrate another way of viewing notions of truth and beauty, and of recognising intuition also as a significant category of knowledge.

A reading of these essays will, it is hoped, prepare our readers to receive yet another volume on the subject from the pen of A.K. Coomaraswamy's *Transformation of Nature into Art*. A.K. Coomaraswamy too examines these categories but from a very different standpoint and a different language of discourse. The perusal of a revised edition of the 'Transformation of Nature into Art' (under publication by IGNCA) will enable our readers to see the convergences between the modern dialogical frame-work and the reflections on the subject by the exponents of traditional theories of Art in Asia, particularly India and China as also those of one stream of European thought. A discerning reader will easily observe that there have been and are perennial concerns in many streams of thought. In India, reflections on the nature of the artistic act reached an unparalleled degree of sophistication at its stage of 'experience', prelinguistic unformed (*arūpa*), the process of manifestation in artistic form or forms (*rūpa* and *pratirūpa*) and the evocation of an experience through the very specificity of the form (*rūpa*), which transcends form (*parārūpa*). The theories of Chuang Hao of the Tang period in China, those of Zeami in Japan are close parallels and are echoed in the Christian scholastic tradition, particularly those of Meister Eckhert, St. Augustine and St. Aquinas. Since all art tends towards creating a perfect dialogue between the mind of the artist, the formal language of art and the resonance in the spectator, it has been compared to a mystical experience of perfect concord and thus comprehended as the work of God in the Islamic and Christian traditions. The master Chiah Tzu Yuan had exclaimed "when a painting has reached divinity (*shên*) there is the end of the matter". St. Thomas believed "it is of the essence of art to bring back into order the multiplicity of Nature and it is on this sense that it prepares all creatures to return to God". The language of discourse of these traditional masters may at first sight appear different and remote from that of the disciplines of modern philosophy, phenomenology or even semiotics yet in essence, it is an endeavour to re-establish the whole and to re-open the dialogue of 'relational thinking' beyond the 'I-It', to the 'I-Thou'.

IGNCA seeks to identify these diverse perceptions and tools in cultures, historical periods and disciplines, all with a view to expand this area of knowledge and the depth of dialogue.

We are thankful to Dr. Goutam Biswas for having offered his manuscript to the IGNCA.

I would also like to record my appreciation of the willing help and assistance of Prof. B.N. Saraswati, Prof. S.C. Malik and the co-publisher in the production of the monograph.

December 14, 1994 **KAPILA VATSYAYAN**

New Delhi

Acknowledgements

A PART of this work was conceived and written during a Fellowship at the Indian Institute of Advanced Study, Shimla. I tender my sincere thanks to the Institute for offering me the Fellowship and hosting me in the beautiful silence of Shimla hills. The work was further revised, altered and enlarged after my return to the University of North Bengal. I should like to record in this connection my unreturnable debt to Prof. Pabitra Kumar Roy for introducing me to the domain of aesthetics and inspiring me to get into this particular project.

My meeting with Maurice S. Friedman, Professor Emeritus of San Diego State University and a chief exponent of the Philosophy of Dialogue at Indira Gandhi National Centre For the Arts, New Delhi in January 1992 benefited me immensely to pursue Martin Buber's Phenomenology of Dialogue and from Philosophical Anthropology to Aesthetics. I am highly indebted to him. I express my deepest gratitude to Dr. Kapila Vatayayan, Academic Director, IGNCA, for giving me this opportunity to publish this work by the Centre, and agreeing to write the Foreword.

I am extremely thankful to Prof. B.N. Saraswati of the Indira Gandhi National Centre for the Arts, New Delhi, for his keen interest in the publication of this book.

My sincere thanks are due to Ms Emu Foning, State Institute of Education, Government of Sikkim for going through some major part of the manuscript and suggesting corrections.

I am indebted to my friends Rekha Jhanji, S. A. Sayeed, Bijoy Boruah, V.K. Bharadwaj and Chinmoy Goswami for discussing some important issues and sharpening my arguments.

I am deeply indebted to my mother Mrs. Nilima Sarkar, Prof. S. C. Malik, U.G.C. Research Scientist in Anthropology, Nehru Memorial Museum & Library and Prof. S.A. Shaida of A.M.U., Deptt. of Philosophy, whose constant encouragement led to the completion of the manuscript. I am also thankful to Prof. Malik for taking care of the editorial aspects of the Mss. and getting it ready for publication. To Shri Susheel Mittal of D.K. Printworld, for expediting this publication, my thanks.

However, for any shortcoming in the matter presented here I alone am responsible.

Goutam Biswas

Contents

Introduction

THE phenomenology of aesthetic experience marks a significant direction of thinking in the history of modern philosophy. The writings of Moritz Geiger, Jean-Paul Sartre, Raymond Polin, Martin Buber, Martin Heidegger, Maurice Merleau-Ponty, and others have contributed immensely towards phenomenological formulations of issues and insights relating to art and aesthetics. Sedulous research in this area has produced seminal works like that of Roman Ingarden and Mikel Dufrenne.[1] The realisation that a philosophy of art without an account and analysis of aesthetic experience is inadequate and lifeless is because of this trend of thought and research. Doubts concerning the general philosophical assumption that an object without an actual or possible reference to experience is abstract, and experience without any content is empty seem to make no sense and are philosophically unproductive. Phenomenologically speaking, experience consists in the directedness of consciousness upon some object, be it an object of cognition, emotion or imagination. The expression of any experience is dependent upon the way consciousness is related to the object. A scientific formula or theory is an expression of some experience of an object or phenomenon. The universe of discourse that is shaped by this scientific method stands apart from the universe of discourse that is formulated by artistic experience and expression. Philosophy not only synthesises different types of experience according to the different ways consciousness is related to its object — and thereby envisages a general theory of experience at various levels — but it also explores into the uniqueness of each type and imbibes insights from it. Keeping the latter task of philosophy in mind, art experience is visualized as an important area of study for the philosopher.

Today, the triad of consciousness, aesthetic object and art expression, therefore, determines the scope of a philosophy of art. Art experience is definitely the primal source of this philosophy, since it is an exudation of consciousness from the cloister of its privacy to the world. This is why embalming works of art in archives has little to contribute to any philosophy of art. Heidegger admitted that all works of art do have a "thingly character" and they are "shipped like coal from the Ruhr and logs from the Black Forest". But, he said, "shippers or chairwomen in museums may operate with such conceptions of the work of art. We, however, have to take works as they are encountered by those who experience and enjoy them".[2] Sartre would perhaps agree that works of art in archives or museums are **beings-in-themselves**, unencountered, and susceptible to oblivion. This is the reason for which he held that a work of art is 'unreal' as compared to an object or **being-in-itself** which is 'real'. "There is no realisation of the imaginary, nor can we speak of its **objectification**. Each stroke of the brush was not made **for itself** nor even for the constructing of coherent real whole (in the sense in which it can be said that a certain lever in a machine was conceived in the interest of the whole and not for itself). It was given together with an unreal synthetic whole and the aim of the artist was to construct a whole of real colours which enable this unreal to manifest itself."[3] But a work of art as something unreal paradoxically becomes very real for human consciousness as it promises an escape from superfluity and contingency of our day-to-day empirical world. Perhaps Sartre's commitment to a dualistic ontology of **being-for-itself** (*Pour-soi*, human subjectivity) and **being-in-itself** (*En Soi*, object) did not permit him to ascribe any reality to art objects. But his contention implies that they enjoy a privileged status, a sort of reality with a difference.

Taking the clue from Sartrean ontology of **being-for-itself** and **being-in-itself** Dufrenne assigns a quasi-subjectivity to aesthetic object with a revelation of 'for itself' in it. He says: "The aesthetic object bears its meaning within itself and is a world unto itself. We can understand this kind of object only by remaining close to it and constantly coming back to it. Because it illuminates itself in this way, it is like a for-itself. Or rather it is like a for-itself of the in-itself, that is, a taking up of the in-itself into the for-itself. The aesthetic object is luminous through its very opacity — not by receiving an alien light by which a world is outlined, but by making its own light spring from itself in the act of expression. Thus we shall call the aesthetic object a 'quasi-subject'."[4]

The conception of an aesthetic object as a 'quasi-subject' leads to the problem regarding the ontological status of art objects. While art objects act and exist as **beings-for-themselves**, contribute to and enrich the human experiential perspective in a way so that they can be differentiated from their mere physical factual being (as human subjects are distinguished from their dead bodies) they at the same time retain their identity as separate from artists, beholders and critics, i.e., from human subjects. This problem seems to be unresolvable and the unique mode of existence of art objects appears inexplicable. But it is so only in the context of an ontological bifurcation of aesthetic experience into the subject of such experience and its object. Concepts of dialogue and communion may be invoked in this case to suggest an alternative ontology. In dialogue the 'space' between the experiencing being and that which is experienced becomes ontologically significant. I should like to suggest that art experience is basically a dialogue between the creator, the beholder and the critic on the one hand, and the art object on the other. The understanding of an art object is possible within this experiential context which is constituted by the relational sphere or the 'space' between **I** (the artist, beholder, critic) and **thou** (the art object). The primary task of the phenomenology of aesthetic experience could then be one of showing the way to a transcendence of the disjunction of subjectivity and objectivity in art, and of explicating the nature of dialogue and communion not only as a means of this transcendence but also as an end, i.e., the consummation of art experience. This work is an attempt to perform this task.

The practice of dialogue can be comprehended in two different ways, viz. as **dialogue in language**, and as **dialogue preceding and overpassing language**. With the former the scope of interpretation and understanding of a phenomenon of art is limited because interpretative activity, in this case, cannot break through the conceptual barrier of language as a mediating factor in recreating and re-enacting the artist's experience or articulating one's own aesthetic experience. By 'language' I understand any kind of symbol or sign which is an exteriorization of a form of relationship between man and reality. But when language becomes a definite social institution with conceptual, semantic, and syntactic constraints involved in it, it can hardly be generous to art activities wherein a suspension of the commoner's mode of cognizing the reality and silence play a major role. One can say that the language of art is an obvious deviation from empirical, ordinary language but not by fully relinquishing the garb of ordinary language. The language of art carries a deeper and newer meaning than that is traceable in language which is more an instrument and less an expression of being. In dialogue, being is, in Buber's language, 'relation's own being' and the meaning of dialogic communication or expression can be gathered from this relational sphere of **I-Thou**. Aesthetic meaning and communication which, according to the contention of this book, is dialogic by nature springs from this experiential realm. Silence or suspension of verbalism is its initial insignia. Following S. N. Ganguly we can say, 'Silence', in this context, is to be taken in the Indian sense of *Śāntam* which signifies "very many things like quiet, peace, silence, restful etc.".[5] The practice of dialogue in and through language alone renders the mediation of language a prerequisite and it lays aside its pre-linguistic and trans-linguistic dimensions. It falls into a contradiction by mixing language in its non-dialogical and instrumentalistic sense with dialogue. Language, in a dialogical framework, cannot be separated from the being of dialogue. A dialogic communication is different from normal communication which, as S.C. Malik points out, "takes place in a conditioned form of knowledge".[6]

Dialogue preceding and overpassing language starts from experience, proceeds through language, and reaches beyond language. This is a broader notion of dialogue encompassing pre-linguistic, linguistic and trans-linguistic frame-work of the relation between man and art. 'Dialogue' in this second sense is inclusive of the first sense. The distinction between the two senses of the concept of dialogue corresponds to the distinction between Gadamar's concept of dialogue as a fusion of two horizons through the mediation of language on the one hand, and the concept of dialogue as explicated by Martin Buber. I have subscribed to Buber's views on dialogue as more fundamental, more open, and pervading diverse spheres of human encounter. Michael Polanyi's concept of **I-Thou** relationship too yields a concept of dialogue in its non-linguistic and tacit dimension. In this work I have tried to propound the view that art experience is dialogic in all its pre-linguistic, linguistic and trans-linguistic aspects. In arguing for this view I have drawn support from many sources and various thinkers who are perceptive of this problem. The problem and method of understanding aesthetic experience as it is outlined here has been stretched further in evoking a standpoint in order to re-understand some of the contemporary Indian philosophers' approach to art. I found the ideas of Rabindranath Tagore and Radhakrishnan most suited to the frame-work of phenomenology of dialogue.

This book does not propose any definite and closed theory of art; it discusses the relationship between man and art, and various issues concerning aesthetic experience. In the course of discussion a complementary relation between philosophy of art and philosophical anthropology has been worked out. The complementarity is natural as it is man himself who becomes dialogic in his aesthetic experience and art as such becomes a dialogue for him. The concept of art as dialogue goes alongside the concept of man as being in dialogue or **I-Thou** relationship rather than in **I-It** relationship. The co-presence of philosophy of art and philosophical anthropology has been highlighted in contemporary Indian philosophical perspective too. It has been discussed in the essays on Tagore and Radhakrishnan. Art is, indeed, a fundamental concern for man in his search for newer images in it. The readers of this book will decide how much of that concern has been reflected and found a voice herein.

Notes and References

1. Some of the important works of Roman Ingarden are : (i) *The Cognition of the Literary Work of Art*. Translated by Ruth Ann Crowley and Kenneth R. Olson. Evanston, Ill., North-Western University Press, 1973. (ii) *The Literary Work of Art: An Investigation on the Borderline of Ontology, Logic, Theory of Literature*; Translated by George G. Grabowicz. Evanston., Ill., North-Western University Press, 1973. The well-known book by Mikel Dufrenne is *The Phenomenology of Aesthetic Experience*, 1973, North-Western University Press, Ill., often referred to in this monograph.
2. Martin Heidegger : *Poetry, Language, Thought*; Translation and Introduction by Albert Hofstadter, Harper Colophon Books, Harper & Row Publishers, 1975, p. 19.
3. Jean-Paul Sartre : "The Work of Art", In Harold Osborne (Ed.) *Aesthetics*, Oxford University Press, 1972, p. 33.
4. Mikel Dufrenne: *The Phenomenology of Aesthetic Experience*; Translated by Edward S. Casey *et al.*, North-Western University Press, Ill., 1973, p. 146.
5. S. N. Ganguly : "Culture, Communication And Silence", In *Philosophy & Phenomenological Research*, Vol. XXIX, 1968-69, pp. 182-200.
6. S. C. Malik : *Modern Civilization: A Crisis of Fragmentation*, Abhinav Publications, New Delhi, 1989, p. 69.

2

The Phenomenology of Aesthetic Experience

A Dialogical Perspective

IN Owen Barfield's *Poetic Diction: A Study in Meaning* we come across an intriguing statement: "In the moment of knowing, which is also the real moment of poetic creation the knower ceases to exist as subject at all; and conversely, when he comes fully to himself, as subject, he ceases to know".[1] The statement accords a special cognitive status to poetry implying the inapplicability of subject-object dichotomy of traditional epistemology to any analysis of this kind of knowledge. An important task of philosophy is to elucidate the meaning of certain items of knowledge which may indeed fall within the finitude of time and space of the commoner's world and are capable of rational demonstration in a certain way and to a certain extent, but which at the same time are called transcendent with respect to this time and space. "There are", writes Baudelaire, "moments of existence when time and space take on extra depth, and the feeling of existence is immensely amplified".[2] Music too gives us another example of transcending the fact-based time.

If philosophy can fulfil that task, it may enable us to take a heirarchical leap from one level of existence and reality to another without necessarily falsifying one and verifying another but signifying a continuity of reality through different levels. The philosophy of art comes forward in highlighting such items of knowledge. It may render a significant contribution to philosophy as a whole by implying that the epistemic ability and range of human faculties like perception, reason and imagination are not confined to any particular heirarchical level of reality. The images of poetry, painting, sculpture and architecture, the world and life as transfigured and transubstantiated in music, dance and all the other arts constitute such items of knowledge. They are to be known by participating in that realm of reality and transcending the bifurcation of a subject knowing an object and the object being placed at a lower logical level as an **in-itself** sunk into the oblivion of its facticity or fact-oriented meaning. Barfield's remark on poetic creation is valuable in this very sense and can be taken as a clue to our understanding all the other art forms and art activity as such.

The basic theme of this chapter may be indicated by questions like (a) What is our relation with works of art? (b) What is the relation between man as an artist and his creations? (c) What is the nature of the creative process? (d) How is the meaning of a work of art determined? (e) What is the ontological status of a work of art? While such questions could be considered by taking the specific art forms into account my objective is primarily an epistemological one so that a general frame-work for dealing with these questions is anchored. One can quite legitimately hold that there are considerable variations and differences in the manner of presentation, in the degree of sensuousness, flexibility, opacity, materiality, and in the role of medium, etc. so far as different art forms are concerned. Such variations and differences do impair one's aesthetic consciousness and experience. Reflections on the specificities involved in our perception of individual art forms may result in philosophies of painting, poetry, music, dance, etc. But whatever the individual art form may be, its relationship with the spectator or the artist is a fundamental or universal phenomenon which has its own ontology. Its discovery may not only provide answers to the questions above but lead us to envision a common platform on which all arts may stand together.

II

My concern has been epistemological in the sense that whenever we create or enjoy or evaluate a work of art an awareness of something comes on its way to take a shape. This awareness has certain indeterminacy about it and is likely to change in course of time. The indeterminacy is there, because in the realm of art we do not interact with an object having a fixed meaning and suggestion, i.e., an object which is a 'spoken fact'.[3]

A 'spoken fact' has a prevailing meaning-content in the commonsensical world. One can speak of it only with reference to or a presupposition of this content. In other words one can speak of it as already spoken of. A work of art is identified by an absence of facticity of this kind. Its meaningfulness is dependent not on any factuality, but on surpassing the inflexibility and *status quo* of the meaning-contents of facts and the inertia of life and culture. Appearances of such things as buildings, pots, rivers, mountains, etc. are abstracted from their material existence and transformed into visions, forms and images in art. According to Susanne Langer, art forms are purged of their actual material and factual context and they acquire a different context; a picture is made with pigments on a piece of canvas, but the painting that emerges does not consist of pigment-on-canvas. The painting comes with its own structured space, not the actual space. Langer called it 'virtual space'. For her, painting presents 'virtual space' music 'virtual time' and literature 'virtual life'.[4] It is in this sense that an art object cannot be a 'spoken fact'. Yet it is a symbol of a particular relationship between the human and the world; it is both significant and speakable.

III

A thing becomes a work of art by generating a new set of meaning—categories beyond the prevalent meaning—contents of the world of spoken facts on the basis of this particular relationship between the human and the work or the world to be transfigured in it.

A work of art has a continuous existence and identity like a human being. Like a human being it is a **no-thing**. The continuous identity of a person, say, 'Mr. Sayeed' or 'Mr. Stephen' does not debar one to have a fresh dialogue with him to know the person anew and construct a new meaning of life for both the persons. Though an art object is not really identical with a human person, it contributes to our being — not as our possession — but by pointing to a way of our becoming. Music, for example, is an art form which is non-representational and essentially of temporal nature. But it has a sensuous element in it by virtue of which it appears to us as something like a 'subject'. It is perhaps because of this element that the heart of Indian music is conceived as *rāga* and the meaning of the concept of *rāga* is elucidated as being 'that which colours the minds' (*Ranjayati iti Rāgaḥ*). Ravi Shankar, the noted Indian musician, says: "To me, a *rāga* is like a living person, and to establish that intimate oneness between music and musician one must proceed slowly. And when that oneness is achieved, it is the most exhilarating and ecstatic moment like the supreme heights of the act of love or worship. . . .".[5] This sensuous element is present in other art forms too. However it is wrong to identify the 'sensuous' with the 'physical' or 'mundane'. The physical or the mundane might be the material basis of a work of art, but, it is not 'sensuous' which is an outcome of the image-making process in a relational perspective of man and the work or the world to be transfigured in it. An art object speaks for itself without necessarily referring to physical or mundane reality. It is real and concrete by itself. Human sensibility finds its 'alter' in this for a dialogue with it, and a dialogue is surely different from any business talk. The meaning of a poem, for example, is considered to be all absorbed into and communicated through sensuous imagery. Without a dialogue with such an imagery, its meaning cannot be grasped. Ezra Pound contrasted poetry with 'general expressions in non-concrete terms' which are more a 'laziness' ; "they are talk, not art, not creation".[6] 'Concreteness' is to be understood in a particular sense in the context of poetry, literature and art. The meaning of the concept of the 'concrete' applied to an art object, poetic imagery or any segment of the world looked at aesthetically as a 'vision' is to be explicated on the ground of how powerfully and forcefully the object or the form may enter into a relationship with human selves; and, pose itself to human perception and imagination as dearer and more real than the physical, factual and mundane reality. This is why the poet is so extremely choosy to pick up the right word; the musician struggles to sing the right note, and the sculptor sometimes travels extensively to find out the right sort of stone. It is not a sheer 'perfectionism', and if it is 'perfectionism' at all it is due to a very strong artistic proclivity wishing to deflect from the fact-ridden reality.

IV

The object of art experience is, therefore, really **no object** or **no thing**. A depletion and displacement of material and factual reality is a necessary prerequisite to artistic creation and aesthetic experience. But does 'art' or 'art object' not have a public meaning? And once meant, is it not an 'object' of knowledge and reflection? When a critic, and not an enjoyer, experiences an object of art, the standard or criterion of his evaluation is surely not utility and information. He keeps the object at a distance and away from the periphery of his personality so that there is no distortion of what is the case — that which he is studying and on the basis of which he has to give his judgement. Is it then possible to have a so-called 'objective' and 'impersonal' critique of a work of art? An impersonal evaluation is at the same time an impassioned one so far as a work of art is concerned. An inner tension between art experience and the retreat in which the judgement is made constitutes the essence of art criticism. It consists of a double movement of one's going forth to the experience of the art form concerned and stepping out of the experiential dimension. A work of criticism communicates this tension. A sharp distinction between the two cannot be made. An art criticism can be called a dialogic discourse, i.e., a discourse based on dialogue with the work.

The critic has to bear in mind the character of an art object and its difference from other objects of direct mundane significance or relevance, the objects which are 'spoken facts'. It is never a finished product. Not being a finished product does not mean that the work of art is an 'incomplete work', like Keats' incomplete poem "Hyperion". Nor does it mean 'imperfect'. What I mean by 'never a finished work' is that there is no fixed, fully enclosed or exhausted, fully actualised content in the work of art because it essentially admits of appreciation in terms of ever unfolding possibilities of meaning. There is no one particular appreciation of a work, nor can the work's content be exhaustively brought out. The work is an 'unfinished product' insofar as it is a source of unfinished possibilities for appreciation and interpretation. It is an 'unfinished product' to the extent that it is unlike, say, a finished product available in the market, namely a car, a toy, a chair, a box and so on. From the standpoint of the creator-artist, the work **may** be a finished product; but even to the artist, let alone to spectators, the work is 'unfinished' in the sense that it assumes an 'open-textured' character by becoming an ontologically peculiar entity. While a car or a chair can have a definable meaning the meaning-content of a work of art eludes any straight-jacketed definition. Functional artifacts like a car may be defined functionally, which gives meaning to the functional terms. But works of art are afunctional and their meaning-contents can never be confined to limited possibilities.

The critic is a spectator as well who needs to exert his imagination to be able to appreciate the art object which **seems to be finished**. Sartre's remark is notable in this context : ". . . the imagination of the spectator has not only a regulative function, but a constitutive one . . . it is called upon to recompose the beautiful object beyond the traces left by the artist".[7] A work of art surpasses the ostensive references of spoken discourse by opening-up possible modes of being, a whole new world over and above any restricted situation. The critic cannot stay away from interpreting a work and imagining its possible modes of being. The roles of the artist, the beholder and the critic thus overlap. 'Art' means the **phenomenon** of art which is not merely the finished **product** of art activity or art activity alone. It means a relational network comprising man, world and the work. A work of art comes into being in the totality of this phenomenon.

V

It is not possible to describe a phenomenon of art as something entirely independent of our awareness of it. Nor is it possible to absorb it totally into our consciousness and bring it under the terms of an idealistic thesis. As Alfred Hofstadter says: "... the subjective self on the one hand and the objective things of the world on the other, are jointly operative and jointly revealed in the work".[8] This operation and revelation, however, cannot be considered in terms of any 'agent point of view', because agency is a part of the relational network — the entirety of the phenomenon of art.

What is common to all art experiences is such a relational perspective where neither the subjective nor the objective stance holds. Hence a general frame-work beyond subject-object or observer-observed dichotomy is required to understand and realize what thc phenomenon of art is. This is possible only if we turn to the experiential dimension of art. In our art experiences we owe our agency to this relational realm.

The dilemma and controversy of objectivistic and subjectivistic aesthetics may be traced back to the

Pythagoreans and the Sophists. While Pythagoreans argued for aesthetic objectivity in terms of harmony, order, proportion, measure and number which are the objective basis of beauty, aesthetic subjectivity was a natural implication of the Sophists' thesis "Man is the measure of all things".[9] In later philosophies of art in the west, from Greek through the medieval to the modern, this opposition was carried on within different kinds of theories like the conceptual realism of Plato, rationalism of Descartes, empiricism of Hume, critical rationalism of Kant, idealism of Hegel and so on.

Some medieval thinkers, however, tried to bring about a reconciliation between these two concepts giving rise to two extremely different approaches to art. St. Basil and St. Thomas Aquinas, for example, held that beauty is a property which certain objects possess but in relation to the subject. It was a kind of dialectic between subject and object which, for them, was constitutive of our experience of the beautiful. Aquinas reasoned his relationalistic approach to beauty by placing it in the context of human cognition : ". . . beauty relates to the cognitive faculty; for beautiful things are those which please when seen. Hence beauty consists in due proportion; for the senses delight in things duly proportioned, as what is after their own kind — because even sense is a sort of reason, just as is every cognitive faculty".[10] Such a contention had the potency to mature and endorse a concept of the primacy of the spectator's and the artist's point of view in determining the nature of aesthetic awareness. It did not suggest any transcendence of subject-object dichotomy but it was an insightful attempt to juxtapose both the frames of reference in a third perspective which focuses on aesthetic cognition. But the possibility of an ontological shift from the subject to the object or the other way round always remained open even with Aquinas's third perspective, because the ontological basis of this perspective was not worked out. As a result, the dichotomy continued and conflicting theories of art kept on coming into the scene. Even Kant, whose immense contribution in the field of aesthetics is beyond question, and who in his *Critique of Judgement*, was the first to give a clear and convincing argument for the autonomy of art, could not get over this dichotomous trend; he owed the autonomy of art to human subjectivity which is capable of achieving a psychical distance as a factor of art and aesthetic principle.

It cost Kant underplaying the empirical or the sensuous. For him, art experience is autonomous to the degree it is independent of its empirical moorings. The 'subjective' has an exalted significance in Kant's schema, 'a dance of bloodless' (*a la* Bradley) understanding and imagination in tune with each other. The subjective is the *a priori* consciousness, reflexively realizing itself in delight. Aesthetic delight in Kant is not a delight in something other than or out of the consciousness, rather it is the harmony of the two cognitive faculties, quite apart from the representation that might have occasioned the state of harmony.

So, for Kant, as far as the quality of a judgement of taste is concerned, 'aesthetic' means "that whose determining ground can be no other than subjective".[11] Aesthetic object is a subjective existent. The universality of an aesthetic judgement is subjective. But Kant's contentions are based on arguments which do not defy the subject-object dichotomy. Even the communicability of a judgement of taste is subjective. The consciousness of a "mutual subjective harmony of the cognitive powers with one another in the judgement of taste"[12] is the basis of such communicability. It is ultimately the transmissibility of one's state of mind to another which counts in a Kantian frame-work: "The subjective universal communicability of the mode of representation in a judgement of taste, since it is to be possible without presupposing a definite concept, can refer to nothing else than the state of mind in the free play of the imagination and the understanding (so far as they agree with each other, as is requisite for cognition in general)."[13]

In tune with this dominant role of human subjectivity the attitude of the spectator succeeds to an important place in Kantian aesthetics. For contemporary and future aestheticians it had certain major implications: (a) From Kant's point of view, an aesthetic object became essentially a perceptual or experiential object, (b) Disinterestedness of the perceiver was considered to be an aesthetic virtue, (c) the disinterested attitude of the beholder characterised the nature of aesthetic perception as such and any aesthetic object as non-mundane or non-utilitarian.

Besides these implications which served rather as directives for the emergence and development of theories of art, Kant's system offered a few challenges to his successors. One of them is worth mentioning in the present context as it shows that an urge to transcend the subject-object paradigm was felt among some post-Kantian aestheticians. Let me put it in the words of Monroe Beardsley: "Kant's system attained its precarious stability through the delicate adjustment of certain oppositions — between the matter of experience which is given, and the form, which is contributed by understanding : and between the phenomenal world, which we can know empirically, and the noumenal world of things-in-themselves which lies beyond knowledge but somehow is the source of the given in experience. The resulting dualisms appeared to the idealists as a demand to be overcome, or overridden. . . .".[14]

The transcendental idealism of Freidrich Wilhelm Von Schelling was an attempt to meet this demand. For him the problem of transcendental philosophy was to show how the inner harmony of nature and the self can be made manifest to the self. His aesthetics, though imbibed largely from Kant, represents this trend: "Every aesthetic production starts from an essentially infinite separation of the two activities (the conscious one of freedom, and the unconscious one of nature — drawn from Kant's treatment of Art in relation to Genius) which are separated in all free productions. But as these two activities are to be represented in the product as in union, this product represents an infinite in finite form. The infinite represented in finite form is Beauty".[15] Such attempts are made after taking the separation for granted in all experiential contexts. It is generalized into an axiom without any proper basis. At least in art, 'free productions' are impossible other than from a relational perspective. To think that the object of experience is always transcendent in relation to the experiencing consciousness is a realistic dogma. Its counter-thesis, namely, 'the experiencing consciousness is transcendent of the object represents idealists' dogma. Art transcends this either-or category. In the words of Ernst Cassirer: "when absorbed in the intuition of a great work of art we do not feel a separation between the subjective and the objective worlds".[16]

Without much digression into the history and the detail of such theories let us now look at the source of such contrary theories of art as aesthetic realism and aesthetic idealism, and the central problematic.

VI

The source is a slicing of the total phenomenal sphere of our aesthetic experience in terms of two ontologies, viz. Ontology of the subject and that of the object. There is no reason to presume that such a division is not a product of some theoretical enterprise on our part. When we talk about someone being 'cooperative' we already know what it is to be 'non-cooperative'. Similarly when we describe something as 'blue' we know that it is 'not yellow' or 'not green'. Besides differentiating one object of knowledge from another we also differentiate 'object' from the 'subject', i.e., the 'known' or 'knowable' from the 'knower'. This is taken for granted in many theories of knowledge. Knowledge through differentiation merely amasses representations and accumulates information about something or other. It may acquire sophistication by ordering them in terms of sets and categories. But it remains dissociated from life. It may be 'correct' but not 'concrete' because the moment man thinks with reference to such sets and categories his existence is fragmented; what is knowable and sayable is determined by them. But aesthetics experience takes place in one's being-in-the-world. To speak in Gadamar's term, it is like 'play' which is a way of our being-in-the-world. The characteristic feature of play lies in a relationality of the player and the play. There is neither a subject nor an object in it. Gadamar says : "The mode of being of play does not allow the player to behave towards play as if it were an object. The player knows very well what play is, and what he is doing is 'only a game'; but he does not know what exactly he 'knows' in knowing that."[17] With this concept of play as a clue Gadamar held that it is not aesthetic consciousness, but the experience of art or art experience which is more important .... "the work of art is not an object that stands over against a subject for itself. Instead the work of art has its true being in the fact that it becomes an experience changing the person experiencing it".[18] Like play the ontology of art focuses on the totality. The epistemological significance of it lies in a transcendence of subject-object dichotomy.

Segregation of the work from our experience of it or the creative agency from the spatio-temporal perspective and mode of creation, or, for that matter, subjugation of one aspect to the other replacing their conjugation is an obstacle to our understanding of the phenomenon of art. This is the central problematic. To conceive this conjugation in terms of subjectivity alone will be a mistake. The argument for such conception would be that this experience is an experience by some subject. Such an argument takes us away from the experience itself and treats it only discursively — as an 'It'. An objective law devised in terms of some specific ingredients of this experience cannot explain the experience as a whole. Any attempt to do so would result in another mishandling of the experience. The point, therefore, is to retain its first-order character is any discource on it. For this purpose, we have to start with 'philosophy **in** art' rather than 'philosophy **of** art'. Let me formulate it in the light of Maurice Natanson's distinction between 'philosophy **in** literature' and 'philosophy **of** literature' which, I think, could be applied to art as such.[19] 'Of' leads to problems in formal aesthetics, 'in' marks a dimension of art which informs us philosophically. 'Of' raises questions about the categories of different art forms and their relationship to the particular modes of being of respective art works, or categories of any work of art. 'In' presents the realized work and summons us to an appreciation of its implicit philosophical achievement, or 'in' may present the world or any segment of it for any further shaping of it into an art work. Every artist, in this sense, is a philosopher who accepts the experiential world as an integral part of his being. His philosophy grows out of his being **in** the art experience. K.G. Subramanyan's memoir of Ramkinkar, the sculptor and painter, tells us : "He wanted now to go for that elusive reality behind visible fact, the intangible life-force behind tangible form; the form was only a vehicle for that thing behind. This did not mean that he turned his eyes away from what he saw, he never could. He found the visible world irresistible. What he wanted was to get into it and lay hold on its magic. In Rabindranath's words he wanted to jump into the sea of forms and come up with the pearl of formless. So art became an odyssey, an adventurous search; he had to negotiate its whirlpools and quicksands, its cyclops and sirens."[20] This is a philosophy **in** art. It turns to the very experience given in art and attempts its reconstruction and reinterpretation. It is a reflective as well as a living extension of art experience. It is a movement from existence to thought but without any breach, because the movement aims at making existence more thoughtful.

Ultimately, the 'of' and 'in' distinction ends if we, the philosophers of art, do not feel inhibited to incorporate the experiential dimension of art into any thought on art, if we start from scratch — from where the artist works and the beholder enjoys and interprets. This will lead us to a more comprehensive and evidenced philosophy of art. It will be more comprehensive in the sense that the epistemology implicit in this methodological stand will accommodate all sorts of art experience; hence there can be a philosophy of art based on art experience as such. It will be evidenced because the methodology will retain the first order character of art experience. There can always be a philosophy of painting, music, etc. But, now, these individual philosophies of art based on experiences and reflections related to specific art forms will have a place in the general ontology of art. Alfred Hofstadter's remark is worth quoting in this connection. "The history of aesthetics is littered with doctrines that, like expression theory, were the conceptualized voices of the art impulses of their day: art as imitation, art as wisdom, art as catharsis, art as the reflection of beauty, art as the presentation of harmony and concinnity, art as the expression of taste, art as embodiment of sentiment, art as symbol of morality, art as integration of finite and infinite, art as mystic identification with the Infinite, art as Dionysian play. . . and so on. Such doctrines, each an aesthetic in the sense of being an option for one among the many possibilities opened up in the form of being constituted by art and each, therefore, constituting the conceptual counterpart of a possible form of art, are products of authentic spiritual forces. But they must not be confused with aesthetics, or with the theory of fine art, whose aim is not to speak for a single kind of art but to understand art in all its forms and dimensions. Theory of art must begin not with one selected kind of art experience but with the whole aesthetic-artistic life of man so far as that is accessible to us from historical investigation, contemporary experience, and imaginative penetration into the lives of other men, other cultures, other times. It must try to bring to view the total context and the pulsing heart of artistic actuality, of which such a phenomenon as expressionist creation and experience and its counterpart in the conceptual form of a theory are but one manifestation".[21]

VII

For placing philosophy of art in a general perspective like this we have to explore the nature of experience itself that persists in our art activity. While it is possible to exclude this experiential dimension in our dealings with facts—the dealings which are discursive by nature, art is characterised by this dimension only. One can argue that literary works of art do have a discursive aspect as it is essentially mediated by language. But this view does not go very far. There are different types and levels of experiences and expressions which do not always fit into the prevalent conceptual schemes. Such expressions consists in what is called in Indian poetics 'suggestible meaning' or *vyaṅgyārtha* as different from 'ordinary, conventional meaning' or *vācyārtha*.[22] To speak in the light of Susanne Langer, what is important here is not the literal assertion made in a literary work of art but the way in which it is made.[23] Literary works of art do not record experiences in a sheer descriptive, photographic manner. They record them interpretatively and leave a penumbra of silence around the written words and sentences so that there remains scope for further interpretation. Like other visual arts it presents a forms (*rūpa*)—a configuration of sensuous images the perception of which is extraordinary (*alaukika*) as it is a perception of something non-mundane. In the case of a painting or sculpture one does not merely have a physical perception of it but one becomes a 'spectator' by looking into the meaning of it within and beyond appearances, and, perception gets mingled with imagination. According to Susanne Langer an art object is an image; it is a 'virtual object', 'abstracted from the physical and causal order'. Hence its perception must differ from ordinary perception. In her discussion on aesthetic perception with particular reference to classical Indian aesthetics Rekha Jhanji holds that aesthetic perception has a *sui generis* character and it is essentially different from ordinary perception. In this context she quotes approvingly from Abhinavagupta : "... . the form of perception differs from correct (*samyak*) perception, mistaken (*mithyā*) perception, doubt (*saṁśaya*) and similitude (*sādṛśya*). . ."[24] Citing the example of poetry Abhinavagupta says: ". . . there occurs in a qualified person a perception transcending the words of the poem . . . there appears, immediately after the perception of their literal sense, a perception of a different order (an inner *mānasī*) perception, consisting in a direct experience (*sākṣātkāra*). . . .".[25] In literary works of art images are mirrored upon the 'inner eye' of the artist and/or the reader; it is acclaimed as *dṛṣti*, a way of looking at the universe so far as the interpretation of life's experience is concerned. This is a personal encounter. Even general truths are reached or realised in poetry and literature on the basis of a personal encounter and awareness and rarely through pure reasoning. Hence a literary work of art is never a monologue, it is always a dialogue; it presents different modes of relationality. The non-discursive aspect of it is quite apparent in this form of art.

VIII

But one may raise question concerning the historicity of art. If some art work is at the same time a crucial historical evidence or a landmark of some phase of history, is it not reified as a fact and thereby a symbol for discursive thought? The question brings about a pseudo-conflict between the theory that a work of art is always a **phainomenon** the **logos** of which is manifest in ever new modes in different cases of experience and the one which maintains that art cannot be treated as something ahistorical. The first view can be exemplified with reference to some eminent Indian thinkers from classical period to this century. (1) Abhinavagupta said: "In aesthetic experience, what happens is,... the birth of the aesthetic tasting of the artistic expression. Such an experience, just as a flower born of magic, has, as its essence, solely the present, it is correlated neither with what came before nor with what comes after."[26] (2) Radhakrishnan conceived poetry as a form of knowledge but with a difference from other kinds of knowledge which are discursive by nature. The difference, for him, consists in its here-and-now spatio-temporal character: "Poetry, it is sometimes said, is but a reaction to environment. Historical factors can easily account for it. A statement of origins is not, however, an explanation of the phenomenon. Origins may help us to understand the pathology of art, its failures, but not its normal creativity".[27] (3) Rabindranath Tagore also had the same view. In 'The Religion of an Artist' he tells us "... directly a poem is fashioned, it is free from its genesis, it minimizes its history and emphasizes its independence".[28] But there is no real contradiction between this phenomenology of art and historicity of art. Even when some piece of art is marked as an emblem of history or known to be significant as an axial skeleton of some phase of history the past thrives in it as the present. It is enacted and re-enacted in human imagination. Its original meaning achieves new significances through new interpretations. First of all it is **present** to an experiencing eye, and then it is contextualised, but only tentatively, because, it is never left alone. It lives in humanity for further decontextualisation and contextualisation. Hence historicity does not mean 'known past'. As Gadamar says : "... a hermeneutics that regarded understanding as the reconstruction of the original would be no more than the recovery of a dead meaning".[29] According to

Gadamar true experience is that of one's historicity, and this means placing the experience in a continuity, i.e., in the context of a tradition. Gadamar says: "The hermeneutical experience is concerned with what has been transmitted in tradition. He explains it further : "But tradition is not simply a process that we learn to know and be in command of through experience; it is language, i.e., it expresses itself like a 'Thou'. A 'Thou' is not an object, but stands in a relationship with us. . . tradition is a genuine partner in communication, with which we have fellowhsip as does 'I' with a 'Thou'."[30] The phenomenological concept of temporality signifies a continuity. A past which is integrated into the total phenomenon is not a dead past; it adds to the experience. Gadamar's concern of historicity does not explain a work of art in terms of certain facts. History of a work of art or its creation can be relevant to one's present experience of it to the extent it is amenable to an integration into the present experience. In that case history would rather mean 'biography' of the artist or the work. If a fact is totally integrated, it becomes a biographical fact in relation to the work. If it remains outside and influences the art experience it is history in a reductionistic sense. To quote from Gadamar again: "Neither the separate life of the creating artist — his biography — nor that of performer who acts a work, nor that of the spectator who is watching the play, has any separate legitimacy in the face of the being of the work of art".[31] As I have already mentioned, the phenomenon of art means a totality, and the phenomenology of aesthetic experience cannot defy this totality.

IX

The intention of the artist is also a fact associated with any work of art. The question is; whether it is relevant or not. A problem arises when such an intention is taken to be a private factor enclosed within the mind of the artist, and the concept of intention is understood in a psychological sense as isolated from the total phenomenon of art. A theoretically serious but easily disposable thesis against intention in art is perhaps that which is propagated by Wimsatt and Beardsley in their paper "The Intentional Fallacy".[32] It has two major points: (i) we cannot really discover the artist's intentions and (ii) even if we could, it is irrelevant to the mening of the work. The thesis seems to be imposing, and it a debars us from realizing the symbiosis of man and the world, the artist and his creation, the beholder and the work. This realisation is a pre-requisite for us to understand the deeper unity between man and the universe, as an aesthetically important phenomenon.

The thesis of Wimsatt and Beardsley treats intention as something private and knowable only to the person himself. Giving a counter argument, David Best writes : "It is strange that the prejudice persists that the person himselfhas infallible knowledge ofhis intentions and thus is necessarily in the best position to say what they are. For quite apart from Philosophical Considerations, it is contrary to common experience. For instance, a psychoanalyst's task may be to help a patient to recognize that he has misconstrued his intentions."[33] Best points out further that a person's action is the principal criterion for what his intention is : "This point was well illustrated in a talk I once heard by Ron Geesin, an artist who creates the most extraordinary sounds out of the most ordinary by an ingenious use of tape-recorders. After one illustration, a member of the audience asked him what he had originally intended to produce. He looked puzzled for a moment, and then, gesturing to the tape-recorder, he said that was what he had intended. The questioner was not satisfied, and said that he knew that was what was eventually produced, but what had been his original intention. Ron Geesin looked even more puzzled for a time, then burst out: 'That was my intention, you've just heard it".[34]

Best's argument shows that there cannot be any breach between intention and creation. Interpretation in art experience is possible when creation bears the mark of intention as a continuum of consciousness. Intention thus becomes a part of art experience as such. According to Margaret Chatterjee, intention in art provides means to distinguish the art object from the natural object. Besides that, as she points out, it is a necessary condition of hermeneutics in art : "To leave out intention would be to deprive us of any means of distinguishing the art object from the natural object. Questions of interpretation are adjudicated upon by bringing in many considerations of which intention is surely one. To leave it out is to leave out the point where the hermeneutic circle begins — the creator of the art object."[35] Chatterjee, in the same article, characterizes our response to a work of art as a response to a live communication. This is, for her, because of the intentions a work embodies She says: "The response to a work of art is a response to live communication. The focus is no doubt on the quiddity of the 'object' ".[36]

The intentional background of art is made alive by a 'sympathetic respondent' or *sahṛdaya*. It is such a respondent who forms the scope of hermeneutical understanding of art. The consciousness of the respondent is also intentionally directed to the artist through the work and a dialogic situation is created. It means a relationship with the work and also with its creator. As artist's consciousness is directed to the world and through its transfigured image to the work and then to the beholder; thus, the beholder's consciousness also takes an intentional turn. This relationship or dialogue yields an understanding and a re-understanding of the work and the human image (the artist and/or the beholder) in it. Without this relation one cannot comprehend what a work of art embodies. This is also a mode of intentionality in art. I call it the 'dialogic mode of intentionality'. As intention cannot be treated in isolation from the work, the work too cannot be separated from it. To oppose intention is to fall into the fallacy of the 'finished product' as if it is just the final product which is all that counts. But it is the total phenomenon which includes the past, lives in the present and projects the future; it does not exclude the intention of the artist. In order to answer the question about 'intentional fallacy' it is necessary to reiterate the distinction between history as biography and history as a kind of reductionism. While there are some intentions extraneous and irrelevant to art experience, there are intentions which may be biographical in relation to the work of art and integral to its experience.

X

Thus, a phenomenological symbiosis of the perceiver and the perceived, man and the world, is essential if one is to overcome the epistemological (and eventually ontological) bifurcation of subjectivism and objectivism, idealism and realism in the realm of aesthetics. And it is the concept of the phenomenon of art rather than the work of art or the human agent as discrete items of aesthetic cognition which is more appropriate in this regard. The phenomenon of art includes the object or the work, its modes of giveness and acts of agency, and that which binds them together as one experiential whole. It means both creation and response, and thereby it signifies the relation between the beholder and the work, the artist and the world. The phenomenologist of aesthetic experience explores the **logos** of this phenomenon.

There is a natural affinity between our art experiences and the phenomenological technique. Having selected a certain area for study such as beauty or human freedom, the phenomenologist aims to grasp what is actually experienced — the object in its pure experiential dimension, and to describe it faithfully. To do this he has to free his perceptions from all cultural determinations and all theoretical constructs. This is what is called 'phenomenological reduction'. But this is not a reduction in the sense of narrowing down the experience to certain precepts of atomic facts. Phenomenological reduction differs from all reductionistic philosophies such as the sense-datum theory in that the phenomenologist proposes to face, without any manipulation, the thing itself in all its purity and potentiality. This is how he withdraws himself from the naturalistic attitude — the attitude which abstracts the objects of experience from the experiencing agent, i.e., from the sphere of experience as such and locates them in the world of 'in-itself'. The reduction, on the other hand, bring the things back to their experiential dimension and renews the world as a lived world. As a methodological device, phenomenological reduction keeps man open to all possible modes of perception of the object in question. In art there is a spontaneous reduction of phenomenological kind, i.e., reduction in the sense of bringing the particular area of study or world as a whole to its lived reality. Art suspends the world as a 'spoken fact', the world beset with definite characterisations, scientific abstractions and so on. This is a parallel of phenomenologists' returning to things temselves. As Merleau-Ponty said: "to return to things themselves is to return to that world which precedes knowledge, of which knowledge speaks and in relation to which every scientific schematization is an abstract and derivative sign-language as is geography in relation to the countryside in which we have learnt what a forest, a prairie or a river is".[37]

Art renews what was a cliche in ordinary language or day-to-day event like sunrise or sunset or a much used thing like a pair of shoes in a transcendental perspective with the intention of knowing it in a new way. It poses itself as a challenge to the ordinary modes of cognising reality. In Sartrean sense, it takes a 'magical' view of the content of experience.

XI

The relationalistic approach which I am trying to articulate here is not of the Aquinas's kind. The interplay between consciousness and the world through the creation and perception of art objects has no 'inner' and 'outer' reality. It is real as it is — as an independent phenomenon. The phenomenological symbiosis that I have talked about is natural in terms of a complementarity that may hold between two biological organisms and this complementarity, in the process, acquires an ontological status by itself. The discovery of this one ontology will determine the constitution of our aesthetic expericnce. Or we can say, the factor constitutive of our art experience is a kind of dialogue between man and world. The mode of intentionality in aesthetic experience can be characterised as dialogic only, because the intentional acts of consciousness with regard to our aesthetic experience do not emerge from consciousness as a centre or ego, or from the art object alone. These acts flow from the interplay itself — from the dialogue. The concept of dislogue is, therefore, methodologically significant for us, it needs a further elaboration.

'Dialogue' is a philosophico-anthropological notion which points to an unfolding of man's being in relation to the other in ever new modes. Our non-dialogical interactions with fellow human beings and nature reveal aspects of humanity in a split, fragmentary fashion. In such interactions, consciousness is the consciousness **of** something; it turns all objects of experience, including other human beings, and all possible knowledge-contents as things. They can be put into order, systematized, but they have to leave the depth of the existence of the person untouched. This form of relationship is known as an **I-It** relationship. In this form of relationship with the world we are never in the presence of our objects of knowledge. Here we know the reason of their existence in terms of causality. But we do not know how we are related to them because of the sharp boundary line which exists between the world of the knower and the world of the knowable. It is, therefore, more a division than a relation.

The subject-object polarisation is a necessary condition for acquiring knowledge. Knowledge, in this sense, involves consciousness **of** something. But this is not the only way to knowledge. We can take a leap from this dual nature of thought by simply diffusing our consciousness in and through the object. This is consciousness in the very domain of experience to which our intentional acts owe. In dialogue alone, we hold the complete being of ourselves to the other and await our unfolding in an in-between sphere of **I-Thou**. This unfolding is creative as it is rich with the unbound possibilities which cannot be realized either by the man who is confined to himself as knower or by the man who is reified as an object by the other's look. This is relation in its true sense. Knowledge of relation cannot be had in an abstract manner. For this we have to **be** in relation. Participation in the object of knowledge and the object participating in our consciousness—these two things together form a unique phenomenon. Those who remain confined to the **I-It** form of cognition alone may ask: "How can the object participate in consciousness?" In the case of our knowledge of other persons, other persons do participate in our consciousness. The success of a philosophical anthropologist depends on how warm he is in inviting the other to participate in that knowledge-situation and how sincere he is in his effort to transcend his own conceptual and cultural barrier. In anthropological knowledge-situation the world of knowables is the world of people in different groups, societies and with different individual purposes. We cannot bring them under fixed meaning-categories. So the cultivation of mutuality is a necessary condition for the study of man by man : "The fundamental paradox of ontology that man is a being in whom the world participates as experience and who participates in the world as existence is the point of departure for philosophical anthropology".[38] These two poles can be synthesized in the notion of dialogue which means a realm of 'the between' where both knower and the knowable stand face to face — in relation to each other. It is its own ontology. Knowledge is generated not from any of the units of relation, but from and in the phenomenon of relation itself—from and in the sphere of **I-Thou**.

'Dialogue' is not only the realm of the **between** bearing its own ontological signification, it is a method as well : A holistic view of man in terms of the unification of divergent aspects of him envisioned through an integration of his states of becoming both in **I-Thou** and **I-It** forms of relationship has to be sought. This is possible only by using dialogue itself as a method. Man is capable of entering into both **I-Thou** and **I-It** relationship. In observing man as a third person (as **he**) in his knower-aspects, I reduce him to an **It**, because a 'third person' approach is always indirect and inherently incapable of taking into account the 'second person' aspect of man, which makes him truly a person capable of having a direct access to other second persons. In a dialogical method I know the other as a **thou**, and hence grasp directly his capacity for both **I-It** and **I-Thou** forms of relationships and knowledge.

XII

But can this relationality which is constitutive of our knowledge of man be assigned to our aesthetic experience as well? In other words, can we talk 'participation' of the work of art or the world in our experiential context? Can it 'participate' as a living entity? We raise these questions which are basically questions concerning the nature of art object by separating the work of art from the purview of aesthetic experience. This is generally the difficulty with regard to any reflection. The detachment of the reflective self from the context of reflection is always presupposed. This is in conformity with subject-object dichotomy. But reflection may take place also within the context of the experience. I have discussed it above.

What sort of experience is this? There are surely experiences which are basically dichotomous. Most of our experiences belong to this kind. This led Jaspers to hold that what one experiences as being resides always in the whole of the subject-object dichotomy.[39] We have seen that the transcendence of this dichotomy becomes an imperative for us so far as our knowledge of man is concerned. As regards art, the nature of experience and the object within the experiential dimension demand the same transcendence. Philosophical anthropology and philosophy of art thus map on to each other's area both methodologically and ontologically.

We experience a sort of 'companionship' with the world when we are engaged in transfiguring some segment of it, or our life in it, in a work of art. And the same experience is also felt by us in appreciating a work of art. Just as we 'enter into' the depth of the expressed world or life, so does the world or life so expressed 'enter into' our consciousness. This noetic-noematic co-ordination is essentially dialogical. Each retains its identity, but at the same time their respective identity lies in the sphere of the **between**.

Surely a work of art is brought about by human endowment, that is to say, the artist creates it. But when the creative endowment is completed and the work is presented to the sensitive beholder, it evokes a penumbra of thoughts and feelings in him in its own right. And there is indeterminacy in the ranges of thoughts and feelings; it is the indeterminacy of the intentional content which is derivable from the work. In other words, there is an endless possibility of thoughts and feelings that can accrue from a work of art. From this we can say that the work, once completed, takes on a life of its own, so to speak. It would therefore be appropriate to regard a work of art more in the way we regard something as a **being-for-itself** than we treat something as a **being-in-itself**. The work creates in us new feelings and ideas, fresh insights and understandings, thus demanding from us a recognition of it in terms of what I call quasi-conscious existence. Certainly this point defies clear explanation. In this connection we might be able to glean some helpful insight from the remark made by Mikel Dufrenne : "The aesthetic object carries the world which it reveals within itself. Rather than referring to the world which it reveals within itself, as things do — e.g., as a cloud refers to rain — the aesthetic object refers to itself alone and is for itself its own light . . . aesthetic object is a quasi for itself".[40] Thus a work of art is identified as something which expresses itself in its own light. It is this self-expressive autonomy of the work, as one might put it, that seems to require a quasi-conscious characterization. Once this characterization of the work is admitted, it is natural to describe aesthetic experience as involving a kind of dynamic interplay between the human subject and the (quasi-subjective) work of art.

XIII

From the phenomenological standpoint, an aesthetic experience is composed by two absolutely co-related movements viz. (1) the specific intentional act of the artist's and/or the beholder's consciousness, and (2) its directedness towards an art object. The object undergoes a process of definitizations just as a piece of music assumes a structure and stretches over time through its bits. The end of it is really not the end, but a consummation of a work of art. While the creative consciousness approaches this object as its 'existential correlate', the object calls on such consciousness for congealing a definite form. None of the two poles of this relational frame-work constitutes a sufficient condition for there being an aesthetic experience. But it is the interplay between them which is both necessary and a sufficient condition of aesthetic experience. A phenomenology of aesthetic experience describes the way man moves on towards an envisioned possibility which is so fully realized that it is made as present as existence. This is the special mode or the structure of intentionality which I have called 'dialogic mode of intentionality'.

The phenomenological method demands a suspension of all stereo-typed 'isms', mundane considerations and cultural preoccupations in our aesthetic experiences.This suspension perhaps pushes us back to the primitive silence which seizes us between idea and reality, conception and creation. But this helps us to start afresh, to have a true and open meeting with the object before us. The bewildered state goes off slowly and a clear and new understanding emerges. This is dialogue. It never remains fact-ridden, but contributes to culture beyond the point seen by us. In a dialogical perspective the meaning of art does not get hardened into an **It**. Hence, the meaning which art communicates is flexible, renewable, and changeable. In dialogue, we gather newer and newer meanings. It renders the impossible possible.

Notes and References

1. Owen Barfield : *Poetic Diction : A Study in Meaning*, Faber & Gwyer, London, 1928, p. 244.
2. As quoted by Roger Cardinal in *Figures of Reality*, Barnes & Noble Books, Totowa, New Jersy, 1981, p. 129.
3. K. C. Bhattacharya; The eminent Indian idealist philosopher employed this concept in the context of his neo-Vedāntin philosophy of subject which was to show the possibility of a gradual and critical self-withdrawal from the world of facts and consequently a realisation of spiritual freedom. See K. C. Bhattacharya *Studies in Philosophy*, Motilal Banarsidass, Delhi, Vol. II, Chapter 1, Section 10. In his explication of the concept of subject as freedom. Bhattacharya makes a distinction between 'spoken of' and

spoken' to show the difference between 'spoken as **meant**' (as information) and 'spoken not as meant but as only **symbolised**' (e.g. 'I am' in which I is not spoken **of**, but only spoken). *Ibid.*, Vol. : II, pp. 465-66.

Quite consistently with his philosophy of subject, Bhattacharya's aesthetics was an analysis of aesthetic enjoyment; Bhattacharya held the aesthetic object remains that relative to the subjectivity of the beholder/artist, See *Ibid.*, Vol. I, pp. 349-63. Though any purely idealistic or realistic approach is not acceptable in our frame-work I have used the concept of 'spoken fact' only in its relevant sense here, and stipulated it to the extent it is required.

4. Susanne Langer: *Problems of Art*, Charles Scribner's Sons, New York, 1957, p. 28. See also Langer's *Feeling and Form*, Routledge & Kegan Paul Ltd., London, 1953.
5. Ravi Shankar : *My Music, My Life* (with an introduction by Yehudi Menuhin), Vikas Publishing House Pvt. Ltd., New Delhi, 1982. p. 57.
6. As quoted by Elizabeth Drew in her *Poetry : A Modern Guide to Its Understanding And Enjoyment*, Dell Publishing Co., Inc., New York, 1959, p. 87.
7. Jean-Paul Sartre : *What is Literature?* Harper & Row, 1965, p. 41.
8. Alfred Hofstadtr : *Truth and Art,* Columbia University Press, New York and London, 1965, p. 25.
9. Wladyslaw Tatarkiewick : 'Objectivity and Subjectivity in the History of Aesthetics', *Philosophy and Phenomenological Research,* Vol. XXIV, December, 1983, No. 2.
10 Monroe C. Beardsley : *Aesthetics From Classical Greece to the Present,* The Macmillan Co., New York, pp. 101-02.
11. Immanual Kant : *Critique of Judgement,* trans. by J. H. Bernard, Hafner Publishing Co., New York and London, 1968, p. 37.
12. *Ibid.,* p. 53.
13. *Ibid.,* p. 52.
14. Monroe Beardsley : *op. cit.,* p. 230.
15. Bernard Bosanquet : *A History of Aesthetics,* George Allen & Unwin Ltd., London, 1966, p. 319.

16. Ernst Cassirer : 'Art' in *Problems in Aesthetics,* ed. by M. Weitz, Macmillan, New York, 1959.
17. Hans-George Gadamar : *Truth and Method,* The Seabury Press, New York, 1975, p. 92.
18. *Ibid.*
19. Maurice Natanson: 'Phenomenology And Theory of Literature', In *Literature Philosophy and the Social Sciences: Essays in Existentialism and Phenomenology* by Maurice Natanson, Martinus Nijhoff, The Hague, 1962.
20 K. G. Subramanyan : 'Recalling Ramkinkar — Artist and Man', In *The Visva-Bharati Quarterly,* New Series, Vol. 2, Nos. 1-4, p. 106.
21. Alfred Hofstadtr : *op. cit.,* p. 21.
22. Anandavardhana : *Dhvanyalok,* Flash 1, *Ślokas* 2, 3, 4, 9, 10 and 13 Commentary Abhinavagupta, Bengali translation from Sanskrit by Subodh Chandra Sengupta & Kalipada Bhattacharya; A. Mukherjee & Co. Pvt. Ltd., Calcutta 1986. See also the English translation by Krishnamoorthy, Karnataka University, 1974.
23. Susanne Langer: *Philosophy in a New Key,* Harvard University Press, 1963, p. 260.
24. Rekha Jhanji: *Aesthetic Communication,* Munshiram Manoharlal Publishers, New Delhi, 1985, p. 28.
25. R. Gnoli: *The Aesthetic Experience According to Abhinavagupta,* Chowkhamba Publication, Varanasi, 1963, pp. 53-54.
26. *Ibid.,* pp. xxxiii-xxiv.
27. Sarvepalli Radhakrishnan : *An Idealist view of Life,* Unwin Books, 1961, pp. 144-45.
28. Rabindranath Tagore : 'The Religion of An Artist', In *Angel of Surplus,* ed. by Sisir Kumar Ghose, Visva-Bharati, 1978, p. 16.
29. Hans-George Gadamar : *op. cit.,* p. 149.
30. *Ibid.,* p. 321.
31. *Ibid.,* p. 113.
32. Wimsatt and Beardsley : 'The Intentional Fallacy', In *Philosophy Looks At Arts,* ed. by J. Margolis, Scribner, New York, pp. 91-105.

33. David Best : *Feeling and Reason in the Arts,* George Allen & Unwin, London, 1985, pp. 122-25.
34. *Ibid.*
35. Margaret Chatterjee : 'Must we be for or ãgainst Intention in Art', In *Diotima,* 9, Part I, 1981, Athens, pp. 67-72.
36. *Ibid.*
37. Maurice Merleau-Ponty: *Phenomenology, Language & Sociology,* Selected Essays, ed. by John O'Neill, Heinemann, London, 1974, p. xxii.
38. Goutam Biswas : 'Martin Buber's Notion of Dialogue', In *Journal of Indian Council of Philosophical Research,* New Delhi, Vol. III, No. 1, Autumn, 1985.
39. Karl Jaspers : *The Way to Wisdom,* trans. by Ralph Manheim, New Haven Yale University Press, 1954.
40. Mikel Dufrenne: *The Phenomenology of Aesthetic Experience,* trans. by Edward Casey *et al.,* North-Western University Press, Evanston, 1973, p. 227.

3

Martin Buber's Concept of Art as Dialogue

The abyss and the light of the worlds,
Time's need and eternity's desire
Vision, event and poem:
They were and are dialogue with you.
— **Martin Buber**

The contribution of Martin Buber to contemporary phenomenological movement in its struggle to overcome the impasse between subjectivity and objectivity and envision the epistemic range of man beyond this dichotomy has been of immense significance. Dialogue which for Buber was the only means to make a road through this impasse and also an end in itself as a consummation of human existence became an indispensable philosophical category in his writings. Beginning from the early history of epistemology until the present phenomenological approach to human knowledge the dicthotomy continued. As a corollary to this, the concept of man has always been explicated in a knower-known perspective at the cost of our awareness of man in his wholeness. Even the phenomenological theory of intentionality of consciousness which originally attempted to bridge the gulf between the thought-oriented approach and the reality-oriented approach to knowledge, it continued to remain under the sway of the disjunction of the relativity of object to consciousness (Husserl) and that of consciousness to object (Sartre). According to Buber, while the directionality of consciousness can be conceived on the ground of a bifurcation of reality into man and man, and man and the world, it can also be understood in terms of another mode of intentionality which consists in dialogue alone. In the former case the support of the directionality of consciousness is **Ego** — transcendental or pre-reflective. Buber called it the relational sphere of **I-It** where consciousness is always a consciousness **of** as per the well-known phenomenological slogan: 'consciousness is always a consciousness **of** something'. In the latter case the support of the directionality of consciousness is the relation itself. This is the realm of the **between** where consciousness is a consciousness **in** the relation. Buber called it the relational sphere of **I-Thou** the ontological status of which can be described in Buber's term as 'relation's own being'. Buber thus initiated and led a new trend of thought which gives priority to existence, experience and the image of the human that proceeds and develops through every type of personal encounter we have with the other.

Buber's entire scheme was to answer the famous Kantian question: 'What is Man',? comprehensively and in a holistic perspective. The **I-It** or subject-object dichotomy does not yield any knowledge of the whole man because man is capable of both forms of relationship, viz.

I-It and **I-Thou**. But **I-Thou** or dialogical relationship reveals man known as a **Thou** in his entire capacity to **be** in both ways, as a being who does not merely possess power over the **It** (the object of knowledge) but can also switch over to a Thou-orientation to it. Hence the best way of characterizing Buber, as Maurice Friedman has suggested, is that he is a philosophical anthropologist.[1] Buber's phenomenological ontology of the **between** was developed in the context of answering questions about man. But this ontology and man's cognitive competence related to it has further ramifications in other human studies and disciplines where disclosure of man's being in the world is of a primary concern. Such a frame-work is brought about very prominently by the phenomenon of art. Art, from Buber's point of view, reveals man's capacity to enter into a dialogue even with the so-called recalcitrant, inanimate nature — the world of things; man comes out of his ego-sense with a directed choice to confront, shape, and give a form to the world. The prospect of a Buberian aesthetics can be traced to this human capacity of being in a dialogical relationship with the world. Dialogue as a major concept of Buber's philosophical anthropology and the basis of knowledge of man by man thus becomes the ground of artistic creation and aesthetic experience as well.

II

The concept of art as dialogue and its phenomenological formulation is most perspicuously present in the writings of Martin Buber. Buber's aesthetics is an extension of his philosophy of dialogue. Dialogue, for him, is essentially a reality and a method in and through which man is known by man. It forms the perspective of **I-Thou**. 'Dialogue' signifies **relationship** between man and man, a live communication rather than a sheer exchange of meaningful words. It is a communication based upon communion from where words may follow but words do not constitute it. Or, one can say that words become identical with the specific mode of existence. According to Buber **I-Thou** is a 'primary word' which is 'spoken from the being'.

Both methodologically and ontologically 'dialogue' is a very important concept in our philosophico-anthropological enterprises. No monologue can yield any concept of man in a comprehensive way. The moment we raise the question: 'How is knowledge of man by man possible,? we have to set ourselves in relation to each other, and consequently, to the entire world lived by us.

But what kind of relation is this? Is it a kind of relation that we have with objects? Or are we related to each other as pure sujectivity? Since man is always more than what he is at a certain spatio-temporal point, he as a knowable subject cannot be reduced to a 'spoken fact' with a fixed meaning. Nor can he be treated as pure subjectivity from the purview of knowledge. The concept of man as pure subjectivity results in unknowability of man as such. The man-in-himself cannot be known. But can there ever be a man-in-himself? Is he not always in a communicative state — in relation to someone real or imagined? Even a recluse or *yogī* seeks to unite himself with **The One**. We always strive to establish the meaning of our existence by discovering our relation with the universe. But such discoveries cannot remain isolated within the precincts of an individual life. Their verity or versimilitude must be tested and ensured in a human social perspective where each individual is in relation with the other.

Martin Buber bifurcated this relational reality into two dimensions viz. **I-Thou** (man-man) and **I-It** (man-object). But the most primitive mode of existence for human creatures is **I-Thou**. The primitive function of knowledge contains no analysis or reflection which brings separation. It knows only 'relation', and not any 'object' or 'thing' as an independent being having its very own structure. Here neither the subject nor the object but the relation itself is the "category of being, readiness, grasping form, mould for the soul".[2] An anthropological investigation puts it this way : "For modern, scientific man the phenomenal world is primarily an 'It', for ancient and also for primitive man it is a 'Thou'... The world appears to primitive man neither inanimate nor empty but abundant with life ... ".[3] The child's self too, according to Buber, is enabled through his personal relation with other human beings; it comes to the knowledge of external reality as **It** when it is enabled to differentiate between that which is a **Thou** to the child and that which does not speak to him but acquires a meaning in terms of his certain use of it. Buber's statement in this regard is quite revealing : "The development of the soul in child is inextricably bound up with that of this longing, with the game of his experiments and the tragic seriousness of his perplexity".[4]

But which of these two ways should we follow in knowing man who is capable of both ways of living? To put it a bit differently : 'How is knowledge of man by man possible?', the question is a methodological and ontological one. We have already seen that it is not possible to view man either as an **It** (object) or as pure subjectivity (a lone **I**) in a Buberian perspective. Hence methodologically Thou-orientation, i.e., dialogue is the only alternative left for us. Ontologically too Buber thinks that there is an 'in-born thou' within us which unfolds itself in our relationship with the other. This 'in-born thou' obliges us to know the other in his or her essentiality, as a **Thou**, and not as an **It** or a **He** or **She**. In our act of addressing the other as **Thou** we address the whole being of the other. But when we refer to the other as **he** or **she**, i.e., in third person, we reduce the other to an **it**; we treat him or her as an object with some definite aspects. While in **I-Thou** form of relationship the whole being of man is addressed, **I-It** form reveals only aspects of him. The whole being of man includes the inexhaustible competence of men to be in both modes of existence, viz. **I-Thou** and **I-It**. The dialogical approach to man involves the anthropologist too in an **I-Thou** mode of existence. This enables him to envision man in his entirely which takes into account also man as forming meaning even of the world of **it**.

As Buber contented, even the world of **It** owes its origin to **Thou**. In his book *Martin Buber : The Life of Dialogue* Maurice Friedman writes : "Only **I-Thou** gives meaning the world of **It**, for **I-Thou** is not reached in time but is there from the start, originating and carrying-through."[5] Meaning, which we can talk of or assign to objects, facts, or events that may be physical or psychical is in course of time hardened into an **It** and estranged from any direct human participation. To be in a human world, "again and again that which has the status of object must blaze up into presentness and enter the elemental state from which it came, to be looked on and lived in the present by man".[6] Man has a personal existence where he is not identified by any of his manifest aspects but from the core of which he offers himself to the world in newer relations and thereby changes the meaning of a fact-ridden world. The personal existence of man creates a demand within him to relate himself to the world in ever new ways and not always with reference to a given meaning-structure. If the world of **It** is not renewed time and again by a Thou-orientation, it ceases to be in the human world. Unlike animals man does not remain satisfied simply by using things. He desires also to enter into personal relationship with things and to imprint on them the saga following from his relationship. Here lies the origin of art.

According to Buber the art form being assigned to a thing the thingly nature of the thing is transcended : "It ceases to be accessory to a tool and becomes an independent structure". But this independent structure is not to be dissociated from the purview of relation; it beams only in the light of relation. Artistic creation and awareness proceeds from our dissatisfaction with the stringent meaning-contents of the world of **It** and our urge to elevate it to a level of intimacy with our own being. Buber says : "The form indicated by even the clumsiest ornament is now fulfilled, in an autonomous region as the sediment of man's relation to things. Art is neither the impression of natural objectivity nor the expression of spiritual subjectivity, but it is the work and witness of the relation between the *substantia humana* and the *substantia rerum*".[7]

The aesthetics of Martin Buber consists primarily in an investigation into the origin and *raison de'etre* of art wherein his philosophical anthropology is heavily drawn upon. As Lous Z. Hammer points out : "The fact that some men are artists is to be grasped, within the framework of Buber's thought, not as a mere accident, but rather as an outcome of what man essentially is".[8] Also, that his question concerning art is a philosophico-anthropological one is clear from its very formulation: "What can be said about art as about a being that springs from the being of man?"[9] Buber starts his essay 'Man and

His image-work' by pinpointing this relation: "The question of the connection between the essence of man and the essence of art must be posed anew. That means that art must be regarded as the image-work of man, the peculiar image-work of his peculiarity. We ask about the connection between what is essentially peculiar to man and what is essentially characteristic of art."[10] The connection can be articulated within the frame-work of Buber's philosophical anthropology. In *A Believing Humanism : Gleanings* Buber maintains that the centrality of human existence is sought in man's relation to all existing beings : "What appears here as the Humanum, as the great superiority of man before all other living beings known to us is his capacity of his own accord, hence, not like the animals out of the compulsion of his needs and wants but out of the overflow of his existence, to come into direct contact with everything that he bodily or spiritually meets — to address it with lips and heart or even with heart alone. In distinction from the animal, man can grasp all that encounters him on his life's way as a being existing in itself beyond his own interest. He can enter into relationship with this independently existing other. By knowing and acknowledging the other at times as a whole, he can at times himself relate to is as a whole".[11] For Buber the essential characteristic of art too consists in this meeting which is of dialogical kind. Man cannot come into direct contact with things as long as they remain under the purview of knowledge which forms the world of **It**, i.e., knowledge which is non-dialogical by nature : ". . . one misses the basic nature of art . . . if one moves it so close to knowledge, indeed directly, subsumes it under the latter".[12] Here 'knowledge' means knowledge of — a discursive mode of awareness without meeting or encounter. The overflow of man's existence does not find any outlet in the world of **It** because man is here confined to the border of necessity. In conformity with what Buber depicted as 'the great superiority of man before all other living beings known to us' in a non-utilitarian urge to 'meet' and 'address' all beings as 'independently existing others', his reflection on art activity says : "Perception draws out of the being the world that we need: only vision and, in its wake, art transcends need and makes the superfluous into the necessary".[13] Transcendence for Buber is dialogical which consists in a personal meeting between **I** and **Thou**. For Buber both anthropological knowledge and aesthetic cognition require a Thou-orientation. Knowledge through dialogue is basically a non-judicative comprehension of the real; it is not discursive, it is immediate. It is not so much an achievement of the knower; nor is it indicative of any property of the object. It records the vision and negates the bifurcation of language and reality, and knowledge and the object of which it is a knowledge are fused into one relational whole. Its veracity is established within the perspective of relation alone through a continuous self-giving, by discharging one's being to give shape to the 'object' and thereby accruing a so far unknown identification from that 'object' which is really **no object but a partner** in the process. It happens so not only in case of our knowledge of man but also our art experience. Man enters into a dialogical relation with his image-work; the created form is taken up into the meeting of **I** and **Thou** and not left out as a detached object of observation, use and analysis. In Buber's words : ". . . all art is from its origin essentially of the nature of dialogue". [14]

In a Buberian perspective the complementarity between philosophical anthropology and philosophy of art can be understood in the following terms: (i) The method of philosophical anthropology is incorporated into our understanding of art experiences and art objects. About the phenomenon of art Buber says : "It is, indeed, neither the mystery of the things nor that of the spirit that is represented in art, but the relation between the two".[15] (ii) Our art activities point back to the peculiarity of human nature which consists in a relational reality of **I** and **Thou**. Buber's aesthetics endorses the view that man is essentially dialogic. It is interesting to note what Buber says regarding man's art activity : "The artist is the man who instead of objectifying what is over against him forms it into an image. Here the nature of the action in which perception takes place no longer suffices: the working must play a substantial part if that which stands over aganist him is to become image. That which stands over against, I say; that does not mean this or that phenomenon, this or that piece of the external world, some complex of appearances given to the sight or hearing in the actual experience, but whatever in the whole possible world-sphere enters into that sense with which this particular art is associated, the whole possible world-sphere of sight, the whole possible world-sphere of hearing".[16] Since the image-work (i.e., the art object) is encompassed by the whole possible world-sphere of sight or hearing depending on the sense with which it is associated, the scope of hermeneutical understanding remains open with the art appreciator or critic. The meaning of a particular art object cannot keep fixed as the whole possible world-sphere percolates through it generating new meanings for the beholder or the critic. It happens so because we are in an unending dialogue with the image-work under perception. This bringing forth of oneself in one's creative move to the world through art and art through world triggers us back to man's beginning in relation, his trust in it, and finally his mission to **be** in it. (iii) Buber equates the ontology of man with the ontology of the **between**. For him the real is relational: "In the beginning is relation", and "the aim of relation is relation's own being, that is, contact with the **Thou**". This relational realm is the realm of the **between**. Man as a whole with his inexhaustible spirit is real only in this realm. In the world of **I-It** we extract knowledge from things about their constitution, use etc., we thereby 'win experience' from them — the experiences that belong to things. The things may be physical or psychical but as Buber says : "Inner things or outer things, what they are but things and things".[17] The concept of experience, in this sense, gets along with a concept of man as a collector or manipulator of experiences from things; the **logos** of man is lost in the **logos** of things, man appears before man with a camouflage. Man himself is thus reified to a thing. Only in an **I-Thou** perspective does man's being find its own locus which is 'the relation's own being'.

Methodologically, Thou-orientation to man suspends all of his third person aspects (It-aspects) like his being a tool maker, an engineer, an office bearer, a rational animal, a member of a social class, etc., and focuses upon the fundamental phenomenon of his being in the relation, i.e., man as a **phainomenon** who can simply be faced and addressed. This dialogical method yields our knowledge of man; the specificities of man are linked with this **Humanum** and assessed on its basis. Ontologically Thou-orientation places the reality of man in the reality of relation and its manifestations. This phenomenological ontology of Buber does not suffer any profanation in his treatment of art. For him the ontology of art is to be sought in man's relation with the phenomenon of art, i.e., in the ontology of the **between**. "The common principle that we find effectively present in sufficient concreteness in each of the arts" is envisaged, according to

Buber, by taking this relational dimension into account, i.e., man's relation to the image-work accomplished or unaccomplished so far.[18] In *I and Thou* Buber says: ". . . a man is faced by a form which desires to be made through him into a work (of art)".[19] Like a **Thou**, an art form encompassed by the whole possible world-sphere (of sight or hearing) has a reality-character: "This form is no offspring of his (man's) soul, but is an appearance which steps up to it and demands of it the effective power . . . if he speaks the primary word out of his being to the form which appears, then the effective power streams out, and the work (of art) arises".[20]

As regards our anthropological knowledge-situation, Buber holds that the situation is relational and the relation consists in mutually : "Relation is mutual. My Thou affects me, as I affect it".[21] But does the image-work or the form which is yet to be transformed into an image reciprocate our feelings as does the other human being in an anthropological knowledge-situation? Is there any mutuality in our relationship with the being of art? On the one hand Buber maintains that the being of art springs from the being of man, and on the other hand he holds that art (which includes works of art within the purview of human perception) has a 'reality-character' and it needs to be addressed as **Thou**. But if the being of art is parasitic upon the being of man, can it be said to have a life of its own? In what sense is art real and is its reality manifested in sufficient concreteness in each of the arts and works of art? These are some of the problems which must arise so far as the co-implication between philosophical anthropology and philosophy of art goes in a Buberian perspective. I think these problems centre mainly around the concept of the being of art in the context of aesthetic experience. While Buber's contention that the being of art cannot be isolated from its experiential dimension is quite in the spirit of the contemporary phenomenology of art and should draw the attention of researchers in this field, we have to bear in mind that his concept of the being of art as springing from the being of man is proposed primarily in the context of anthropology of art in its philosophical sense and it must not be isolated from art's being and it's 'reality-character' manifested in the sphere of human cognition. To take the example of a child, a child is given birth by his parents and his growth is dependent on them in many ways but he cannot be denied his own being. I make this distinction between the two sense of being for understanding Buber with more clarity and to dispel the confusion, but any of these senses cannot be really isolated from the other. In fact these two senses of being are knitted together in Buber's writings. Art is real only in the context of its relationship with us; its ontology is the ontology of this relation. Buber holds that the question concerning the being of art as springing from the being of man "is an anthropological one in the philosophical sense of the world", and "every anthropology of a subject touches on its ontology, hence . . . . every investigation of a subject in its conditioning by the manner, the nature, the attitude of man leads us towards this subject's place in being and its function in meaning".[22] At the same time he says that the question concerning the relation between being of man and being of art "must begin in the sphere in which the life of human senses dwells; it is that in which the dependence of man on the existent properly constitutes itself and that which determines the reality-character of all art so that no mental and no emotional element may enter into art otherwise through becoming a thing of senses".[23] What Buber perhaps means is that man's consciousness in art activity is first directed to something which the consciousness is not, and then gradually the being of art becomes manifest in view of its relation to consciousness within human experiential dimension. As its reality-character is undeniably apparent man is bound to put faith on this, and his whole being is involved in his meeting with the art form encompassed by the whole possible world-sphere. The same is true regarding any particular art form which could never be conceived without being in relation to man. The independence of the two poles, viz. man and art, is not of primary importance. What is primarily important is there being a relation between the two. But is this independence not a necessary condition for there being a relation? From Buber's point of view independence is asserted in relation. The co-implication between philosophical anthropology and philosophy of art is rather a follow-up of the relationalistic ontology of Buber. The being of art cannot be placed beyond it. Hence questions or doubts regarding the reality-character of a work of art, or in Buber's term, the 'image-work' arise only in the **I-Thou** relational frame-work where a 'lively' role of the work is a natural expectation.

III

We have seen in the preceding section that there is not only a complementarity between Buber's philosophical anthropology and his philosophy of art but this relation is considered to be necessary for the understanding of art as a human phenomenon. This is further substantiated by Buber's phenomenology of dialogue which incorporates the being of art within aesthetic experience in a non-isolationistic way.

Buber's inquiry into our art experience has a clear phenomenological orientation as he does away with psychologism on the one hand and objectivism on the other, i.e., the concept of art as representing the mystery of the spirit or that of things. Art, for him, represents relation's own being. According to Buber it is the intentional act of human consciousness moving towards its object forms the basis of all kind of awareness. This is what he means when he says: "Our behaviour rests upon innumerable unifications of movements to something and perceptions of something. There is no movement that is not directly or indirectly connected with a perception, and no perception that is not more or less consciously connected with a movement. There is nothing in and of us that is fully removed from this base; even the images of fantasy, dreams, madness draw their material from it . . ."[24]

In art this movement figures in 'meeting' or 'dialogue'. By 'experience' we cannot anymore mean 'experience of' so far as our experiencing something in a relational realm is concerned. In Buber's dialogic framework 'experience' would mean **living the life of that which is being experienced**. According to Buber the eternal source of art is "a man faced by a form which desires to be made through him into work", and in the sustaining source of an **I-Thou** relationship aesthetic cognition must yield to the need for exclusiveness, for sacrifice, so that the work appears in its wholeness and concrete uniqueness. He says: "The work does not suffer me . . . to turn aside and relax in the world of **It**; but it commands. If I do not serve it aright it is broken, or it breaks me. I can neither experience* nor describe the

* By 'experience' Buber here refers to the usual concept of 'experience of something'.

form which meets me, but only body it forth. And yet I behold it, splendid in the radiance of what confronts me, clearer than all clearness of the world which is experienced. I do not behold it as a thing among the 'inner' things nor as an image of my 'fancy', but as that which exists in the present... And the relation in which I stand to it is real, for it affects me, as I affect it".[25]

Meeting makes the form in its presence. The transition from the level of the experience **of** something to experiencing something wherein the intentional acts of consciousness are submerged is shown here. It is a landmark of Buber's contribution to contemporary phenomenology. Maurice Friedman in his introduction to Buber's **The Knowledge of Man** says : "To Kant's statement that we can only know of the 'thing in itself' that it is, Buber adds for modern man the assertion 'and that the existent meets us' ".[26] This mode of intentionality is such that it does not simply allow one to speak of the exclusive importance of subject or object. Cartesian dualism has always prompted us to ask whether aesthetic experience is subjective or objective, and then led the way either to subjectivism or objectivism. A work of art is not objectively set afar from man. Nor is the human agency inclined against the world which is its canvas or the work which awaits a meeting with man. The recent distinction between the work of art and the aesthetic object does not occur in Buber's writings, but it is implied when he said : "The work produced is a thing among things, able to be experienced and described as a sum of qualities. But from time to time it can face the receptive beholder in its whole embodied form".[27] Obviously Buber's concern is with the work in its experiential dimension. It does not have any aesthetic value as a thing among other things — 'inner' or 'outer'. Hence Buber would agree with what Mikel Dufrenne says : "The work must offer itself to perception: it must be performed in order to pass, as it were, form a potential to an actual existence".[28] For Dufrenne the being of the work of art is not dependent on being experienced, while the aesthetic object exists only as experienced by a spectator. The work of art, from this standpoint, is the enduring structural foundation for the aesthetic object. As an unaccomplished, unfulfilled form it is within the domain of aesthetic experience; after creation it sinks back into an **It** but awaits a **Thou**, — the artist or the beholder, to become an 'image-work' which is the aesthetic object.

Now the sphere of aesthetic intentionality is such that it has to be dialogic in character because the aesthetic object which is **no-object** defies any other description, use or analysis than being confronted as a **Thou**. The phenomenological symbiosis of **I** (man) and **Thou** (the aesthetic object) determines the being of art. This symbiosis cannot take place until the intentional mode in our experience **of** something passes on to a dialogical level where that something demands a 'Thou-orientation' from us. In fact it is this communion between man as an artist and/or spectator and the art object which forms the central problematic of Buber's phenomenology of aesthetic experience. Its relevance to recent studies in phenomenological aesthetics becomes apparent with Mikel Dufrenne's observation: "The aesthetic object bears its own signification within it, and by entering more profoundly into communion with the object, one discovers its signification, just as one understands the being of others by virtue of friendship. The communion is indispensable. Without it, the aesthetic object is inert and meaningless, just as without performance (when it requires one) it is only imperfectly existent".[29] The aesthetic object does not signify anything beyond itself. This is the function of any **signifying**

object which according to Dufrenne is different from aesthetic object. An aesthetic object is **expressive**. It is the artist's gesture towards us. According to Dufrenne it is an "originally speech which, instead of bringing forth a conceptual meaning, simultaneously awakens a feeling and conjures up a presence".[30] But in spite of Dufrenne's emphasis on communion, he holds that this communion becomes apparent through the feeling which reveals subjectivity. For him aesthetic expression reveals this subjectivity. Buber's aesthetic philosophy does not admit of any such priority to any subjective or psychological element like feeling. His stand is exceptional because, for him, communion or **I-Thou** relationship is the most fundamental phenomenon which cannot be subsumed under the category of subjectivity or feeling or objectivity. Communion or **I-Thou** relationship precedes feelings. It is not the feeling which conjures up the aesthetic presence. It is the other way round; communion in simultaneity with the presence conjures up the feeling. Aesthetic experience without this relation is inconceivable. As we have discussed above, the being of art can be conceived concretely in relation, i.e., in the experience **in** art.

From Buber's standpoint, I. A. Richard's concession to the phenomenon of art as merely emotionally significant is intolerable. Also, Croce's conception of a true creative work as the inner intuition and the formulation of the work of art as emotionally charged image, the embodiment of which in any external material being purely an affair of technical skill and not an essential part either of the creative act of the inner expression or of the finished work of art resplendent in the inner light of the creator-mind, this is not acceptable in the relationalistic frame-work of Buber. On the same ground Buber's view can be contrasted with Collingwood's expressionist theory of art according to which the essence of art is in the expression of emotions, or Susanne Langer's concept of the work of art as a virtual image reflecting a pattern of feeling.

There may be different modes of aesthetic presence depending upon the interplay between the perceiver and the perceived. Accordingly there may be innumerable interpretations and ways of reception and presentation of an art object. But, from Buber's dialogical standpoint, the Thou-orientation is the fundamental condition for hermeneutics in art. This condition is not formal, logical; it is existential. It is there as an unshakable ground on which the community of taste grows. Under the purview of dialogical mode of intentionality an art object does not remain a mere object of our free acceptance or rejection. In Buber's phrase, 'it commands'. In the words of Hans George Gadamar: ". . . . we must admit that the world of artistic tradition — the splendid contemporaneousness that we gain through art with so may human worlds — is more than a mere object of our free acceptance and rejection."[31] According to him an immediate truth-claim proceeds from the art object itself and an alienation into aesthetic judgement takes place on our part when we withdraw ourselves and "are no longer open to the immediate claim of that which grasps us". For Gadamar, "our senstive-spiritual existence is an aesthetic resonance chamber that resonates with the voice that is constantly reaching us, preceding all explicit aesthetic judgement."[32] This resonance shows a primordial, common accord between man and man, man and the world.

A concretisation, renewal and interpretation of this accord is possible through our aesthetic experiences. Martin Buber's aesthetic suggests that the heremeneutics in art has its legitimacy on this ground — the ground of our saying **Thou** to the form, the image-work. In Buber's philosophy of dialogue the addressed or 'Thou' is not necessarily a human being though the relation is in one way understood in a human model. The possibility of a dialogical relationship between man and nature or inanimate things is acceptable in the Buberian frame-work by holding nature or things in dialogue. In other words, though there is no mutuality in a relation between man and nature or a thing the **I-Thou** dimension of reality is conceivable in that context; Buber says: "Each thing and being has a twofold nature: the passive, absorbable, usable, dissectible, comparable, combinable, rationalizable, and the other, the active, non-absorbable, unusable, undissectible, incomparable, non-combinable, non-rationalizable. This is the confronting, the shaping, the bestowing in things. He who truely experiences a thing so that it springs up to meet him and embraces him of itself has in that thing known the world."[33] In his *Martin Buber : The Life of Dialogue* Maurice Friedman explicates this point in clearer terms with particular reference to art works : "Though natural things may 'say' something to us and in that sense have personal relations with us, they do not have the continuity, the independence, or the living consciousness and consciousness of self which make up the person. A tree can 'say' something to me and become my Thou, but I cannot be a Thou for it. This same impossibility of reciprocity is found in the work of literature and art which becomes Thou for us, and this suggests by analogy that as the poem is the 'word' of the poet, so the tree may be the 'word' of Being over against us, Being which is more than human but less than personal . . . . this view alone allows to non-human existing beings their true 'otherness' as something more than the passive objects of our thought and categories and the passive tools of our will to use."[34] This act of addressing involves the whole of our being as well as the being of art. They together form the "relation's own being". In the realm of art the dialogic move is self-consciously taken; the art object is addressed and through the act of addressing the modality of its existence in its own right is established. It becomes real, but unlike the reality of an object our knowledge of the reality of an art object remains unfinished. It is so because it as an indefinite **x** and without any definite meaning-content meets us in our art experience. So its reality-character can be talked about in the context of one's perception from one's contact with being. As Maurice Friedman elaborates on this point : "The sense world is a preliminary stage on the way to artistic vision and vision is figurating faithfulness to the unknown and does its work in cooperation with it. The meeting of the artist and world is not an encounter between perception and sense-object, but between the being of the artist and the being of the **x** . . . The artist fashions the sense world anew through his figuration in vision and in work — not through trying to penetrate behind the world of senses, but through completing its form to the perfect work of figuration."[35] In this experiential dimension (of the dialogical kind) the being of art is established concretely. The anthropological significance of art can be sought in the channellisation of the creative competence of man into this experiential dimension, i.e. the dialogic form of intentionality and the reality-character of the form or image-work. But, unlike Gadamar, Buber would maintain that the speakability of this experience, i.e., the experience in art does not yield any alienation. Such a speakability itself involves creativity as the language of common sense does not suffice to depict the experience. Thus for Buber the hermeneutics in art proceeds from our grasp of the immediate truth-claim of the work within the spell of a dialogic mode of intentionality; it matures through newer and newer modes of presence of the object to one's presence. These modes become transparent to us for the interpretative element in our understanding of it. To take the example of Hindustani classical music, the same *rāga* is executed in different styles by different *gharānās* (schools) though the notes remain identical. Each way of presenting the *rāga* has a unique impact on the audience. Perhaps there is no end of interpreting the specified notations of *rāgas* in the available texts of Hindustani classical music. Interpretation always involves an otherness to which man has to set himself in a relation. Each relation means a unique kind of communion which changes the context of a literary text, a mural, a sculptor, or any work of art. To speak in a different way, every context of the interpretative understanding of a work of art involves a suggestion making its decontextualization possible. An image to be embodied or a work to be appreciated is, from this standpoint, a **Thou** which is not bound by the precincts of strict meaning. It cannot be known through or inferred from anything which is already meant or defined.

The creator or beholder must have a direct access to the art object. The possibility of different interpretations of one and the same object is there even in cases of our understanding of objects belonging to the ordinary commonsensical world and the statements made with regard to them. But this possibility is mostly in terms of changes of space and time, practical interests and biases, contexts and pretexts, and above all, a given meaning-structure. An artistic creation, on the other hand, unfolds itself in terms of its own space and time transcending the ordinary day-to-day world. Even the entire world, from the point of view of this single creation, is seen in a different way — in an intimate perspective of the creator and/or beholder overpassing the border of observed facts which can be adjusted to a general scientific outlook or a commonsensical structure of meaning.[36] Despite an essential difference from the Buberian approach we can recall on this point Susanne Langer's distinction between "symbols which express facts for discursive thinking" and "artistic symbols". She says : "Artistic symbols . . . are untranslatable. Their sense is bound to the peculiar form which it has taken . . . though the material of poetry is verbal, its import is not the literal assertion made in the words, but **the way the assertion is made.**"[37] Interpretation of an art form requires an entry into this way, and thereby a transcendence of the naturalistic attitude. The aim of such interpretation is not to **explicate** the art form (as we do in cases of geometric symbols), but to **describe** as it exists in relation to man. This relation is important for interpretation because the form in this case has to be **in the presence of** man and man too has to be **in the presence of** the form. **Being in the presence of** is a necessary requisite for interpreting art objects. We can outline a phenomenology of aesthetic experience keeping this dialogic mode of intentionality as our focal point and thereby delineate all other dimensions of a phenomenon of art in its light. According to Buber art is one of the forms of **I-Thou** relationship. It responds to human onlookers in an unspoken language the translation of which is possible through dialogical interpretation; a translucency is created and the speakability of the unspoken comes up from the depth of dialogue itself. Thus, from Buber's point of view, a dialogic discourse on art is possible. One major task of contemporary philosophy of art is to articulate it, and elevate the level of language by relating it to the being of art and the being of man.

Notes and References

1. Maurice Friedman: "Introductory Essay", In Martin Buber's *The Knowledge of Man*, edited with an introductory essay by Maurice Friedman, tr. by Maurice Friedman and R. G. Smith, London, George Allen & Unwin Ltd., 1965. Henceforth, *KM*.
2. Martin Buber : *I and Thou*, tr. by Ronald Gregor Smith, Charles Scribner's Sons, New York, 1958, p. 27.
3. H. and H. A. Frankfort, John A. Wilson and Thorkild Jaccobson : *Before Philosophy*, Maryland, Baltimore, 1968, pp. 13-14.
4. Martin Buber : *I and Thou*, p. 28.
5. Maurice Friedman : *Martin Buber: The Life of Dialogue* Harper & Row, New York, 1960, p. 67.
6. Martin Buber : *I and Thou*, p. 40.
7. Martin Buber : *KM*, p. 66.
8. Louis Z. Hammer : "The Relevance of Buber's Thought to Aesthetic", In *The Philosophy of Martin Buber*, ed. by Maurice Friedman and Paul Arther Schilpp, Henry Tudor, 1961.
9. Martin Buber : "Man and His Image-work", In *KM*, p. 149.
10. Martin Buber : *KM*, p. 149.
11. Martin Buber: *A Believing Humanism: Gleanings*, tr. by Maurice Friedman, Simon & Schuster, New York, 1969, p. 120.
12. Martin Buber : *KM*, p. 152.
13. *Ibid.*, p. 160.
14. Martin Buber : *Between Man and Man*, tr. by R. G. Smith, Kegan Paul, London, 1947, p. 25.
15. Martin Buber : *KM*, p. 165.
16. *Ibid.*, p. 160.
17. Martin Buber : *I and Thou*, p. 5.
18. Martin Buber : *KM*, p. 150.

19. Martin Buber : *I and Thou*, p. 9.
20. *Ibid.*
21. *Ibid.*, p. 15.
22. Martin Buber : *KM*, pp. 149-50.
23. *Ibid.*, p. 150.
24. *Ibid.*, p. 156.
25. Martin Buber : *I and Thou*, p. 10.
26. Maurice Friedman : "Introductory Essay", In *KM*, p. 55.
27. Martin Buber : *I and Thou*, p. 10.
28. Mikel Dufrenne: *The Phenomenology of Aesthetic Experience*, tr. by Edward S. Casey, Evanston, Ill. North-Western University Press, 1973, p. 79. Henceforth, *PAE*.
29. *Ibid.*, p. 228.
30. *Ibid.*, p. 135.
31. Hans-George Gadamar : "The Universality of Hermeneutical Problem", In *Contemporary Hermeneutics* by Joseph Bleicher, Routhledge & Kegan Paul, 1980, p. 129.
32. *Ibid*, p. 132.
33. Martin Buber : *Pointing the Way*, ed. and tr. with an introduction by Maurice Friedman, Harper Torchbooks, New York, 1963, p. 27.
34. Maurice Friedman : *Martin Buber : The Life of Dialogue*, Harper & Row, New York, 1960, p. 171.
35. Maurice Friedman : "Introductory Essay", In *KM*, pp. 55-56.
36. Compare : "Each painting, each book, is a rediscovery of the totality of being." Jean-Paul Sartre, *What is literature?* Harper & Row, 1965, p. 51.
37. Susanne Langer: *Philosophy in a New Key*, Harvard University Press, 1965, p. 260.

4

Michael Polanyi's Aesthetics

A Phenomenological Study

THE philosophy of Michael Polanyi presents us with a frame-work within which the relationship between man and his discoveries, his object of knowledge and creation can be seen in a new light, it enable us to overthrow the positivistic perspective of human knowledge and ensure its personal dimension. Knowledge, for Polanyi, can be accounted for in view of man's faith and commitment, intellectual passion and existential urge to bring forth the universal intent in his discovery. This dimension is of some fundamental importance as it brings the free human individual with his creative competence closer to the world; it makes him responsible for it, and generates a commitment in him to discover the so far unknown forms of reality within the world. This specific output of Polanyi's philosophical programme is in consonance with his statement that he turned from physical chemistry to philosophy in reaction to the scientific outlook producing a 'mechanical conception of man and history in which there was no place for science itself' (as a free human enterprise).[1] The alternative frame-work of knowledge proposed by him has great relevance not only to philosophy of science — an alteration of which was the initial thrust of his writings — but also to philosophical anthropology,[2] philosophy of art and, for that matter, to contemporary culture as a whole. In this chapter, I propose to focus on Polanyi's theory of art in terms of a notion of intentionality envisioned in his concept of personal knowledge and its underlying structure. For this purpose, I wish to proceed by giving (i) a brief outline of Polanyi's epistemology of personal knowledge in terms of its salient features, so that (ii) a new mode of intentionality can be envisaged to explain not only our achievement of meaning at the level of our interaction with impersonal objects but also (iii) the nature of meaning be-spoken by the works of art. This chapter will, in this sense, attempt to give an interpretative and critical study of Polanyi's approach to art. I call this study 'phenomenological' as it concerns the phenomena of art in the irreducibility of their meaning and coherence accomplished through the dynamics of personal knowledge. We shall also see that this dynamics entails a concept of consciousness, the intentional acts of which consist in self-transcendence to be sought in a meeting or dialogue between man and the world. Aesthetic intentionality comes under the purview of this notion of consciousness.

I

A Critique of Objectivism

While Polanyi does not deny the objectivity of our knowledge, he assigns a new meaning to it and frees it from the clutches of objectivism. Objectivity of any knowledge-claim is on a par with its universality, which can be achieved only through a personal commitment of the knower. For Polanyi science is impossible without a presupposition of the existence of something hidden from its view. The knowability of it is a faith to be pursued. This faith leads the scientist to commit himself to discover it, to unveil its structure, and depict it with clarity, precision and proof. The commitment situation is formed by the scientist's search for the hidden reality and it controls the entire knowledge-process. The questions concerning truth and falsity, validity and invalidity, precision and imprecision, clarity and ambiguity are all meaningless, if we do not relate them to a commitment situation and point to the right or wrong steps of science in its way of discovery. As Polanyi remarks: "A passionate comprehension necessarily appreciates the perfection of that which it comprehends".[3] The relation between man and the world in the perspective of human knowledge is not to be seen in a psychologistic, subjectivistic or objectivistic fashion. It is animated by the human personality stepping out to the unknown, and thereby widening its own horizon and enriching its own identity. Subjectivism is not the alternative of objectivism. A proper critique of objectivistic, positivistic, and impersonal approach to human knowledge can be accomplished, according to Polanyi, by spelling out its 'personal co-efficient' persisting in every form of human knowledge. This co-efficient, as Polanyi contends, bridges 'the disjunction between subjectivity and objectivity', and "implies the claim that man can transcend his own subjectivity by striving passionately to fulfil his personal obligation to universal standards".[4] An important contribution of Polanyi is that he rejects any ontology of the subject or the object in this regard. If 'ontology' means a **theory of what there is**, then such ontologies themselves are based on some ontical assumptions. But these assumptions cannot be used to give a one-sided version of knowledge and reality. 'What there is' can be systematically theorized and put into some propositions. But this would be an abstraction devoid of any relation to the very act of theorizing and systematizing. The concepts deployed in a theory will then be without any foundation. Polanyi's concept of knowledge does not leave aside the dynamic aspect of it which thrives through a constant interaction between the knower and the known, knowing and being. Its ontological import lies, first, in a transcendence of any dichotomy of the two into a reality in an active, animate manner, and, secondly, in guiding us to comprehend something real. The way the personal being of man is tied up with reality in the formation of knowledge as a meaningful and coherent achievement is furhter envisioned by Polanyi in terms of what he calls subsidiary and focal awareness.

Subsidiary Awareness and Focal Awareness

Knowledge, for Polanyi, is an action which requires skill. Its articulation is a skilful shaping of a coherent meaning performed by subordinating a set of particulars as clues or a tool to it. All acts of knowing are constituted by three interrelated factors : (a) the **person,** (b) who integrates **subsidiary clues,** (c) to **focus** on a **coherent meaning**. We become aware of these clues subsidiarily within our focal awareness of the coherent entity that we achieve. To cite an example given by Polanyi : "When I receive information by reading a letter and when I ponder the message of the letter, I am subsidiarily aware not only of its text, but also of all the past occasions by which I have come to understand the words of the text, and the whole range of this subsidiary awareness is presented focally in terms of the message. This message or meaning, on which attention is now focused, is not something tangible: it is the conception evoked by the text. **The conception in question is the focus of our attention, in terms of which**

we attend subsidiarily both to the text and to the objects indicated by the text. Thus the meaning of a text resides in a focal comprehension of all the relevant instrumentally known particulars, just as the purpose of an action resides in the co-ordinated innovation of its instrumentally used particulars".[5]

Similarly, when one plays a musical instrument to perform a composition which is a coherent entity, one's **focal** target is to achieve that coherent entity, i.e., to present the audience with the composition as a whole, though, during the performance, one is **subsidiarily** aware of the particular clues like the right movement of fingers on the instruments, pitch, etc. which lead the process of performance to the consummation of a piece of art. As Polanyi says: "Subsidiary awareness and focal awareness are mutually exclusive. If a pianist shifts his attention from the piece he is playing to the observation of what he is doing with his fingers while playing it, he gets confused and may have to stop. This happens generally if we switch our focal attention to particulars of which we had previously been aware only in their subsidiary role".[6] They are mutually exclusive, but they cannot be divorced from each other. None of these two kinds of awareness is reducible to the other. Each of them has to be given its due to account for the entire knowledge-process. The relation between the two is accountable in terms of the extension of the personal being of the knower through the subsidiary clues to form the knowledge into a coherent whole. The person integrates and indwells these clues to form knowledge. The subsidiary clues are treated by Polanyi as extensions of our bodily equipment. Such an extension is a dynamic factor which involves a certain change in our being. The entire knowledge-situation is activated by this dynamism — the movement of the personal being from its own locus through the subsidiary clues to the focal target. Thus, the concepts of subsidiary and focal awareness give a personal dimension to human knowledge, and point beyond the traditional bifurcation of the subject and the object in epistemology. We can conceive of a meaningful knowledge only by keeping it under the purview of the human personality : "The theory of personal knowledge offers an interpretation of meaning. It says that no meaningful knowledge can be acquired, except by an act of comprehension which consists in merging our awareness of a set of particulars into our focal awareness of their joint significance. Such an act is necessarily personal, for it assimilates the particulars in question to our bodily equipment; we are aware of them only in terms of the things we are focally observing."[7]

The Tacit Dimension of Knowledge

Our knowledge of the subsidiary clues is always in terms of what we become aware of focally. But our knowledge of those clues themselves in the process of knowing is ineffable and prelinguistic : "When arts of knowing are explained by maxims, these never disclose fully the subsidiarily known particulars of the art, so that the powers of articulation are already restricted at this stage .... This ineffable domain of skilful knowing is continuous in its inarticulateness with the knowledge possessed by animals and infants, who also possess the capacity for reorganizing their inarticulate knowledge and using it as an interpretative frame-work... We may say in general that by acquiring a skill, whether muscular or intellectual, we achieve an understanding which we cannot put into words and which is continuous with the inarticulate faculties of animals".[8]

Inarticulate intelligence which gropes its way by plunging from one view of things into another and which, therefore, is **preverbal** and **a-critical** can be detected, according to Polanyi, among human infants and animals very easily.[9] But what is more important is that Polanyi proves this to be the foundation of our articulate, explicit knowledge. In his *The Study of Man*, he starts with a logical oddity which man faces when he tries "to discover knowledge that will stand up, by itself, objectively" and "the moment he reflects on his own knowledge he catches himself red-handed in the act of upholding his knowledge", Polanyi says: "He finds himself asserting it to be true, and this asserting and believing is an action which makes an addition to the world on which his knowledge bears. So every time we acquire knowledge we enlarge the world, the world of man, by something that is not yet incorporated in the subject of the knowledge we hold, and in this sense a comprehensive knowledge of man must appear impossible."[10]

To offer a solution to this Polanyi brings about the notion of **tacit knowledge** as preceding our knowledge which is usually "set out in written words or mathematical formulae". The vain pursuit of reflecting ever again on our own reflection to catch hold of our knowledge 'objectively' ends here with the distinction between tacit, unformulated knowledge and explicit knowledge, because, "we may say that **we always know tacitly that we are holding our explicit knowledge to be true**".[11] Here Polanyi comes up with his concept of truth. He says : 'P is true' declares that I identify myself with the content of the factual sentence P, and this identification is something I am doing, and not a fact that I am observing.[12] This tacit component prevails in every experiential perspective of man. We always move from the level of our knowledge of what we are doing and how we are doing (which is unformulated, tacit) to the level of our awareness of what we have achieved (in an explicity, formulated shape). To confirm that which we have known we either go back recapitulating our process of knowing or put it to some other test. In either case, we indulge in a kind of action which itself cannot be put into an explicit linguistic formulation. This entire perspective of human knowledge is summarized in Polanyi's statement : **'We can know more than we can tell'**.[13] The recognition of the tacit component of human knowledge makes us realize that we are not confined to the **metier** of formulated, systematized, and articulate domain of knowledge. Knowledge has a depeer dimension where our personal being is actively involved.

II

To this brief introduction to Polanyi's epistemology we should add his warning against a tendency to identify the pervasive substructure of all intelligent behaviour that he calls the unformulated, tacit dimension of knowledge with subconscious or preconscious awareness or with the fringe of consciousness.[14] This warning can be justified by recalling, first, what Polanyi himself said about the subsidiary awareness which goes through a process of tacit integration : "The relation of subsidiaries to that on which they bear is a logical relation similar to that which a premise has to the inference drawn from it, with the great difference that the inferences arrived at here are tacit. Subsidiary awareness can be fully conscious, as that of a pointing finger or a pair of pictures viewed in the stereoscope, though in other cases our consciousness of subsidiaries may be on a very low level and may be altogether subliminal. Such is the case, for example, when sensory clues inside our eyes and inner ear are integrated to a precept. Such variations in their level of consciousness in no way affect the functions of subsidiary elements in contributing to an act of tacit knowing."[15] Secondly, 'pre-reflective' is an appropriate adjective for the tacit way of knowing rather than 'pre-conscious' or 'subconscious', because, though we are very much conscious of our acting tacitly to form the subsidiary clues into a coherent meaning, we do not stop to reflect upon it. The conscious process at this level is more akin to 'non-thetic' or 'non-positional' in Sartrean sense of the terms.[16] Tacit knowing is a doing of our own. To be aware of it is "an essential part of our existence as sensuous active persons".[17] Thirdly, according to Polanyi, all tacit operations of mind "consist in comprehending experience, i.e., in making sense of them".[18] For example, a man unequipped with any map enters a new land to explore it. In his fumbling progress through a hitherto uncharted domain, he tries to make sense of every bit of his discovery and then record it with indications to be decoded by future explorers. Now such an active participation of the human person cannot remain cloistered in the preconscious or the subconscious. On the contrary, to do full justice to this foundational aspect of our knowledge and to show that it is intrinsically tied up with our being and becoming and not with the knowing subject or knowable object alone in isolation from one another, Polanyi stipulates the notion of 'understanding' by which he means **comprehending** or **making sense** of our experience from tacit to the explicit level through the tacit operations of our consciousness. Thus, experience, for him, becomes a unified phenomenon without any split between the knowing subject and the knowable object. This gives us a new insight into the nature of human intentionality. Polanyi's reflections on knowledge is in several senses important for and relevant to the questions concerning phenomenological notion of intentionality. What we **intend** to know is for him a major constituent of knowledge. It signifies the role of consciousness in a directional or projective sense. From this point of view, the intentional acts of consciousness have a definite non-psychological character as they start with a trust in the existence of something to be known or discovered, something that exists as independent of consciousness. With his intellectual passions man pours himself into new forms of existence, and aims it a correct shaping of knowledge gained in each form. The task of knowing something is thereby regarded as a pre-existent one: "The sense of a pre-existent task", says Polanyi, "makes the shaping of knowledge a responsible act, free from subjective predilections".[19] Thus, man **meets** the world, not from any unconscious or subconscious depth, but from the depth of his fully conscious state, his personality. Polanyi calls it a **fusion**: "It seems reasonable to describe this fusion of personal and the objective as personal knowledge".[20] With a professional phenomenologist the objective status of a thing to which the intention may not correspond becomes a problem when we consider the intentional structure involved in assertive judgements, not otherwise. The 'object' intended, for Husserl, is 'real' only insofar as it is real for me. This problem can be avoided by taking a Polanyian approach to it, because, for Polanyi, meaning is not to be taken for granted; meaning is an achievement through our doing with what is real. The real is independent of me, and I trust it to be so. My interaction with it is a kind of 'meeting' which makes it real not only for me but for everyone by assigning a meaning to it

The modes of intentionality that we are generally acquainted with in the writings of Husserl and Sartre are still under the sway of subject-object dichotomy, and so unable to account for the experiential forms where the observable or knowable has a conscious or quasi-conscious role to play. The basic purpose of phenomenology was to bridge the gulf between thought-oriented approach and reality-oriented approach seizing both the subject and the object in the intentional network. But this network fails to get rid of the disjunction between subjectivity and objectivity. In Husserl, we find that the support for all intentional acts of knowing and the knowable entity is 'transcendental ego', and the knowable is relative to it via the intentional acts. Ultimately, for Husserl, the entire structure of intentionality becomes parasitic upon such a formally segregated concept : "I must lose the world by epoche, in order to regain it by universal self-examination".[21] In Sartre, 'the transcendence of the ego' signifies the relativity of consciousness to object. Though his conception of consciousness as having no other substantive dimension than a non-thetic and non-positional one is closer to our day-to-day existence, its streaming down into *en soi* or object-in-itself shows Sartre's emphasis on objectivity rather than subjectivity. However, the primacy of either subjectivity or objectivity debars us from entering the **reality as a whole** and having an undistorted and unbiased self-perception in the process of knowing. Polanyi's theory of knowledge warns us against any such split between our experiencing ourselves and the world. It points to a concept of consciousness in and through **understanding**. What it intends is the knowable, but indefinite and inarticulate till now, waiting for the knower's interference. This intention is not the private whim of the knower. It involves his trust in an objective, independent, and impersonal existence of something to be known. His noetic activities are initiated by this belief. To speak from Polanyi's standpoint, a complete phenomenological suspension of the world for a right knowledge of it is, in fact, a hindrance to such knowledge. Husserl was right when he vouched for the difference between judging as "meaning — and as a rule, merely supposing — that such and such exists and has such and such determinations", i.e., the judgement (what is judged) as "a merely supposed affair or complex of affairs; an affair or state of affairs, as what is meant", and, contrasted with this, a "preeminent judicative meaning, a judicative having of such and such itself" which he called 'evidence'.[22] This is what he identified with scientific intuition. For Husserl evidence is 'experiencing' of something itself. But steeped in Cartesianism he made this experiencing 'a mental seeing of something itself'.[23] According to him, no judgement can be accepted as scientific '**that I have not derived from** evidence'.[24] This is the basis of objectivity in science from Husserlian standpoint; it becomes purely reflective. But the structure of tacit knowing tells us about a more primordial form of intuitive capacity which is sensuous in character — like a 'hunch' guiding us to discover something through steps that are unspecifiable. As Polanyi says : ". . . in the structure of tacit knowing we have found a mechanism which can produce discoveries by steps we cannot specify. **This mechanism may then account for scientific intuition, for which no other explanation is known so far. Such intuition is not the supreme immediate knowledge, called intuition** by Leibnitz or Spinoza or Husserl, but a work-a-day skill for scientific guessing with a chance of guessing right."[25]

This chance leaves us in a bit of uncertainty. The object of knowledge is not entirely **my** intentional constitution. There is always a risk of failure, a chance of delusion which sharpens our intellectual passion for correction, validation and perfection : "The anticipation of discovery, like discovery itself may turn out to be a delusion. But it is futile to seek for strictly impersonal criteria of its validity. . . To accept the pursuit of science as a reasonable and successful enterprise is to share the kind of commitments on which scientists enter by undertaking this enterprise. You cannot formalize the act of commitment, for you cannot express your commitment non-commitally".[26]

In Polanyi's frame-work, a perpetual exteriorization of self through subsidiary clues as bodily equipment and an interiorization of the world giving it a semantic dimension go together; it is not a suspension or bracketing out of the world but taking a plunge into it which is more important. Here the intentional network of human knowledge consists not in the primacy of *noesis* over *noema* or its reverse, but **in a continuous to-and-fro relationship**; in the function of understanding which Polanyi expands "into that of what we **intend**, what we **mean** or what we do".[27] The intentional acts of consciousness begin with an intellectual passion to discover — from proximal, interiorized particulars to the integration of a coherent, distal whole. This is the functional import of tacit knowing. The bearing of particulars on a total pattern producing the phenomenon of pattern constitutes the **phenomenal** aspect of tacit knowing. Thirdly, the particulars bear on what they **mean** — the coherent whole which they signify. This is its **semantic** aspect. And, as this whole of parts is something **real** whose significance in many respects ranges beyond the specifiable particulars or even beyond the presently visible outline of the whole, there is an **ontological** import of this structure of knowing.[28] Thus, the pre-theoretic and the theoretic mode of understanding are combined in Polanyi's epistemology. When the latter becomes alienated from the former, knowledge is reified into a set of explicitly formulated systems. This epistemology integrates the knower with the known, the articulate with the inarticulate, the unmeant with the meant. One may call it an integral view of knowledge and reality.

We have seen how meaning is achieved through tacit integration. This takes place at different logical levels of our relation with the object concerned. The level which we have discussed so far is that of the relation between a personal knower and the impersonal object. Polanyi calls it 'fusion'. We have called it 'meeting'. 'Meeting', of course, has an interpersonal connotation which cannot be characteristic of our relation with an object. But, if by 'object' we mean something which is meant, then we do not really have any interaction with any object at the tacit level. Our knowledge of objects which are objects in the sense of having been meant is preceded by our tacit awareness of that which is not yet meant. We can call it a 'meeting' in the sense that here the visionary act of the experiencing person is submerged in the experience itself. The assertion of the experience in terms of a conceptual frame-work at an explicit, verbal level becomes a discovery presenting the discoverer with an elation of mind, a satisfaction of his intellectual passion. Now this relation with an object is, for Polanyi, such that here the object is placed at a lower logical level than the knower. He calls this relation as an 'I-It' relation. He contends also that there are knowable entities of higher categories. When we pass on from the tacit or preverbal level of awareness to a verbal or explicit level, we make the passage with an implicit faith in the existence of others who have the same rational competence to understand it and participate in our shaping of knowledge in the same way. We seek the universal validity of our knowledge with this basic faith of man in man. And when we approach man himself for our anthropological knowledge, we translate this basic faith into a more articulate fashion, i.e., in terms of a mutual recognition of each other's autonomy, rationality, freedom and responsibility. This is the level where "mutuality prevails to such an extent. . . that the logical category of an observer facing an object placed at a lower logical level become altogether inapplicable. The I-It situation has been gradually transformed into an I-Thou relation."[29] At this level, it is not only the knower who intends the known, but the known too intends to know the knower and offers himself to be known. The play of intentionality changes here. Through the act of addressing the other as **Thou**, I also become addressible as **Thou**. The 'Thou-orientation' resolves the subject-object dichotomy into a phenomenal sphere of dialogue and meeting between two personal knowers. The meaning that we achieve here is not by reifying the experience of meeting into the impersonality, facticity, and objectivity of the assertion made in the context, but by intensifying the very experience of meeting. But, for Polanyi, even the objective assertions regarding the meant entities cannot be completely dissociated from meeting and indwelling as the discovery of meaning is based on it, and the discovery itself becomes a 'celebrated fact' in its relation to the intellectual passion.

Hence we can talk about 'meeting' and 'meaning' at two levels and in two senses:

(a) Meeting in the sense of indwelling of the personal knower in the impersonal object leading towards achievement of meaning at the explicit verbal level in an impersonal fashion; and

(b) Meeting in the sense of indwelling of the personal knower in another person leading towards

> achievement of meaning at the explicit level but in terms of dialogical agreement and in an open-ended fashion.

Accordingly, human intentionality alternates between (a) and (b). But, as Polanyi would assert, the difference between the two is more a matter of degree than a real one. The concept of intentionality, as we have tried to spell out within the context of personal knowledge, is such that it signifies not merely intention **toward** but a participation **with**. There is an act of communion involved in such an intentional act. In both (a) and (b) there is a measure of companionship between the knower and the known. In (b) it is more intense. The achievement of impersonal meaning that we have talked about in (a), however, is also dependent upon a personal act, a personal mode of establishing and asserting it. In one way or the other, a dialogue between man and the world, man and man constitutes the basis of meaning. The word 'meaning', according to Polanyi, describes the entity toward which the person is pointed or directed. As Bruno V. Manno describes it : "By interiorizing or pouring ourselves into or dwelling in objects as subsidiaries directed towards a focal purpose, one makes them mean something." And the functional relation of the subsidiary to the focal target "involves the intentional or vectorial quality, the outward displacement of meaning. This intentional act is an act of self-transcendence, for the meaning act uses the experience of a person's senses as clues which transcend this experience by embracing a vision of reality beyond the impression of the senses."[30] Polanyi always tries to assert a continuity between meeting-and-meaning in senses (a) and (b) as cited above, and he classed both our knowledge of other human beings and our aesthetic awareness under (b), i.e., the **I-Thou** form of awareness as a sign of transition from natural sciences to the study of humanities: "The difference is only a matter of degree : indwelling is less deep when observing a star than when understanding men or works of art. The theory of tacit knowing establishes a continuous transition from the natural sciences to the study of humanities."[31] But he seems to stress this continuity more from the standpoint of the participant, and in terms of the nature of the participation than from the perspective of the object. These two perspectives, of course, cannot be set apart from one another. Polanyi's own approach to knowledge and reality demands them to constitute a unified field. To avoid proneness to anyone of them, I have laid greater empahsis on the concept of 'meeting' and a concept of 'meaning' evoked in terms of meeting. We shall see that a concept of intentionality based on meeting through a tacit integration of man's being with reality, may serve as an important clue to our understanding of aesthetic experience and aesthetic meaning.

III

Aesthetic experience can be discussed from the standpoint of the artist as well as the beholder. But their roles overlap. The Greek meaning of **aesthesis** provides a basis for aesthetic experience in the open availability of feeling and perception. The common factor shared by the artist and the beholder is a creative and visionary approach to reality. This involves the entire being of a person in terms of an integration of the subsidiaries as our bodily equipment and directionality of our consciousness to a focal target through imagination and interpretation. Polanyi's concept of 'bodily equipment', however, is very important in this regard as it shows the outward displacement of our being in a very conspicuous manner and implies a notion of intentionality in a mutually relative context where the personal man and the object interact with each other. It somehow resembles what M. Merleau-Ponty says regarding the role of body in the realm of art : "It is by lending his body to the world that the artist changes the world into paintings. To understand these transubstantiations we must go back to the working, actual body — not the body as a chunk of space or a bundle of functions but that body which is an intertwining of vision and movement."[32]

The creative and visionary approach to reality manifests also our capacity for feeling and sensation in a way which goes deep below the common surface of things. The originality and greatness of a work of art consists in grasping the origin, the roots of both ourselves and things. Originality here means, as Heidegger would put it, "that from which and by virtue of which a thing is, what it is and how it is".[33] Polanyi seeks it in the realm of relation so that not only the root or origin of art as such and the art objects but also the change in our being brought about by our reliance on and integration of subsidiaries and movement toward the achievement of a coherent entity is accounted for at a meta-level, i.e., in a discourse. It justifies the need for a participation on the part of the artist. He discovers the world in a special way, and by discovering it he discovers himself too.

The art object, too, after assuming a shape, plays a quasi-conscious role. It stands over against us and invites interpretations. We shall see that Polanyi opposes art objects to mere indicators (words, maps etc.), and identities strived by men. Now such meanings are exemplary in nature in the sense that they are found and inexhaustible by interpretation. It is interesting to note what Sundara Rajan says on this point : "The exemplar has a meaning-content which, however, cannot be exhausted by any specific contextualization of it. Its content transcends all such specifications and serves to suggest ever more fresh and novel specifications. Because of this latent or tacit dimension, an exemplar cannot be grasped in the manner of an objective cognition; rather it is to be 'comprehended' and not known as contextualized instance".[34] Sundara Rajan's way of expressing the notion of 'exemplar' sounds quite like that of Polanyi's notion of meaning as symbols and metaphors. Polanyi, however, stresses the 'lively' aspect of such exemplars to the extent of acknowledging a Thou-character in them. In any case of creation, enjoyment and interpretation, Polanyian frame-work shows relationality as the essential ingredient of the world of art. It becomes a dialogue, if by 'dialogue' we do not mean a sheer exchange of words but also a kind of communion.

Besides the availability of feeling and perception, an organization of them is of utmost importance for the constitution of aesthetic experience. For the artist the material for creation is not yet organized. For him 'the vast territories of space and time must still be marked *terra incognita*. He takes a plunge into it, gropes for a moment in his stream of consciousness to arrest it as an image. In the words of Herbert Read : "The sensibility plays lightning over these dark abysses, and in the flashes gets a brief glimpse of the lineaments of this unknown : the brief glimpse that is the artist's intuition, and which he then strives to communicate to us by the symbols he invents. That is the moment of originality — the moment in which we are made to realize the ethereal shimmering texture of music, 'the shapes that haunt thoughts', 'wilderness' in poetry, the 'beauty wrought out from within upon the flesh' of a painting".[35] This is the pre-conceptual basis for the organization of feeling and perception. Polanyi compares it with our contemplative experience.

From Polanyi's standpoint, what Read calls a 'brief glimpse' is a discovery — an outcome of a search like that of an explorer in an unknown land. The nature of this discovery, however, differs from a scientific one in that it is a contemplative experience which dissolves any conceptual frame-work. According to Polanyi, this framework lies as a screen between ourselves and the observable. Contemplation "stops our movement through experience and pours us straight into the experience; we cease to handle things and become immersed in them".[36] He adds : "And as we lose ourselves in contemplation, we take on an impersonal life in the objects of our contemplation; while these objects themselves are suffused by a visionary gleam which lends them a new vivid and yet dreamlike reality. It is dreamlike, for it is timeless and without definite spatial location. It is not an objective reality; for it is not the focus of an intelligent perception anticipating future confirmation by tangible things, but resides merely in the coloured patches of various shapes which the things present to the eye. Correspondingly, the impersonality of intense contemplation consists in a complete participation of the person in that which he contemplates and not in his complete detachment from it, as would be the case in an ideally objective observation. Since the impersonality of contemplation is a self-abandonment, it can be described either as ego-centric or as selfless, depending on whether one refers to the contemplator's visionary act or to the submergence of his person".[37] This is how Polanyi describes the contemplative communion of the religious mystic, and places art between science and worship. Music, poetry, paintings: the arts — whether abstract or representative —

are a dwelling in and a breaking out which lie somewhere between science and worship".[38] Here Polanyi is unclear whether the impersonality of contemplation is selfless or ego-centric from his own viewpoint. On this point, I wish to recall the synthesis that I have tried to make between the knower's visionary act and his dwelling in the object which he intends to know — the synthesis that has been my endeavour through the concept of 'meeting'.

Meeting may be more or less intense. But it serves as a 'touchstone of reality' and brings it forth in terms of a comprehension of both the participation of the subject in the world as existence and the appearance of the world in the subject as experience, as a complete unsegregated whole in a sphere between them. 'Meeting' always signifies a **between-ness** where it is neither the self nor the other which is important in itself. It is their **coming together** which is important in an ontological sense. The transition from this level to a semantic level is to be understood in consonance with the former so that any split does not take place between 'meeting' and 'meaning'.

In the case of aesthetic experience, the art object remains as a meaningful entity but in an open-textured manner. It has its own space and own time. "We think of it as something that has a 'life' of its own, so to speak".[39] Some recent Indian scholars of aesthetics have compared this experience with love which involves us deeply in a personal encounter with a presence.[40] We can conceive of this encounter at two levels :

(a) The artist delves into an opacity, creates an image both from something which he is not and from within himself through a communion between the inner and the outer. This is the pre-semantic level.

(b) When the art object assumes a shape, it is left open to the beholder for further communion as a requisite for appreciation and interpretation. This is the semantic level.

Here we have a special use of the term 'semantic' which is different from mere 'indication'. Polanyi generally spoke of indicators as words which point in a subsidiary way to that focal integration upon which they bear. Some words, of course, can be replaced by road-signs, telling the way, or by maps or drawings by engineers or by mathematical formulae which serve subsidiarily as indications, as denotative words do. These indicators, (words, maps or mathematical formulae, etc.) are of no intrinsic interest, "while that upon which they bear is the part of the operation that claims our intrinsic interest".[41] They function within a **from-to** relationship, in which the focal target is seen from the self as a centre: "... the self is never carried away in indication; it is never surrendered or given to the focal object . . . indications are always self-centres".[42] Polanyi contrasts this form of semantic meaning with that which consists in a self-**giving** or surrender. For example, a **symbol** — say, a flag — as an object of our focal awareness "is not merely established by an integration of subsidiary clues directed **from** the self to a focal object; it is also established by surrendering the diffuse memories and experiences of the self **into** this object, thus giving them a visible embodiment . . . . Instead of being a self-**centered** integration, a symbol becomes rather a self-**giving** one, an integration in which not only the symbol becomes integrated but the self also becomes integrated as it is carried away by the symbol — or given to it."[43]

Metaphors, like symbols, form another set of semantic meanings which, too, consist in a self-**giving** : "As in the symbol, so in the metaphor; the subsidiary clues consisting of all those inchoate experiences in our own lives that are related to the two parts of a metaphor — are integrated into the meaning of a tenor and a vehicle as they are related to each other in a focal object (a metaphor).* The result is that a metaphor, like a symbol, carries us away, embodies us in itself, and moves us deeply as we surrender ouselves to it."[44] Thus, according to Polanyi, there are three kinds of semantic meanings; indication, symbol, and metaphor. His concern is more with the artificial meanings, contrived by man and manifested as symbols and metaphors, as he intends to establish that these meanings — the coherent entities — which we know as Michaelengelo's *Moses*, Beethoven's *Ninth Symphony* are irreducible and real side by side the meanings which we know as natural : "In order to hold these meanings securely in the reverence they seem to him to demand, contemporary man therefore needs a theory of these meanings that explains how their coherence is no less real than the perceptual and scientific coherences he so readily accepts. He needs to see how his obvious personal involvement with these meanings is necessarily and legitimately part and parcel of the reality they actually have, that his personal involvement is not at all reason to regard them as mere subjective fantasies. These meanings will then not seem to be mere appearness to him. They will seem to be in truth what they 'are'.[45] Polanyi classes the phenomena of art with this group of meanings. "The work of art", as he says, "is a 'something' — a 'reality' with powers of its own".[46] Our consciousness is directed to it, and participates in its life in the process of integrating its parts in

---

* By 'tenor' Polanyi means the subsidiary element, and by 'vehicle' the focal object.

our vision of it. As he maintains, the meaning of a poem "is formed by the integration of its formal pattern with that part of its content that can be expressed in prose".[47] Its prose content is incompatible with the artificial speech of a poem. "Nevertheless, we succeed in integrating these incompatibles — the artificial pattern and the prose content — and by doing this we produce a joint meaning which is the meaning of the poem."[48] ". . . the artist produces from his own diffuse existence a shape circumscribed in a brief space and a short time a shape wholly incommensurable with the substance of its origins. Then we respond to this shape by surrendering from our own diffuse memories of moving events of gifts of purely resonant feelings. The total experience is of a wholly novel entity, an imaginative integration of incompatibles on all sides".[49]

For Polanyi, this achievement of meaning on the part of the artist gets dissociated from the personal life of its maker and starts **living** for other personalities : "A poem can form no part of a poets' **usual** personality. Thus the formal structure of a poem, which has so much of the poem's meaning in it, forms a blockage, insulating the poem from everyday affairs and so also from the poet as a private person. When entranced by a poem, we repeat its words through our lifetime; strictly speaking, it **the poem** that speaks to us, not the poet".[50] By holding this Polanyi seems to mean that the personal life or the autobiography of a poet is not the source of intention in poetry; that would make poetry more a 'private talk' and less a personal encounter.

We enjoy a work of art in itself, not for the satisfaction of any of our personal mundane desire. We accept its suggestions and clues, and integrate them by our imagination for sharing its meaning; we live in this meaning rather than the meaning it would have for us in our ordinary 'interested lives'. A work of art, from this stance, is 'virtual' rather than factual or utilitarian.[51] Our relation with it consists in a play between our imaginative and interpretative approach to it and the emotions and associations evoked by its sensuous form and content.

In experiencing an art object, uptake and interpretation are always based on a meeting — a dialogue between **I** as a spectator and **thou** as an art object. It is in this sense that the art object has a quasi-conscious role to play and the mode of intentionality differes in such experiential spheres. This is why Polanyi holds that aesthetic experience consists of a communion which is more akin to religious mystical experience : "... artistic creation and enjoyment are contemplative experiences more akin than mathematics to religious communion. Art, like mysticism, breaks through the screen of objectivity and draws on our pre-conceptual capacities of contemplative vision".[52] From the general epistemological perspective of Polanyi, the tacit dimension of knowledge is more vivid in this realm, and the logical level of the object is approximated to a higher category — a **Thou** rather than to an **It**. The meaning that it acquires after going through a meeting is, therefore, not tangible. What specific emotions and associations will be evoked by a work of art is not known *a priori*. It communicates through communion. This pre-conceptual, tacit apprehension of a work of art in its creation and enjoyment is not only the basis for its articulate understanding, it pervades throughout our interpretative activities centering around it.

The thesis of intentionality that I have tried to construe in the context of Polanyi's epistemology and his thought in general keeps us in the track of 'meeting-meaning-meeting'. The directionality of concisousness to something and its participation with it in terms of a tacit integration, indwelling in and interiorizing of the clues as proximal terms of our existence and bringing or understanding the image as a meaningful, coherent entity indicates this intentional structure. While creating or appreciating an art object we rely upon subsidiary clues like the manipulation of notes, modulations of the voice, techniques taught by a music master, accompaniments, etc. and strive to articulate and understand the composition as a coherent, meaningful entity. We indwell and interiorize these clues into our personal being as a whole — its past, present and future — with respect to the integration of a distal whole say, a musical composition. There is a movement of our consciousness through the proximal terms, i.e., our bodily equipments to the distal whole by cultivating our relation with them. According to Polanyi, while these clues are enlivened by us, the distal whole, too, has a 'life' of its own. Hence the outward displacement and movement of consciousness is not toward any **It** but to a **Thou**. Aesthetic awareness and meaning, therefore, cannot be called subjective or objective but dialogic. In view of our study of Polanyian aesthetics, art becomes a dialogic constitution.

Notes and References

1. Michael Polanyi : *The Tacit Dimension*, Routledge & Kegan Paul, London, 1967, p. 3, Henceforth, *TD*.
2. Goutam Biswas : 'How is knowledge of Man Possible? — An Inquiry into Philosophical Anthropology', In the *Visva-Bharati Quarterly*, Vol. 47, Nos. 3 and 4.
3. Michael Polanyi : *The Study of Man*, University of Chicago Press, p. 36. Henceforth, *SM*.
4. Michael Polanyi : *Personal Knowledge*, Routledge & Kegan Paul, London, 1958, p. 17. Henceforth, *PK*.
5. *Ibid.*, p. 92.

6. *Ibid.*, p. 32.
7. Michael Polanyi, *SM*, p. 44.
8. Michael Polanyi, *PK*, p. 90.
9. Michael Polanyi, *SM*, p. 15.
10. *Ibid.*, p. 11-12.
11. *Ibid.*, p. 12.
12. Michael Polanyi, *PK*, p. 254.
13. Michael Polanyi, *TD*, p. 4.
14. Michael Polanyi: 'The Body-Mind Relation', In *Man and the Science of Man*, ed. by William R. Coulson and Carl R. Rogers, Charies E. Merrill Publishing Company, Ohio, 1968, p. 87.
15. *Ibid.*, p. 87.
16. J.P. Sartre: *The Transcendence of the Ego*, tr. by Forrest William, The Moonday Press, New York, 1957.
17. Michael Polanyi : *SM*, p. 31.
18. *Ibid.*, p. 20.
19. *Ibid.*, p. 36.
20. Michael Polanyi, *PK*, p. vii.
21. Edmund Husserl : *Cartesian Meditations*, Martinus Nijhoff, The Hague, 1960, p. 157.
22. *Ibid.*, p. 10.
23. *Ibid.*, p. 12.
24. *Ibid.*, p. 13.
25. Michael Polanyi: *Knowing and Being*, ed. by M. Grene, Routledge & Kegan Paul, London, 1969, pp. 143-44.
26. Michael Polanyi, *TD*, p. 25.
27. Michael Polanyi, *SM*, p. 22.
28. Michael Polanyi, K*nowing and Being*, pp. xv, 141-45 and *TD*, pp. 10-13.
29. Michael Polanyi, *PK*, p. 346.
30. Bruno V. Manno : "Creative Imagination as a Basis of Relating the Sciences and the Humanities : The Epistemological Perspective of Michael Polanyi", In *Philosophy Today*, Summer, 1980, p. 174.
31. Michael Polanyi : *Knowing and Being*, p. 160.

32. M. Merleau-Ponty : 'Eye and Mind', In *Aesthetics*, ed. by H. Osborne, Oxford University Press, London, 1972, pp. 57-58.
33. Martin Heidegger : "The Origin of the Work of Art", In *Philosophies of Art and Beauty*, ed. by A. Hofstadter and Richard Kuhns, The Modern Library, New York, 1964, p. 649.
34. R. Sundara Rajan : "Symbols of Transcendence : Notes Towards a Theory of Communication in Art", In *Journal of Indian Council of Philosophical Research*, Vol. IV, No. 2, Spring 1987, New Delhi, p. 60.
35. Herbert Read : *The Origins of Forms in Art*, London, 1965, p. 32.
36. Michael Polanyi : *PK*, p. 197.
37. *Ibid.*
38. *Ibid.*, p. 199.
39. Michael Polanyi and Harry Prosch, : *Meaning*, University of Chicago Press, 1975, p. 66.
40. See, for example, Pabitrakumar Roy's paper entitled "The Concept of Intentionality and the Problem of Aesthetic Response", In *Indian Philosophical Quarterly*, Vol. XII, No. 3, July-September 1985.
41. Michael Polanyi and Harry Prosch : *Meaning*, p. 70.
42. *Ibid.*, p. 74.
43. *Ibid.*, p. 75.
44. *Ibid.*, pp. 78-79.
45. *Ibid.*, p. 68.
46. *Ibid.*, p. 87.
47. *Ibid.*, p. 86.
48. *Ibid.*, p. 86.
49. *Ibid.*, p. 88.
50. *Ibid.*, p. 86.
51. Susanne K. Langer : *Feeling and Form : A Theory of Art Developed from Philosophy in a New Key*, Routledge & Kegan Paul Ltd., London, 1973.
52. Michael Polanyi : *PK*, p. 199.

5

Personal Man and Aesthetic Truth

A Dialogical View of Rabindranath Tagore's Philosophy of Art

SANKHO Ghose, a renowned Bengali poet says: "The truth in poetry has a changing form. The proclamation of certain immutable truths like 'birth is accidental', 'death is inevitable' and 'sex is infallible' is not everything of poetry. The truth of poetry consists in realising the life that rests on such truths in its conflict with diverse experiences."[1] This is a concept of aesthetic truth which requires a personal awareness of the impersonal reality. With Rabindranath Tagore it did not remain static or sterile in a limited frame-work of modernity in terms of sheer conflicts but found its route through such conflicts towards an infinity of the aesthetic consciousness of man.

According to Tagore man establishes truth in his creations and not in the crowd of facts. He made several distinctions like 'truth' and 'fact', 'construction and creation', 'common truth' and 'significant truth'. An aesthetic view of truth thus differs from an ordinary or so-called realistic view of it. And as it is essentially related to man's personal encounter of the real it differs from all non-existentialist, speculative and scientific theories of truth. So long as our understanding of truth is operative in terms of the limitations of natural language merely to confirm what is called 'truth'. Within the frame-work of facts, it cannot even differentiate poetry from prose. Hermeneutics in art must realise the limitation of this frame-work. A dialogical understanding, however, is potently capable of overcoming this limitation, and with its pre-linguistic, linguistic and trans-linguistic dimensions it can account for any creative life-praxis of man.* The presence of an 'other' in the form of a human, an artistic image-work, an all-pervasive ethereal tune or an imaginary counterpart of one's own perception of the world is the **Thou** in our art experience. This **Thou** is a necessary prerequisite for framing a Tagorean philosophy of art.

II

Rabindranath Tagore approached art as signifying a human continuum and having a lively and quasi-conscious character because of its inseparable relationship with human consciousness. This relational aspect of art can be said to be a follow-up of Tagore's conception of the world as a 'life-world' — a world of expressions — and not as an aggregate of things. The world, for Tagore, is a perspective where consciousness releases itself from its self-enclosedness. As a poet, and as one steeped in Upaniṣadic thought, he conceived of this relation as unitary and intimate. It was not man against the world or the world against man, but a **relation** between the two which was ontologically important for Tagore. From this stance, the world becomes a home of humanity having 'some inner value which is not in the extension in space and duration in time'[2],

* Vide 'Introduction' of this volume.

and its existence becomes truthful : "In the region of Nature, by unlocking the secret doors of the workshop department, one may come to that dark hall where dwells the mechanic and help to attain usefulness, but through it one can never attain finality. Here is the storehouse of innumerable facts and, however necessary they may be, they have not the treasure of fulfilment in them. But the hall of union is there, where dwells the Lover in the heart of existence. When a man reaches it he at once realizes that he had come to Truth, to immortality, and he is glad with a gladness which is an end, and yet which has no end."[3] Hence truth, for Tagore, reigns in this relational realm. The inner core from which consciousness takes its direction to the world is, for Tagore, 'personality'. According to Tagore, personality means a "self-conscious principle of transcendental unity within man"[4] by virtue of which man extends himself in the infinite through the increase of his knowledge, love and activities. In the Tagorean frame-work, 'personal man' would mean a man who consciously cultivates his personality and brings it forth to the world in his creative activities. The truth of the experiences the personal man gathers by facing the world as his intimate one would therefore depend on the relation between his personality and the experiences in question. For Tagore 'truth' means **being** 'true'. It is possible to look at truth in an existential sense only when it is lived, and related to the being-becoming of man. This general philosophico-anthropological viewpoint of Tagore projects on his aesthetic. Or one can say in reverse that his basic attitude is aesthetic because he sees man in his 'surplus', i.e., in his creative impulse to move beyond what is immediately given and express himself in newer and newer fashions. The art objects are emblems of human personality and they **are** true in relation to it. So, in this chapter, I lay greater emphasis on the co-implication between philosophy of art and philosophical anthropology as far as Tagore is concerned and, accordingly, between personality and aesthetic truth in his approach to art. The validation of art is always impassioned and within or the realm of art — in an intentional network that holds between **I** and **Thou**. This co-implication has certain important consequences which can be briefly stated as follows :

1. It provides an answer to the question : 'Why is the concept of art open?'
2. It assigns a primacy to the relation between man and the world — a dialogue and communion between them. The artist does not deal with his images as sheer objects for use or information. Relation cannot be impersonal in the realm of art.
3. Truth of our aesthetic experience and judgement is, therefore, relative to this relationality. There, truth is different from the truths of reason and fact. Tagore's distinction between truth and fact comes up in this connection.
4. In his later life, Tagore was keen on treating art-objects more as individual entities having a deeper relation to his personal being and appearing more truthful to him. The world of forms was, therefore, not a dream to the poet in the last phase of his life. It was, as it were, his own identity inscribed in his own blood shed as Truth in all its directness and cruelty.

The entire Tagorean aesthetics can therefore be called a search for truth from the perspective of art. In what follows I propose to elucidate this basic theme in terms of the above-mentioned propositions. The concept of art and its cognate concepts cannot be defined in the way the exact concepts of logic, mathematics and geometry can be defined in terms of their necessary and sufficient properties. Hence the possibility of a theory of art which is understood as art's true definition embracing the necessary and sufficient conditions of art is challenged. To quote from Morris Weitz's celebrated paper 'The Role of Theory in Aesthetics' : "Is aesthetic theory, in the sense of a true definition or set of necessary and sufficient properties of art, possible? If nothing else does, the history of aesthetics itself should give one enormous pause here. For, in spite of the many theories, we seem no nearer our goal today than we were in Plato's time. Each age, each art movement, each philosophy of art tries over and over again to establish the stated ideal only to be succeeded by a new or revised theory, rooted, at least in part, in the repudiation of preceding ones".[5] The concept of 'art' is an **open concept** as distinguished from the **closed concepts** of logic, mathematics and goemetry. Hence it is impossible to identify some of art's necessary properties. New forms of art may emerge. The conditions of the application of the concept of art are also changeable. From this standpoint the task of a philosophy of art is not to specify the essence of art but to elucidate the criteria for the correct use of concepts like 'art', 'expression', 'form', etc.

While this criticism against the traditional philosophies of art seeking a theory of art is quite intelligible, the task of aesthetics proposed in view of it has a serious shortcoming. It reduces the creative competence and activities of human beings to some sets of linguistic and conceptual behaviour. While it distinguishes between **closed** and **open** concepts, it never raises the question "Why is it that the concept of art is open?" with a real rigour for exploration. To say that they are open because they are empirical is not enough. The empirical concepts are constituted in the context of human experience. The constitution is, therefore, never completed. Man, who is a historic being, constitutes and defines these concepts and at the same time consitutes his own identity through such an activity. Concepts like 'art', 'civilization', 'morality', etc. signify a human continuum. The thesis of the analytical aesthetics which stops at the observation that the concept of art is indefinable because it is open and inexact suffers from triviality, lacking any synthetic significance. To search into the continuity and identity of the historic man and relate it to all his experiential dimensions is an important task to be accomplished by philosophical anthropology.

In fact the plurality of art, its open-textured character, on the ground of which the concept of art is declared to be an open one, owes to the human agency in the creation and appreciation of arts. Again this is an agency which is replete with contradictions and paradoxes, susceptible to social norms and religious beliefs, and ultimately deeply concerned with its own identity through different directions of its becoming in relation to the world. Sometimes these directions are chosen by the human agent as a critique of the existing state of affairs. To do justice to this important factor the co-implication between philosophical anthropology and philosophy of art cannot be slurred over in silence. One of the major contributions of Rabindranath Tagore to contemporary philosophy of art is to bring about and establish this co-implication. He did not search for a definition of art, but for the reason for the existence of art. The human significance of the phenomenon of art was brought forth by Tagore in course of his inquiry into this reason. Tagore is an answer to the rigmarole of analytical aesthetics. As he himself was a creative artist, we see in him a continuous feed-back between what he thought and what he did — his theory and practice — which ranges beyond the private spheres of his life to form a *weltanschauung* with a universal human appeal. In this world-view man is essentially a person who constantly overpasses his immediate borders and becomes unique by his creative move towards an envisioned possibility. According to Tagore, man's personality and creativity go together; one cannot be creative without being a person. Personality, for Tagore, is an anthropological category which sets man at a distance from the world of commonsense and commoners over-shadowed by "the tyranny of facts and the impertinence of the insignificant". It then leads him through a way which unfolds his being in terms of his relation with the world in an unconventional, non-utilitarian and intimate sense. This is the way of art. The world of commonsense is split between **I** and **It**, i.e., man and the objects for his use and information. Here the relation between man and the world is conceived more in the sense of a division. There is no sense of communion of man with this world. The personal man renews this world of facts aesthetically; it is then replaced by his world of expression, i.e., his symbols clothed with reality by his consciousness. He gives an independent status to his creation. He has a **dialogue** with it. Its open-textured character demands that the dialogue be unending. Just as there is no end to our knowing a friend, so there is no end to our knowing an art object. While speaking about literature Tagore said : "A good deal of literature is nothing but a go-as-you-like dialogue among friends. A meeting of minds, or an embrace, it is expression and the delight in expression."[6] There is no static conception of truth in this realm. The truth of art is essentially a truth of, and a truth in-and-through, dialogic realization of the personal man. It depends upon **how he relates himself to the art-form.** In the following sections, I attempt to interpret Tagore's view of art with a focus on the relation between human personality and aesthetic truth.

III

The main objective of a philosophy of man is to explore the mode in which man exists in relation to the world. Tagore views this relation basically from an aesthetic point of view. The aesthetic apprehension of reality forms the core of almost all his reflections on man and his world. V.S. Naravane has rightly pointed out : ". . . Tagore does not introduce aesthetics into his world-view in order to complete or systematize his ideas. He allows his deepest thoughts on metaphysical and social questions to be permeated by his aesthetic approach, and even his specific aesthetic opinions. Aesthetics is thus the very foundation of his philosophy, not its coping stone".[7] The experiential forms in the process of human becoming were never conceived by Tagore in a detached and impersonal manner. As a poet he looked at the world as a composite whole charged with human meaning, the understanding of which requires human participation, **abiding within** and in communion with it. He said: "When we experience anything aesthetically, we do not experience only that object. A good poem confers dignity on land, sea and sky, on the whole of the existence."[8] For Tagore, a human being is not merely a member of a species, but a person. Hence the relation that man holds with the world is personal.* For his own spiritual demand,

---

* 'Personal', however, is not to be confused with 'private'.

the personal man extends himself over the world through a creative synthesis and looks for a complement of his own being in the world. Tagore says : "I exist, and everything else exists. There is this union of the two in my existence. If I do not feel anything beyond my own self, I do not feel myself".[9] According to Tagore, the truth of this kind of awareness (aesthetic awareness) has an integral character. It emerges from an in-between relational realm, of man and his world; it is revealed through an integration of man's being with the world. Here 'truth' means 'truthfulness' or 'being true', i.e., how truthfully I become myself in relation to the world. In this process of becoming, the world which is a mere congregation of impersonal facts and things is gradually replaced by a world of expressions. It is the personal man who expresses. He is basically an artist. The truth of an aesthetic experience consists in an authentic presentation of the art-object, revealing a unity or harmony among its different co-ordinates **within the field of the artist's and/ or the beholder's perception**. Such objects and our relation to them constitute the human world. This constitution is based on an awareness of the inadequacies of the natural world as a fact that keeps it from being an art-object. As Maurice Merleau-Ponty says : "The eye sees the world, sees what inadequacies keep it from being a painting . . .".[10]

The facticity is there in a given meaning-structure as well. But, for Tagore, the crux of man's creativity is counterfactual. The artist continually contributes forms to the world of things and objects which are already meant in terms of a given language-structure (or meaning-structure). The world of expressions thus comes in. The latter, for Tagore, is essentially human and man's encounter with it is essentially personal, or else it could not be his own intimate world: "The world and the personal man are face to face, like friends who question one another and exchange their inner secrets."[11] According to him, every man is an artist and a true understanding of the world is possible only in an in ɜntional mode which is creative.[12] Art, for him, has a 'life-growth'. The truth of aesthetic experience does not have any referent beyond the sphere of this intentional mode. Truth and beauty go together; the art object which is an integral part of the experience of it is true and beautiful substantively — not adjectively. To express the truth is the virtue of the artist, and, indeed, of any human being. In it he is not bound either by subjective inclinations or by objects or facts-in-themselves; he is free, what is true is beautiful. What is beautiful is delighting. The freedom of man lies in this delight. To live this life of truth is, for Tagore, the way of man's being.

IV

Tagore did not define art because "definition of a thing which has a life-growth is really limiting one's own vision in order to be able to see clealy" and "clearness is not necessarily the only, or the most important, aspect of a truth".[13] For him this life-growth is anthropomorphic in character, owing its genesis to the personal existence of man, as opposed to his gross physical existence. "This personal man", Tagore says, "is found in the region where we are free from all necessity — above the needs, both of body and mind — above the expedient and useful ... And it has personal relations of its own with the great world, and comes to it for something to satisfy personality."[14] Thus the relation between the personal man and the world consists in a complementarity between the two. This specific intentional mode suffuses all the myriad varieties of human creation. From the aesthetic standpoint, man as a knowing subject is not really free.

The freedom of man, when he is a knower, is relative to the objects of his knowledge. It manifests itself in terms of a conquest of objects and is at most the freedom of a tyrant. It is not a creative conquest by man of his own being. Tagore says: "Man, as a knower, is not fully himself — his mere information does not reveal him. But, as a person, he is the organic man, who has the inherent power to select things from his surroundings in order to make them his own. He has his forces of attraction and repulsion by which he not merely piles up things outside him, but creates himself. The principal creative forces, which transmute things into our living structure, are emotional forces. A man, where he is religious, is a person, but not where he is a mere theologian. His feeling for the divine is creative. But his mere knowledge of the divine cannot be formed into his own essence because of this lack of emotional fire. . . Repetition of the facts that the sun is round, water is liquid, fire is hot, would be intolerable. But a description of the beauty of the sunrise has its eternal interest for us — because there, it is not the fact of sunrise, but its relation to ourselves, which is the object of perennial interest."[14] True freedom is the transcendence of mere being through creative becoming. It is not a state, nor is it a flight from a state, but an adventure. Art is basically the art of existence which invokes the need for a realization of this freedom.

The reason for the existence of art was sought by Tagore in man's creative impulse to move beyond what is given, i.e., in man's freedom. He calls this creative impulse the **surplus in man**. The works of art are the emblems of this **surplus** which enables man to move from quantity to quality, fact to truth, utility to beauty. Man becomes through this surplus. It signifies an evolution from the biological order of human existence to a spiritual order, from object or **I-It** level to a personal or **I-Thou** level. In the biological and objective realm we are confined to the world of facts and face too many 'truths' in terms of our knowledge of those facts. In the world of personality we experience truth in its oneness with ourselves, in its relation to us. In the former case the Sartrean conflict between **Being-for-itself** and **Being-in-itself** goes on for eternity in the form of a chasm between solitary knowers and inert facts or objects which, for Tagore, cannot be real without any relation to us. In this respect his idea resembles Martin Buber's view that the real is relational He says : "The punishment we suffer in solitary confinement consists in the obstruction to the relationship between the world of reality and the real in ourselves, causing the latter to become indistinct in a haze of inactive imagination; our personality is blurred, we miss the companionship of our own being through the diminution of our self. The world of our knowledge is enlarged for us through the extension of our information; the world of our personality grows in its area with a large and deeper experience of our personal self in our own universe through sympathy and imagination."[16] Tagore's philosophy of art looks for an ontology of art which, in his case, is seen to be one with the ontology of man. It envisions a pattern of human becoming which is fundamental to all artistic activities. This pattern is the mode of all specific aesthetic modes. Modes are not facts. Truth in art, therefore, cannot be factual. It has to cohere with the process of that becoming and fit into its entire pattern.

V

A work of art is trans-factual. It takes place in the ordinary world, uses the media of commoners, but surpasses them all by virtue of its beauty unrecorded in any of its specificities in isolation from the whole. This beauty shines forth at the point of unity: "A rose has some petals, a stem, which are of some definite shape and size, and green leaves encircle it. With all these details there exists a principle of unity that transcends such details. We call it beauty".[17] Unlike statements of fact, the truth of it cannot be established or justified by any criterion which is alien to this mode of perception. The judgement 'The rose is beautiful' is not an information about a rose the truth of which would depend on the fact that the rose is beautiful. Like the rose itself, beauty too is a substantive entity, and it cannot be a sheer predicate of something else. The artist purposefully adapts the appearance of rose to its beauty and makes it real. "The truth of such judgement", in Whitehead's words, "is a truth of feeling, and not a truth of verbalization".[18] For Whitehead, truth of this kind becomes 'self-justifying' and it 'derives this self-justifying power from its services to the promotion of Beauty'.[19] Beauty too according to Whitehead, is to be truthful for the perfection of art. He say : "In the absence of truth, Beauty is on a lower level, with a defect of massiveness. In the absence of Beauty, truth sinks to triviality. Truth matters because of Beauty".[20] Tagore also believes in a complementarity between truth and beauty. But he assigns a prior significance to truth. Fore him, truth is lived through a conscious adaptation to the personal self which is transcendent of factual determinations and existential in its free becoming. What is true from this stance is a matter of joy, delight, and, therefore, beauty. What is delicate or fine is not necessarily beautiful, because it is not necessarily true. He says : "There is pain at each and every creative move of our self. But if we say that it is pain alone, then its description remains incomplete, because it is in this pain that there is beauty, there is delight."[21] This proclivity to identify truth as beauty resembles the approach of Gandhi when he said : "People generally fail to see beauty in truth, the ordinary man runs away from it and becomes blind to the beauty in it. Whenever man begin to see beauty in truth, true art arises".[22] Tagore quotes the famous saying of Keats, 'Beauty is truth and truth beauty', more than once, but by reversing the order : 'Truth is beauty, Beauty truth.'[23] This change is important, inasmuch as Tagore understands the complementary relation between truth and beauty in view of a pre-identification of truth as beauty. At the same time he gives an unconventional meaning to both the concepts in congruity with his aesthetic and philosophical-anthropological frame-work. Truth consists in harmony and beauty is revealed through it. But as beauty does not mean for Tagore any sensual appeasement, harmony or truth too does not mean for him a sheer retention of likes and rejections of dislikes.

Harmony does not exclude discord, but transcends it. This is what we experience with good musical compositions. Tagore says : "The very mark of truth is that everything comes under its purview. Despite an apparent discord and disorder in such convergence, there is a great harmony at the depth of it, or else it would have annihilated itself. . . truth has a symmetry without which it cannot hold itself. But this symmetry is not there by laying aside the disproportionate; it accepts the disproportionate and then transcends it".[24] This version of the coherence theory of truth maps on to the aesthetic field. The aesthetic perception of a harmonious whole in an art object is based upon aesthetic intentionality. Harmony is not an attribute of an object as brownness can be the attribute of a table, nor is it a mental entity.

It is a vital core coexistent with our perception of a whole and unspecified in the parts as separated from the whole. Parts dissimilar to and disproportionate with each other form into a whole along with the creation of an art form. The art form does not remain any more an 'object' for a 'subject', but becomes an individual existent for the artist and appreciator, i.e., the personal man. The sharp distinction between substance and its attributes arises within a subject-object frame-work of epistemology. Beauty or harmony is regarded there as a quality or a predicate of a thing or a subject. But within the sphere of aesthetic intentionality, however, the art object is as much a substantive entity as it is a qualitiative form. Hence, it is meant to be appreciated in terms of what it suggests, not in terms of its having any definite property. For Tagore, 'truth', 'beauty' and 'harmony' are interchangeable terms for the phenomena which occur in relation to the personal man. The wholeness of the perceived content cannot exclude him. The moment the distinction between the whole and its parts is made with regard to an art object, it ceases to be an art object. This wholeness is a phenomenological construction within a sphere of dialogue between the personal man and the world.

VI

The aesthetic intentionality destroys the 'thingness' of a thing or 'meantness' of an object and transforms the world of facts and things into a human image-work or world of expressions. The personal self identifies it as its own. The self too grows through it; hence the contribution of the image-work itself in constructing the world of art is no less for Tagore: "When I see the world through music/I come to know it as my own. Then its luminous language fills the sky with love/And its dust speaks its final message".[25] These are, for example, no statements of facts. Nor do they merely **describe** some particular aesthetic experience or realization. They are **uttered with** the realization. The truth of such statements consists in having a **true relationship** with the art form in question. We have knowledge of objects the truth of which consists in empirical confirmation of knowledge-claims. Aesthetic truth consists in a unity of the personal self with the specific experiential form. The former is real from the standpoints of science, commonsense and metaphysics. The latter is real from the standpoints of aesthetics and philosophical anthropology. Tagore says: "Union has its significance not in the realm of **to have**, but in the of **to be**. To **gain** truth is to admit its separateness, but to **be** true is to become one with truth".[26] Thus no aesthetic truth can be drawn from the work of art if the work is treated as an object *per se*. It **happens** and **matures** in a passage between the artist and his work, we the spectators and the work. The work of art itself is an expression of this relation between man and his world. Tagore believed that our "arts and literature are constantly giving expression to this intimate communion of man with his world".[27] He said: "Our creation is the modification of relationship."[28] Such a relation, however, cannot be impersonal. Aesthetic truth reflects an active involvement of human personality in producing and/or appreciating a work of art. It is, therefore, personal.

Unlike propositional truth, aesthetic truth cannot be proved or demonstrated. While truths of fact and truths of reason are determined and proved by means of objective, impersonal criteria, aesthetic truth is confirmed by the authenticity of human expression. The difference between the two is thus stated by Tagore: "It is easy to prove that which is provable. But it is difficult to express that which abounds in joy."[29]

Insofar as truths of fact are concerned, a proposition is true if it reports on an actual state of affairs. From this viewpoint, only a proposition can have truth-value, and the concept of truth becomes parasitic upon the concept of fact. A fact, by its very nature, has to be known, and without being known it cannot remain a fact. A fact-stating statement has to be either true or false on verification. Positivism goes one step further to assert that this criterion of verifiability has no alternative so far as meaningfulness of propositions is concerned. It **reifies** the human world to a world of bare objects, facts, and propositions, and establishes the legacy of human subjects or knowers in terms of their conformity to this pre-given objective universe. As per the principle of verification all the facts of consciousness are to be laid aside as pseudo-statements if they cannot be verified by the facts of experience. The home of truth is thus built upon a very narrow foundation where language corresponds to facts. When extended to aesthetics, this approach assigns only emotive value to statements of art and denies any cognitive meaning to them. From this standpoint, the principal function of lanaguage is to depict what is, and, at most, what is a convincing possibility. But, for the purposes of art, a 'convincing impossibility' is preferable to an 'unconvincing possibility', and art may well be a form of knowledge gleaned by discovering interrelation among things that might happen. Cassirer says: "In the work of the artist these possibilities become actualities; they are brought into the open and take on a definite shape. The revelation of this inexhaustibility of the aspects of things is one of the privileges and one of the deepest charms of art".[30] To answer any question concerning truth in art, analytical aesthetics will quickly indulge in elucidating the use or employment of the concepts 'art', 'truth', 'artistic truth', etc., i.e., in an empirical description of the concrete variations of linguistic behaviour. That the statements of art may have extra-linguistic referents which may subsequently motivate our feeling is an unfounded clause for analytical aesthetics. It discounts the possibility that art is a human acivity which does not cling on to a given language-structure or play the rule-bound conventional games now and then.

As opposed to this notion of truth which is essentially fact-oriented, Tagore contended that the principal task of art and literature is to express, to present us with the taste of the infinite, the real. Expression is the expression of truth which overflows its receptacle that is fact: "Only beauty is not a mere fact; it cannot be surveyed and mapped. It is an expression. Facts are like wine-cups that carry it, they are hidden by it, it overflows them. It is infinite in its suggestions, it is extravagant in its words. It is personal, therefore, beyond science".[31]

VII

What are called 'truths of reason' are essence-oriented. They are divorced from any existential necessity. Both pure science and metaphysics propagate truths of reason. The objective ideal of scientific knowledge dissociates its truths from the human personality. Metaphysics, in its absolutistic sense, rejects everything as 'appearance' or *māyā* and locates truth in an extra-human sphere. Both are, for Tagore, abstractions : "Abstract truth may belong to science and metaphysics, but the world of reality belongs to Art."[32]

The essence of art consists in revealing truth in its relational and integral sense. The deeper the relation between man and his image-work, the truer the whole intentional sphere. Tagore says : "We can make truth ours by actively modulating its interrelations. This is the work of art, for reality is not based in the substance of things but in the principle of relationship. Truth is the infinite pursued by metaphysics; fact is the infinite pursued by science, while reality is the definition of the infinite which relates truth to the person".[33] Here a problem arises concerning aesthetic universality or intersubjective validity of aesthetic judgements. While empirical and rational truths are universally agreed upon with reference to some objective, impersonal criteria, aesthetic truth is not so agreed upon. What should then be the criterion of aesthetic universality? When I say 'this is beautiful', I mean something to be beautiful for everyone and communicate my vision of beauty to other persons. It reminds us of Kant's contention that locutions such as 'X is beautiful for me' or those indexed by personal pronouns are nonsense. Such is the logic of the term 'beautiful'. Aesthetic truth is basically communicable. But where does its intersubjective validity lie? We might try to answer the question briefly in terms of Tagore's aesthetic philosophy. The specific intentional mode indicates a criteriological shift with regard to the intersubjective validity of the specific experiential form which is produced within that intentional sphere. The 'thou-orientation' in aesthetic perception and understanding demands a 'thou-orientation' on the part of the beholder and the critic. They have to have an empathic attitude to the art object. Our understanding and appreciation of art objects, like the creation of them, have a constitutive role in recomposing them beyond the traces left by their creators. We have to enter into the same mode of intentionality required for the creation of art objects. This generates a common basis for making and understanding an aesthetic judgement, i.e., a 'community of taste'. Secondly, it has an existential necessity which belongs to Tagore's concept of true human becoming. The universality of aesthetic judgements consists in a revelation of the uniqueness of man. As Tagore contended, our arts and literature represent the creative activity which is fundamental in man. Aesthetic truth is therefore sharable within the limits of aesthetic intentionality, and the existence of a non-solipsistic world too is presupposed in such a phenomenological construction. In connexion with our distinction between aesthetic truth which is personal, on the one hand, and objective, impersonal truth, on the other, it is interesting to recall what Tagore said about the rational man and the artist: "Our rational man also seeks to simplify things into their inner principle; to get rid of the details; to get to the heart of things where things are one. But the difference is this — the scientist seeks an impersonal principle of unification, which can be applied to all things. For instance, he destroys the human body which is personal in order to find out physiology, which is impersonal and general. But the artist finds out the unique, the individual, which yet is in the heart of the universal. When he looks on a tree, he looks on that tree as unique, not as the botanist who generalizes and classifies. It is the function of the artist to particularize that one tree. How does he do it? Not through the peculiarity which is the discord of the unique, but through the personality which is harmony. Therefore he has to find out the innder concordance of that one thing with its outer surroundings of all things."[34] The intersubjective validity of aesthetic experience and judgements is based on a special mode of cognition which does not abbreviate reality but intensifies it.

VIII

Tagore's writings are full of suggestions and indicative of further philosophical rumination. Our understanding of his theory of art presupposes a phenomenological orientation which is implicit in his writings. Various concepts are fabricated together in his unified approach to man and his world. Hence, besides 'personal man' and 'aesthetic truth' as our main points of discussion, we have touched upon Tagore's concepts of 'surplus in man', 'harmony', 'beauty', 'freedom', etc. and his philosophical anthropology in general. The co-implication between philosophical anthropology and philosophy of art has been stressed, as Tagore held that the *raison d'etre* of art lay in the very nature of man. By 'human nature' Tagore always meant the **true** nature of man. For him the personal self transcends the empirical self as conditioned by man's psycho-physical necessities. The personal being of man transcends the limitations of the empirical self and unites itself with the world as a whole. The meaningfulness of human creations and human life as such consists in this relation between the personal man and his world. Man cultivates this relation through art and literature. This sphere of intentionality consists in a **dialogue** between man and his image-work and the fellow human beings. A transcendence of the ego through aesthetic intentionality is a necessary condition for aesthetic enjoyment. Truth in art is a fruition of such relationship between man and his world, "a release from inner and outer compulsions, and yet surrounded by a grace of sense, a white light still and moving. . ."[35]

IX

The relation between the personal man and aesthetic truth became more intense with Tagore in his later days.

A closer look at the evolution of his aesthetic mode of being and the consequent keenness of his perception reveals that in the last phase of his life he betook himself avocationally to the world of painting. This is peopled by men and women who stare at us demanding individual identities. Disturbing as they might appear to onlookers who are used to encounter grace and charm in painting, Tagore's characters are strong individuals who would just refuse to be reduced to the status of symbols of archetypes. Truly did Coomaraswamy say that with Tagore's painting we come to have our 'modern primitives '.[36] The following lines from Tagore's letter to Jamini Roy are worth quoting in this context: ". . .When I turned to painting, I at once found myself in the grand cavalcade of the visual world. Trees and plants, men and beasts, everything became vividly real in their own distinct forms. Then lines and colours began revealing to me the spirit of the concrete objects in nature. There was no more need for further elucidation of their *raison d'etre* once the artist discovered his role of a beholder — pure and simple. Only the true artist can comprehend the secret of the visible world and the joy of revealing it. . . The artist has a call and must answer the challenge to compel the unperceptive majority to share in his joy of the visible, concrete world — directly perceived. He sings not, nor does he moralize. He lets his work speak for itself and its message is: Look, this is what I am, Ayamaham bho!"[37] Similarly, should one care to peruse the later poems of Tagore (from Purabi onwards), one would not fail to notice a growing concern for individuals in preference to generalities and types. A tree is no longer a mere tree, but an individual tree; a flower is not any flower, but a specific flower. From a world of types Tagore gradually moves on to a world of concrete realities disclosed before a deepened sensibility of aesthetic perception. The essence of a work of art thereby becomes transparent in the work itself, proclaiming its own individual identity before the personal man. Tagore always held that practical modalities of being obscure the richness of the individuals; habitual awareness deadens our sensibility while beauty is revelatory in nature; it discloses a vista of nuances hitherto unnoticed. Aesthetic perception awakens us to a new awareness, a new mode of being.

Notes and References

1. Sankho Ghose : *Sabda Ar Satya* (in Bengali) Papyrus, Calcutta, 1987, p. 31. Translation mine.
2. Rabindranath Tagore : *The Religion of Man,* London, Unwin Books, p. 18, Henceforth, *RM*.
3. *RM*, p. 66.
4. *Ibid.*, p. 75.
5. Morris Weitz: "The Role of Theory in Aesthetics", In *Problems in Aesthetics*, ed. by Morris Weitz, New York, Macmillan, 1959, p. 146.
6. Rabindranath Tagore : *Angel of Surplus*, ed. by Sisirkumar Ghosh, Visva-Bharati, 1978, p. 149.
7. V. S. Naravane : *The Elephant and the Lotus*, Bombay, Asia Publishing House, 1965, p. 211.
8. Rabindranath Tagore : *Sahitya* (in Bengali), Visva-Bharati, 1958, p. 79. Translation of the passage is available in Abu Sayeed Ayyub's *Poetry and Truth*, Jadavpur University, 1970, p. 119.
9. Rabindranath Tagore : "Sahityatattva" (in Bengali), vide *Rabindra Rachanavali*, Government of West Bengal, Vol. XIV, p. 352; translation mine.
10. Maurice Merleau-Ponty : *The Primacy of Perception*, North-Western University Press, 1964, p. 165.
11. Prithwish Neogy (ed.): *Rabindranath Tagore Art and Aesthetics,* Calcutta, Orient Longmans, 1961, p. 22; Henceforth, *RAA*.

12. Tagore says : "... Man by nature is an artist; he never receives passively and accurately in his mind a physical representation of things around him. There goes on a continual adaptation, a transformation of facts into human imagery, through constant touches of his sentiments and imagination", *RM*, p. 83.
13. *RAA*, p. 13.
14. *Ibid.*, p. 11.
15. *Ibid.*, pp. 17-18.
16. *RM*, p. 82.
17. Rabindranath Tagore : *Sahityer Pathe* (in Bengali), Visva-Bharati, Chaitra, 1365, pp. 125-26; translation mine.
18. A. N. Whitehead : *Adventures of Ideas,* Cambridge, Cambridge University Press, 1961, p. 266.
19. *Ibid.*
20. *Ibid.*
21. Rabindranth Tagore : *Atmaparichaya* (in Bengali), Visva-Bharati, 1969, p. 45; translation mine.
22. V. S. Naravane : *The Elephant and the Lotus*, p. 161.
23. Rabindranth Tagore : *Sahitya* Visva-Bharati, 1961, p. 51. Professor Satyendranath Roy made this point of difference between Keats and Tagore in his book *Sahityatattve Rabindranth* (in Bengali), Tagore's Theory of Literature Calcutta, Sanskrit Pustak Bhandar, 1990, p. 84.
24. *Atmaparichaya*, p. 45; translation mine.
25. Opening line of a song of Tagore; translation mine.
26. *RM*, p. 41.
27. *Ibid.*, p. 72.
28. *Ibid.*, p. 83.
29. Rabindranath Tagore : *Sahityer Svarup* (in Bengali), Visva-Bharati, 1969, p. 8; translation mine.
30. Ernst Cassirer : 'Art', In *Problems in Aesthetics,* ed. by Morris Weitz, p. 115. Macmillan, New York, 1959.
31. *RAA*, p. 30.
32. *Ibid.*, p. 48.
33. *RM*, p. 84.

34. *RAA*, p. 23.
35. T. S. Eliot : *Four Quartets*, Faber & Faber, London, p. 16.
36. See Ananda K. Coomaraswamy's foreword to the Catalogue of Tagore's paintings exhibited in New York in 1930.
37. *RAA*, pp. 108-9.

6

Artistic Knowledge

Sarvepalli Radhakrishnan's Phenomenology of Art

INDIAN *Weltanschauung* always placed man as an enquiring being at the centre of the universe and looked for a unity of man and the universe, be it in materialistic terms or in spiritual transcendence. Some major trends of contemporary Indian thought, however, lay less emphasis on the former and makes a sedulous effort to project man as a synthesis of the ideal and the real. It is a search for man's own image as an integral being transfiguring the real and projecting the ideal as an essence of the real. But it is impossible to understand this transfiguration and projection without a concept of harmony of the inner and the outer, man as an experiencing being and the world as experienced. As long as the primacy of the inner, i.e., man as an experiencing being is asserted in comparison with the outer world, consciousness remains fragmented and identified only as a knower; the world gets bifurcated into knower and known. Transcendence, from contemporary Indian standpoint, is conceived in a holistic sense to explicate the centrality of human existence in non-isolationistic terms like 'harmony', 'meeting', 'wholeness', 'relation', etc. According to Tagore, for example, man's joyous meeting and union with the 'Real outside him' is the telos of man. He stated clearly that "reality is not based in the substance of things but in the principle of relationship".[1] Gandhi also believed in being nearer to nature and found that the Indian practice of tree worhsip is symbolic of "true reverence for the entire vegetable kingdom, which with its endless panorama of beautiful shapes and forms, declares to us as it were with a million tongues the greatness and glory of God".[2] In recent years J. Krishnamurti held that the dichotomy of the knower as a censor and experience, and the known, gives a narrow vision of humanity and reality. Citing the example of true love in which there is no observer, Krishnamurti went for a "total abandonment of the observer and the observed".[3] This trend of thought signifies a clear shift from the fact-ridden reality to a non-factual order of being. The factual world is beset with dichotomies and man places in it is understood in terms of geographical boundaries, nations, race, caste and so on. Contemporary Indian thought suggests a suspension and transcendence of the conceptual frame-work provided by facticity—the frame-work that dictates what my self is, what man is, what beauty is, etc.

This philosophy of man based on a holistic vision gives rise to a non-utilitarian attitude to man and his creative work. It is in this context that the distinction between construction and creation was formulated by Tagore : "Construction is for a purpose, it expresses our wants, but creation is for itself, it expresses our being".[4] The contemporary Indian philosophy of art highlights the non-utilitarian aspect of art and thereby of a higher order of man's being in relation to art works and activities. There has always been a concept of man latent in this trend. While Tagore's concept of art is inseparably linked with his concept of 'surplus in man' and 'personality'. Sri Aurobindo upheld art as one of the many evolutionary episodes by which man has sought to express and increase 'his mental, vital, psychical, spiritual existence'. Sri Aurobindo's philosophy of art is a follow-up of his concept of man as a product of a spiritual evolution. He said : "The intellect is not the poet, the artist, the creator within us; creation comes by a supra-rational influx of light and power which must work always by vision and inspiration."[5] The task of art and poetry was for Sri Aurobindo "to liberate man into pure delight and to bring beauty into his life."[6] Ananda K. Coomaraswamy's theory of art proposes a balance between 'the sentimental' and 'the intellectual' dimension of man's being in order to envision the possibility of art.[7] His philosophy of art is based on what he calls a 'normal point of view' according to which art belongs to actual human societies and human state of affairs. The search for authenticity and meaningfulness of art is in vein if art is rootless and estranged from its human tradition. According to Coomaraswamy man is not only 'soulful or sentimental' but also 'intellectual' and the 'normal point of view' is prescriptive too by its relation to a concept of 'whole man' which includes both the selves.[8]

In accordance with their own anthropological approaches all these thinkers dwelt upon the concept of a harmony of the being of art and the being of man. Man's drive into the world of art and literature is basically to establish a new image of himself which is again and again surpassed in course of his journey, and the ideal and the real are blended to constitute a new reality. As Tagore said : "In order to gain himself truly, he (man) is moved towards self-creation and self-transcendence. In the image of the ideal, man makes himself. What are his arts and literature but a reflection of this image?"[9] This is a demand of modernity which tradition as a spell of history and cut off from continuity cannot ignore. Hence Tagore's idea of art as reflecting man's own image perfectly resembles a very modern concept of "image of man" which is "not only an image of what man **is**, but also an "exemplary image of man" that helps him discover, in each age anew, what he may and can become, an image that helps modern man rediscover his humanity".[10] This harmony of the being of art and the being of man as a dominant theme in contemporary Indian reflections on art points to something afar, beyond the world of facts; it heightens man's consciousness in the process of a 'continuous creation of unforeseeable novelty'. This is in the sense that this harmony **deprofanises** art. Beginning from classical Indian literature on art and aesthetics right up to modern Indian thought, art has been conceived as being an experience and always in relation to human consciousness. It was given a special status as a channel through which one could liberate oneself from the clutches of facts, utility and self-centred view of the world. According to Visvanath art experience is analogous to one's experience of Brahman (*Brahmasvādasahodora*).[11] In our time the connection between man and art has been conceived as an essential one and given an ontological and epistemological significance to describe the very nature and scope of the philosophy of art. The phenomenological significance of this harmony consists in surpassing the world of facts and constituting a new reality. Such a reality is, in Husserl's term, 'irreal', and yet relevant in reproducing and re-understanding reality. Radhakrishnan said: "The function of the artist or the poet is to exalt the natural towards its destined spiritual perfection... In true poetry the real is idealised, and the ideal realised, and we have quite a genuine but a higher kind of real object."[12]

II

With his inheritance from the classical Indian tradition Sarvepalli Radhakrishnan shares the contemporary mind too. His awareness of it in depth is most apparent in his first book *The Philosophy of Rabindranath Tagore.* His career as a professional philosopher was therein marked with a togetherness of philosophy and poetry. No wonder that the perennial problem of Radhakrishnan's aesthetics is 'artistic knowledge' which has its source in supra-rational human faculty of intuition. In his treatment the problem of knowledge receives a new look with reference to art and human nature : "Art as the disclosure of deeper reality of things is a form of knowledge."[13] According to Radhakrishnan art has a cognitive value to be determined in terms of correspondence between what is expressed and the truth of the spirit. It is not an empirical verification of a knowledge-claim with reference to external objects or phenomena. Bernard Phillips has remarked: "All knowledge, Radhakrishnan would agree, does indeed arise out of experience and refer ultimately to it, but the delimitation of experience to scientific experience is not **empiricism** but **apriorism**. There is no first principle which permits of the deduction that only through the senses may the real be apprehended."[14] While the truth-value of a statmeent of fact (physical or psychological) is determined externally in terms of a correspondence of what is said with what is the case, a judgement of taste or a poetic statement is rendered true by means of its correspondence with what is actually tasted or experienced in an alive perspective. The latter may be called 'experiential' while the former is 'empirical'. The verification or the determination of the truth-value of a statement of art, if it is possible at all, is possible by comparing such a statement with the 'experiential' basis of it from where it originates. Radhakrishnan called this experience 'knowledge by being' or 'intuitive knowledge'. To study Radhakrishnan's philosophy of art it is a prerequisite to elaborate his concept of 'intuitive knowledge' or 'knowledge by being'.[15] As Radhakrishnan himself said that "in aesthetic experience we have a type of intuitive knowledge, a personal relationship with the object which is essentially different from what is found in intellectual cognition."[16] One important question arises in this context: If aesthetic experience is a sort of intuitive knowledge which consists in a personal relationship between the knower and the known, then its expression and communication seems to be impossible because intuitive knowledge, for Radhakrishnan, is basically non-propositional and non-communicable. Radhakrishnan was aware of this problem and tried to solve it in terms of a complementarity between intuition and intellect as having a common root in 'self' or 'spirit' as a non-substantial life-force of human being.

III

The concept of 'intuitive knowledge' is a key-concept in Radhakrishnan's epistemology that extends the domain of human knowledge beyond sense-experience, science and logic to religious, mystical and aesthetic awareness. Knowledge through intellect or senses alone leaves out the experiential dimension. Knowledge of this is based on differentiation or analysis. Sense-experiences are limited by sense-organs and cannot go beyond them to apprehend the **more** of an object: "Sense experience helps us to know the outer characters of the external world. By means of it we obtain an acquaintance with the sensible qualities of the objects. Its data are the subject-matter of natural science which builds up a conceptual structure to describe them."[17] While knowledge through senses isolates the outer from the inner, knowledge by intellect or logical analysis is "successful only to the extent that it displaces the living flux of reality by a system of static concepts."[18] Intuition knows the whole of an object in an immediate way by diffusing the knowing mind into the experiential realm. In this form of cognition knowing and being are integrated. It is not ordinary sense-intuition of empiricists or itellectual intuition of Plato's type. Rather it comes closer to what Radhakrishnan describes as the "non-mathematical side of Plato's teaching" which upholds "noesis as the highest kind of knowledge, immediate and supra-intellectual".[19] It is a non-discursive mode of cognition which drops the subject-object dichotomy and "comes in a flash as distinct from patient observation or logical analysis . . . It reveals the central feature of the intuited object. The subject and the object in intuition tend to coalesce."[20] Radhakrishnan elucidated the concept of intuition with reference to classical Indian philosophical sources like *Upaniṣads, Yoga-Sūtra, Bhāṣā-Paricceda* and identified it as *Pratibhā* or *ārṣa-jñāna* or *Parā-Samvit.*[21] It could also be called *Yogic* intuition or *Yogaja Pratyakṣa* of Naiyāyika's kind.

According to Radhakrishnan knowledge reflects the deepest convictions by which we live and think and is related to what he called "the living flux of reality".[22] This living reality is not the physical, objective reality of the scientist. This is, for Husserl, the 'environing world' which must be distinguished from the 'natural reality' of natural sciences.[23] Husserl characterized the latter as an 'idealized abstraction' from the 'lived world'. Radhakrishnan's integral philosophy says : ". . . matter, life, consciousness and value are facts of experience studied in their abstract isolation by science, while for philosophy they are all interconnected as in human personality. The experience which philosophy studies is concrete and whole while the subject-matter of science is abstract and partial."[24] Like the Naiyāyikas he thinks that knowledge can be both propositional and non-propositional. The non-propositional knowledge which is at the basis of propositional one is a contribution of intuition. It gives certitude to knowledge. Radhakrishnan says: "If the term 'knowledge' is restricted to what is communicable, what can be expressed in formulas and propositions, then intuitive insight as ineffable and non-propositional is not knowledge. But certainty and not communicability is the truest test of knowledge, and intuitive experience has this sense of assurance or certainty, and therefore, is a species of knowledge."[25] The propositional or communicable knowledge remains imperfect so long as it is not aided by an intuitive grasp of the knowledge-situation. Radhakrishnan's approach to the problem of knowledge thus differs from Russell who said : "... logic is what is fundamental in philosophy, and ... schools should be characterised rather by their logic than by their metaphysics."[26] Certainty in a knowledge-claim cannot be brought about simply by a linguistic formulation of it. A linguistic formulation of knowledge can vouch for its certainty when it is, as Michael Polanyi would say, 'matched against' a direct experience or experimentation or when there is a "confident use of language".[27] The confident use of language is made possible by a practice of directness in knowledge. In other words the act of knowing something in the sense of having an immediate and direct encounter with the object cannot be separated from formulated or verbal knowledge. The theory of knowledge which excludes the former is incomplete and therefore cannot account for any type of knowledge which is different from or transcends logical or empirical categories and thereby expresses a different aspect of human personality. But unlike Polanyi or Sartre, Radhakrishnan would hold that intuitive knowledge is trans-reflective or supra-intellectual and not 'pre-reflective'. For him "intuition is not a-logical but supra-logical". Like Bergson he thinks of intuition not as a primitive sub-intellectual immediacy but a higher immediacy "which supervenes on intellectual analysis".[28] By maintaining that it is supra-logical Radhakrishnan keeps the possibility of moving from the intellectual to the intuitive, and thereby the possibility of expressing intuited knowledge through the intellect, open. Perhaps this is the reason why he calls intuition a 'non-conceptual', integral insight but not non-rational: "Intuition is of two types, **perceptual knowledge** and **integral insight**. Personally I use intuition for integral knowledge." "Intuitive knowledge can be categorised, validated and communicated through the mediation of intellect. Still it transcends conceptual expressions."[29]

What follows is that the non-discursive, non-propositional and non-communicable becomes communicable by the mediation of intellect. The meaning of any knowledge-claim based on intuition, therefore, can be grasped by attending to the same intuition, i.e., the first order experience. Whether the articulation of the experience (intuitive experience) is correct or not can be judged by such a return to the experience. Thus there is a continuity between intellect and intuition. Radhakrishnan says : "There is no break of continuity between intuition and intellect. In moving from intellect to intuition we are not moving in the direction of unreason, but are getting into the deepest rationality of which human nature is capable. In it we think more profoundly, feel more deeply, and see more truly. We see, feel and become in obedience to our whole nature, and not simply measure things by the fragmentary standards of intellect. We think with a certain totality or wholeness. Both intellect and intuition belong to the self. The two are synthesized in the self and their activities are interdependent."[30] Radhakrishnan rejected any substantialist notion of self like the Cartesian concept of 'I' as a thinking substance. A substance cannot create art. Art can only be the art of the spirit in man.

According to Radhakrishnan "intuition which ignores intellect is useless. The two are not only incompatible but vitally united . . . Intuition is beyond reason, though not against reason. As it is the response of the whole man to reality, it involves the activity of reason also. The truths of intuition are led up to by the work of the understanding and can be translated into language of understanding, though they are clearly intelligible only to those who already in some measure have immediate apprehension of them."[31] Thus it is that the self or spirit in man which serves as a principle of integration between intuition and intellect. As a philosophical anthropologist Radhakrishnan offered a holistic image of man whose different faculties are not compartmentalised but integrated with each other as knots in the same network of the spirit. Radhakrishnan comes closer to some trends of theistic existentialism in this regard. His rejection of a substantialist view of self and emphasis on human existence and transcendence as a 'concrete form of experience' makes him adopt an existentialist attitude like that of Jaspers. In his article "The Metaphysical Quest" he mentions approvingly the views of Kierkegaard, Jaspers and Paul Natorp. Even "Sartre's existentialism", Radhakrishnan says, "though avowedly atheistic, lends considerable support to a spiritual view of the universe".[32] Like some existentialists Radhakrishnan was against reason as reified from human personality but not reason as forming an integral part of the human personality. Hence 'spirit', for Radhakrishnan, is the live root or source for all human creations and actions. The complementarity between reason and intuition can be conceived with reference to spirit. D. M. Datta remarks aptly in his reflections on Radhakrishnan's philosophy, "every great work of art, literature or philosophy is touched by the spirit and is rooted in some intuitive apprehension of the spirit".[33]

IV

Despite the complementarity between intuition and intellect, reason and emotion, Radhakrishnan retained their respective identity so that he could explain not only communication and expression but also the silence in artistic creation and aesthetic experience. Hence Croce's view that art experience without an expression of it is meaningless and cannot be called an art experience at all was acceptable for Radhakrishnan with the critical observation that this view "does not seem to take into account the fact that inarticulateness stands between experience and expression for the average man".[34] The inarticulateness is there because the medium through which the experience is given a form and thus expressed is to be handled carefully in a manner which is different from the commoners' use of it. The nature of art experience is such that it is always pregnant with a meaning which may be construed in the context of or with reference to the empirical, factual world but is not derived from it and not based on an one-to-one correspondence between what is experienced and what is the case in fact. The artist has to struggle in silence in order to give expression to this meaning, silence occupies a span of time between experience and its expression. A world of art would surely not be possible without the latter but that does not make aesthetic experience and expression identical. Had the two been identical there would be no need of any creation. The language of art differs from its commonplace counterpart particularly because it conveys something unique, portrays some realisation which is based on the artist's personal encounter. Croce does not make any distinction between 'intuition' and 'expression' and by expression he means language which includes the words of everyday speech, the words of the poet, musical notations, lines, colours, sounds, etc. According to Radhakrishnan intuition is a 'knowledge by being' which transcends the subject-object paradigm of epistemology; it is basically non-propositional. This knowledge is given expression with the aid of a medium like language in order that it can evoke the experience in others, its verbal equivalent is thus developed in it. For him, so long as the artist or beholder is aware of his experience, one may hold that the expression is in some sense contained in the experience itself, but its communication is not possible on this ground alone. In his words : "The moment the poet has the intuition or the experience, i.e., the experience is vividly felt, the intuition unmistakably known, its expression or embodiment is also implicitly present. For the purely formless cannot be known or conceived. The form is present in the experience itself, but the great poet is he whose nature it is to represent experience through words winged with magic, capable of evoking the experience. The experience has its full shape in the words and phrases which clothe it. In the experience itself the expression is only implicit. To the extent to which the poet is perfectly aware of the experience, we may say that his expression is in a sense also complete but certainly its verbal equivalent is not developed in it. Croce seems to ignore the problem of artistic communication".[35]

The encounter is in silence, it is a dialogue between the artist and the art content or the world — a dialogue which is necessary for giving shape to the art form and communicating its essentials to the beholder. The beholder too needs training to understand art expressions or the language of art as such and for that he should be able to grasp the essentials of it through dialogue. This pre-linguistic or pre-symbolic stage of grasping is dropped into oblivion by Croce. The dialogic self of the artist struggles to give a form to his creation in its uniqueness and thus communicates it to the beholder. Even this tension in silence is an experience which Tagore expressed in one of his poems in *Balaka*: "It seems that creation seeks to speak out; it keeps mumbling as though in dream and meaningless sounds keep surging up in darkness".[36] Even if it is accepted that creation is expressive by definition, it does not always succeed in attaining perspecuity. This is because expression is not merely a mental act, but also an achievement. When expression is an achievement it is communicative; it is intentional in the sense that it is directed towards the audience or spectator and the import of the intended meaning is apprehensible. In the words of S. C. Sengupta: "The theory of art as expression and nothing else places the artist on an ivory tower where the air is too rarefied for him to breathe. What does the intuition in his brain consist of? It has passed the stage of vague, indistinct impressions and is a clear and distinct image, that is to say, it is already in a stage fit for communication, for a clear and distinct image is inherently communicable, and although the whole process is imaginal, the artist must be using mental materials from which the appropriate shape is wrought. But even this form is rudimentary, and actual practice would suggest that the artist's intuition develops in course of communication; words call forth words and pigments and clay and marble reveal new possibilities in the process of manipulation".[37] Radhakrishnan's criticism that Croce's intuition-expression equation has underscored the significance of communication in art can be understood with reference to this intentional character of art experience. The self that is expressed in art, for Radhakrishnan, is the individual self, but "not the narrow 'particular' one". Our experience of the beautiful becomes communicative because the experience of universal man incarnates in it. While an art experience is unique and individual, it is also universal in this sense. The juxtaposition of individuality and universality of art experience is possible in Radhakrishnan's philosophical frame-work because of his man-centred approach. As Bimal Krishna Matilal has righly pointed out, Radhakrishnan was deeply influenced by Tagore's thought and "Tagore's intuitive understanding of the synthetic philosophy of what we may call 'universal humanism' inspired Radhakrishnan to write about it".[38] Man, for Radhakrishnan, cannot be fully described by any science. The spirit of man is inexhaustible and not confined to the petty wants of day-to-day living. This is the universal aspect of man. The uniqueness and individuality of aesthetic experience or what Radhakrishnan calls 'artistic knowledge' consists in individual man's striving to rise above his insulated existence through his knowledge of the unusual, the unprecedented form of reality and his giving a shape to it. Hence Radhakrishnan believed that it is by *vairāgya* or detachment from the commonsensical and routine-bound world and its wants the artist can "rise to the calm of universal spirit".[39] To substantiate his position he referred to Kant as well: "In the *Critique of Judgement*, Kant argues that the pleasure we experience as the enjoyment of beauty is individual and in that sense subjective; it is also disinterested, and our judgement concerning it is universal. Deepest poetry has the widest appeal".[40]

The distinction and complementarity between 'intuition' and 'intellect', can be regarded also as a means to combine the individuality and universality of 'artistic knowledge', the phenomenological significance of which lies in 'suspending' the presuppositions of commonsense and focusing the **logos** of art as being essentially related to the intentional nature of the consciousness of the artist and the beholder. Artistic knowledge is based on the artist's intuition in conjunction with his/her communicative intention which brings about artistic expression as an achievement. It is again re-intuited by the beholder, and its universal character is **evidenced** in terms of its **logos**. To re-intuit, on the part of the beholder, through the medium of the expression of the artist's intuition, is in effect a sort of re-identification of the artist's intention. The act of re-intuiting makes the apocalypse complete. It unveils a dialogic situation insofar as the artist's intention is essentially transitive and communicative in character. But if it does not meet with a nodding assent from the beholder the intention would remain suspended in nullity. A song subsists in singing as much as in listening. A dialogue of the twin modes makes for the case that a song happens to be there. It is in this way that aesthetic cognition becomes essentially different from sense-experience and logical knowledge, unique in itself but highlighting the aesthetic realm in its universality.

IV

An analysis of Radhakrishnan's concept of 'artistic knowledge' requires a phenomenological setting. The object of artistic knowledge is either a complete work of art or anything which is intended to be a work of art. The moment it becomes an object of artistic knowledge, it becomes an aesthetic object in a correlational perspective shared by the knowing subject as well. **What** appears and the **way** it appears are conjoined in aesthetic experience or what Radhakrishnan calls 'artistic knowledge'. A phenomenology of aesthetic experience systematically explores into the entirety of this phenomenon. The **way** a thing appears, or briefly, the **thatness** of the thing determines the essence or the **whatness** of it so far as artistic knowledge is concerned. The beauty of something cannot be described, measured or weighed with reference to some definite and fixed, properties of that thing; the **logos** of this beauty is determinable only in terms of its **thatness**.

With Radhakrishnan, this **thatness** is invariably related to the ongoing activity of the spirit in man upon the mystery of the world. He conceived spirit as "life, not thing, energy not immobility, something real in itself and by itself and cannot be compared to any substance subjective or objective". Phenomenologically speaking, this transcendence of the subjective and the objective through a creative participation of the human self in the world is the process of intentionality of consciousness. This non-substantialist notion of self is consistent with Radhakrishnan's rejection of both the naturalistic and the transcendental view of art. "Art is concerned neither with the actual and the imperfect nor with the ideal or the hazy, but with the natural transfigured by the ideal immanent in it". Thus both absolute subjectivism and absolute objectivism are discarded by Radhakrishnan for stipulating the notion of art as an outcome of a harmony of the ideal and the real, the subjective and the objective, the inner core of man and the outer universe. The essence of an art object is to be sought in the revelation of it in a sphere of dialogue and communion of the knower and the known. The programme of a dialogical aesthetics is to give a dialogical description and interpretation of this revelation. Radhakrishnan's views on art are quite congruent with the frame-work of the phenomenology of dialogue. Radhakrishnan was not much concerned with the formal structure of art. His emphasis was on this essence of art which relates straightaway to the experience of the spirit in man. Artistic knowledge, therefore, would not be for Radhakrishnan a sheer reflection of the objective experience. Art, for him, is a form of integral experience wherein a predominance of intuition as a "sublimated knowledge, *jñānam vijñāna sahitam*" is unquestionable. Radhakrishnan was quite unequivocal in upholding the personal dimension of artistic knowledge.

The being in dialogue is man's being in communion with the world. The phenomenology of aesthetic experience highlights this being and its anthropological significance is rather perspicuous in it. But in so doing it does not assign any undue magnificence to man in isolation from his experiential perspective — from the 'others' of his experience. On the contrary the phenomenology of aesthetic experience in its dialogical sense opens new vistas for seeing man with his unending interpretative and creative competence to understand the world and whatever he is not, and thus places him in a relational perspective. Radhakrishnan's philosophical anthropology endorses this view of man in harmony with the rest of the reality. His aesthetics is not merely a supplement to his philosophy of man, but a phenomenological orientation to it shows that his concept of art is an integral dimension of his conept of man and *vice-versa*.

Notes and References

1. Rabindranath Tagore : *Religion of Man*, Unwin Books (Paperback) London, p. 84.
2. D. M. Datta : *The Philosophy of Mahatma Gandhi*, University of Calcutta, 1968, p. 57.
3. J. Krishnamurti : *Freedom From The Known*, ed. by Mary Lutyens, B. I. Publications (Paperback) 1982, pp. 90-91.
4. Rabindranath Tagore : "Construction versus Creation", In *Lectures And Addresses*, Macmillan & Co. Ltd., India, 1970.
5. Sri Aurobindo : *The Human Cycle*, New York, 1949, p. 159.
6. Sri Aurobindo : *The Future Poetry*, Pondicherry, 1991, p. 199.
7. Ananda Coomaraswamy : *Figures of Speech or Figures of Thought*, Luzac & Co., London, 1946. See pages 13 and 182. See also Coomaraswamy's *Christian and Oriental Philosophy of Art*, Dover Publication, New York, 1956, p. 31.
8. *Ibid.*
9. Rabindranath Tagore: *Angel of Surplus*, ed. by Sisir Kumar Ghose, Visva-Bharati, 1978, p. 154.
10. Maurice Friedman: *To Deny Our Nothingness*, The University of Chicago Press, Chicago & London, Phoenix Edition, 1978, p. 17.
11. Visvanath : *Sahitya Darpana*, Chapter 3, Sloka 2, Nepali translation from Sanskrit by Komolnath, Royal Nepal Academy, Kathmandu.
12. Sarvepalli Radhakrishnan : *The Philosophy of Rabindranath Tagore*, Good Companions Publishers, Baroda, 1961, Pages, 89 and 91. Henceforth, *PRT*.

13. Sarvepalli Radhakrishnan: *An Idealist View of Life*, Unwin Books, London, 1961, p. 152. Henceforth, *IVL*.
14. Bernard Phillips : "Radhakrishnan's Critique of Naturalism", In *The Philosophy of Sarvepalli Radhakrishnan*, ed. by Paul Arthur Schlipp, New York, 1952. Henceforth, *PR*.
15. S. Radhakrishnan : *IVL*, p. 109.
16. S. Radhakrishnan : 'Reply to Critics', In *PR*, p. 793.
17. S. Radhakrishnan : *IVL*, p. 105.
18. *Ibid.*, p. 113.
19. *Ibid.*, p. 102.
20. S. Radhakrishnan : *The Brahma Sutra : The Philosophy of Spiritual Life*, George Allen & Unwin, London, 1960, p. 107.
21. *Ibid.*, p. 106.
22. S. Radhakrishnan : *IVL*, p. 113.
23. Edmund Husserl : *Phenomenology and the Crisis of Philosophy*, tr. by Quentin Lauer, Harper Torchbooks, New York, 1965, p. 153.
24. S. Radhakrishnan : *IVL*, pp. 176-77.
25. *Ibid.*, p. 114.
26. Robert R. Ammerman : *Classics of Analytical Philosophy*, Tata-Mcgraw-Hill Publishing Co. Ltd., Bombay/New Delhi, 1965, p. 5.
27. Michael Polanyi : *Personal Knowledge*, The University of Chicago Press, 1962, (Paperback) pp. 249-53.
28. S. Radhakrishnan : *IVL*, p. 116.
29. S. Radhakrishnan : *PR*, p. 791 & 794.
30. S. Radhakrishnan : *IVL*, p. 120.
31. S. Radhakrishnan : "The Spirit in Man", In Radhakrishnan (ed.) *Contemporary Indian Philosophy*, London (George Allen & Unwin Ltd.) and New York (Humanities Press Inc.) 1966, p. 486. Henceforth, *CIP*.
32. S. Radhakrishnan : *Religion and Culture*, Orient Paperbacks, New Delhi & Bombay, 1989, p. 105.

33. D. M. Datta : *The Chief Currents of Contemporary Philosophy*, The University of Calcutta, Third Edition, 1970, p. 146.
34. S. Radhakrishnan : *IVL*, p. 148.
35. *Ibid.*, pp. 148-49.
36. Rabindranath Tagore : *Balaka*, English translation of the particular poem mentioned is available as "The Swans", In *Tagore For You*, ed. by Sisirkumar Ghose, Visva-Bharati, 1984, pp. 142-44.
37. S. C. Sengupta : *Towards A Theory of Imagination*, A. Mukherjee & Co., Pvt. Ltd., Calcutta, 1989, pp. 212-13.
38. Bimal Krishna Matilal: "Ideas and Values in Radhakrishnan's Philosophy", In *Radhakrishnan, Centenary Volume*, ed. by G. Parthasarathi & D. P. Chattopadhyaya, Oxford University Press, 1989, p. 23.
39. S. Radhakrishnan : "Reply to Critics", In *PR*, p. 793.
40. S. Radhakrishnan : *IVL*, p. 152.
41. S. Radhakrishnan : *CIP*, p. 492.
42. S. Radhakrishnan : *PRT*, p. 88.

Index